COMMERCIAL ACTIVITIES AND DEVELOPMENT IN THE GANGA BASIN

About the Editor

V.K. Shrivastava is a Professor of Geography at the University of Gorakhpur, Gorakhpur, India with a teaching and research experience of over three decades. He has written and edited more than a dozen text-books and research monographs. He is currently the Chairman of the International Geographical Union Commission (IGU) on Geography of Commercial Activities. Also, he heads the NAGI Commission on Geography of Marketing in India.

In addition to attending a number of conferences in India and abroad, Dr. Shrivastava has organised four I.G.U. International Conferences at Gorakhpur and three in France, Japan and Czech Republic. He is the Chief Editor of the *Indian Journal of Marketing Geography* since its foundation in 1983, which is an internationaly known journal.

COMMERCIAL ACTIVITIES AND DEVELOPMENT IN THE GANGA BASIN

Edited by
V.K. SHRIVASTAVA
Professor and Head
Department of Geography
Deen Dayal Upadhyay University of Gorakhpur, Gorakhpur

Foreword by
ALAIN METTON
Vice-President, de l' Union Geographique Internationale
Department de Geography, University de Paris
Val De Marne, 94010, Creteil Cedex, France

CONCEPT PUBLISHING COMPANY, NEW DELHI - 110059

Chief Editor :
Prof V.K. Shrivastava

Editors :
Dr. P.R. Chauhan
Dr. S.K. Dixit

ISBN 81-7022-779-8

First Published 1999

Published and Printed by
Ashok Kumar Mittal
Concept Publishing Company
A/15-16, Commercial Block, Mohan Garden,
NEW DELHI - 110059 (India)
Phones : 5648039, 5649024
Fax : 091-11-5648053

IN THE MEMORY OF

Late Shri Vir Bahadur Singh

18-2-1935 — 30-5-1989

A Sketch of Late Shri Vir Bahadur Singh

Late Shri Vir Bahadur Singh was one of the persons who define a category of their own. Unmatchable, unconceivable and extra-ordinarily humane. Such human beings quietly pass off the crowd before the world realises that it has been a witness, a friend, a foe, a teacher, a son, daughter or father etc. to a legend. This was Vir Bahadur. He had indomitable courage, unmatched vision, extreme humility and an extra-ordinary understanding of political phenomena at national and international levels. He was always the master of the arena he was asked to manage, be it administration, organisation, planning or any thing that the exigency of the situation required. Probably it was this capacity and this potential in him that cost his life. I have no hesitation in giving him a likeness of Subhash Bose or Shastri ji.

He was born on February 18, 1935, at a village called Harnahi, south of Khajani Town, a block headquarters of Gorakhpur district of Uttar Pradesh, twenty minutes drive from the centre of Gorakhpur city. His father, late Shri Raghunandan Singh, was a farmer. The land which gave birth to this towering personality bears the imprints of Guru Gorakhnath, Lord Buddha, Lord Mahavir, Baba Raghav Das, Shaheed Ram Prasad Bismil, Shaheed Bandhu Singh, Shri Devarha Baba and others.

Vir Bahadur entered active politics when he was hardly twenty years of age. It seems he was destined to be a politician. He was appointed the President of the district unit of All-India Youth Congress in 1954. Undeterred by his commitment to active politics he pursued his studies and obtained the Degree of Master of Arts in Geography, in 1965 as a regular student from the Department of Geography, University of Gorakhpur, Gorakhpur. In the university life he was through and through a student. He never utilised his political affiliations for any gain in the university life, though Gorakhpur University, at this time, was a breeding ground of potential political personalities among students. Apart from the still untouched heights achieved by Vir Bahadur, quite a few of them are now dominating the national political scene, a bit behind the charm and dynamism of the late leader.

Soon after obtaining a degree he entered the electoral platform and was first elected a member to the State Legislative Assembly in 1967, a feat which he repeated five times. His administrative capacity and political understanding won him a place in the cabinet of ministers of Uttar Pradesh as a Deputy Minister in 1970, and as a Minister of State in 1976. He was later appointed a full-fledged Cabinet Minister in 1980. In contunity he later ruled as the Chief Minister of Uttar Pradesh from 1985 to 1988. The regin of his chief ministership was the reign of regional development in national perspective. He knew the land and the people from the grassroots. His experience matched with his imagination and a God-gifted sense in implementing schemes which promoted human welfare in general. It was a period of intense developmental activities from planning a filmland to establishing a city business complex. The now neglected *Ramgarh Tal Pariyojana* is a dream of dreams for the world planners. Basically being developed to preserve the heritage of Lord Buddha, who attained his *Parinirvan* 52 km east of Gorakhpur at Kushinagar, and Lord Mahavir who also meditated at Pawapuri near Kushinagar, the project enhances and conserves the utility of a lake ecosystem. It comprises of a quiet and extensive park, a lake, a floating restaurant, five star hotel, a planetorium, a conference complex and what not, comparable to George Pompeidu Centre of Paris. Gorakhpur Town, a prestigious seat of eastern Uttar Pradesh, was thus being converted to an international tourist centre with modern transportation, communication, sanitation, planned market complexes, with drinking water and drainage facilities and a healthy living environment. A pointer to this imagination is the development of parks, places of entertainment and libraries. He treated the population of the whole region as his own family and took care to cater to the needs of children, youth, mature and old-age persons. Gorakhpur was being given all imaginable facilities of a metropolis.

Almost when he was through his skillfully carved developmental schemes he was called upon to join the central cabinet of ministers under the Rajiv Gandhi Government. He joined as Cabinet Minister of Information and Broadcasting, in June, 1988. There again his acumen came to the fore. Besides organising his party and government at national level he became instrumental in evolving liberal and advanced policies and programmes, telecommunications network in the country. This gave a boost to the national economy and augmented the convenience and information system of the rural masses. He visited foreign countries a few times. The last was his visit to France in connection with a conference on telecommunications where he breathed his last suddenly at Paris on the fateful day of May 30, 1985.

Curriculum Vitae of Late Shri Vir Bahadur Singh

Name	:	Shri Vir Bahadur Singh
Birth Place	:	Village-Harnahi (Madurao) Block - Khajni Tahsil - Bansgaon District Gorakhpur, Uttar Pradesh
Date of Birth	:	February 18, 1935
Father	:	Shri Raghunandan Singh
Mother	:	Smt. Uda Singh
Wife	:	Smt. Champa Devi
Brothers	:	Shri Uma Prasad Singh Shri Gulab Singh
Sons	:	Fatah Bahadur Singh, Jitendra Singh Vikram Singh
Daughters	:	Kamla Singh, Indu Singh, Neelam Singh
Education	:	Primary-Bahuripar, Khajni Jr. High School-Piprauli High School & Inter — J.L. Nehru Inter-College, Bansgaon B.A. —Gorakhpur University, Gorakhpur M.A. (Geography) University of Gorakhpur, Gorakhpur, 1965

Political Career

President, District Youth Congress	:	1954
Member, U.P. Legislative Assembly	:	1967
Deputy Minister, U.P. Government	:	1970
Minister of State, `U.P. Government	:	1976
Cabinet Minister, U.P. Government	:	1980
General Secretary, U.P. Congress Party	:	1977-1980
Chief Minister, Uttar Pradesh	:	September 25, 1985 to June 24, 1988
Cabinet Minister, Govt. of India	:	September 25, 1988 to May 30, 1989
Death	:	May 30, 1989, Paris

Foreword

The spatial manifestation of commercial activities highlights the regional contrasts and imbalances in human welfare. It is through commercial activities that the wealth is generated. Human welfare is imbedded in the effective distributional aspects of the generation of wealth. If the distributional pattern follows the dictum of territorial justice then development occurs. Human welfare is the ultimate goal of all developmental activities. In this context the present book embodying the proceedings of the IGU Symposium on the Role of Commercial Activities in the Economic Development of the Ganga Basin, held at no less a place of ancient importance than Gorakhpur, rightly deserves a place among the books dealing with human activities, culture and development.

It was in 1984 that I happened to know of Dr. V.K. Shrivastava at the International Geographical Union Commission meeting in Paris. He organised the first ever Congress of the IGU Commission at Gorakhpur in 1985, followed by the IGU Regional Symposium on the Ganga Basin in 1990. This symposium of the Commission focussed on the Ganga Basin covering Bangladesh, India and Nepal so it naturally attracted the attention of geographers and scientists from these countries. It thus turned out to be an international symposium for which Prof. Shrivastava deserves congratulations. The publication of this volume goes a long way in carrying the message of the IGU, i.e. to disseminate geographical knowledge and strengthens the performance of the Commission on commercial activities.

Geographers of the world in general and scientists, planners, politicians, administrators in particular and all those concerned with human welfare will note the rich contents of this book. Ganga Basin, the most populous region of the world has been studied in all possible dimensions with the perspective of geography. The seven themes have been integrated through scholarly works of eminent geographers which has a fairly good share of young scientists, I have been told. The book covers a variety of topic ranging from commercial agriculture to industries, infrastructure, human resources, public policy and their developmental implications. Energy, environment and resources trio is the key for economic development. I am happy to note that the conference papers have amply contributed to this theme.

I am confident that the readers will find in Prof. Shrivastava's book substantial evidence of the two way relationship between commercial activities and economic development. On behalf of the International Geographical Union (IGU) and on behalf of the prospective reader I offer my greetings to Dr. Shrivastava and to members of editorial board for bringing out this excellent publication in the service of humanity. I equally congratulate the publishers for this book which is worth their title 'Concept'.

ALAIN METTON
15, Rue Carle Hebert
92400 Courbevoie
France

Preface

The book in hand is the outcome of the deliberations of the IGU Symposium on the theme held in January, 1990, at the University of Gorakhpur, Gorakhpur. The symposium was held under the auspices of the International Geographical Union Commission on Commercial Activities. It was supposed to be a regional symposium but since the great Ganga herself washes the pious lands of three nations—Bangladesh, India and Nepal, it naturally turned out to be an international one. Incorporating the objectives of the IGU Commission attention was focussed on the economic development of the Ganga Basin, one of the most populated and yet the economically most backward parts of the world. The rich heritage of the area and the deep involvenment of scientists and researchers in its multifarious activities generated a numer of papers which were organised under five themes, i.e. Commercialization of agriculture, Agro-industries, Infra-structure and Economic development, Public policies and regional trade and Human resources and manpower planning.

The impact of infra-structural developments, land and water management is reflected in the income levels of farmers which in turn has promoted commercialization of agriculture. Thus a clear shift from subsistence to commercial agriculture in the area emerges. The growth of the secondary sector in the Ganga Basin is itself a sign of the trend of commercialization. The bases of agro-industries are being eroded due to the conflict between large and small scale industries. Infra-structural changes in Bangladesh, India and Nepal have emerged on a large scale particularly in irrigation, river basin management and transport and communication etc. This has given a boost not only to agricultural produce but also to distribution system. The development of regulated marketing, the growth of periodic markets, the commercial dynamism of urban fringe of cities, changes in tribal marketing systems and socio-economic impact of such changes has been duly assessed throgh many studies. This naturally calls for planning of commercial activities in the area of study. Planning suggestions must take into account the public policies and programmes. It has been observed that there has been a growth of tertiary sector of the economy, particularly in villages, but development is yet to take its roots. The ecological balance has to be handled with caution. Unless human resources of the area are well assessed and the potential of resources is examined in context of ecological constraints real development may not take place.

The book contains painstaking results of sincere researchers and teachers, most of whom belong to geography. The encyclopaedic contents of the book will provide useful material to readers, inspiring methodology to researchers and new dimensions of planning to administrators, it is hoped.

V.K. SHRIVASTAVA

Contents

THEME — II

AGRO-INDUSTRIES AND ECONOMIC DEVELOPMENT

THEME — III

INDUSTRIALIZATION AND ECONOMIC DEVELOPMENT

THEME — IV

INFRASTRUCTURE AND ECONOMIC DEVELOPMENT

THEME — V

HUMAN RESOURCES, ENVIRONMENT AND ECONOMIC DEVELOPMENT

List of Contributors

Bhuiyan, Rejuan Hossain, Research Scholar (Bangladesh), Department of Geography, Aligarh Muslim University, Aligarh, U.P.

Chauhan, P.R., Reader, Department of Geography, University of Gorakhpur, Gorakhpur.

Das, Debashish, Reader, Department of Geography, Viswa Bharti Santiniketan, Birbhum, West Bengal.

De, N.K., Professor, Department of Geography, University of Burdwan, Burdwan, West Bengal,

Dixit, R.S., Reader, Department of Geography, I.T. College, Lucknow, U.P.

Dikshit, S.K., Reader, Department of Geography, University of Gorakhpur, Gorakhpur, U.P.

Dube, R.S., Professor & Head, Department of Geography, Dr. H.S. Gour University, Sagar, M.P.

Fazal, Shahab, Research Scholar, Department of Geography, Aligarh Muslim University, Aligarh, U.P.

Hinge, P., Department of Geography, Government Arts and Commerce College, Indore, M.P.

Jaiswal, J.P., Department of Geography, University of Gorakhpur, Gorakhpur, U.P.

Jain, A.K., Asstt. Librarian, Govt. Indira Gandhi Engineering College, Sagar, M.P.

Jain, C.K., Survey Assistant, Department of Geography, Dr. H.S. Gour University, Sagar, M.P.

Katare, S.S., Professor & Head, Department of Geography, Govt. P.G. College, Mandla, M.P.

Khan, Nizamuddin, Department of Geography, Aligarh Muslim University, Aligarh, U.P.

Mahatam Prasad, Department of Geography, Bapu Degree College, Peppeganj, Gorakhpur, U.P.

Mandal, A.K., Department of Commerce, Patna University, Patna, Bihar.

Misra, O.P., Reader, Department of Geography, M.L.K. (P.G.) College, Balrampur, Gonda, U.P.

Mitra, Champa, Professor, Department of Geography, University of Burdwan, Burdwan, W.B.

Phanse, V., Professor & Head, Department of Geography, Government Arts & Commerce College, Indore, M.P.

Poudel, P.C., Department of Geography, Tribhuan University, P.N. Campus, Pokkhra, Nepal.

Rai, J.P., Reader, Department of Geography, D.C.S.K. (P.G.) College, Maunath Bhanjan, Mau, U.P.

Rai, R.N., Department of Geography, Nehru P.G. College, Chhibramau, Farrurkhabad, U.P.

Sarkar, A.K., Scientific Officer, National Atlas and Thematic Mapping Organization (NATMO), Govt. of India, Calcutta.

Shanker, Rolee, Department of Geography, Dr. H.S. Gour University, Sagar, M.P.

Sharma, S.C., Reader & Head, Department of Geography, M.L.K. (P.G.) College, Balrampur, Gonda, U.P.

Sharma, O.P., Reader & Head, Department of Geography, D.A.V. Degree College, Lucknow, U.P.

Sharma, Nandeshwar, Professor & Head, Department of Geography, L.N. Mithila University, Darbhanga, Bihar.

Sharma, K.D., Reader, Department of Geography, Punjab University, Chandigarh.

Shrivastava, V.K., Professor, Department of Geography, University of Gorakhpur, Gorakhpur, U.P.

Shrivastava, K.R., 19Ka, Hirapuri Campus, Gorakhpur University, Gorakhpur.

Srivastava, R.C., Reader, Department of Geography, P.P.N. College, Kanpur, U.P.

Srivastava, S.P.L., Department of Geography, Bapu Degree College, Peppeganj, Gorakhpur, U.P.

Shukla, S.K., Reader, Department of Geography, Dr. H.S. Gour University, Sagar, M.P.

Singh, Abha Lakshami, Professor, Department of Geography, Aligarh Muslim University, Aligarh.

Singh, R.S., Department of Geography, University of Gorakhpur, Gorakhpur, U.P.

Singh, U., Mehmoorganj, Varanasi

Sinha, B.R.K., Reader, Department of Geography, Viswa Bharti Shantiniketan, Birbhum, W.B.

Sultana, Razia, Reader, Department of Geography, Jahangirnagar University, Savar, Dhaka, Bangladesh.

Sur, Suchit, Reader, Department of Geography & Applied

Geography, North Bengal University, Darjeeling, W.B.

Tiwari, K.N., Department of Geography, Degree College, Mallikpura, Ghazipur, U.P.

Tripathi, D.N., Reader, Department of Geography, M.L.K. (P.G.) College, Balrampur, Gonda, U.P.

Tripathi, M.P., Reader & Head, Department of Geography, Tribhuan University PN Campus, Pokhra, Nepal.

Verma, S.S., Reader, Department of Geography, University of Gorakhpur, Gorakhpur, U.P.

Verma, J.S., Reader, Department of Geography, L.B.S. Degree College, Anandnagar, Mahrajganj, U.P.

Vishwa Nath, Reader, Department of Geography, Budha Vidya Pith Degree College, Naugarh, Siddharthnagar, U.P.

Address by Vice-Chancellor
Professor Dr. (Mrs.) Pratima Asthana

Learned Delegates and Friends,

It gives me immense joy to greet the delegates who have come to participate in the Symposium on the Ganga Basin organised by the Department of Geography, University of Gorakhpur. I have been told that this Symposium is one of the three symposia that are proposed to be organised at Gorakhpur in ensuing years under the banner of the International Geographical Union. It is commendable on the part of Geography Department to begin the series and the organizers deserve all praise and admiration in their endeavour to stimulate the geographers in particular and the intellectuals in general.

The city of Gorakhpur is associated with *Guru Gorakhnath*, the doyen philosopher of the *Nath* cult in India. The region is rich in spiritual legacy as well as material prospects. It has been the *Karmabhumi* of saints like Kabir and Buddha and finally their resting place. With a glorious past and a promising future Gorakhpur has rightly been selected to be the venue of this Symposium. In recent years a number of national and international seminars and conferences have been held here which shall be remembered as landmarks in the history of Gorakhpur University.

Geography is unusual among Social Sciences, and yet it does belong to the discipline of Science. However, in its concern for the interconnections between the environment and society, and between resources and economy, it is more or less a subject covering science and scientific enquiry. The interrelationship of environment and society interact. In studying environment and society, constitute the study of modern Geography when specialists correlate their own observations with the findings of physical and social sciences. The geographers do create an understanding of the environment in which human groups live. Geographers are also aware of the economic, social and historical relationship that extends beyond the immediate area where environment and society interact, the geographers constantly discover and follow threads of connection between people and places. We may recall here the words of Archibald MacLeish in describing the famous photograph of the Earth taken by Apollo VIII mission "To see the earth as we now see it, small and blue and beautiful in that eternal silence where if floats, is to see overselves as riders on the Earth together." These words amply reflect today, the integrating spirit that is the core of geography.

The focus of this symposium is the Ganga Basin, one of the most fertile and populous parts of the world. Ganga is the most sacred river not only of India, but probably of the whole world. While the physical characteristics of the Ganga have influenced the material life in the plains, its sanctity has influenced the religious life of the people. The *Puranas* narrate a legend that King Bhagirath came near *Vindu sarovar* for the sake of Ganga and lived there for a number of years. Goddess *Tripathaga* or the Ganga was first initiated there. The innumerable stars in the milky way are nothing but the Goddess *Tripathaga.* This *Tripathaga,* having flowed in the sky came down upon the Earth, and after being harnessed through Lord Sankara's Yoga, fell down upon his head. At the same time, Lord Sankara saw that King Bhagiratha had grown pale and thin due to hunger and thirst and in the state of penance or *Tapasya* for his love for Ganga. Having realised the strong desire of the King, Lord Shiva allowed *Tripathaga* to flow down upon earth. The entire course of the river was then divided into seven streams, the seventh being the *Bhagirathi* or the Ganga.

The length of Ganga is about 2580 km which is slighty less than the length of the Indus and the Brahmputra. The length of a river is significant in determining its navigability and its uniting force in respect of culture and civilization, locations of settlements and roads etc. From all these view points the singnificance of the Ganga from Gangotri to Ganga Sagar is tremendous. Ganga has great tributaries flowing both from the plains and through the peninsular uplands south to it. The approximate area of the Basin, as may be known to the experts gathered here, is approximately 9 lakh square kilometres. It is made up of thousands of feet deep alluvium deposits. Its regime is marked by monsoonal character. River terraces are frequent in the Himalayas and have provided sites for human settlements. Rocky stratum of the peninsular region have given rise to defensible settlements like Mirzapur, Chunar, Munger, Bhagalpur etc. Another important feature of the streams of the Ganga Basin is the occurrence of natural levees. These levees are commonly developed along the Ganga and its tributaries in U.P. These levees are the highest points of the plain and remain dry during the floods. Large villages are located on such levees. Many of its tributaries are characterised by frequent floods. The river Kosi is known as the Hwangho of Bihar. Flood zone is almost continuous along the course of the Ganga and its tributaries. Floods have influenced the changes in the course of rivers and have consequently played remarkable role in the shifting of settlement sites and land use characteristics.

It is for the experts assembled here to brood over the real problems of floods and droughts, agriculture and industry, energy and resources of the Ganga Basin. These facts are very well known to geographers. I am confident that many other aspects would be discussed in various technical sessions of the symposium. The antiquity, the origin and evolution of settlements, society and culture of this region must also be borne in mind. As a student of History I am spontaneously reminded of the *Janpadas* lying along the Ganga and described in the *Puranas* as *Kuru, Panchala, Kosala, Videha, Anga, Malla, Madra* etc. Of these the *Janpadas* of *Malla, Videha, Magadh* and *Anga* belong to the middle Ganga valley in which the region of Gorakhpur is located. The *Malla Janapada* coincided with the doab of the Gandak and of the Rapti-Ganga, while the *Videha Janpada* extended upto Kosi. The capital cities of the *Malla Janpada* were Pawa and Kusinagar, about 50 to 60 km east of Gorakhpur city. *Videha* was the capital city of *Videha Janpada.* Similarly the capital city of *Magadh* was *Rajgarh* of *Rajgiri* and that of *Anga* was *Campa* near Munger. The people of the *Janpadas* were known after the name of the particular Janpadas where they resided. Practically all capital cities were located on major rivers and occupied a site on their levees or high banks. Such sites had the advantage of strategic locations as well. These settlements directed the route pattern of the Ganga plain. The trunk route from Puskalavati to Sravasti followed the belt avoiding the *Tarai* region. The route from Indraprastha to Tamralipti was the forerunner of the Grand Trunk Road. These routes were connected to the South, i.e., Indraprastha-Ujjaini, Kosambi-Vidisa outlining the basic network of roads in the country. A geographical study of the Ganga Basin, focussing mainly on commercial and economic activities would provide a useful and practical knowledge for the development of our country.

Examples of the international application of geography in business can be seen in the progress made by U.S.A., U.K., Japan, West Germany, France etc. In Geography planning for economic, urbaan and regional development has been widely accepted as the watch-word. A competent geographer has ideas, tools and experience to make substantial contribution to the understanding of economic development. I expect in this context from the participants of the present symposium that they would make fruitful contribution to highlight the economic and development process of our society as a whole.

Geography illuminates many aspects of the world we live in. It can make strong and necessary contribution to international knowledge. It can help in creating a favourable international climate for peaceful settlement of disputes and for productive measures to ameliorate the burning global problems. Geography also plays a key role in the field of citizen education. There is a great need for improving our geographical literacy so that we may deepen our knowledge and comprehension of national and international events and enhance our performance in peaceful and developmental activities.

With these words I feel happy to inaugurate your symposium.

KEY-NOTE ADDRESS

THE ROLE OF COMMERCIAL ACTIVITIES IN THE ECONOMIC DEVELOPMENT OF THE GANGA BASIN

PROFESSOR MOHAMMAD SHAFI

There is no alluvial basin in the world so vast and so fertile and level as the plain of the Ganga Basin. It is one of the most densely populated regions of the world and constitutes the granery of India. The people, however, depend mainly on agriculture producing chiefly cereals and cash crops including pulses, sugarcane, potatoes, oil seeds, cotton and tobacco, but maintain a low standard of living and an inadequate nutritional level. Poverty leads to low nutritional intake which in turn leads to ill-health, and this results in low productivity which leads to poverty. The farmer of the Gangetic plain is thus caught in a vicious circle and the major question is how to take him out of the web of poverty.

The farmer of the Ganga Basin is basically a subsistence farmer excluding the small grops of farmers who have relatively large farms, resort to mechanization and have adopted new agricultural technology. The subsistence farmers produce a substantial part of their own food requirements and utilize the production of a surplus for sale and the cash income helps the farmers to pay their rent or taxes and also in meeting their requirements of consumer goods. So the difference between subsistence and commercial farmers lies in the degree to which they participate in the market. However, there is an important and critical threshold beyond which a farmer ceases to base his strategy of production on the need to provide food for his household and relies on the market not only for the sale of the bulk of his produce but also for the purchase of the greater part of his household.

An examination of the cropping pattern of the Ganga Basin will show that the physical factors have mainly influenced the distribution of the crops. However, the technical factors like irrigation, improved varieties of seeds and modern technology have produced changes in the traditional cropping pattern. The introduction of high yielding varieties of wheat seeds accompanied by increases in infra-structural facilities ushered a revolution in the production of two cereal crops particularly wheat and rice. Food crops including cereals and pulses cover more than 75 per cent of the total cropped area in the basin, while the non-food crops, oil seeds both edible and non-edible account for about 10 per cent, sugarcane, potato, cotton, tobacco and jute constitute the remaining of the cropped area.

The extent of commercialization leading to economic development according to Abercromblie falls into four stages: *Stage I* where production is used entirely for subsistence. *Stage II* where barter transaction or sales take place and the emergence of a small surplus above the subsistence requirements may be largely unintentional, perhaps the result of an occasional particularly favourable agricultural season. *Stage III*, the regular production of marketable surplus is aimed at deliberately, but the main emphasis is still on subsistence production. In the *final stage*, production for the market predominates over subsistence. The Ganga-basin agriculture falls in the third stage and farmers who grow cash crops like sugarcane, potatoes, cotton, oilseeds, tobacco and jute are in the final stage but these constitute a small percentage of the total farmers of the Basin.

The introduction of new agricultural technology has led to the use of modern inputs which the farmers have to purchase, unlike the farm grown seeds, and the organic manures obtained from the farmyard. In 1981-82 the share of the inputs was about 40 per cent of the total value of agricultural output. In order to procure these inputs, the farmer has to sell a substantial part of his produce.

The spread of New Agricultural Technology has accelerated the dependence of the farmer on market for the procurement of the inputs and a substantial part of his produce for sale, and this has sharpened the process of commercialization of agriculture. Another factor which has further helped this process is Government policy leading to the announcement of procurement prices of cereals before the sowing operations begin. The price policy is a crucial factor in the commercialization of agriculture. The announcement of assured minimum price is an incentive to the farmer for sustained agricultural production. Moreover, the price policy ensures that the relevant income levels of the farming community are not eroded by continuing unfavourable terms of trade between agricultural sector and non-agricultural sector.

The survey, which S.S. Madalgi of the Reserve Bank of India, carried out in respect of monetisation of the Indian economy can well be applied to examine the trends of commercialization of agriculture in the Ganga Basin. The study of Madalgi was confined to foodgrains only. He points out that the proportion of quantity as well as value of marketable surplus to gross production between 1961-62 and 1970-71 varied between 33.4 per cent and 38.4 per cent except in two years 1965 and 1966-67. It was within the same range between 1971-72 and 1974-75 and this phase coincided with the increasing adoption of the new agricultural technology. A break-up of the contribution as from the various groups of the farmers showed that small farms in the size group of 0-2 hectares contributed 26 per cent of the total marketable agricultural surplus in 1950-51, their contribution came down to 16 per cent in 1960-61. The share of the middle class farm in the size group 2-4 hectares was over 20 per cent of the total marketed agricultural surplus in 1950-51, but declined to 17 per cent in 1960-61. On the other hand the share of large farmers having 4 hectares and above who accounted for half the surplus, increased to three-fourths of it during the corresponding period. It must be noted that increase in agricultural production in the seventies and eighties has been the result more of improvement in yield than of extension in area. Commercialization of agriculture requires surplus agricultural production and for surplus production large scale application of New Agricultural Technology is needed.

I am conscious of the charges which have been levied against the Green Revolution Technology. It is said that the new technology is discriminatory. The Green Revolution has increased the economic inequality and thus aggravated social conflict. The profit of the big farmers has led to the eviction of small farmers and many small farmers have sold their lands to the large farmers and this has increased the landless work-force resulting in poverty for this section of the population. The use of machinery has displaced labour and created unemployment.

The force of these arguments against the application of new technology is no stronger to my mind than the charge which was levelled against the steam engine when it was invented in Britain. Western Uttar Pradesh in the Ganga Basin, and Punjab and Haryana outside the Basin are the areas where the Green Revolution had the widest impact. It has been shown that in Western Uttar Pradesh and particularly in Ganga-Yamuna Doab per capita income grew at about 3 per cent annually during the sixties and seventies and 25 per cent of the population was below the poverty line as against 46 per cent for India. For an efficient marketing system and setting the pace towards commercialization of agriculture in the Ganga Basin and perhaps for the country as a whole, liberal credit facilities should be made available particularly to the small and marginal farmers.

Mention should be made of NABARD which was established in 1982, for providing credit for the promotion of agriculture, small scale industries, cottage and village industries, handicrafts and other economic activities in rural areas. This National Bank for Agricultural and Rural Development has taken over the functions of the erstwhile Agricultural Credit Department (ACD), and Rural Planning and Credit Cell of the Reserve Bank of India (RPCC) and Agricultural Refinance and Development Corporation (ARDC). It is an apex institution accredited with all matters concerning policy, planning and operations in the field of credit for agriculture and other economic activities in rural areas. This brings us to the important questions of marketing of surplus agricultural produce, storage, transportation, grading, marketing efficiency and development of infrastructure and the establishment of agro and processing industries commonly designated as agri-business.

It would be worthwhile to examine in depth the nature of relationship specially between the size of holding and the marketed surplus. Dharam Narain of the Institute of Economic Growth in his findings points out that the marketed proportion of output came down from 33 per cent for the 4-10 ha size group of holding to 23 per cent to holdings less than 2 ha and then rose up to 50 per cent for the large farms size group exceeding 10 ha. The *proportion* of marketed output on small holdings, it will be seen, is quite high and it has been interpreted as reflecting "distress sale". However, the marketed proportion of output rises steadly with increase in farm size. The geographers taking groups of villages in varying agro-climatic conditions may well investigate this phenomenon as it has an important bearing on the formulation of agricultural price policy. Another question which would be worthwhile investigating is whether marketed supply increases more than proportionately with output and whether, if output falls, marketed supply falls more than proportionately.

Again while considering the agricultural marketing organization, it should be noted that the marketing channels for wheat, pulses and millets are similar with some regional varieties but for paddy/rice they differ owing to the process of rice milling and its marketing is closely linked with rice milling industry which also performs the function of storage and wholesale distribution. In case of wheat the medium and large farmers in Uttar Pradesh store wheat during the *rabi* season while the private traders are by far the most important agents of storing foodgrain. It would be a useful study in food systems to examine at the village level as well as the traders level the length of storage of different commodities, the storage losses and their causes.

Marketing efficiency refers to the sensitiveness of the market of a particular commodity spatially as well as temporally in response to the availability and the demand of the commodity. Higher the sensitiveness, greater is the efficiency of the marketing system. In order to assess the marketing efficiency, correlation coefficient between the time series of prices prevailing at different wholesale markets should be worked out. If the correlation coefficient is close to unity, the marketing system is efficient. Such a study would help in planning the supply in relation to the demand of the commodity spatially. In order to assess this efficiency, one has to study the structure of 'the market, marketing practices and the market performance.

Ladies and Gentlemen

Green Revolution in India paved the way towards commercialization of agriculture, and the agro-processing industry is a big step in giving stability to monetization of agriculture. Processing industry has not made big strides in the Ganga Basin as it has done in Punjab and Himachal Pradesh. Government policies are mainly responsible for the introduction of processing of fruits into various types of saleable products. However, in the Ganga Basin there are various agricultural commodities which may usher a revolution in the marketing system and may lead to monetization of agriculture in the Basin if their processing and subsequent processes are carried out on an organized and scientific basis. Processing simply implies the rendering of a produce to-make it fit for maximum sale value. Cleaning, grading and standardization are the most essential components of processing. Even after these operations, further processing needs to be done for example: wheat to flour, whole pulse to *dal*, paddy to rice, cane to sugar and most of these processing operations are in the private sector, while the co-operatives hold a small share in the total processed quantity of each commodity. It is necessary to set up more well-organized and efficiently operated processing units in the co-operative sector so as to produce not less than 50 per cent of finished goods and these co-operatives should be linked up with the provincial co-operative markets on the one hand and the consumer co-operative markets on the other.

Rice processing undergoes various operations—cleaning, storage, drying, para boiling, shelling, hulling and polishing. These processes in villages are carried out by hand pounding, huller mills and sheller mills with capacity ranging between 1 and 2 tonnes per hour but these are inefficient and entail much losses and at the same time the cost of milling per tonne is high. These mills operated by entrepreneurs need modernization for which procurement, sale and pricing policies of the government are important.

Similarly, the dehusking of pulses is done by the traditional methods and the average yield of *dal* from pulses, ranges from 65 to 75 per cent. These methods are time consuming and inefficient and the product has a low nutritive value due to friction. The National Commission on Agriculture reports that the Central Food Technological Research Institute (CFTRI) has developed an improved method of processing *dal* which is semi automatic and the average yield of *dal* by this method is 10 to 20 per cent higher than the traditional method. The modernization of the traditional method would make the marketing system favourable to the farmer.

Ladies and Gentlemen

It is not the purpose of this address to recount all the commodities in regard to the agro-processing industry. What needs to be emphasised is that marketing and commercial activities would play a vital role in the economic development of the Ganga Basin if the activities are properly organized. The problems of small units of agro-industries as well as small and cottage industries flow from their scale of operation, lack of standardization, inadequate market intelligence, competition from technically more efficient units, insufficient holding capacity. The marketing strategy needs to be reoriented to meet the consumer needs. In order to achieve this, diversification of markets is necessary. Other measures which would be fruitful are introduction of modern marketing technique, better inventory control, better management practices, exploring new markets, keeping the cost of marketing low, and efficacious use of mass media for consumer education and market promotion. These measures would lead to a fuller utilization of human resources and usher a new chapter in the economic development of the Ganga Basin.

REFERENCES

Abercombie, K.C. (1961), The Transition Subsistence to Market Agriculture in Africa South of the Shara, F.A.O., *Monthly Bulletin of Agricultural Economics and Statistics*, Vol. 10, No. 2, quoted in Jakhade, V.M. and Majumdar, N.A. (1963), Subsistence Sector in Indian Agriculture, *Reserve Bank of India Bulletin*, Vol. 18, No. 9.

Dandekar, V.M. (1988), The Indian Society of Agriculture Economics, *The Next Stage*, Bombay.

Dantwala, M.L., Agrarian Structure and Agrarian Relations in India, in *Indian Agricultural Development Since Independence*, Indian Society of Agricultural Economics, New Delhi.

Findlay, Allan, and Anne Findlay, (1987), *Population and Development in the Third World*, London.

Government of India (1985), *Seventh Five Year Plan*, 1985-1990, Vol. 2, Planning Commission, New Delhi.

Government of India (1987), *India: A Reference Annual*, 1987, Publication Division, Ministry of Information and Broadcasting, New Delhi.

Government of India, Ministry of Argiculture and Irrigation (1976), *Report of the National Commission on Agriculture*, Vol. XII and XIII, New Delhi.

Indian Council of Social Science Research (ICSSR) (1980), *Alternatives in Agricultural Development : In ICSSR Working Group Report*, Allied Publishers, New Delhi.

Jakhade, V.M. and N.A. Majumdar, (1963), Subsistence Sector in Indian Agriculture, *Reserve Bank of India Bulletin*, Vol. 18, No. 9.

Khusro, A.M. (1968), *Readings in Agricultural Development* (Edited), New Delhi.

Law, B.C., (1968), *Mountains and Rivers of India*, National Committee for Geography, Calcutta.

Madalgi, S.S. (1976), Trends in Monetisation in the Indian Economy 1961-62 to 1974-75, *Reserve Bank Staff Occasional Papers*, Vol 1, No. 1.

Minhas, B.S. (1970), Rural Poverty, Land Redistribution and Development Strategy, *Indian Economics Review*, Vol. 5, No. 1.

Nanavati, Manilal, B. and J.J. Anjaria, (1970), *The Indian Rural Problem*, Indian Society of Agricultural Economics, Bombay.

Narain Bharam (1961), Distribution of the Marketed Surplus of Agricultural Produce by Size Level of Holdings in India, 1950-51, *Occasional Paper No. 2*, Institute of Economic Growth, Delhi.

Pancey, Arnold and Philip Payne, (1985), *Agricultural Development and Nutrition* by Arrangement with F.A.O., London.

Raj, K.N. (1975), Agricultural Development and Distribution of Land Holdings, *Indian Journal of Agricultural Economics*, Vol. 30, No. 1.

Raj Krishna (1979), Small Farmers Development in Desai, M.B. (ed.), *Intervention for Rural Development : Experiences for Small Farmers Development Agency*, Indian Institute of Management, Ahmedabad.

Sidhu, D.S. and A.J. Singh, (1986), Technologyeal Change in Indian Agriculture in Dantwala, M.L. (ed.), *Indian Agricultural Development Since Independence*, New Delhi.

Subbarao, K. (1986), Agricultural Marketing, *Ibid.*, 1986.

A Report — IGU Regional Symposium

THE ROLE OF COMMERCIAL ACTIVITIES IN THE ECONOMIC DEVELOPMENT OF THE GANGA BASIN

(January 27-29, 1990)

The symposium on the role of commercial activities in the economic development of the Ganga Basin was organised under the auspices of the International Geographical Union Commission on Geography of Commercial Activities. The Symposium is one of the series of three symposia planned to be held at SAARC level in 1991 and at international level in 1992. In all 46 papers were presented in this symposium and 52 delegates from Bangladesh, India and Nepal participated.

PROCEEDINGS

Inaugural Session, 27.1.90

The *Inaugural Session* was presided over by Professor Mrs. Pratima Asthana, Vice-chancellor, University of Gorakhpur. Professor A.B. Mukerji was the Co-chairman. Mr. A.P. Verma, I.A.S., Commissioner, Gorakhpur Division, was the Chief Guest. Professor M. Shafi, Professor Emeritus, Aligarh Muslim University and Vice-President, International Geographical Union, was the chief speaker.

The inaugural session commenced with a prayer song in honour of the Goddess of learning, Saraswati, followed by a welcome song in honour of the guests and delegates present.

Dr. V.K. Shrivastava, Director of the symposium and Member of the IGU Commission, introduced the aims, objects and organisation of the symposium. He highlighted the work of the Commission on Geography of Commercial Activities under the leadership of Professor A. Metton of France. It was brought to the notice of the audience that the Commission has brought out a number of publications, newsletter and has been able to organise many symposia in various parts of the world.

Professor Mrs. Pratima Asthana inaugurated the symposium by lighting an earthen lamp. In her address she dwelt upon the place of geography among the social sciences and highlighted the importance of the river Ganga. She stressed that a geographical study of the Ganga Basin, focussing mainly on commercial activities and economic development will be practical and useful both. She further added that there is a great need for improving geographical literacy in order that we might deepen our knowledge and comprehension of national and international events and enhance our performance in peaceful and developmental activities.

Mr. A.P. Verma, the chief guest of the session, lauded the role that geographers can play in the economic development of areas. He emphasised the need of commercialization of agricultural and development of agro-industries for the economic development of the Ganga Basin. He asserted that geographers can fruitfully advise administrations in coming over hurdles of plan implementation etc.

Professor M. Shafi delivered the Key-Note address. Professor Shafi said that there is no alluvial basin in the world so vast, so fertile and so level as the plain of the Ganga Basin. The economy of the basin depends on subsistence agriculture characterised by a large percentage of cereals and some cash crops. He highlighted the vicious circle of poverty, low nutritional intake, ill health and low productivity in which the farmers of the Ganga Basin have been caught and posed the question of taking the farmers out of the web of poverty. Professor Shafi explained the four stages suggested by Abercromblie of commercialization leading to economic development. The Ganga Basin, according to him, falls in the third stage where the regular production of market oriented surplus is aimed at but the main emphasis is still on subsistence production. He mentioned the efforts of National Bank for Agricultural and Rural Development (NABARD), Agricultural Credit Department (ACD), Rural

Planning and Credit Cell of the Reserve Bank of India (RPCC) and Agricultural Refinance and Development Corporation (ARDC) for providing credit for the promotion of agriculture. The economic development of the Ganga Basin can be accelerated if aspects such as marketing of surplus agricultural produce, storage, transporations, grading, marketing efficiency and development of infrastructure and the establishment of agro-processing industries are looked into. The marketing strategy needs to be re-oriented to meet the consumer needs. He concluded that marketing and commercial activities would play a vital role in the economic development of the Ganga Basin if the activities are properly organised. Dr. J. N. Pandey thanked the audience on behalf of the Department.

Technical Session I

Chairman — Prof M. Shafi
Co-Chaiman — Prof. N. Sharma
Rapporteaur — Dr. Debashis Das

Theme — Commercialization of Agriculture and Economic Development.

Dr. Mrs. Abha Lakshmi Singh (Aligarh) in her paper 'Impact of Prices on Area Under Crops in Upper Ganga-Yamuna Doab' examined the issue of correlation between the extent and trend of price rise and those of area under concerned twelve selected crops. The paper examined the responses of farmers to changing patterns of cropping due to economic profit. Positive and negative correlations were noted in specific crops.

The second paper was presented by Professor (Ms) Champa Mitra (Burdwan). She discussed the significance of processing industry related to agricultural products in her paper on 'Agro-Processing and Economic Development in West Bengal'. She remarked that agro-processing is significant in view of export based agriculture and for generating employment outside agriculture.

Technical Session II (27.1.1990)

Chairman — Prof. A.B. Mukerji
Co-chairman — Prof. Suchit Sur
Rapporteaur — Dr. R.C. Srivastava

Theme — Agro-Industries and Economic Development

Dr. A.K. Sarkar (Calacutta) presented a paper 'Agro-Industries and Economic Development in Burdwan: A Case Study in Remote Sensing Techniques'. Dr. Sarkar stressed on the use of satellite imageries and areal photographs in the identification of land systems zones. The potenital land resource zones can then be identified.

The second paper was presented by V.B. Singh and S.S. Verma (Gorakhpur). The paper 'Horticulture and Rural Development: A Case Study of Ghazipur Tahsil' was based on primary data generated after interviewing 400 farmers of 16 selected villages. The authors observed that horticulture plays an important role in economic development by adding to the income of the farmers.

Technical Session III (28.1.1990)

Chairman — Prof. H.H. Singh
Co-chairman — Dr. Noor Mohammed
Rapporteaur — Dr. (Ms) Abha Lakshmi Singh

Theme — Industrialisation and Economic Development

Dr. S.C. Sharma and Dr. D.N. Tripathi (Balrampur) presented a paper on 'Industrialisation and Economic Development: A Case Study of Amethi Tahsil'. The Role of existing industries in the economic development of Amethi Tahsil, part of former Prime Minister's constituency, was explained in details. Suggestions were given for further industrial development.

Prof. N.K. De (Burdwan) analysed the industrial structure of 24-Paraganas in his paper 'Industrial Potential and Economic Development in the District 24-Pargana, West Bengal'. The components of industrial resources were analysed and possibilities of development were explored.

Dr. M.P. Tripathi and P.C. Poudel (Nepal) analysed the

role of agriculture in the economic development in their paper on 'Agricultural Pattern and Economic Development in Ganga Basin: A Case Study of Western Development Region in Nepal'. Migration and means of irrigation were identified as main factors in controlling agriculture.

Dr. Suchit Sur (Darjeeling) emphasised the role of horticulture for economic development through his paper entitled 'The Role of Specific Crops in North Bengal in the Regional and State's Economy'. He highlighted the role of plantation crops and mulberry in the region. Aspects of tea plantation were discussed in details.

Technical Session IV (28.1.1990)

Chairman — Prof. N.K. De
Co-chairman — Dr. M.P. Tripathi
Rapporteaur — Dr. B.R.K. Sinha

Theme — Infrastructure and Regional Trade

The first paper was presented by Debashis Das (Santiniketan) on 'Problems and Prospects of Mandis in Ajoy-Kopai Inter-riverine Tract of Birbhum District, West Bengal'. The spatio-temporal orgnization of mandis, the process of marketing, problems and prospects were discussed. Dr. (Ms) K.R. Shrivastava (Gorakhpur) discussed 'Periodic Markets, Central Places and Regional Development: A Case Study of Baghelkhand Region'. The nature of market cycles, spatial gaps in service areas and the role of markets in socio-economic development was discussed. Mr. O.P. Sharma (Lucknow) discussed the role of regulated markets in the process of development through his paper on 'Regulated Markets as Focal Point of Economic Development: A Case Study of Mohibullapur Mandi, Lucknow'. Dr. V.K. Shrivastava touched various un-noticed aspects of rural market-transport relationship through his investigations in the lower order means of transportation and market activities. His paper 'Socio-Economic Implications of Rural Market-Transportation Relations: A Case Study of the Middle Ganga Valley' highlighted empirical aspects and their theoretical implications. Dr. Miss P. Hinge and Dr. Miss V. Phanse discussed the 'Hierarchy of Service Centres: A Case Study of

Ujjain District' with empirical data and relevant maps. Dr. M.P. Tripathi and Dr. P.C. Poudel presented examples from Nepal regarding the role of commercial activities in rural development through their paper on 'Commercial Activities and Economic Development in the Ganga Basin: A Case Study from Nepal'. Dr. (Ms) Razia Sultana (Dhaka) explained the characteristics of market cenres of Bangaladesh through her paper entitled 'A Geographical Analysis of Market Centres of Satkhira Upzila, Bangladesh'. The random location of markets and its implications in the process of development were highlighted through maps and excellent discussion. Dr. Noor Mohammad (Delhi) explained how the socio-economic disparities can be reduced through citing examples from his paper on 'Levels of Agricultural Development in Uttar Pradesh'. Four levels of development were identified and their character was explained. Dr. V.N. Lal (Pokhari Quli, Garhwal) drew attention towards the significance of rural markets in the economic development of Hill areas through his paper 'Profile of a Rural Hilly Market of Garhwal Himalaya: A Case Study'. Dr. J. N. Pandey (Gorakhpur) and Dr. Bharat Pandey (Ballia) elaborated how land consolidation is influencing crop pattern through their paper on 'Impact of Consolidtion on Commercial Crops'. Dr. M.D. Shulkla (Balrampur) discussed 'Transportation Planning for Eco-development: A Case Study of Balrampur, Gonda District.'

Technical Session V (28.1.1990)

Chairman — Dr. S.C. Sharma
Co-chairman — Dr. S.S. Katare
Rapporteaur — Dr. A.K. Sarkar

Theme — Role of Infrastructure and Regional Trade in Development

Dr. N. Sharma (Darbhanga) discussed a valueable model through his paper on 'Planning Commercial Activities in North Bihar: A Desired Developmental Dimension'. Dr. R.C. Srivastava (Kanpur) highlighted the problems of retail periodic markets in million cities in his paper 'Periodic Markets in Million Cities of the Ganga Basin: A Case Study of Kanpur'. Dr. K.D. Sharma (Chandigarh) presented his paper on 'Some

Questions on the Persistence of Periodic Markets in Economically Developed Areas'. He raised the questions on the persistence of periodic markets in view of the changes in threshold and the nature of economy. Do markets really represent historical heritage, he asked. Miss Alpana Chandra (Gorakhpur) analysed the role of periodic markets in agricultural development in her paper 'Impact of Periodic Markets on Agricultural Development in Deoria District'. Miss Rekha Pandey (Gorakhpur) highlighted the 'Socio-economic Facilities and Economic Development in Pratapgarh District' of Uttar Pradesh. The viability of handloom industry vis-a-vis powerloom was examined by S.S. Singh (Maunath Bhanjan) in his paper on 'Characteristics of Household Textile Industry in Azamgarh and Mau Districts'. P.R. Chauhan and V.K. Chaudhary (Gorakhpur) analysed 'Commercial Activities in a Rural Market of Urban Fringe of Gorakhpur Town'.

Technical Session VI (29.1.1990)

Chairman — Prof. Ghampa Mitra
Co-chairman — Dr. K.D. Sharma
Rapporteaur — Dr. P.R. Chauhan

Theme — Human Resources, Manpower Planning and Economic Development

Dr. Ajit Jain (Sagar) analysed the movement pattern of traders of Vidisha plateau in his paper 'Spatio-Temporal Organisation of Tertiary Sector: A Meso-Regional Study'. He concluded that trader movement has become radial from the place of origin, though previously it was peripheral. Dr. S.S. Katare (Jabalpur) preseneted an analysis of 'Geography of Violent Crimes of the Lower Chambal Valley'. He highlighted that the terrain governs the incidence of crimes in the study region. The spatial pattern of crimes and the habitats of criminals were anaylsyed in details. Dr. S.K. Dikshit (Gorakhpur) discussed his paper on 'Socio-economic Influence on Electroal Participation in Eastern U.P.' and noted that the Indian political system can function in essentially traditional social system and can still serve the modern political goals. He tested the influence of literacy, urban population and male population on electoral participation. Dr. B.R.K. Sinha (Shanti

Niketan) identified the levels of human resource development and their relation with economic growth in his paper on 'Levels of Human Resource Development and Economic Growth in a Segment of the Middle Ganga Plain'. Dr. H. Lal and Dr. C.B. Verma (Gorakhpur) discussed the evidences of marked growth of urban population and its extreme concentration within built up areas of selected urban centres in their paper on 'Dimensions of Urban Population Pressure and Development in U.P.' Dr. J.N. Pandey (Gorakhpur) remarked that population control and conservation is the immediate need in his paper on 'Human Resource Planning and Economic Development in Saryupar Plain of U.P.' The pattern of performance of family planning measures was discussed jointly by Dr. H. Lal and Miss Madhu Yadav (Gorakhpur) in their paper 'Family Planning Performance and Socio-economic Development in the Ganga Basin'.

Technical Session VII (29.1.1990)

Chairman — Dr. S.K. Shukla
Co-chairman — Dr. G.P. Shrivastava
Rapporteaur — Dr. H.R. Yadav

Theme — Energy, Environment and Resources

Dr. S.N. Singh (Gorakhpur) explained the identification of levels of industrialisation through census data in his paper entitled 'Levels of Industrialisation in Eastern Uttar Pradesh'. Dr. Mahatam Prasad and Dr.S.P.L. Srivastava (Peppeganj) in a study based on primary data remarked that shop owners of weaker sections of the society are engaged in less income generating business in their paper on 'Socio-economic Structure of Shop Owners in Peppeganj — A Market Town'. Dr. H. Lal and Dr. D.P. Yadav (Gorakhpur) presented an account of sample rural markets lying in an urban fringe through their paper 'Geographical Personality of a Rural Urban Fringe Market and its Impact on the Economic Conditions'. Dr. J.S. Verma (Anandnagar) and Dr. V. N. Chaudhary (Naugarh) discussed the 'Transformation of Tharus in Gorakhpur Tarai' and highlighted the cultural transformation of Tharus and its impact on the economy of the region. Dr. J.S. Verma further highlighted the

'Changing Scene of Rural Environment: A Geographical Assessment' taking examples from the Tarai region of U.P. Mr. V.K. Chaudhary (Gorakhpur) analysed the 'Ecological Complex and Market Development in Garhwal Himalayas'. Dr. V.K. Shrivastava (Gorakhpur) discussed 'Policy Responses to Spatial Inequalities: A Case Study of Uttar Pradesh'. The Role played by agricultural pricing policy and the implementation of developmental schemes was highlighted. Mrs. Sharmila Mazumdar discussed the project outline on 'A Geographical Study of 24-Parganas on Energy, Environment and Development'.

A few supplementary papers were also presented. Dr. J.P. Rai (Maunathbhanjan) and Dr. R.N. Rai (Chibramau) discussed the 'Spatial Distribution of Market Centres in Middle Son Basin'. Shahab Fazal (Aligarh) presented his study on 'Impact of Price Movement on Area Under Sugarcane in Saharanpur District'. The district registered 230 per cent increase in sugarcane production in about 25 years due to price rise. Dr. V.K. Pandey, Dr. S.C. Singh (Bhabhnan) and Dr. S.S. Verma (Gorakhpur) assessed the 'Impact of Irrigation on Agricultural Development in Gorakhpur District'. Dr. S.S. Verma and Dr. L.C. Yadav (Gorakhpur) further emphasised the 'Impact of Water Management on Agricultural Development: A Case Study of Rohilkhand Plain'. Dr. P.R. Chauhan, Dr. Ram Surat Singh and Mr. Chandra Shekhar (Gorakhpur) discussed examples of 'Wholesale Agricultural Markets and Rural Development from Middle Ganga Plain'. Nizamuddin Khan (Aligarh) highlighted the 'Role of Periodic Markets on Agricultural Marketing System in North India: A Case Study of Faizabad District'. Dr. H. Lal, (Gorakhpur), Dr. H.R. Yadav (Bhatpar Rani) and Dr. O.N. Misra (Bansi) discussed a strategy for 'Transforming Spatial Inequality' through a case study.

Panel Discussion (27.1.1990)

Chairpersons — Prof. L.B. Tripathi
Prof, A.B. Mukerji

Panel Members — Dr. Pandey B.B. Lal, Dr. C.P. Singh, Prof, Mrs. Champa Mitra

Theme — Dimensions of Development

A Panel Discussion was organised in the evening of the first day of the conference. The chairpersons included Professor L.B. Tripathi (Gorakhpur), a psychologist and Pro-Vice-Chancellor, University of Gorakhpur, and Prof. A.B. Mukerji (Chandigarh). The panel members included Dr. Pandey B.B. Lal, Principal, Engineering College, Gorakhpur, Dr. C.P. Singh (Department of Geography, Delhi School of Economics), Member, Commonwealth Geographical Bureau, and Prof. Champa Mitra (Burdwan).

Dr. V.K. Shrivastava, Director of the Symposium, introduced the panel members to the audience. As development is a multi-dimensional value loaded concept, he said, it was felt necessary that experts from various field were invited to share their thoughts with geographers. He welcomed the participation of Mr. G. Singh, Manager, State Bank of India, who sponsered the panel discussion.

Initiating the discussion Professor L.B. Tripathi pointed out that development is a very complex concept. It carries surplus meaning and it may carry two different meanings even for two persons belonging to the same discipline. The country decided about four decades back to start activities that could lead to development. Development is a multi-dimensional concept and its conspicuous aspects will be discussed by the specialists. He called upon Prof. Mukerji to direct further discussions. Prof. Mukerji emphasised that we can understand development through the ideas given by shcolars of various disciplines. He elaborated the horizontal concept of development in the form of balanced regional development and vertical concept which incorporates inter-sectoral development. A balanced development of different sectors leads to the formation of rural and urban economy. Various regions are linked together through the process of production, distribution and consumption. Balanced regional development should be seen in the context of production, distribution and consumption.The ultimate decision about development is not taken through the models that geography or economics are producing but by the political will of the party in power. The balance between various sectors of development in primary, secondary, tertiary and quarternary sectors (in third world countries the first three sectors are more important) is also necessary. The vertical and horizontal sectors need integration. Dr. C.P. Singh emphasised that development should be looked from the point of view of the human beings and their environment in which they live. In the Gandhian concept, development was oriented towards the individual, the down trodden men. The word 'socialism' emnated from our Constitution due to the very need of production of what, distribution where and consumption by whom. Geographers are mainly concerned with who get what and where. There is a continuous conflict in post-independent India between development and environment. The question is can we have development with environmental conservation or is it that development carries within it-self the seeds of the destruction of environment. Professor Champa Mitra (Burdwan) said that economic development is proportional to the degree of technology adoption. Some times technology is infused in various regions without assessing their resources. At times development planning can not be implemented in remote regions because of lack of integration with the people residing there. Developmental planning in many cases cannot be implemented because of the psychological reactions of people residing in the area and because of the ignorance of the environmental conditions prevailing in the area of implementation. Dr. Pandey B.B. Lal (Gorakhpur) stressed the role of planning for irrigation in the Ganga Basin for speedy development. In flood prone areas like eastern Uttar Pradesh, water management is very important as every year immense loss occurs to cattle, crops and human beings. He highlighted the role of big storage dams in controlling floods and providing water for irrigation. Dr. Pandey lamented the opposition to the construction of Tehri Dam in U.P. hills by a section of people under the cover of Gandhian thoughts. Gandhi had much broader vision of development and the opposition to Tehri dam is politically motivated. For development planning for agriculture, irrigation and industries is essential in the Ganga Basin, he added. The development projects must be modernised and new technology should be brought in for better results.

Professor A.B. Mukerji later invited reactions from the delegates. Dr. B.R.K. Sinha (Shantiniketan) said that development should incorporate natural, human and cultural resources. Human resource should be developed as social resource. Professor N.K. De (Burdwan) emphasised that geographers should concentrate on land, air and water in their attempts to contribute to studies of development. The resoruces should be properly utilised to accomodate growing population. Dr. Noor Mohd. (Delhi) was of the opinion that sustainable development must take place. It should be for the enhancement of quality of life. We should have development in which environment is not under the stress beyond the limits of recovery. We should develop in a manner so that our social fabric is not destroyed. Dr. Asit Sarkar (NATMO, Calcutta) drew attention on physical, economic and social constraints in development. All these factors put together hinder the process of development. Dr. S.K. Shukla (Sagar) emphasised the need for involvement of people in the process of development. The concept of target group in development, i.e. the development for whom, should be adequately taken care of.

Professor L.B. Tripathi summarised the scenario of four decades of developmental efforts in India. He said that the focus of development should be the man and the environment in which he lives.

Field Session (28.1.1990)

The commercial profile of Gorakhpur town was discussed by the delegates in the afternoon session on 28th of January. The trip commenced from the southern tip of the town where the international Buddhist Tourist Complex is in the offing known as 'Ramgarh Tal Project'. The establishment of 'Transport Town', New Gorakhpur Town and the huge tourist complex-cum-residential areas points to the potential shift of the commercial hub of the town to the south. From south the field trip proceeded to the mid-west commercial areas and the modern and recently developed commercial areas of 'Golghar'. The newly constructed shops, parks and wide four-lane roads during 1987-89 period when the state of U.P. was ruled by a geographer Chief-Minister have generated a re-alignment of business activities. Most of the double storey building are attracting agencies, offices, afternoon bankers, computer companies and show-room business in the upper storey blocks. The growth of hotels, restaurants and eating places has also taken place. The field trip route then traversed the most densely populated part of Dharamshala Bazar which generates very heavey traffic rather throughout the day due to its strategic location as a linking point of the northern and western parts of the twon. Surveying its afternoon daily vegetable markete the delegates were taken around the 'Gita Garden' which is world famous for bringing out the cheapest religious and cultural books through 'Gita Press'. The field trip then passed through the eastern parts of the town through 'Railway Colony' to the newly developing shopping areas of Mohaddipur. The trip then culminated at the famous 'Gorakhnath Temple' after which the town is named. It was the occassion of an annual fair at the temple and the variety of goods, entertainment and people around there were studied with keen interest. The field trip later concluded with an evening session where the outcome of the field trip was discussed and a few papers were also presented.

Planery Session (29.1.1990)

The planery session was presided over by Dr. Jagdish Singh, Head, Department of Geography, Gorakhpur University. Dr. V.K. Shrivastava, Director of the Seminar, called upon the speakers to suggest recommendations and give their impressions about the three-days Symposium. Dr. Hira Lal Yadav presented a brief summary of the proceedings of various technical sessions. Professor Udai Raj Rai, Dean, Faculty of Law, University of Gorakhpur, was the chief guest of the session. Following Dr. Hira Lal, Prof. A.B. Mukerji examined the entire organisation of the Symposium in context of the two forthcoming symposia at SAARC level and at the international level. Lauding the academic output of the symposium he emphasised that local level seminars on the theme should be held focussing on small rural areas so that they could be linked with the IGU. The information generated by young geographers working in these areas should be strengthened by conceptualisation by experts. He called upon the geographers to carry out more research on rural marketing systems in the country.

Professor Udai Raj Rai, emphasised that a systematic and well planned marketing system can help in the development of the economy of the Ganga Basin. He said that the law related to the exchange economy should be biased in favour of the peasants. The artificaial trade barriers between states should be removed and a common market for agricultural produce shoud be provided. The farmers should get real profit form their produce which is now being shared by whole-sale agents and traders. The economic development of the Ganga Basin depends upon the development of the farmers, he said. Dr. Jagdish Singh summarised the research potential that can be utilised in studying the economic development of the Ganga Basin. Lastly, Dr. V.K. Srivastava proposed a vote of thanks to all who contributed for the sucess of the Symposium.

Recommendations

The following recommendations were unanimously adopted:

(i) Commercialization of agriculture in the Ganga Basin should be given top priority in agricultural policy.

(ii) Indian rural markets should be studied in details.

(iii) An atlas of rural markets should be prepared.

(iv) The bias in public policy to make more grains available to urban population should be reduced.

(v) A law should be enacted to make the whole country as one common market by removing all artificial barriers of boundaries or of commodities.

(vi) Universalization of western models is dangerous to research.

(vii) Rural development can be accelerated by bringing the balance of market profit in favour of the farmers.

V.K. Shrivastava
Director

Introduction

The book in hand is the outcome of the proceedings of the International Geographical Union Regional Symposium on the Role of Commercial Activities in the Economic Development of the Ganga Basin. The symposium was held at the Department of Geography, University of Gorakhpur, Gorakhpur in January, 1990, under the ageis of the International Geographical Union Commission on Commercial Activities. Under the chairmanship of Prof. Alain Metton a series of meetings, seminars, symposia and conferences were organised all over the world. The Ganga Basin symposia was one such academic event.

The selection of the theme had a simple reason behind it. The integrative nature of commercial activities is best reflected in the level of economic development of a region. The relation between commercial activities and economic development is mutual. Hence, the study of economic development would call for a detailed discussion and analysis of the main objective of the Commission. Secondly, the selection of the focal region, i.e. the Ganga Basin, was also deliberate. IGU activities are normally expected to be international in the sense that more academic interaction should be generated. The Ganga Basin is inherently international as it encompasses three nations — Bangladesh, India and Nepal. It is also one of the major river basins of the world and has been one of the cradles of civilization. This region has given to the world the oldest literature of mankind, i.e. the *vedas* and the *puranas*. The region has been a witness to two great epics, *the Ramayana* and the *Mahabharata* which represent scientifically advanced and culturally matured stages of man. It is also one of the most densely populated parts of the world with rich natural and human resources. The waters of the Ganga (Ganges) coupled with rich natural, human and animal resources have provided a natural context for the development of commercial activities from agriculture to industry and infrastructural aspects. Thus the focal region has been generating commercial activities since ages and the symposia provided a platform to scientists, academicians, administrators, planners and politicians to deliberate upon the theme.

II

Commercial activities are of a catalyst nature. They stimulate the forward and backward linkages of the existing economic system and initiate transformations. The weak economic processes are unable to sustain the invigorating impulse and wane. The economic activities which re-configurate and re-adjust with changing techno-economic conditions develop and mutually strengthen the economic processes leading to economic growth. Economic growth leads to polarisation of economic development and a series of growth points and growth poles develop. The growth poles then start disseminating development impulses to the region they serve. Thus the process of economic development is initiated.

Economic development alone will not result in sustainable development. It is because economic development is usually oriented to mass production and accumulation of wealth. The development is polarised lacking integration with non-economic processes. Also, economic development is an endless process leading to the extraction of resources to the extent that either they are exhausted or they are commercially unviable. Economic development generally ignores human dimensions. In a way it exploites environmental resources and leads to pollution of environment. This in turn endangers the society. Economic development must be sustainable. For sustainable development a balance in resource use and environment is necessary. This needs a global out look rather than a regional one. Levels of human resource development and economic growth must be mutually conducive. Only then economic development can have some meaning.

Economic development is of the people and for the people. This fact is rather ignored in the blind race of development. Such ignorance leads to social tensions, crimes and disturbs peace. Trade war is the ultimate result which overshadows political warfare. Thus socio-economic implications of development become more important than economic development alone. The Ganga Basin with a major chunk of world's population and a longer history of human survival than most parts of the world thus presents a suitable context for examining the theme of the symopsium.

III

Commercialization of agriculture and economic deveopment focusses on rural development in general. This theme is initiated with the exposition of the grographical personality of the Ganga Basin by U. Singh. It is followed by three analytical papers by R.S. Dube on marketing potential, by Abha Lakshmi Singh and Shahab Fazal on pricing system and by Suchit Sur on the role of specific crops in raising the income of farmers. The relationship between commercialization of agriculture and economic development in plateau region of the Ganga Basin has further been examined by C.A. Jain and A.K. Jain followed by a discussion of food distribution system in peri-urban space by V.K. Shrivastava.

IV

Agricultural development would be vertically reflected in agro-industrial development. The relationship between agro-industries and economic development have been highlighted by A.K. Sarkar and N.K. De. They have applied remote sensing technique in assessing the potential of development. Bangladesh is a unique entity of the Ganga Basin and Rejuan Bhuiyan has made an indepth analysis of the role of agro industries, particularly sugarcane industry, in Bangladesh. Emperical studies alone cannot guide the destiny of a subject unless supported by theoretical underpinnings. The paper by Champa Mitra focusses on such a theme when she analyses agro-processing and economic development through a case study.

V

The level of industrial development is an indicator of economic achievement. The focal region, i.e. Ganga Basin, is primarily an agricultural area where large scale heavy industries are not viable. But human enterprises seem to possess an inbuilt mechanism of expanding its entrepreneurship to the maximum within limitations. The Hooghly region of the Ganga

Basin is an area where large scale industrial development based primarily on agricultural resources has been studied from this perspective by messers N.K. De and A.K. Mandal. Industrialisation is now a widely recognised phenomena in this rich agricultural region. It is truly reflected in the case studies by S.K. Shukla and Rolee Shankar on Madhya Pradesh and in one of the most backward but politically most significant part of the Basin, i.e., Sultanpur district in the paper by messers D.N. Tripathi, S.C. Sharma and O.P. Mishra.

VI

The theme which attracted attention of most of the participants is the role of infrastructure in economic development. It includes a wide range of papers on periodic markets, regulated markets, central planes, hierarchy and planning etc. Razia Sultana has attempted a sophisticated analysis of rural markets of Satkhira Upzila of Bangladesh. The role of regulated markets in eastern and central Uttar Pradesh has been discussed by P.R. Chauhan and R.S. Singh and by O.P. Sharma respectively. The core concept which emerges from these papers is that regulated markets play a significant role in the process of economic development. This theme has further been examined by M.P. Tripathi and P.C. Poudel in Nepal, by R.C. Srivastava in Kanpur metropolis and by Debashish Das in Birbhum district. It is followed by a micro-level case study of the anatomy of betel leaf market by R.S. Dixit. Nizamuddin Khan has elaborated the role of periodic markets in agricultural marketing system, providing an insight as to how an element of exhange functions within a system of which it is an integral part. Such micro-level studies include a discussion of the socio-economic characteristics of shop owners of Peppeganj market of the pioneer fringe of the Ganga Basin, i.e. Uttar Pradesh tarai, by Mahatam Prasad and S.P.L. Srivastava.

Spatio-Temporal aspect of infrastructure of any region have a direct bearing on its economic development. These aspects have been duly emphasised in the papers by Vishwa Nath on Awadh Plain and by A.K. Jain and C.K. Jain on a meso region of Madhya Pradesh. Vijaya Phanse and Pragati Hinge have worked out the hierarchy of service centres and have emphasised how economic development is controlled by functional compatibility of such centres. Socio-economic implications of rural market-transportation relations have been highlighted by V.K. Shrivastava and K.N. Tiwari, through a case study of Ghazipur district of middle Ganga valley. Planning is basic to all developmental efforts. J.P. Rai and R.N. Rai have put forward the integrated rural development planning of middle Son Basin. Nandeshwar Sharma has exposed the dimension of development for planning of commercial activities in north Bihar. Perodic markets persist with whatever level of economic development there may be. Periodic markets themselves reflect low level of economic activity but they persist even in highly developed areas. K.D. Sharma has examined this unique phenomena from economically developed areas. The role of periodic markets as central places and their role in regional development has been highlighted by K.R. Shrivastava through study of north-eastern peninsular region. Thus an adequate analysis of infrastructure and economic development has been presented to emphasise the infrastructural elements of economic development.

VII

Economic development is the outcome of the mutual relationship between human resources and environment. The levels of human resource development and economic growth has been the focus of study of the paper by B.R.K. Sinha. Similarly, Sheo Shankar Verma has made a comparative study of socio-economic development in the upper and middle Ganga valley. Development is the out come of human efforts and human desires which are reflected through the political system created and followed by the people of a region. S.K. Dikshit has presented this vital theme of socio-eonomic influence on electoral participation in eastern Uttar Pradesh. Economic development leads to changes in rural environment and it is evinced in a study made by J.S. Verma. The development is not devoid of social tensions as well. S.S. Katare has exposed the geography of violent crimes of the lower Chambal Basin.

Thus the proceedings of the symposium on the role of commercial activites in the Ganga Basin presents a comprehensive picture of commercial activities and their impact on environment, society and development.

Theme-I

Commercialization of Agriculture and Economic Development

ONE

Geographical Personality of Ganga Basin

U. SINGH

The Ganga plain, the eastern portion of the Great Plain of India is a unique geographical region of the world. It extends between the Himalayan-Tibetan area in the north and the Deccan plateau in the south, between the river Yamuna backed by the Delhi ridge, the northern most portion of the Aravallis, in the West and Bengal Delta in the east, and covers the major portions of three largest states of Uttar Pradesh, Bihar and Bengal. The plain is unique in the sense that 'it is of overwhelmingly predominant importance to the well-being of the people and peace of the subcontinent. The plain has been known as the heart of India (Madhya Pradesh) possessing the richness and resources of par excellence. The advantage of its geographical location provided it a background for racial, cultural and politico-economic interactions and assimilation since time immemorial.

Its uniqueness lies in the fact that here, perhaps nowhere else in the world, one single river system (i.e. the Ganga river system) has influenced the life pattern of the people of not only of the region but of the whole Indian sub-continent.

Structure, Relief and Landform

The plain, bounded by the 'boundary faults' of tertiary foot hill zone in the north and the spurs of the Deccan plateau in the south, is made of very thick alluvial deposits. Its depth has been recently estimated as 1300 to 1400 m. The alluvial deposits consists of silt, clay and sand intermingled with gravels.

The height of the plain decreases from the Himalayan foot hills in the north (100m) to the plateau river in south and from west (100m) to 30m in the middle and 3m further down in the deltaic region. It slopes with an average gradient of 9.5 cm per km from west-north-west to east-south-east with local variations caused by the changing courses of rivers and the resultant deposits or erosion of sediments in their flood plain.

Thus the plain has a dead flat surface lacking visual relief features (Fig. 1.1).

Ganga, the life line of the plain, takes its rise from its catchment area in the snowy Himalayas and following that general line of the land flows in south-south easterly direction against the plateau spurs beneath. Hence all along its course from Allahabad to Rajmahal the right bank of the river is steep and 8 to 15m high. West of Allahabad the Yamuna which runs along the Delhi Ridge, strikes the plateau rim around Agra. Hence Geddes terms Ganga and Yamuna as the rim rivers.

It may be mentioned here that all important cities of the Ganga plain lie on the right bank of the river close to the plateau spurs. Allahabad, Varanasi, Patna, Bhagalpur grew on the right bank of the Ganga being comparatively higher and broader and generally safe from floods, while Delhi and Agra developed in the Yamuna meanders. But the northern tributaries of the Ganga, though receiving their waters from the snowy Himalayas, are sluggishly flowing rivers. They form a type of inland delta at their confluence which Geddes terms as 'cone'.

The flood plains of the river basins are dotted with *tals*, oxbow lakes and deserted channels of rivers.

The drainage pattern is dendritic in general and most of the rivers meet at acute angle and form parallel or sub-parallel lines to the main stream. Braidings and meandering of rivers are the common features and the sandy shoals are often liable to flood during the monsoon when changing and shifting of river channels are common features. Gomati, Ghaghara, Rapti, Gandak and Kosi are notorious for shifting of their beds (Fig. 1.2).

The most important tributary meeting the Ganga from the south is the Son forming a narrow flood plain dotted with eroded hillocks, sometimes projecting on the river bank.

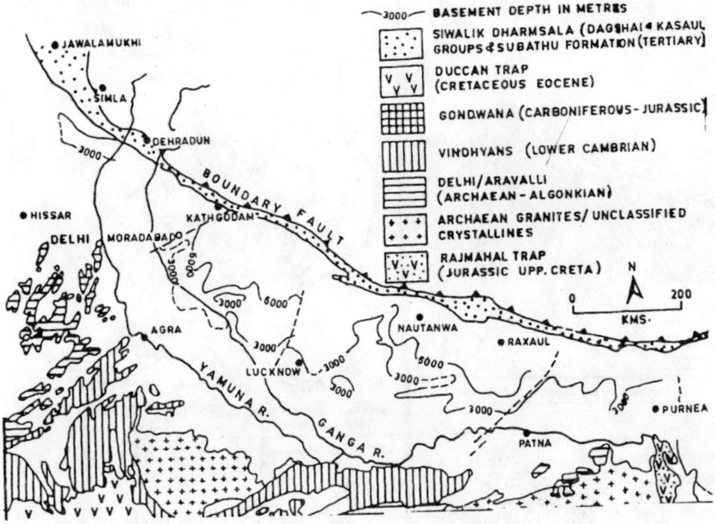

FIG. 1.1: The Basement Structure and Depth of Indo-Gangetic Plain

Further east, the Ganga traverses south-south east wards against the Rajmahal hills, the north-eastern spur of the peninsular plateau. Here it is divided into two large distributaries, the Bhagirathi or Hooghly running due south, and the Padma flowing to south easterly direction. The deltaic plain here is characterised by low elevation from 30m in the north to 4.5m in the south. Even 7m high tide is sufficient to submerge the region upto Calcutta. The delta proper has a gradient of less than 2cm per km and is the land of dead and decaying rivers. To its south is the stretch of Sunderbans.

The topographical and drainage differences have brought significant changes in the soil morphology. They differ in texture from drift sands to fine and heavy clays. They are rich in minerals and organic plant-food but normally deficient in nitrogen. The coastal soils are the interactions of river and tides and are saline and alkaline containing generally half decomposed materials.

Climatically, the plain ranges from sub-humid in the upper to humid in the middle and humid sub-continental type in the lower plain. In the upper plain January mean is 16°C but maximum temperature sometimes in June goes upto

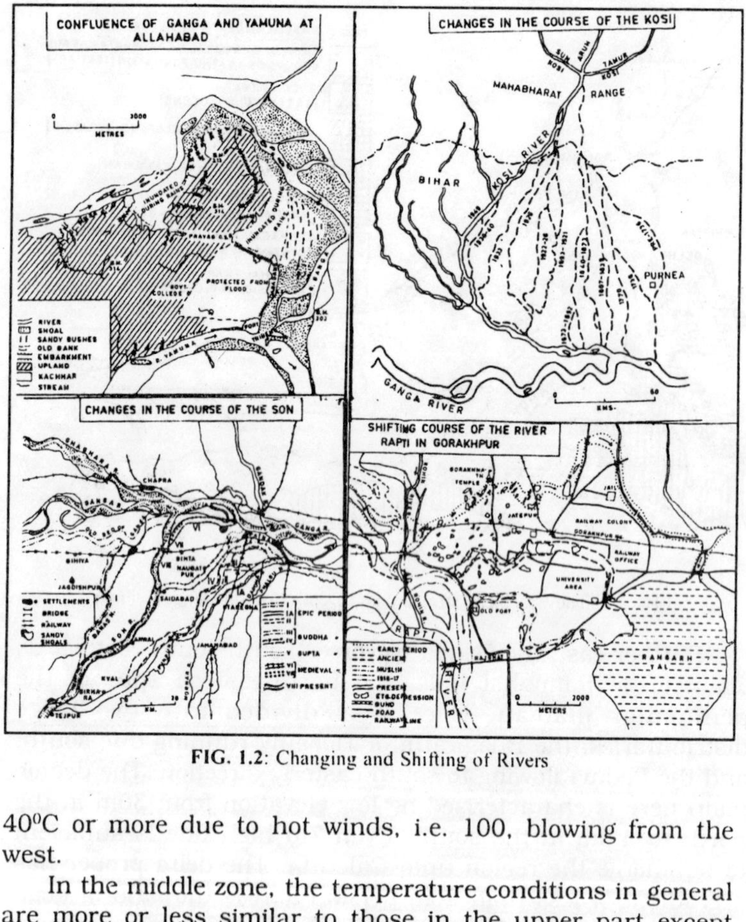

FIG. 1.2: Changing and Shifting of Rivers

40°C or more due to hot winds, i.e. 100, blowing from the west.

In the middle zone, the temperature conditions in general are more or less similar to those in the upper part except the range of temperature is slightly lower.

In the lower plain, no doubt, climate is little different from its counterparts in the north-west. In January, the coldest month, temperature ranges between 17° to 21°C increasing southwards, while in May, the summer maximum ranges between 37° to 39°C. The monsoon starts in the first week of June, lowering the temperature all over the plain.

Heavy down pour is characteristic of the monsoon period. Rainfall, in general decreases from east to west, e.g. Allahabad 90cm to Agra 68cm but increases to north and northwest, e.g. Saharanpur with 75cm to Gonda, Bahraich with over

100cm. But the coastal parts, e.g. Calcutta, receives 200cm. In winter the upper regions receive little more rainfall (3.9%).

Thus, the Ganga plain is commonly divided in three zones—the Upper Ganga plain, the Middle Ganga plain and the Lower Ganga plain. The Upper region is clearly demarcated in the west by the Yamuna. But its eastern limit lacks any physical boundary. However, 100cm isohyet appears to be a suitable demarcating line between the upper and middle plain. In the east the middle Ganga plain is structurally delineated by the Rajmahal spurs from where the Ganga turns to the south.

Process of Occupance and Extension of Human Settlements

Evidences from ancient literature show that during epic period greater part of the Ganga Valley was densely forested and a few principalities and kingdoms occupied the forest clearings in the north of the Ganga, mostly in the river 'cones' above the annual flood level. This drainage system was easier to cross at some favourable points. Middle Ganga plain north across the Ghaghara, Gandak and Kosi rivers was perhaps more attractive for the early settlers and Mithila, Kashi, Koshal were the important kingdoms there. Later the movement was towards the west in the fertile but dry lands of Ganga-Yamuna Doab. Here Kurus and Panchal extended their empires. The Aryan invaders found it easier to advance across the Ghaghara, Gandak and Kosi cones avoiding the marshy tract immediately to the north of the Ganga and the *Bhabhar* land of the *Tarai* further north (Fig. 1.3).

It were the Aryans who extended their power to the south of the Ganga and the Yamuna in the west and east respectively and the area witnessed a parallel line of advancement south of the Ganga and the Yamuna in the west. It provided a gateway to Ujjain through the Chambal Valley.

The Son core was occupied later. Ganga, Bodh Gaya, Rajgarh, Nalanda, the Buddhist centres and Pavapuri, the Jain centre in the Son plain bear testimony to the fact. The Magadh rulers encouraged the trade relations with the lower Ganga sea coast through the Deccan plateau. It provided a gateway to advance Buddhism to Sri Lanka. It is significant to note that a land route tc Nepal had become very important during the Mauryas and the Gupta period (300 A.D. to 500

A.D.) and Buddhism had taken a root in Tibet and China through Kapilvastu and Vaishali.

In the beginning of 12th century, the Ganga plain faced several Islamic invasions making the local kingdoms weeker. In several cases the invaders themselves became the local rulers. However, the whole plain including the Bengal delta became the part of the Moghal Empire (1200 to 1758) administered by their Viceroys.

By the middle of the 18th century the British, with their stronghold in Calcutta, advanced through the Hooghly with a major thrust in the Ganga Valley. The Agra region was ceded to the British in 1803 while the *Audh* Kingdom was finally annexed to the British territory in 1856. The increased transportation and irrigational facilities resulted in agricultural development and in the revival of old cities as district headquarters. Kanpur emerged as the largest industrial city in the Upper Ganga plain on one hand and Howrah and Calcutta Industrial-cum-Commercial cities in the lower Ganga plain. Hence a large section of people from the middle Ganga plain moved to Calcutta and Kanpur in search of jobs.

Thus the plain has witnessed a great racial integration and migration of people during British reign specially after 1857.

From the point of view of human occupation, expansion and cultural, racial and religious interactions and assimilation the plain has passed through braodly in the following his-

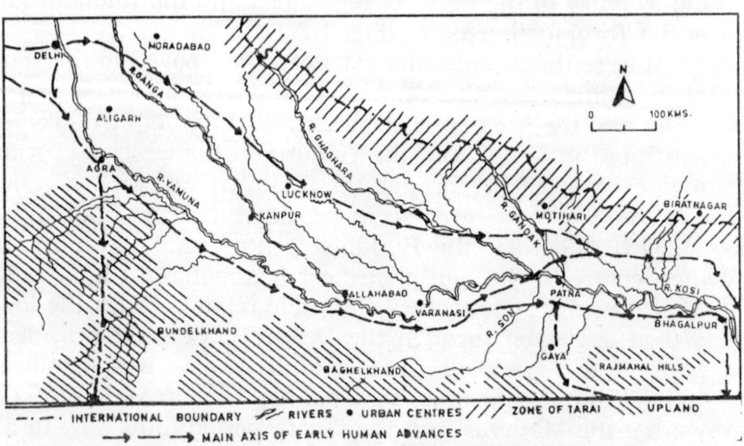

FIG. 1.3: Main Axis of Early Human Advances

torical stages :

(1) Early Vedic Period — Before 2000 B.C.
(2) Epic Period or Ramayana and Mahabharata Age — About 2000 B.C. generally settled by tribal people, rise of some territorial powers such as the Kurus and the Panchal in the West, Kashis, Koshals and Videh in the middle plain north.
(3) Aryan Advancement and Occupation — Upto 500 B.C. The Aryans from the West occupied the favourable portions of the western plain. This was perhaps the era of confusion and chaos both culturally and economically.
(4) The Golden Age of the Indian History — 500 B.C. to 350 A.D. Tirhut and Magadh territorial expansion.
(5) The Dark Age of Indian History — 350 to 1200. Successive raids with signs of decay.
(6) The Moghal Occupation — 1200 to 1757. Though the territory remained a part of the Moghal Empire, greater part of the plain was ruled by local chiefs, nawabs etc.
(7) The British Period — 1757 to 1947.

The reign saw the agricultural development, growth of rail and road transport, educational institutions, a few industrial and commercial centres and a greater movement of goods and services and people.

Thus the plain has witnessed a great racial integration and migration of people during the British regime specially after 1857. As English education first started in Bengal, educated Bengalis were generally employed as clerks in government, semi-government offices and in the railways on one-hand, while highly qualified persons and scholars occupied high positions in government services and educational institutions. As Bengalis are very proud of their language culture and traditions, they often formed their separate colonies wherever they went. Most of the cities of the Ganga plain possess a *Bangali Tola*. Thus during the early British rule the valley witnessed a east-west migration of population.

Calcutta industrial complex, later attracted the economically backward persons generally from the middle

Ganga plain as labourers in jute mills, railway workshop, ports and harbours or even as domestic servants. But a greater majority of such persons returned home after their retirement and seldom stayed there permanently.

After Independence Punjabis came to the region in large numbers. They have permanently settled in most of the cities of the Upper Ganga plain and are generally engaged in trade and commerce. Like Bengalis they often have formed their residential pockets.

Thus, the valley has witnessed the movement and diffusion of different cultures within last several centuries where Hinduism, Buddhism, Jainism, Islam religions have even now very strong influences in people's mind and their life style. Yet a diversity in physique, language, culture and life style is clearly noticeable in different geographical zones of the valley. Bengalis for example, said to be of Negroid and Mongolide origin, are to be easily recognized by their dress, language and accent, and by diet of rice and fish. In the northern part of the middle Ganga plain, in ancient Mithila territorial unit, people are distinct by their yellowish colour, prominent check bones and Maithili language and dilect and rice culture. In Magadh Dravidian's influence on the physique, language and culture is clearly noticeable. Here they generally speak Magadhi or better known Bhojpuri which is similar to *Audhi* spoken further — west on the western margin of the middle Ganga plain. From here noticeable change in the diet of the people is well marked in the sense that bread made of barley or wheat or Bajra is often accompanied with rice. A marked change in the housing is also noticeable. The tapering thatched roofing of Bengal and Bihar begain to disappear giving place to tiled roofing.

The upper Ganga plain, approximately west of Allahabad-Faizabad line, with drier climate, better irrigation facilities and improved agricultural technique appear to be an extension of the Punjab plain. The people are comparatively tall and robust and speak mixed Hindi and Urdu. The area belongs to ancient pastoral races who have been changing their activities with the time. Here the tiled roofing of the western middle zone give place to flat mud roof as an evidence of the dry climatic regime. Similarly bread forms an important item of food while rice becomes a delicacy. Turban or *Pagri*, which is now fast disappearing, form an essential part of the man's dress to protect him against the sun.

Acknowledgements

I thankfully acknowledge the assistance of Dr. Shri Prakash Asthana, M.A., Ph.D., Department of Geography, Banaras Hindu University, Varanasi in redrawing the maps and diagram being reproduced in this chapter.

TWO

Marketing Potential of Foodgrains in The Ganga Basin, West of Bihar, India

R.S. DUBE

The Ganga Basin in India, West of Bihar lies mainly in Uttar Pradesh and Madhya Pradesh north of the Vindhya-Maikal Divide in Central India. Its westward extension into eastern Rajasthan covers only a small proportion of the total area of the basin and has hence been excluded from the following study.

The basin covers about 53 million hectares of land in India (about 16 per cent of the total area of the country), and accommodates about 167 million persons or about one-fourth of the total population of the country. Its area compares that of France or Thailand, while its population number compares with that of the whole West European region. Such a huge area and demographic size possesses substantial scope for intra-regional trade of foodgrains surpluses in different parts of the basin.

The region under study is a much diversified morphometric, edaphic and hydrometeorological unit of the country. The spinal zone of the basin is formed by the Ganga Plain, which is a homogeneous fertile alluvial plain of the Ganga and its numerous tributaries. On the northern limb of the basin are the Himalayan mountainous and sub-mountainous areas, while the southern counterpart is formed by the hills, plateaus, uplands and valleys of the Indian Foreland, where soils vary from the rich alluvial and black cotton soils to several forests and lateritic soil groups. Sharp thermal and hydrological variations have been recorded in different parts of the basin. These physical complexities have contributed to a varied agricultural landscape in different parts of the basin.

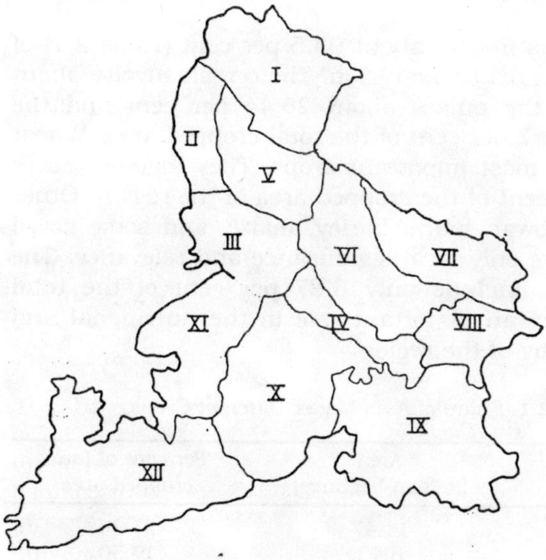

I	Himalayan Region	
II	Upper	Ganga-Yamuna Doab
III	Middle	
IV	Lower	
V	Rohil Khand	
VI	Gomti Plain	
VII	Sarjupar Plain	
VIII	Purviya Plain	
IX	Baghelkhand	
X	Bundelkhand	
XI	Madhya Bharat Plateau	
XII	Malwa	

FIG. 2.1: Physiographic Regions

The Agrarian Scene

A greater part of the land in the basin has been brought under cultivation. The cultivated area covers about 27.51 million hectares of land or about 51.90 per cent of the total area of the basin. About one-third of the cultivated area has been brought under multiple cropping.

The foodgrains involve about 93.5 per cent (Table 2.1) of the total cropped area of the region. The cereals involve about 66.18 per cent, the pulses about 20.44 per cent and the oilseeds about 6.87 per cent of the total cropped area. Wheat and rice are the most important crops. They together cover about 48.80 per cent of the cropped area of the region. Other cereals include jowar, bajra, barley, maize, and some small millets. They have only local significance and relevance. The oilseeds, though, include only 6.87 per cent of the total cropped area play an important role in the nutritional and industrial economy of the region.

TABLE 2.1: Share of Area Under Different Crops

Crops	Area (million hectares)	Per cent of total cropped area
Wheat	11.47	31.30
Rice	6.43	17.50
Jowar	3.03	8.26
Bajra	1.19	3.25
Barley	0.98	2.67
Maize	2.00	5.45
Small millets	0.68	1.85
Total Cereals	24.25	68.33
Pulses	7.49	20.44
Oilseeds	2.52	6.87
Others	—	4.36

The proportion of cultivated area and that under different crops show marked spatial variations in this region. Over a greater part of the region more than three-fourths of the total area has been put to cultivation of different crops (Fig 2.2). The areas where proportion of cultivated area is relatively smaller include the Himalayan areas, and a few districts in the Gomati Plain, Baghelkhand, Bundelkhand and Madhya Bharat plateau.

Over a greater part of the basin in Uttar Pradesh in the north, and central Vindhyan Scarpland region in the south wheat includes more than 30 per cent of the cropped area (Fig. 2.3). The areas where wheat involves very small (less than one-fifth of the cropped area) proportion of the cropped area include Western Malwa and Baghelkhand regions of Madhya Pradesh.

The areas where rice land covers more than 30 per cent

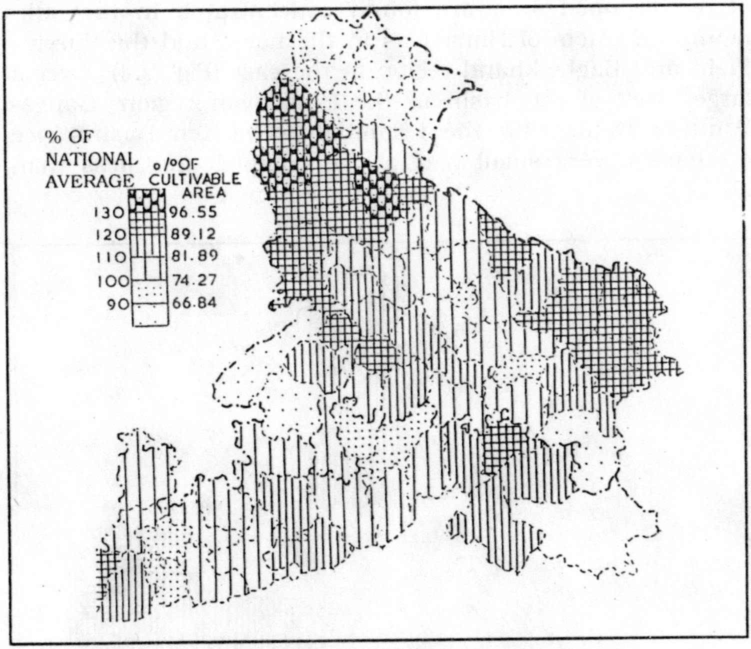

FIG. 2.2: Cultivated Area (% of Total Area)

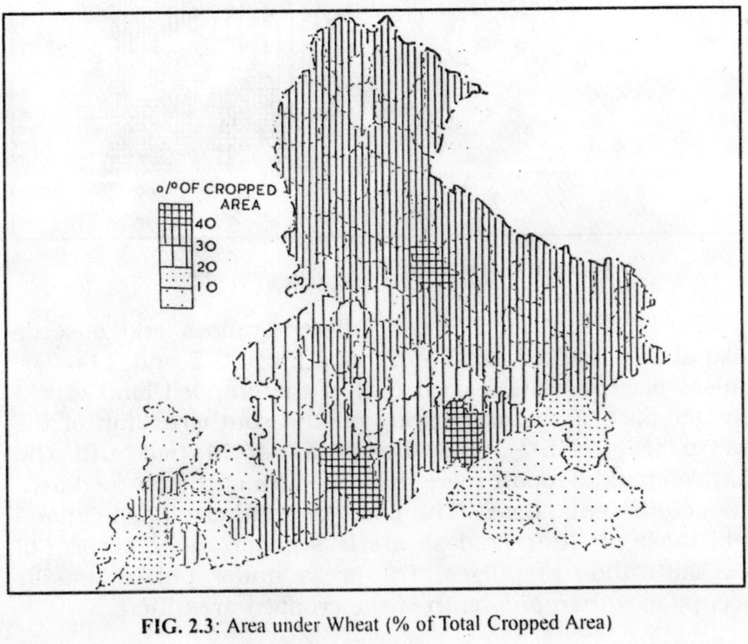

FIG. 2.3: Area under Wheat (% of Total Cropped Area)

of the cropped area are found concentrated in the sub-mountain tracts of Himalayas in the north and the Purviya Plain and Baghelkhand region in the east (Fig. 2.4). Over a larger part of the basin in the Himalayan region, Ganga-Yamuna Doab, and the Chambal-Betwa-Ken Basins rice occupies a very small part of the cropped area (less than 20%).

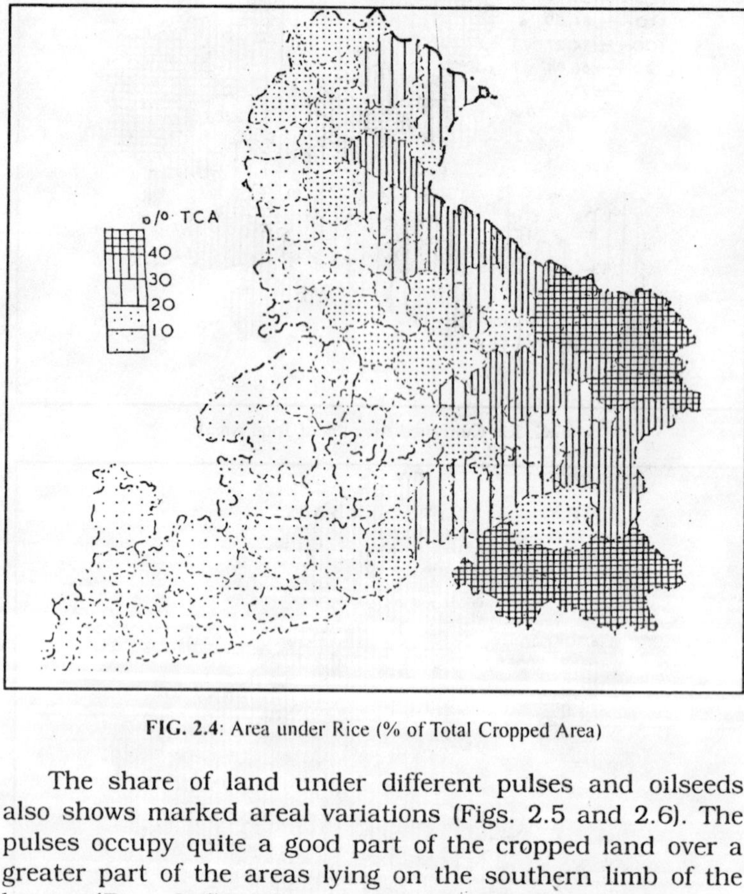

FIG. 2.4: Area under Rice (% of Total Cropped Area)

The share of land under different pulses and oilseeds also shows marked areal variations (Figs. 2.5 and 2.6). The pulses occupy quite a good part of the cropped land over a greater part of the areas lying on the southern limb of the basin (Fig. 2.5). Here the areas of Malwa and the Bundelkhand support more than one-fifth of the cropped area under different pulses. The parts of southern Baghelkhand and those of Uttar Pradesh are less important in respect of the cultivation of pulses. The areas under pulses usually occupy less than one-tenth of the cropped area there.

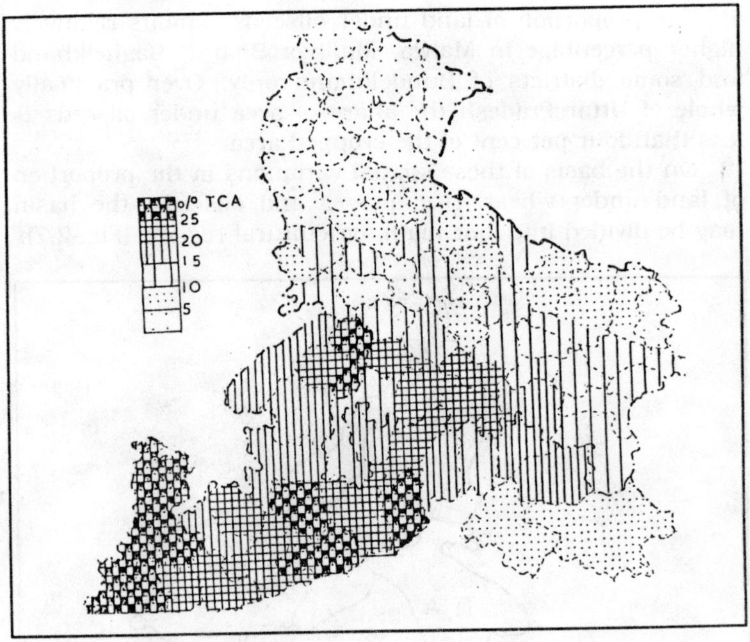

FIG. 2.5: Area under Pulses (% of Total Cropped Area)

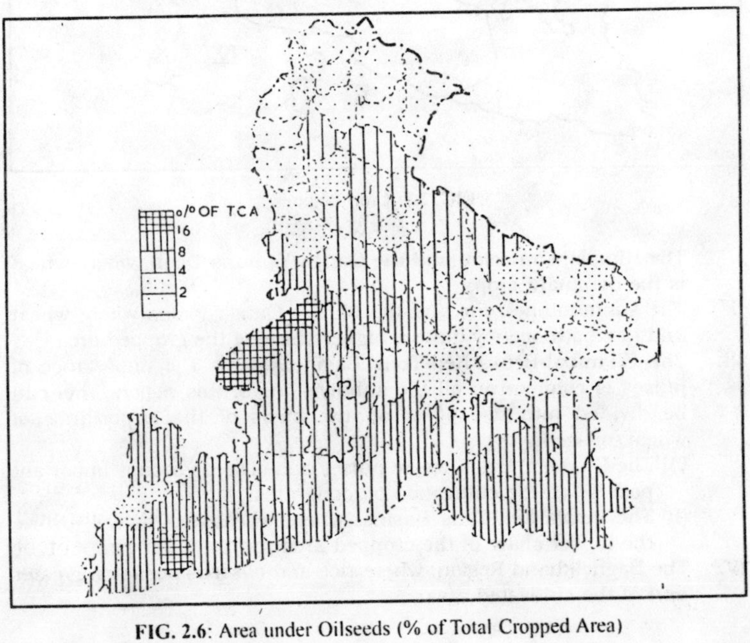

FIG. 2.6: Area under Oilseeds (% of Total Cropped Area)

The proportion of land under oilseeds exhibits relatively higher percentage in Malwa, Madhya Bharat, Baghelkhand and some districts of Bundelkhand only. Over practically whole of Uttar Pradesh the share of area under oilseeds is less than four per cent of the cropped area.

On the basis of these spatial variations in the proportion of land under wheat, rice, pulses and oilseeds, the basin may be divided into four main agricultural regions (Fig. 2.7):

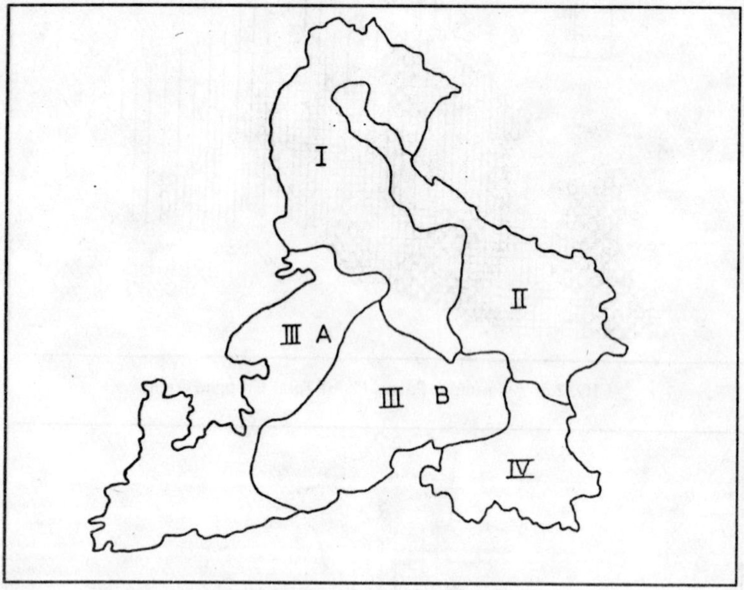

FIG. 2.7: Crop Regions

I. The Himalayan Region and the Ganga-Yamuna Doab, where wheat is the dominant crop;

II. The submontane zone and the Middle Ganga Plains where wheat and rice both occupy quite a higher share of the cropped area;

III. The Chambal-Betwa-Ken-Tons Basin System: The importance of pulses is common in all the subdivisions of this region. This can be divided into two parts on the basis of the importance of wheat/oilseeds:

(A) The Chambal Basin where pulses and oilseeds occupy important position in the cultivation of foodgrains.

(B) The Betwa-Ken-Tons Basins, where wheat and pulses involve the higher share of the cropped area.

IV. The Baghelkhand Region, where rice and oilseeds occupy a greater part of the cultivated area.

The Surplus-Deficit Patterns of Foodgrains

The areas of Ganga Basin, west of Bihar produce abut 37.77 million tonnes of foodgrains a year. This equals about 28.33 per cent of the total foodgarin output in India. The cereals (23.50 million tonnes) comprise about 22.58 per cent and pulses (4.18 million tonnes) about 36.34 per cent of the total produced in India. Among the cereals wheat shares about 16.05 million tonnes or 46.72 per cent of the total foodgrains produced in the basin, or 42.87 per cent that produced in the country as a whole. Rice contributes about 6.20 million or about 27.20 per cent of the total foodgrains produced in this region. The relative share of different foodgrains produced in the region under discussion is appended in Table 2.2.

TABLE 2.2: Share of Foodgrain Production

Foodgrain	Output (million hectares)	Per cent of total foodgrain production
Wheat	16.05	42.49
Rice	6.20	16.42
Jowar	1.84	4.87
Bajra	0.85	2.25
Barley	1.87	2.87
Maize	1.54	4.08
Small Millets	0.70	1.85
Total Cereals	27.50	72.80
Pulses	4.18	11.06
Oilseeds	1.26	3.33
Total Foodgrains	37.77	100.00

The surplus-deficit conditions of cereals, pulses and oilseeds in different districts of the region have been worked out by comparing their per capita daily availability with the recommended standard dietary requirement of an individual. A district has been classed surplus if its production of cereals/pulses/oilseeds has been found in excess of the required dietary amount recommended for an average individual. The district has been classed deficit if the availability of the grains was less than the recommended standard requirement. The per capita per day availability of the grains in various districts of the region has been worked out by constructing the food balance sheet following the procedure preferred by Dube and Misra (1984). The figures so obtained have been classified and mapped. The class-boundaries have been determined by finding out per cent variations from the national averages.

Cereals

The availability of cereals has been depicted on (Fig. 2.8). A close analysis of the patterns that have emerged on this figure shows that some 45 districts of the region have been classed surplus of which about one-fifth of the total districts have registered adequate surplus for exporting cereals. It may also be pointed out that quite a few districts (about one-sixth of the total districts) are classed under the deficit categories in respect of the availability of cereals. The surplus districts of the region are frequently distributed in the Himalayan zone, Rohilkhand, Upper and Middle Ganga-Yamuna Doab, Chambal Basin and Betwa Basin. Practically whole of the region east of the Rohilkhand, the Middle Ganga-Yamuna Doab and the Betwa Basin has been marked deficit with regard to the availability of cereals.

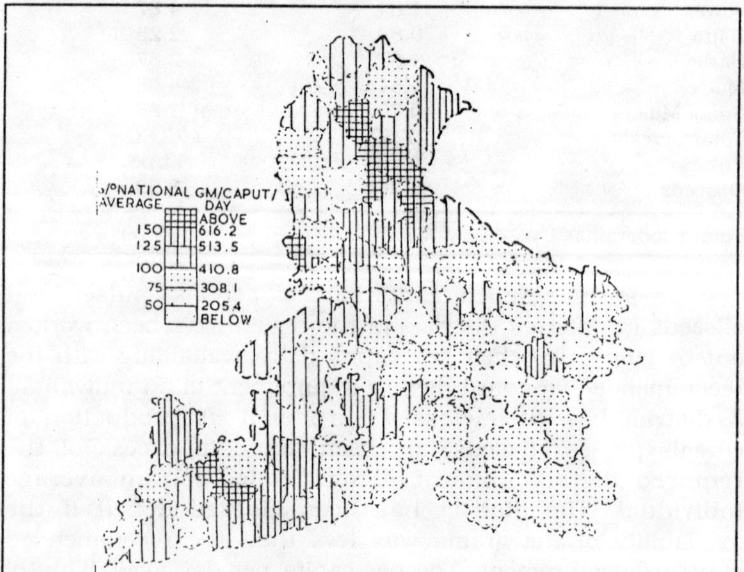

FIG. 2.8: Availability of Cereals

Pulses

The level of avilability of pulses in the region shows greater spatial contrasts as campared with those of the cereals. A casual look on Fig. 2.9 would show that practically whole of the areas in Chambal-Betwa-Ken basins have registered marked surpluses of pulses. The areas of Baghelkhand and those of Uttar Pradesh north of the Trans-Yamuna zone have evidenced pronounced deficit of pulses. Such sharp spatial concentrations of surplus and deficit districts are likely to stimulate flow of trade in pulses between different parts of the basin.

Oilseeds

We do not have adequate data for estimation of the availability of consumable fats from the non-foodgrain sources in this region. It is hence quite difficult to classify districts into

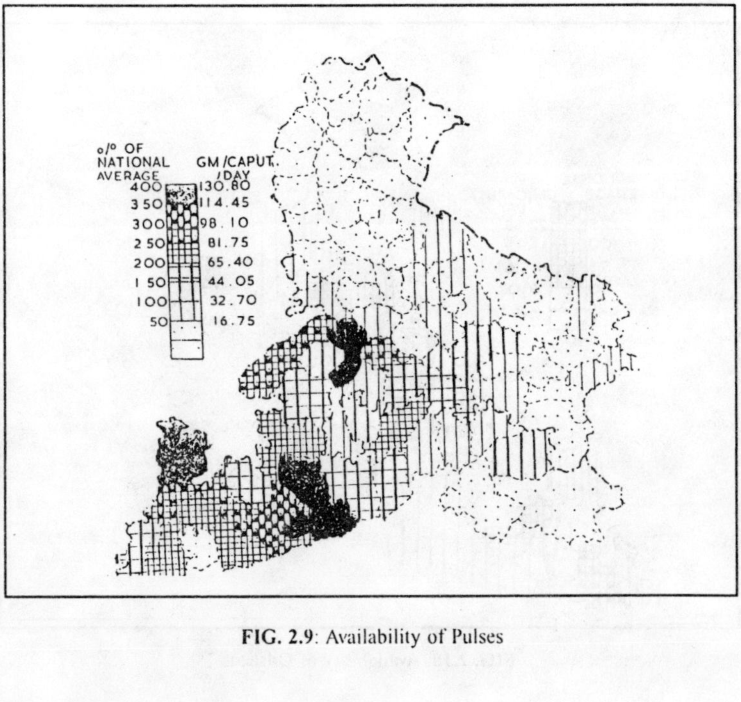

FIG. 2.9: Availability of Pulses

surplus-deficit categories regarding the production of oilseeds in different parts of the region. The availability worked out for oilseeds that has been shown on Fig. 2.10 is, however, quite suggestive about the spatial variability and export-import potentials of different areas. It may be seen from the figure that only a few districts in the Chambal basin have registered availability of oilseeds higher than the national average of 18.15 grams. In fact, practically whole of the region stands deficit in this respect and more than half of the districts have conspicuously low availability of less than 4.53 grams per capita per day, i.e. less than 25 per cent of the national average availability. Such districts are more concentrated in the Himalayan Region, Upper-Middle Doab, Gomti Plain, Saryupar plain, Purviya Plain and Trans-Yamuna Plain. The region hence possess substantial prospects for inflow of the oil seeds, but there are little possibilities for substantial inter-regional flow of trade in oilseeds.

The region may hence be divided into two broad regions in respect of the availability of cereals, pulses and oilseeds —the surplus West and the deficit East, the line of

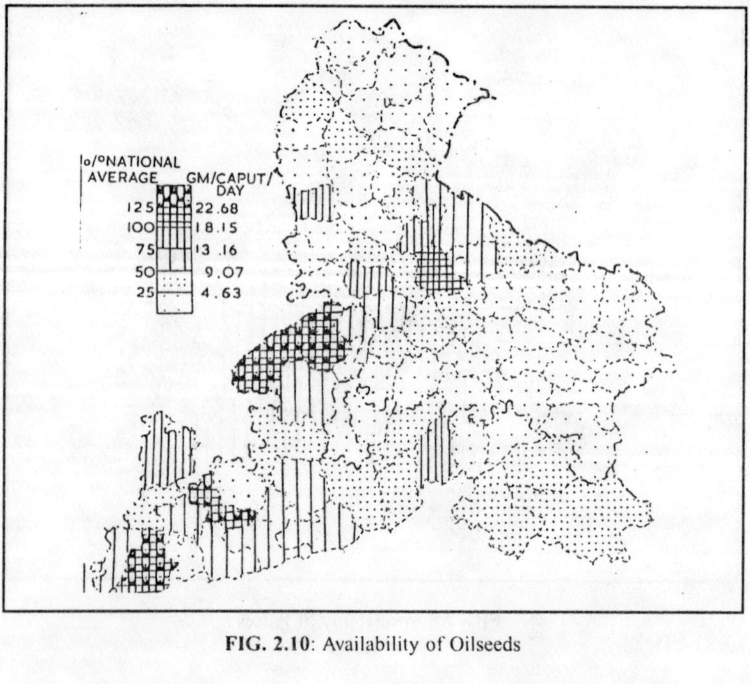

FIG. 2.10: Availability of Oilseeds

demarcation running roughly along the eastern borders of Rohilkhand, Middle Doab and Betwa Basin. The surplus zone may be further divided into regions on the basis of the types of foodgrains marked surplus (Fig. 2.11).

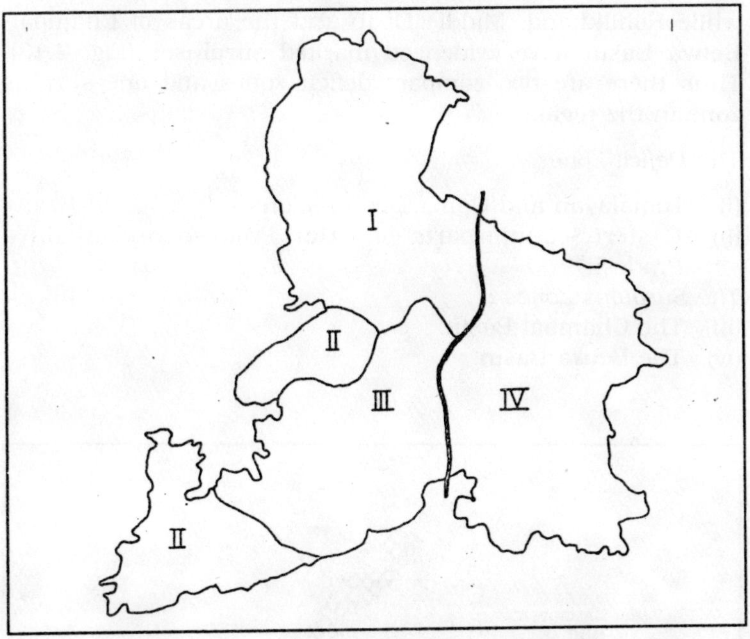

FIG. 2.11: Foodgrain Availability Regions

I. Western Uttar Pradesh, which has registered the surplus of cereals only.

II. The Chambal Basin, which has evidenced the surplus of all the foodgrain classes, i.e. cereals, pulses and oilseeds.

III. The Betwa Basin where cereals and pulses have registered surplus production.

IV. The Eastern Zone, where cereals, pulses and oilseeds all have registered deficit production.

The Qualitative Surplus-Deficit Patterns

A composit picture of the surplus-deficit of foodgrains may be provided by the evaluation of their availability in terms of food-energy. The per capita per day caloric availability of foodgrains has been depicted on the Fig. 2.12. It may be seen from the map that quite a larger part of the region stand deficit in respect of the availability of energy from foodgrains. The northern and eastern areas of Uttar Pradesh and eastern counterparts of the basin in Madhya Pradesh have registered deficiency of caloric availability of foodgrains, while Rohilkhand, Middle Doab and the areas of Chambal-Betwa Basin have evidenced marked surpluses (Fig. 2.13). Thus there are two compact deficit zones and one surplus zone in the region:

The Deficit Zones

(i) Himalayan and Upper Doab regions

(ii) Eastern counterparts of Uttar Pradesh and Madhya Pradesh.

The Surpulus Zones :

(iii) The Chambal Basin

(iv) The Betwa Basin.

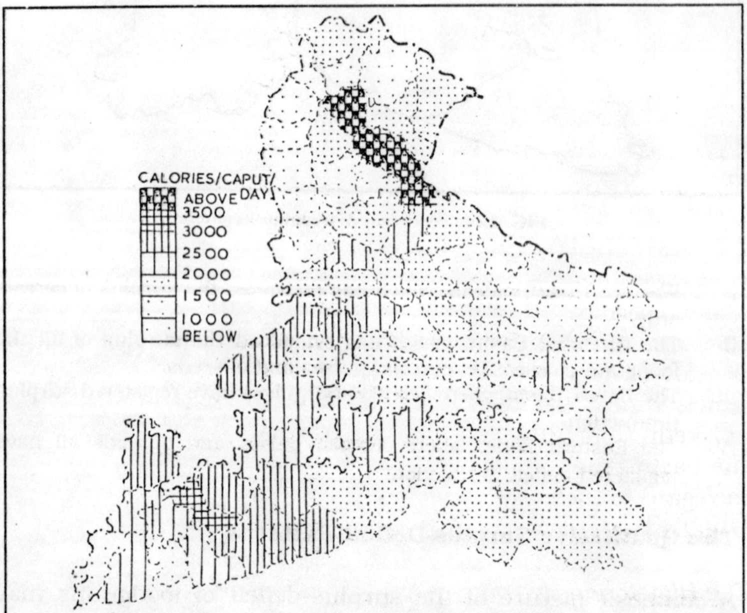

FIG. 2.12: Availability of Food Energy

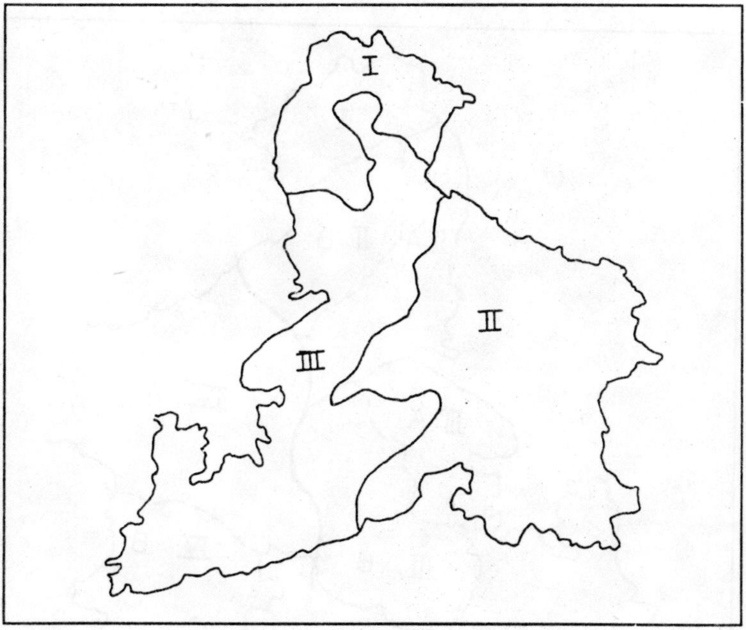

FIG. 2.13: Food Energy Availability Regions.

I The Himalayan Region
II The Upper-Middle Doab and Rohilkhand
III The Chambal-Betwa-Ken Basins
IV The Eastern Zone

The Marketing Potentials

The preceeding discussions of the availability of foodgrains in their quantitative and qualitative terms suggest sharp division of the region into the western surplus and the eastern deficit zones and also of the sharp areal contrasts in the marketing potentials of farm produces in different parts of the basin. The region may be divided into four main regions in regard to their potentials for export-import of the foodgrains (Fig 2.14).

The Himalayan Region

This is the wheat dominant agricultural region with

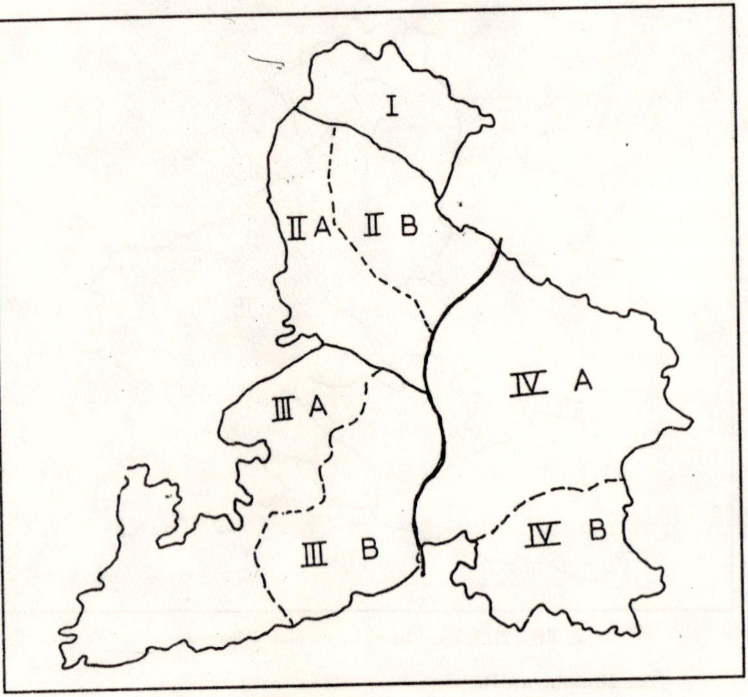

FIG. 2.14: Foodgrain Marketing Potential Regions

quantitative surpluses in the production of cereals. It stands deficit in the caloric availability of foodgrains. As such it does not possess enough potential for export of the cereals.

The Upper-Middle Doab and Rohilkhand

This is the western half of Uttar Pradesh. Wheat is the dominant crop in the Doab region, while in the Rohilkhand both wheat and rice, share a sizeable part of the cropped area. The production of cereals has been marked surplus in the Doab and Rohilkhand both, but availability of food energy from foodgrains has been found deficit in the Upper Doab areas. The Doab and Rohilkhand region possesses adequate potentials for the export of wheat and rice both.

The Chambal-Betwa-Ken Basins

These regions occupy the western parts of the southern limb of the Ganga basin. The Chambal basin is essentially the pulses and oilseeds growing region, while in the areas of Betwa and Ken Basins wheat and pulses occupy the greater part of the cropped area. The cereals, pulses and oilseeds are grown in surplus in the former, while only cereals and pulses have registered surplus in the latter region. Availability of food energy from the foodgrains has given surpluses in both the zones.

The Chambal region possesses substantial potential for the export of cereals, pulses, and oilseeds. The Betwa region also has the export potential for cereals and pulses. (Fig. 2.14).

The Eastern Zone

This is the deficit part of the basin. It covers whole of the eastern Uttar Pradesh and eastern counterparts of the areas in Madhya Pradesh. Wheat and rice are the dominant crops in the northern areas, while rice and oilseeds are the important crops in the southern Baghelkhand region. This zone has registered marked deficit of cereals, pulses and oilseeds both in their quantitative and qualitative aspects. The region, therefore, possesses substantial scope for import of cereals, pulses and oilseeds.

Miscellaneous Observations

The export-import movements of foodgrains are governed not merely by the surplus-deficit status of areas. They are stimulated by the spatial variability of crop types also. The areas of Ganga basin contain the spatial variations of not only crop productivity; it also exhibits sharp variations of crop types also. The intra-regional flow of trade in foodgrains must not be seen merely in the context of food availability status of areas only. It must be also evaluated in the context of crop variations as well. The Easterny Zone though classed as the deficit zone may be possessing the potential of exporting such farm produces as rice, which may be having good marketing prospects in the areas where it is not adequately produced. The potential of the region for intra-regional marketing of foodgrains does not lie hence merely on the surplus-deficit status of areas; it also lies in the spatial variability of cropping patterns in different parts of the basin. The Ganga basin as discussed earlier possesses sharp areal contrasts on crop composition, which affords substantial intra-regional scope for trade in different foodgrains produced in the region.

THREE

The Impact of Price on Area under Crops in Upper Ganga-Yamuna Doab

ABHA LAKSHMI SINGH and SHAHAB FAZAL

Area under crops is largely governed by physical, cultural, technological and economic factors. Physical factors specify the range of crops that can be grown in a region. It describes the production possibilities of crops and offers many choices but they don't determine which crop is most profitable for a particular area. The economic factors have a determining influence on cropping patterns. It determines the particular kind or combination of crops that are most profitable to produce on the farm.

Generally, cropping patterns followed in India are based on traditional systems of subsistence farming, where the farmer is trying to produce everything he needs like cereals, pulses, vegetables etc. The cropping pattern has risen out of necessity of the farmer to become self reliant. But after the introduction of technology in agriculture, the production possibilities have increased with the use of costly inputs. The farmers have started producing surplus with the result that they think of maximizing the returns from their lands. The price which the farmers get for his produce became of vital importance for them.

This chapter seeks ot examine the impact of price on area under tweleve crops namely rice, jowar, maize, wheat, bajra, gram, arhar, mustard, potato, sugarcane and cotton in the upper Ganga-Yamuna Doab from 1960-61.

Material and Methods

The Upper Ganga-Yamuna Doab, comprising of the five

districts of Saharanpur, Muzaffarnagar, Meerut, Ghaziabad and Bulandshahar, is the seat of Green Revolution and that is why it was chosen as the study area. This region is agriculturally prosperous, fertile and highly irrigated north-western part of Uttar Pradesh. It lies between the rivers Ganga and Yamuna and spreads from 28°4' to 30°24' north latitudes and 77°2' to 78°29' east longitudes. It is a flat, monotonous and productive plain. The total area of the study region is 2,055,373 hectares of which, 76 per cent is net sown and 125 per cent is gross cropped area. The net irrigated area is 88 per cent of the sown area. Of which, 67 per cent is irrigated by tubewells and 32 per cent by canals.

Cultivation of crops has been the main occupation. The economic classification of the population shows that about 70 per cent are non-workers and 30 per cent are main workers. Among the main workers, 40 per cent are cultivators and 22 per cent are agricultural labourers and the rest are employed in household industries and other occupations. Though the bulk of the farmers belonged to the marginal category (<1 ha.), but their proportion is comparatively lesser than the rest of Uttar Pradesh. Farmers having semi-medium (2-4 ha.), medium (4-10 ha.) and large holdings (>10 ha.) are found here. In terms of operation of holdings, it was the large and medium farmers who predominate.

The farmers of the study region are prosperous and they grow a variety of crops during both *kharif* and *rabi* season. The four dominating crops of this region covering large per centage of gross cropped area are wheat (33 %), sugarcane (23 %), maize (9 %) and rice (6 %). These crops cover more than 70 per cent of the gross cropped area of the study region (1985-86). This is the wheat belt of the country. In 1960-61, wheat was the second ranking crop, but after twenty five years it became the first ranking crop and there was substantial increase in area under this crop. Rice was the first ranking crop in 1960-61, but now it is the fourth ranking crop. The area under maize and pulses remained stagnant. While the area under other coarse cereals like jowar, bajra and barley declined. Although the area under mustard was negligible but it registered a slight increase. There was drastic increase in area under sugarcane and potato.

The analysis is related to responsiveness of area under a crop to changes in the prices of that crop. For this purpose twelve important crops of the study region were selected. Here we assume that the farmer will react to the higher prices after a season, so to take account of time lag we have related the prices with area of that particular crop in the immediately following year. The correlation co-efficient between area and prices have been calculated. Regression analysis was worked out to establish the statistical relationship. Such a relationship is usually of Cobb Douglas type and is expressed as:

$$Y = A X^b$$

Which when expressed in logarithm would be

$$\log Y = a + b \log X$$

Where X = Price of a crop.
Y = Area under a crop.

All the data have been taken both from primary and secondary sources. The data of prices have been taken from Farm Harvest Prices, Directorate of Economics and Statistics, Ministry of Agriculture, New Delhi. The data of area under the different crops have been taken from Agricultural Statistics of Uttar Pradesh, Directorate of Economics and Statistics, Lucknow. Both the data have been taken for the years 1960-61 to 1985-86.

Discussion

An attempt has been made to discuss the responsiveness of area to price changes in each district of the study region separately (Tables 3.1 and 3.2).

Saharanpur District

The district of Saharanpur, nestling in the foothill of the Himalayas, has a rich farming belt. During the last twenty-five years the area under mustard, potato, sugarcane, maize, wheat, rice and cotton registered an increase while the area under rest of the five crops namely jowar, bajra, barley, gram and arhar declined. There was more than hundred per cent increase in area under mustard and potato, more than fifty per cent increase in sugarcane, maize and wheat and only a slight increase in rice and cotton. The prices of all the crops recorded an increase. More than thousand per cent of increase

Table 3.1: Change in Price and Area of Crops in Upper Ganga Yamuna Doab (1960-61 to 1985-86)

Districts/ Crops	Saharanpur/ Prices	District/ Area	Muzaffar-nagar/ Prices	District/ Area	Meerut/ Prices	Distt./ Area	Buland-shahar/ Prices	District/ Area	Ghaziabad/ Prices	District /Area
Rice	1,315	14	1,186	29	1,299	-3	1.269	33	87	-3
Jowar	992	61	1,105	-93	955	-75	865	-73	55	-3
Bajra	908	-89	852	-96	835	-77	851	-30	58	13
Maize	1,107	86	1,047	-7	996	-14	961	104	115	15
Wheat	1,131	83	952	73	1,134	10.1	1,112	130	51	29
Barley	1,116	-49	1,158	-82	1,122	-87	1,141	-70	76	-29
Gram	2,729	-98	2,720	-95	2,914	-94	2,695	-85	234	-72
Arhar	1,691	-20	1,969	97	1,572	-35	1,778	-25	126	237
Mustard	1,482	984	1,636	113	1,476	84	1,592	378	25	92
Sugarcane	1,258	88	1,407	77	1,310	20	1,314	0.5	95	20
Potato	1,508	113	1,379	222	1,681	76	1,916	326	168	61
Cotton	839	4	1,792	15	1,717	-71	1,631	-81	96	-9

Source: 1. *Farm Harvest Prices*. Directorate of Economics and Statistics, Ministry of Agriculture, New Delhi (1960-61 to 1985-86).

2. *Agricultural Statistics of Uttar Pradesh*. Directorate of Economics and Statistics, Lucknow (1960-61 to 1985-86).

Table 3.2: Relationship between Price and Area of Crops in Upper Ganga-Yamuna Doab

Districts crops	Saharanpur District Regression Equation	*r*	*t*	Muzaffarnagar District Regression Equation	*r*	*t*
Rice	$\log_e' Y = 11.217 + 0.0516 \log_e' x$	0.39	Yes	$\log_e' Y = 10.303 + 0.072 \log_e x$	0.24	No
Jowar	$\log_e' Y = 5.50 + 0.0858 \log_e x$	0.43	Yes	$\log_e' Y = 11.619 - 1.3666 \log_e' x$	-0.73	
Bajra	$\log_e' Y = 13.77 - 1.1205 \log_e' x$	- 0.8		$\log_e' Y = 14.671 - 1.674 \log_e' x$	-0.92	
Maize	$\log_e' Y = 10.306 + 0.0381 \log_e' x$	0.13	No	$\log_e' Y = 10.473 - 0.139 \log_e' x$	-0.64	
Wheat	$\log_e' Y = 10.866 + 0.253 \log_e' x$	0.76	Yes	$\log_e' Y = 10.984 + 0.196 \log_e x$	0.74	Yes
Barley	$\log_e' Y = 9.712 - 0.493 \log_e' x$	0.66		$\log_e' Y = 9.465 - 0.742 \log_e' x$	-0.77	
Gram	$\log_e' Y = 15.295 - 1.228 \log_e' x$	- 0.87		$\log_e' Y = 14.761 - 1.229 \log_e x$	-0.82	
Arhar	$\log_e' Y = 5.634 - 0.074 \log_e' x$	0.16	No	$\log_e' Y = 3.976 + 0.300 \log_e x$	0.69	Yes
Mustard	$\log_e' Y = 2.578 + 0.812 \log_e' x$	0.90	Yes	$\log_e' Y = 4.618 + 0.357 \log_e' x$	0.86	Yes
Sugarcane	$\log_e' Y = 10.947 + 0.276 \log_e' x$	0.90	Yes	$\log_e' Y = 11.283 + 0.257 \log_e x$	0.87	Yes
Potato	$\log_e' Y = 5.890 + 0.259 \log_e' x$	0.56	Yes	$\log_e' Y = 5.545 + 0.451 \log_e' x$	0.77	Yes
Cotton	$\log_e' Y = 9.191 + 0.150 \log_e' x$	- 0.26		$\log_e' Y = 8.984 - 0.120 \log_e' x$	-0.20	

Table 3.2 *(Contd.)*

Meerut District Regression Equation	r	t	Bulandshahar District Regression Equation	r	t
$\log_e'$ Y=10.080 - 0.023 $\log_e'$ x	-0.24		$\log_e'$ Y=8.223 + 0.213 $\log g_e$ x	0.23	No
$\log_e'$ Y=13.228 - 1.291 $\log_e'$ x	-0.77		$\log_e'$ Y=12.495 - 0.802 $\log_e'$ x	-0.89	
$\log_e'$ Y=13.281 - 0.919 $\log_e'$ x	-0.80		$\log_e'$ Y=11.643 - 0.271 $\log_e'$ x	-0.72	
$\log_e'$ Y=11.529 - 0.178 $\log_e'$ x	-0.39		$\log_e'$ Y=9.752 + 0.373 $\log_e'$ x	0.23	No
$\log_e'$ Y=11.953 + 0.035 $\log_e'$ x	0.01	No	$\log_e'$ Y=10.498 + 0.346 $\log_e'$ x	0.79	Yes
$\log_e'$ Y=12.754 - 1.147 $\log_e'$ x	-0.74		$\log_e'$ Y=12.401 - 0.481 $\log_e'$ x	-0.82	
$\log_e'$ Y=14.515 - 1.063 $\log_e'$ x	-0.84		$\log_e'$ Y=12.918 - 0.706 $\log_e'$ x	-0.85	
$\log_e'$ Y=9.280 - 0.499 $\log_e'$ x	-0.23		$\log_e'$ Y=9.158 - 0.179 $\log_e'$ x	-0.03	
$\log_e'$ Y=4.957 + 0.252 $\log_e'$ x	0.85	Yes	$\log_e'$ Y=4.696 + 0.562 $\log_e'$ x	0.92	Yes
$\log_e'$ Y=11.702 + 0.084 $\log_e'$ x	0.67	Yes	$\log_e'$ Y=10.961 - 0.016 $\log_e'$ x	0.15	No
$\log_e'$ Y=7.683 + 0.194 $\log_e'$ x	0.38	Yes	$\log_e'$ Y=6.192 + 0.642 $\log_e'$ x	0.77	Yes
$\log_e'$ Y=12.138 - 0.684 $\log_e'$ x	-0.81		$\log_e'$ Y=12.969 - 0.809	0.76	

Table 3.2 *(Contd.)*

Ghaziabad Distrcit Regression Equation	r	t
$\log_e' Y = 10.960 - 0.408 \log_e x$	0.63	
$\log_e' Y = 9.251 - 0.395 \log_e x$	-0.49	
$\log_e' Y = 9.507 + 0.051 \log_e x$	0.17	No
$\log_e' Y = 10.219 + 0.078 \log_e x$	0.37	No
$\log_e' Y = 10.426 + 0.244 \log_e x$	0.62	Yes
$\log_e' Y = 9.514 - 0.307 \log_e x$	-0.43	
$\log_e' Y = 14.758 - 1.268 \log_e x$	-0.79	
$\log_e' Y = 2.360 + 1.613 \log_e x$	0.98	Yes
$\log_e' Y = 1.982 + 0.714 \log_e x$	0.56	No
$\log_e' Y = 10.188 + 0.241 \log_e x$	0.82	Yes
$\log_e' Y = 7.107 + 0.361 \log_e x$	0.89	Yes
$\log_e' Y = 10.615 - 0.57 \log_e x$	-0.8	

in prices was recorded by all the crops except for that of jowar, bajra and cotton which recorded an increase of more than eight hundred per cent.

A perusal of Tables 3.2 and Figs. 3.1 and 3.2 shows a strong positive relationship between area and prices of mustard (r = 0.9, significant at 1 per cent level), sugarcane

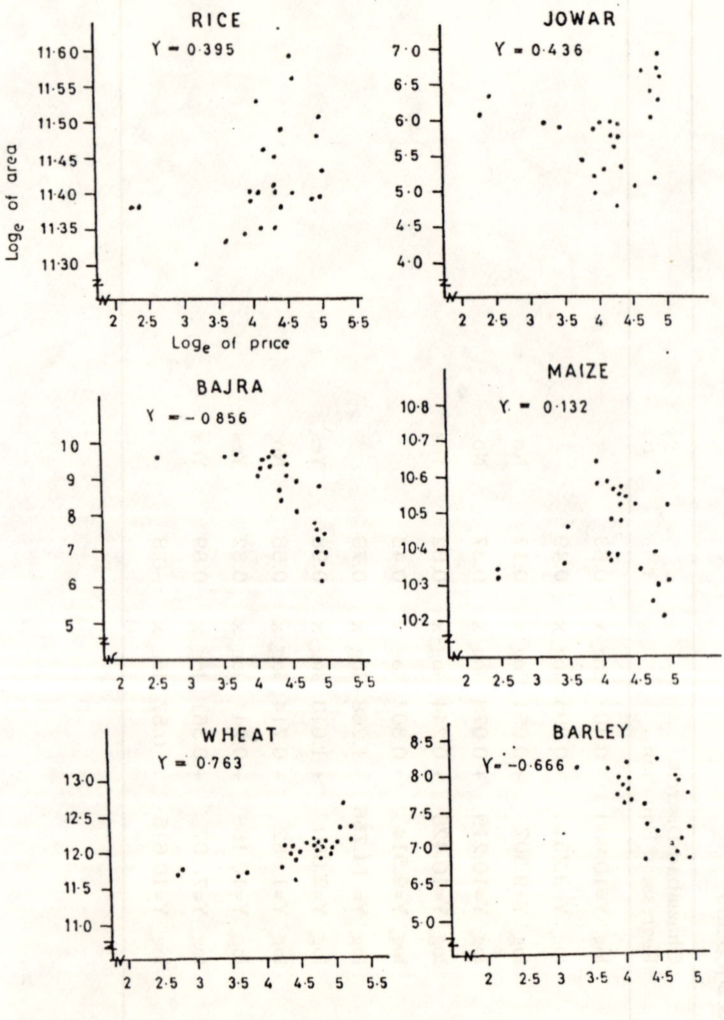

FIG. 3.1: Saharanpur District: Relation between Price and Area of Important Crop

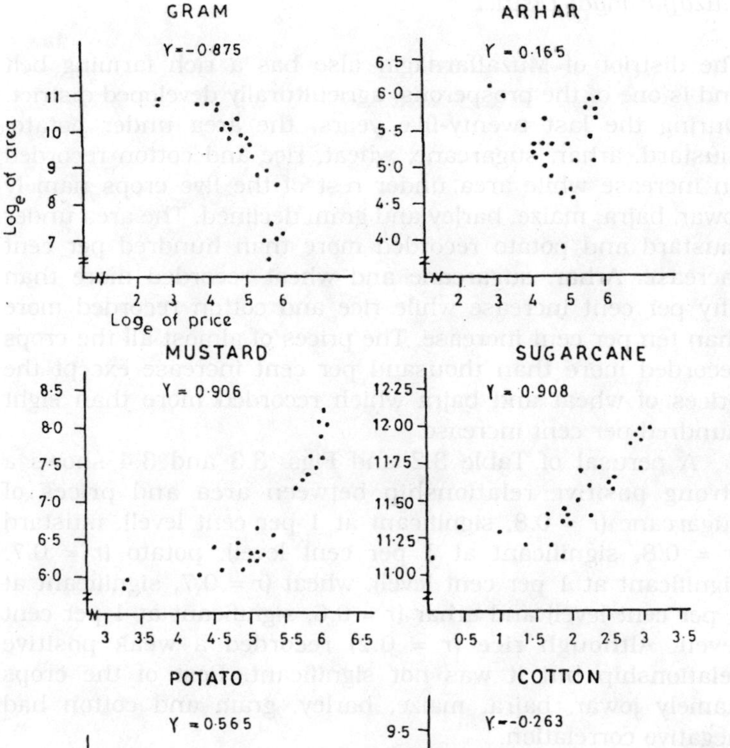

FIG. 3.2: Saharanpur District: Relation between Price and Area of Important Crop

(*r* = 0.9, significant at 1 per cent level), wheat (*r* = 0.7, significant at 5 per cent level), potato (*r* = 0.5, significant at 1 per cent level) Jowar (*r* = 0.4, significant at 5 per cent level) and rice (*r* = 0.3, significant at 5 per cent level). Although arhar (*r* = 0.1) and maize (*r* = 0.1) recorded a weak positive correlation but they were not significant. Rest of the crops like bajra, barley, gram and cotton showed negative correlation.

Muzaffarnagar District

The district of Muzaffarnagar also has a rich farming belt and is one of the prosperous, agriculturally developed district. During the last twenty-five years, the area under potato, mustard, arhar, sugarcane, wheat, rice and cotton recorded an increase while area under rest of the five crops namely jowar, bajra, maize, barley and gram declined. The area under mustard and potato recorded more than hundred per cent increase. Arhar, sugarcane and wheat recorded more than fifty per cent increase while rice and cotton recorded more than ten per cent increase. The prices of almost all the crops recorded more than thousand per cent increase except the prices of wheat and bajra which recorded more than eight hundred per cent increase.

A perusal of Table 3.2 and Figs. 3.3 and 3.4 shows a strong positive relationship between area and prices of sugarcane (r = 0.8, significant at 1 per cent level), mustard (r = 0.8, significant at 1 per cent level), potato (r = 0.7, significant at 1 per cent level), wheat (r = 0.7, significant at 1 per cent level) and arhar (r = 0.6, significant at 1 per cent level). Although rice (r = 0.2) recorded a weak positive relationship but it was not significant. Rest of the crops namely jowar, bajra, maize, barley, gram and cotton had negative correlation.

Meerut District

The district of Meerut has been influenced by its nearness to the National capital, hence there is rapid urbanization and a shift of emphasis from agriculture to industries. The area under most of the food grains has not increased during the last twenty-five years. Only the area under mustard, potato, sugarcane and wheat recorded an increase. Rest of the eight crops namely rice, bajra, jowar, maize, gram, arhar, barley and cotton area declined. More than seventy-five per cent increase in area under mustard and potato and more than ten per cent increase in area under sugarcane and wheat was observed. Whereas the prices of all the crops recorded an increase of more than thousand per cent except the prices of maize, jowar and bajra which recorded more than eight hundred per cent increase.

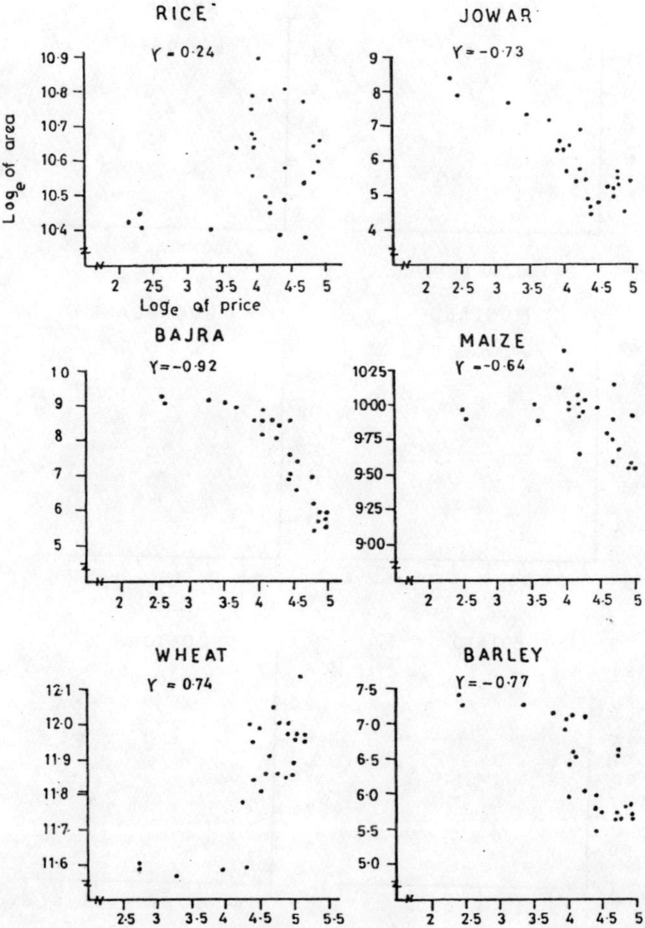

FIG. 3.3: Muzaffarnagar District: Relation between Price and Area of Important Crop

A perusal of Table 3.2 and Figs. 3.5 and 3.6 shows a strong positive correlation between prices and area of mustard ($r = 0.8$, significant at 1 per cent level), Sugarcane ($r = 0.6$, significant 1 per cent level) and potato ($r = 0.3$, significant at 5 per cent level). Wheat ($r = 0.01$) recorded a weak positive correlation which was not even significant. Rest of the crops namely rice, jowar, bajra, maize, barley, gram, arhar and cotton recorded negative correlation.

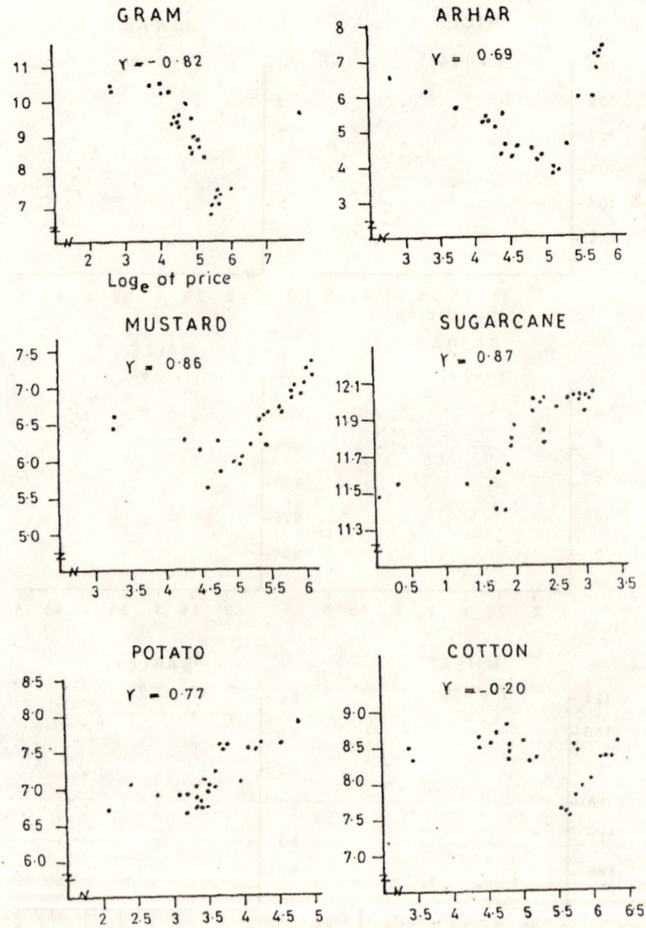

FIG. 3.4: Muzaffarnagar District: Relation between Price and Area of Important Crop

Bulandshahar District

Bulandshahar district is agricuturally very rich and prosperous. Although the farmers of this district have a rough time with its lack of irrigation facilities and land grabbing by vested interests. Due to this the value of agricultural land decreased in this district. The area under mustard, potato,

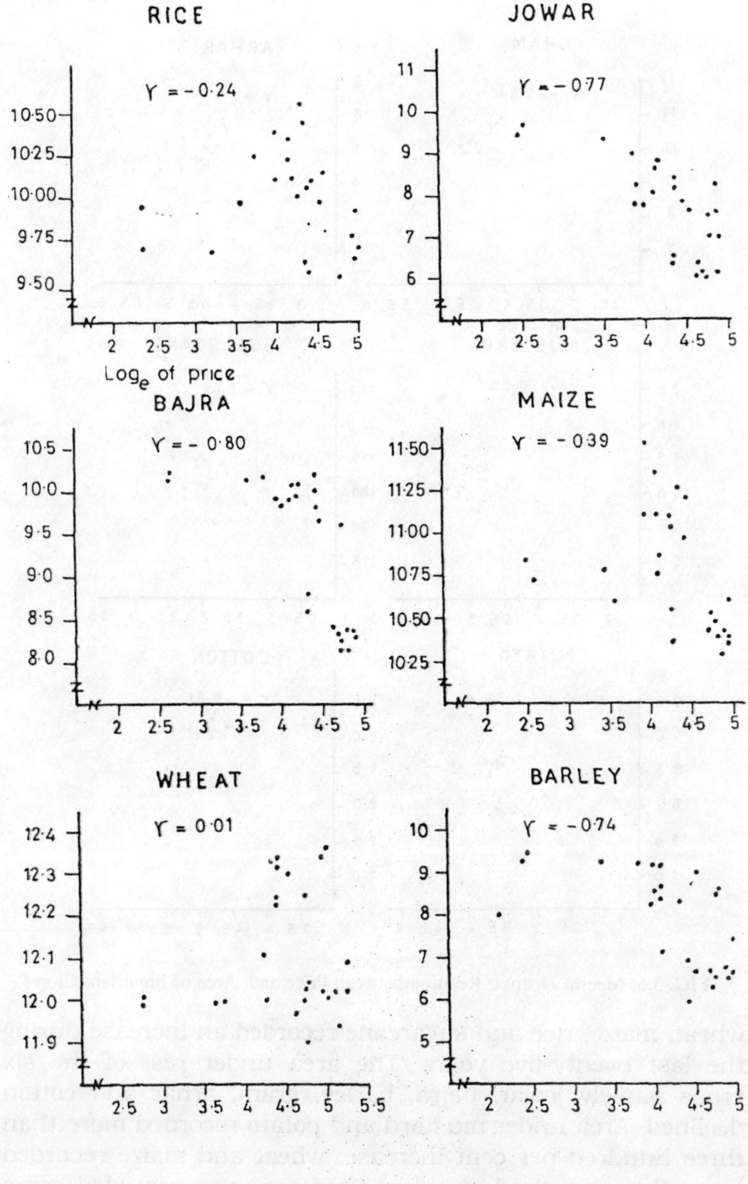

FIG. 3.5: Meerut District : Relation between Price and Area of Important Crop

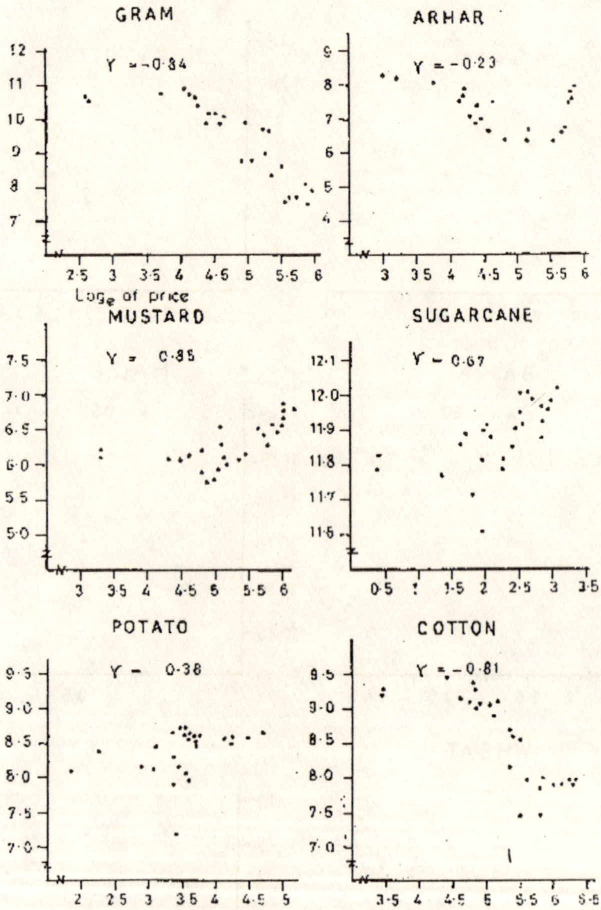

FIG. 3.6: Meerut District: Relation between Price and Area of Important Crop

wheat, maize, rice and sugarcane recorded an increase during the last twenty-five years. The area under rest of the six crops namely jowar, bajra, barley, gram, arhar and cotton declined. Area under mustard and potato recorded more than three hundred per cent increase, wheat and maize recorded more than hundred per cent increase, rice recorded more than thirty per cent increase and sugarcane recorded only marginal increase. Prices of all the crops increased by a thousand per cent except the prices of maize, bajra and jowar which recorded more than eight hundred per cent increase.

A perusal of Table 3.2 and Figs. 3.7 and 3.8 shows a strong positive relationship between prices and area of mustard (r = 0.9, significant at 1 per cent level), potato (r = 0.7, significant at 5 per cent level) and wheat (r = 0.7, significant at 1 per cent level). A weak positive relationship was seen in the case of rice (r = 0.2), maize (r = 0.2) and sugarcance (r = 0.1) which was not even significant. Negative correlation was seen in jowar, bajra, barley, gram, arhar and cotton.

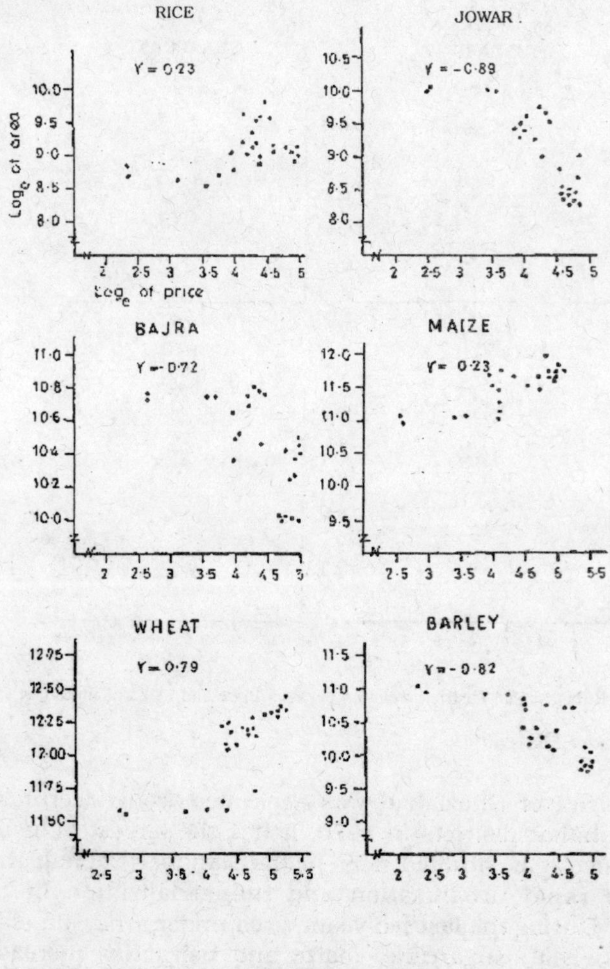

FIG. 3.7: Bulandshahar District: Relation between Price and Area of Important Crop

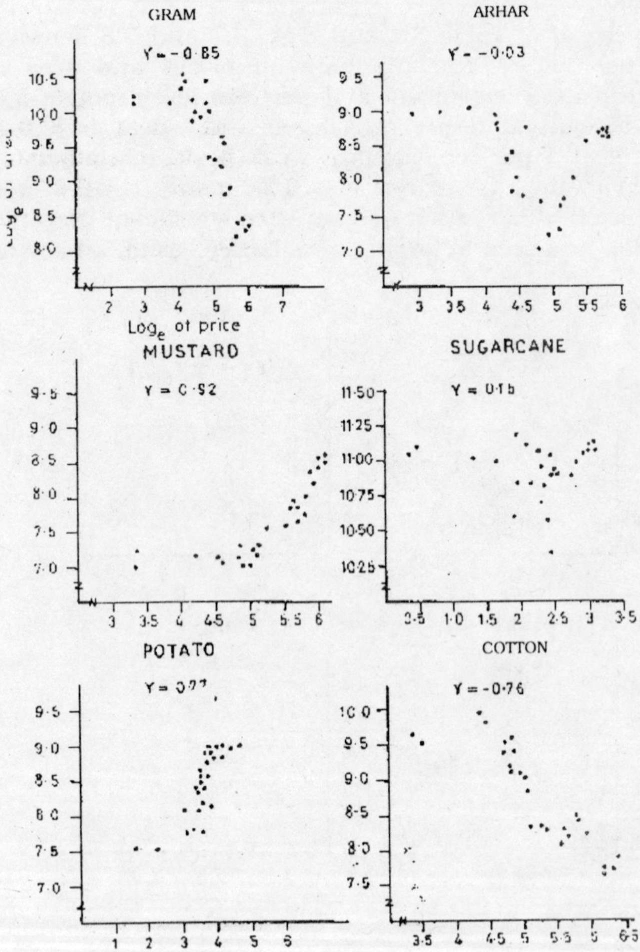

FIG. 3.8: Bulandshahar District: Relation between Price and Area of Important Crop

Ghaziabad District

The district of Ghaziabad was separated from Meerut and Bulandshahar districts in 1976. It has the largest industrial belt. Since it is situated near to the National Capital, there is both rapid urbanization and industrialization in this district. During the last ten years, area under arhar, mustard, potato, wheat, sugarcane, maize and bajra has increased. While the area under rest of the five crops namely rice, jowar, barley, gram and cotton has decreased. There was more than two hundred per cent increase in the area under arhar, more than fifty per cent increase in the area under mustard and potato and more than ten per cent increase in wheat, sugarcane, maize and bajra. Prices of almost all the crops recorded an increase. The prices of gram, potato, arhar and maize recorded more than hundred per cent increase, rest of the crops recorded more than fifty per cent increase.

A perusal of Table 3.2 and Figs. 3.9 and 3.10 shows a strong positive correlation betweenm prices and area of arhar (r = 0.9, significant at 5 per cent level), potato (r = 0.8 significant at 5 per cent level), sugarcane (r = 0.8, significant at 1 per cent level) and wheat (r = 0.6, significant at 5 per cent level). A weak positive correlation was recorded in the case of mustard (r = 0.5), maize (r = 0.3) and bajra (r = 0.1) which was not even significant. Rest of the crops namely rice, jowar, barley, gram and cotton showed negative correlations.

Conclusions

The foregoing analysis reveals the following facts:

1. Regarding prices, it was observed that in the study region, the prices of all the twelve selected crops registered an increase during the last twenty five years. The increase in prices were drastic as compared to increase in area. Highest increase in prices was recorded by gram. More than two thousand per cent increase was recorded by it. Rice, wheat barley, arhar, mustard, sugarcane, potato and cotton recorded more than thousand per cent increase. While the prices of jowar, bajra and maize increased by more than eight hundred per cent. These three crops recorded lowest increase in prices.

2. Regarding area under the twelve selected crops of the study region, it was observed that during the last twenty five years all the crops did not register an increase in their area. This shows that prices did not bring any variations in the total sown area but it brought a shift in allocation of area between crops. Wheat, mustard, sugarcane and potato registered significant increases in their area in the whole of the study region. While marginal increases in area was registered by maize, rice, cotton and bajra in some districts

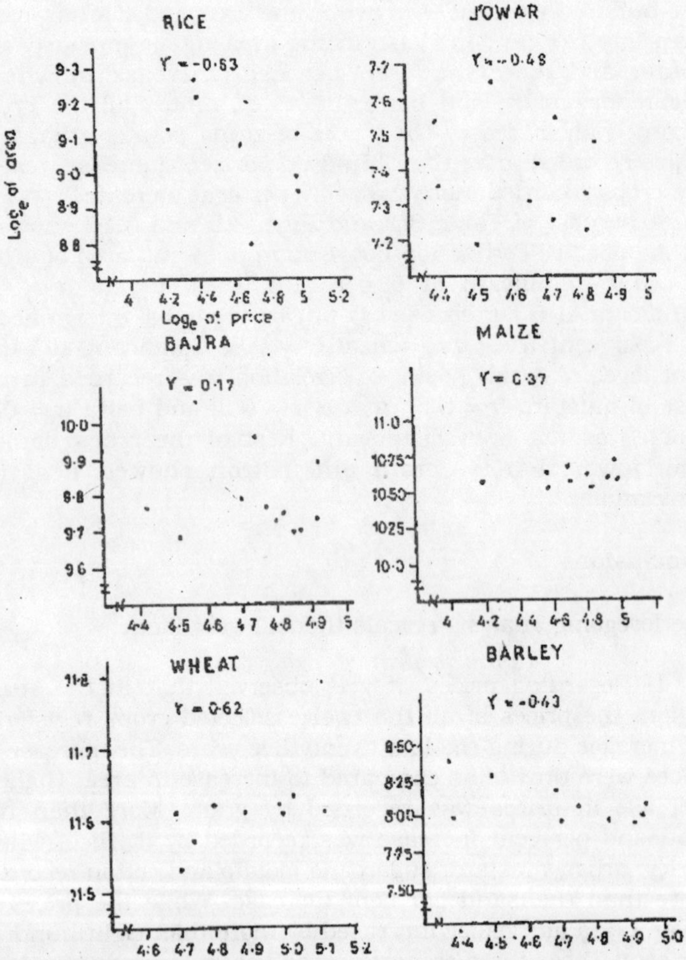

FIG. 3.9: Ghaziabad District: Relation between Price and Area of Important Crop

of the study region. Increase in area under maize was observed in the districts of Saharanpur, Bulandshahar and Ghaziabad. Increase in area under rice was observed in the districts of Saharanpur, Bulandshahar and Muzaffarnagar. Cotton area increased in Saharanpur and Muzaffarnagar and bajra area increased in Ghaziabad district. The crops which

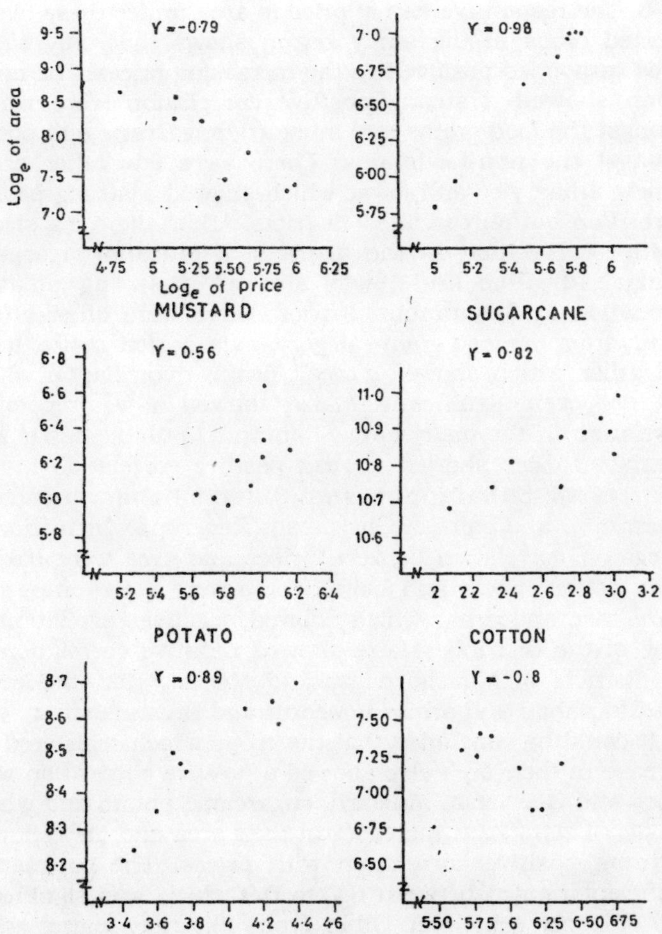

FIG. 3.10: Ghaziabad District: Relation between Price and Area of Important Crop

did not register any increase or just a marginal increase were gram, barley, bajra, jowar, cotton, arhar, maize and rice. Thus, a shift in cropping pattern, from the cultivation of coarse cerals and pulses to the cultivation of wheat, mustard sugarcane and potato was observed during the last twenty five years.

3. The responsiveness of price to area under these twelve selected crops in the study region shows that only a few crops responded positively to the increasing prices. The crops which showed a strong positive correlation were wheat amongst the food grains and mustard, sugarcane and potato amongst the non-foodgrains. There were few other crops namely arhar, rice and jowar which showed a strong positve correlation but only in a few districts. Arhar showed a strong positive correlation in the districts of Muzaffarnagar and Ghaziabad. Rice and jowar showed a strong positive correlation in Saharanpur district. There were other crops, mainly from the food grain category, namely rice, maize, bajra and arhar which showed a weak positive correlation which was not even significant. Maize showed a weak positive correlation in the districts of Sharanpur, Bulandshahar and Ghaziabad. Rice showed a weak positive correlation in the districts of Saharanpur and Bulandshahar, arhar in Saharanpur and bajra in Ghaziabad. The crops which showed a negative correlation between prices and area were barley, gram, cotton, jowar and bajra. There were some crops like maize, rice and arhar which showed negative correlation in some of the districts. Maize showed negative correlation in the districts of Muzaffarnagar and Meerut, rice in Meerut and Ghaziabad and arhar in Meerut and Bulandshahar.

It could be concluded that the crops which registered an increase in their area also showed a positive correlation with prices and vice-versa. Mustard, sugarcane, potato and wheat registered significant increases in their area and also showed a strong positive correlation with prices. The correlation coefficient ranged between 0.7 to 0.9 which was significant at 5 or 1 per cent level. Other crops like rice, maize, arhar and bajra which registered only marginal increase in their area showed a weak positive correlation. In their case, the correlation coefficient ranged between 0.1 to 0.3 which was not even significant. The crops which did not register any increase in their area showed negative correlation with prices. With the exception of cotton which registered marginal increase in its area in the two northern most districts but it showed a negative correlation with prices.

In a region like upper Ganga-Yamuna *Doab*, where several crops are sown farmers are seen to respond to prices. The area under cultivation of different crops depends upon several factors like climate, technology, prosperity of the farmers etc. But the most important factor, which has emerged now, is the profitability of the crop. The farmers like to sow that crop which is more profitable. This does not mean that there will be a total switch from foodgrains to sugarcane and from sugarcane to mustard. As cash crops are more profitable than the cultivation of foodgrains, the farmer of the study region devotes a significant proportion of his land to raise his own requirements but in sowing his 'surplus' land he looks to the market. Some crops like wheat, mustard, sugarcane and potato is primarily produced for money. Wheat is an important crop of this region which is partly grown for farmers need but is mostly grown for market. It is generally the preferred crop because of its price support, massive procurement by the Government on farmers doorstep, cash payments, technological advance and sale of wheat straw. The farmers of the study region are shifting from cultivation of coarse cereals to mustard because it requires only two watering, it is high yielding and more remunerative. There is only marginal area under mustard. During the last twenty five years area under mustard has increased due to its increased prices. Similar was the case of sugarcane and potato. Prices have influenced area under these crops as the farmers want to get maximum returns from his lands.

The coarse cereals like jowar, bajra, maize and barley are mainly grown for self consumption and partly for market. They depend upon rains and can do without irrigation waters, without other inputs and now-a-days even in rural areas people do not like to eat coarse cereals but they go for wheat. So these are the reasons as to why in spite of increasing prices the area under coarse cereals have declined. Area under pulses have remained stagnant or it has decined in spite of its soaring prices. The Government has increased the prices of pulses drastically mainly to goad the farmers to raise more pulses. But cultivation of pulses is not popular in the study region because of its low yields, non-availability of high yielding variety of seeds, it is susceptible to pests, disease and weather fluctuations, there is inadequate facilities to store them and still traditional methods of processing, dehusking and milling pulses into *dal* is carried on. But now with the introduction of early maturing strains of arhar, a change in the cropping pattern was observed because it can be cultivated in the normal cropping pattern as a bonus crop. Short duration arhar takes about five months and is usually grown in rotation with wheat crop in the study region.

In this study we cannot neglect the behaviour of the farmers because it is the farmer who responds to the increasing prices by allocating acreages to different crops. If the farmer is prosperous, educated and aware of the returns which he gets from his lands, he will sow only those crops from which he will be getting maximum returns. Most of the farmers of the study region have large, medium or semi-medium holdings and they are commercial minded because they have surplus to sell. Hence they respond to the increasing prices. While the small and marginal farmers with hand-to-mouth existence do not benefit from increasing prices. This is one of the reasons of poor response to increasing prices by these farmers. In the study region, price is found to influence acreage allocations and the study definitely shows that the farmers of this region respond significantly and positively to price changes.

FOUR

The Role of Specific Crops of North Bengal in the Regional and State's Economy

SUCHIT SUR

Northern part of West Bengal is the traditional producer of a number of fruits and other cash crops that have state level as well as of national and international importance like large cardamom, tea, orange and medicinal plants (100 % of the state), tobacco and pineapple (90 % of the state), mulberry (68 % of the state), mango (40 % of the state) and so on. But all are not well with the cultivation, marketing and processing of the crops. Cultivation is mostly traditional with less application of inputs (except tea), marketing is defective and controlled mostly by money lender, middlemen and commission agents for which the original cultivator actually receives less price. Not only that there are infrastructural and administrative problems but demand fluctuations, international relations and politics also sometimes affect the marketing of crops and their products like tea, organe and pineapple. Most of the processing plants have developed entirely on private initiatives and there is a virtual lack of governmental efforts (State) for providing guidance, research and development and setting up of processing complexes (except tea) without which their prospects seem extremely limited even in the domestic market.

Five districts of West Bengal, viz. Darjeeling, Jalpaiguri, Koochbehar, West Dinajpur and Malda situated north of Ganga together constitute the 'North Bengal region' of the state. It is one of the poorest regions of the state in terms of per capita domestic product (Rs. 756.00 at 1970-71 prices in comparison to Rs. 923.00 for the South Bengal). This relative poverty of the region is mainly due to its underdeveloped secondary and tertiary sectors with 75 per cent of population depending on primary sector in comparison to 51.5 per cent in South Bengal. Except Malda, productivity of cereal crops remained constant or even below the 1960-61 index level and it was also substantially below the state's average and even South Bengal districts. However, potentiality remains and given more inpurts and with the removal of age long neglect and constraints the region holds much prospects in future.

The variety of terrain, climate, soil and tradition of agricultural practices provide suitable and favourable environment for the production of a number of horticultural and other commercial crops like Mandarin Orange, Plum, Peach, Pear, Mango, Pineapple, Medicinal plants, Cardamom, Black pepper, Mulberry, Tobacco, Tea and Jute. In fact North Bengal produces 100 per cent of state's orange, plum, pear, large cardamom, tea and medicinal plants, 90 per cent of tobacco and pineapple, 68 per cent of mulberry for sericulture, 40 per cent of mango and around 25 per cent of jute as well as a substantial quantity of ginger (Fig. 4.1). Among them pineapple, cardamom, ginger, tobacco, medicinal plants and mulberry for sericulture have commercial importance in the national market and tea, jute and silk have commercial importance both in the national and in the international markets. The chapter briefly discusses and analyses the production, marketing, problems and future prospects of cultivation of these crops and their impact on the region *vis-a-vis* state's economic development.

Orange

It is the 'mandarin orange', delicious in taste, that has been cultivated in the Darjeeling hills long before its occupation by the East India company. It can be noticed that the area and production have been increasing through the years (Table 4.1). But the marketing of the produce is almost entirely (70-80%) controlled and conducted by a group of middlemen and commission agents through a system of forward trading. Therefore, the poor orchard owners hardly get 30 per cent of the final sale proceeds. Other problems associated with this crop are — 50 per cent of orchards are over 50 years old,

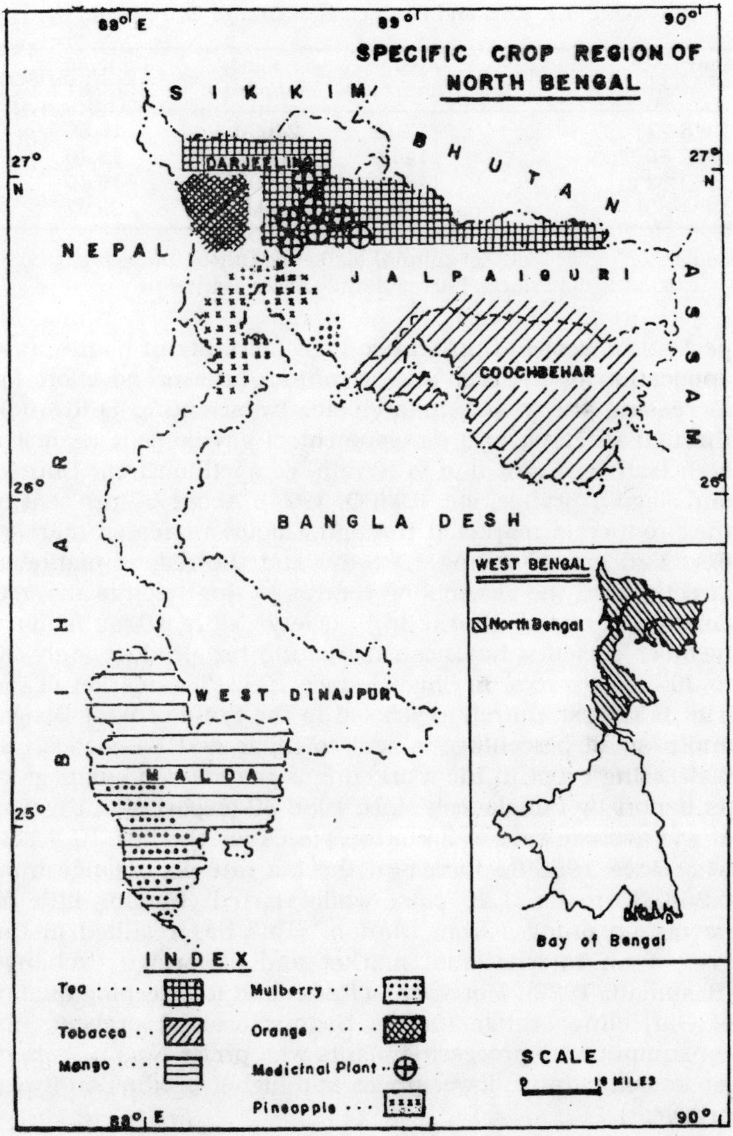

FIG. 4.1: Production of Horticultural and other Commercial Crops in North-Bengal

Table 4.1: Area and Production of Orange in Darjeeling

Year	Area (in ha.)	Seedlings supplied	Production (in M.T.)
1976-77	.912	24000	10.56
1979-80	1144.9	36000	13.40
1982-83	1489.2	33000	15.40
1984-85	1733.2	N.A.	25.67

Source: (i) Dist. Agricultural Marketing Officer, Darjeeling.
(ii) Principal Agricultural. Officer, Darjeeling.

pest and disease attack cause high mortality of plants, rare application of fertilizer and irrigation, little or no effort for increasing the yield, quality, etc. by scientific cultivation through research and development of government agencies, high transport cost due to terrain, competition from Bhutan and Nagpur orange, etc. (CMPO, 1974). About 60 per cent of the produce is marketed through Siliguri regulated markert (Rs. 2.25 crores during 1988-89) and the rest is marketed directly from the assembling centres to the Calcutta market. One co-operative marketing society[1] with 10 subsidiary member societies has been marketing the product (only 20 to 30% of growers) in Siliguri since 1982. The market of the fruit is almost entirely restricted to the State of West Bengal and a small percentage is sent to Bihar and Bangladesh. A distressing event in the marketing is the sudden stoppage of its import by Bangladesh since 1988-89 (export quantity was at the average rate of 2.9 crore pieces for the last 10 years) who since 1988-89 increased the tax rate on organge from 0.25-0.30 to Rs. 1.20 paise while started charging little or no tax on oranges from Bhutan.[2] This has resulted in the loss of an international market and of foreign exchange (Basumati, 1989). Moreover, softness and low keeping quality of Darjeeling orange (unlike Nagpur orange) prevents its consumption by processing plants who prefer Nagpur variety for its comparative lower prices and higher production (twice in a year).

Cardamom

It is the 'Amomum Subulatum Roxburgh' (or large cardamon

or *Bara Elaichi*) variety that is mainly grown in the sub-Himalayan Sikkim and West Bengal and to a smaller extent in North Eastern States. Darjeeling district of West Bengal is the second largest producer in about 2200 ha. in 1988-89 (Cardamom Board). Area and production have remained more or less constant*. About 98 per cent of the produce is marketed and about 581 matric tonne was exported to Calcutta, Delhi, Kanpur, Amritsar and other markets during 1982-83 (District Agricultural Marketing Office, 1985), mainly through Siliguri assembling centre. Middlemen, *fariahas* and commission agents reap most of the profits though the Spices Board (formerly Cardamom Board), Government of India, has come forward in recent years with some subsidy oriented schemes for production, curing and marketing of the crop. Cultivation is still done by traditional methods and about 90 per cent of growers still use traditional method of curing (Spices Board, 1989). The estimated value of production in 1983-84 was Rs. 2.52 crores. Soil erosion and landslips are problems that occassionally cause large scale destruction of plants.

Ginger

This cash crop is mainly cultivated in the hills of Darjeeling district. Area and production are found steadily increasing and have doubled in the period between 1974-75 and 1984-85 (649 ha. and 5.84 metric tonne in 1974-75 and 1207.40 ha. and 13.55 metric tonne in 1984-85) (Principal Agricultural Officer, 1985-86). During 1983-84, the total value of ginger produced was estimted as Rs. 61.83 crores. But all is not well in ginger production. Through forward trading the middlemen, *fariahas* and commission agents control the production, procurement and marketing. One co-operative society[3] is marketing only 3-4 per cent of the marketed surplus of production and also providing some inputs. About 75 per cent of the total production is exported outside the district and the main markets are Delhi and Amritsar (50%), Calcutta (30%), Lucknow and Bihar (20%). About 200 truck loads (10 tonnes weight each) of ginger is annually exported

* Production figures of Agricultural Marketing Department, Darjeeling and Spices Board, Government of India, do not tally

from Siliguri regulated market of which 25 truck load goes to Bangladesh (which mainly imports ginger from Singapore). Therefore, the total value of ginger exported is about Rs. 60.96 crores (of which about Rs. 7.62 crores is exported to Bangladesh) annually.[4] Enquiry at Siliguri regulated market revealed that only 100 truck load of ginger used to be exported from this market during the year 1980-81.

Pineapple

North Bengal (only Darjeeling, Jalpaiguri and West Dinajpur districts) is singularly important for pineapple (big 'Singapuri' variety) in India's commercial horticultural map with about 33 per cent and 90 per cent of National and State's production, respectively in 1984-85 (IIM, 1988). Commercial cultivation took rapid strides during 1970-75 when the acreage stood roughly at 10,000 (complete gardens) (Sur, 1982). Further increase took place till 1977-78 (estimated to be 14,000 acres) but problems like absence of state's effort in marketing, stoppage of bank credit, cut-back of purchase by U.S.S.R. and others, road and rail transport dislocation during floods of 1987-88, cut-back of demand by processing plants (local specially) for increasing cost of inputs and duty, increasing cost of scientific cultivation, etc. had caused decrease of acreage and production after 1978 and at present (1988-89) the acreage and production stand at 9400 acres (estimated) and 2-10 lakh tonnes (IIM, 1988), respectively. Many big garden owners (of West Dinajpur) have already switched over or are in the process of switching over to tea-leaf production in anticipation of better prospect in that (Basumati, 1989).

The estimated capacity of the local canning industries is only 3 per cent of the total sales output which ought to have been 20 to 30 per cent for maintaining the trend of production of fresh fruits. According to a survey conducted by the Indian Institute of Foreign Trade 'the pineapple industry in India has a long way to go to catch up with the advanced countries like USA and Philippines. The success of the industry in these countries can be attributed in the main to the vertical integration of operations, ranging from cultivation of the fresh fruits to marketing of the finished products. Besides, the expensive modern equipment used and the constant attention paid to research have greatly contributed to economise the cost of production'. There is no rapport between the grower and the canner, a very vital issue so far as quality control is concerned. Input prices are always variable, there is practically no control over the quality of sugar and other essential inputs. Every approach is casual, planning is defective with no fixed goal in front (Biswas, 1990). In Table 4.2 utilisation of pineapple for export production by North Bengal canning industries has been presented for the year 1981-82 and 1982-83.

Table 4.2: Pineapple Utilization by North Bengal Processing Plants during 1981-82 and 1982-83 for Export

(metric tonnes)

Name of Unit	1981-82		1982-83	
	Export Prod.	Pineapple utilisation	Export Prod.	Pineapple utilisation
M/s Amarnath Fruit	200	400	350	700
M/s Darjeeling Fruit Pvt. Ltd.	500	1000	1200	2400
M/s Siliguri Canning Ind.	200	400	—	—
M/s Himalayan Fruit Preserver	80	160	210	400
M/s Pal's Fruit Products	75	150	120	240
M/s Hindusthan Fruit Processing	125	250	150	300
M/s Indus Fruit Processing	50	100	50	100
M/s Gita Mango Processing Factory	100	200	250	500
M/s Mahadeo Fruit Processing Industry	500	1000	600	1200

Medicinal Plants

Darjeeling hills have the reputation for production of certain medicinal plants and herbs and for the Quinine producing unit, since the British period. But the indigenous species have largely been lost due to massive deforestation (IIM, 1988). The Directorate of Cinchona (Government of West Bengal) has developed cinchona, ipecac and dioscorea plantation of 1800 acres, 1400 unit and 1800 acres, respectively and has also set up factories (3) for the production of herbal based drugs but progress has been dismal (Government of West Bengal, 1986). Similar is the rate of progress of the West Bengal Pharmaceutical and Phytochemical Development Corporation who has taken some efforts for the cultivation of medicinal and aromatic plants and has set up one Fractionation unit. It also proposes to set up one phytochemical complex in collaboration with U.S.S.R. for many downstream products having international demand but competition from S.E. Asian countries, Brazil as well as Punjab, Uttar Pradesh and Tamil Nadu in coming future is worthnoting.

Tobacco

Andhra Pradesh, Gujrat and West Bengal are the three big producers of tobacco in India. The yield rate per hectare varies greatly with 962 kg. for Andhra Pradesh, 1627 kg. for Gujrat and 1100 kg. for West Bengal. North Bengal region was cultivating the crop even before British Colonial administration took control of this part of Bengal. While the northern part of West Bengal produces more than 80 per cent, the share of Koochbehar district alone is about 65 per cent followed by Jalpaiguri (12%). Koochbehar's share of production is more than 67 per cent of the state (on average).[5] Tobacco is by far the best crop of North Bengal with largest concentration in Koochbehar where some police stations like Sitai, Sitalkuchi and Dinhata record between 13.5 to 16.5 per cent of gross-cropped area in Tobacco (Bagchi and Mukherjee, 1983). Typewise, the cigar and cheroot varieties are mainly grown in West Bengal with 55 per cent of Nicotiana Rustica species. North Bengal produces four varieties viz. wrapper, filler and *jati* (of tobacum group) and *motihari* (of rustica group). Production of *motihari* tobacco is a virtual monopoly of North Bengal with about 17,500 ha. of the total of 22,000 ha. of West Bengal. Again North Bengal has about 80 per cent and Kochbehar has about 60 per cent of *jati* tobacco area of West Bengal. The area under wrapper and filler tobacco is very limited and the production is also small (150 tonne) but even then Koochbehar produces more than 90 per cent of these varieties in India which are good in aroma, burn and other desirable qualities (Bagchi and Mukherjee, 1983). Taking all varieties and species together and considering the average price of both export and inland market per kg. of tobacco, the total value of tobacco produced in Kochbehar alone during 1985-86 will be around Rs. 13-14 crores. Though area is decreasing but production has been found increasing over the years due to higher yield rate achieved in recent years obviously through the improved method of practice and irrigation facilities as provided by the Central Tobacco Research Institute (ICAR) and state government (Bagchi and Mukherjee, 1983).

Tobacco of all types require heavy inputs of manures and fertilizers and therefore, input cost is high but the return is respectable considering the fact that it occupies the field for 3½ to 4½ months, leaving other crops to grow on it. About 98 per cent of the produce is marketable surplus but the benefits are shared by middlemen, labourers and government agencies (through excise duty). Marketing is also affected by the wide fluctuation of price over the months, increasing quantum of excise duty over the years, indebtedness of farmers, absence of a definite marketing policy by the government (Central) (Staff Reporter, 1989), closer of cheroot factory at Dinhata and so on. In spite of such constraints about Rs. 12.50 crores was earned in 1988 through exporting '*hukkah* tobacco paste' to the Gulf countries (Staff Reporter, 1989). The Central Tobacco Research Station has been making commendable efforts in improving the method, yield and curing of tobacco through research and training but unless a Tobacco Board like Tea, Coffee and Spices Board is set up for production, curing and marketing of the crop the economy of the already languishing crop may deteriorate further in the face of vast potentiality (Staff Reporter, 1989).

Mango

Though mango is grown all over the country but better varieties are largely grown in a fiew areas including Malda district of West Bengal where the area coverage (about 40% of the state) stood at 20234 ha. in 1986 (Dist. Statistical Officer, 1986). Out of this area, Fazli variety covered 75 per cent and the rest by other varieties. The other district of North Bengal that has some area under mango is the West Dinajpur. In Malda, Englishbazar P.S. has the highest coverage (19% of gross cropped area), followed by Malda (8.1%) and Ratua (5.1%). Compared to 1944-45, the area under mango has shrunk considerably in both Malda and West Dinajpur during 1981 (on average 32.35 to 29.27 per cent in Malda and 700 to 367 per cent in West Dinajpur) (Bagchi and Mukherjee, 1983). Production and productivity depend much on vagaries of weather and wide fluctuations of output are noticed with every 3-4 years yielding a bumper crop (the variation is between 1 lakh tonne and 20 thousand tonne). The Table 4.3 gives an estimate of area, production, export and value of Malda mango.

Table 4.3: Area, Production and Export of Malda Mango

Year	Area (in ha.)	Prod. (in M.T.)	Quantity of Export (M.T.) By Rail	By Road	Estimated value of export (Rs. lakh)	Places of export
1968	18063	82500	24600	32700	203.91	Assam (32%), Calcutta (27%), Delhi-Allahabad (16%), Coalfield (15%), others (10%)
1969	18225	50600	13800	23500	177.84	Assam (38%), Calcutta (39%), Coalfield (5%), Delhi (4.5%), others (13.5%)
1970	18225	24979	9400	11600	144.29 234.47*	Assam (30%), Calcutta (35%), Delhi etc. (15%), Coalfield (7%), others (13%)
1977	N.A.	80000	N.A.	N.A.	780.00*	N.A. N.A.
1983	N.A.	82000	N.A.	N.A.	429.12*	N.A. N.A.

Source: Report of the fact finding survey of Malda district (West Bengal), United Bank of India, 1971.

* Maldar Am: Amer Malda — M. Choudhuri, *Madhuparni* (Bengali), Malda District special, 1985.

The total value of the crop varies between Rs. 10 crores to Rs. 4.5 crores. Mangoes of West Dinajpur are mostly consumed locally in North Bengal but 85 per cent of the produce of Malda is exported outside and even to the international market of U.S.S.R. (about 2/3 amount of total export in the form of mango pulp and juices used to be taken by this country but has recently cut-back the amount of purchase) and the domestic demand hovers around 60 thousand tonnes (IIM, 1988). The mango trade is almost wholly controlled by the *mahajans* and *aratdars* through *fariahas*. About 40 thousand persons get seasonal employment annually in various stages of production and marketing of the crop (CMPO, 1974). Large number of tiny household units have come up for processing both green and ripe mango in Malda. But in spite of its importance as a valuable cash crop the problems noticed are— very little attention is given to the proper maintenance, scientific replantation and extension of orchards, financial difficulties and risk factor prevent owners to do anything but lease out the orchards to *fariahas*, drought and other weather vagaries do considerable damage, shortage of railway wagons, booking difficulty and road closure due to collapse of bridge and culverts on roads and railways during floods, lack of serious effort on the part of government for export of the crop to the international market, uncertain future of processing plant consuming Malda mango, loss of acreage due to conversion of Mango orchards into other uses and so on. There are however, a few government co-operatives and private organisations who are making some efforts to help the growers, exporters and processing units.

Mulberry and Sericulture

Sericulture involves operations in two different sectors that are intimately linked together. They are: (a) agro-based and (b) industrial. North Bengal districts are primarily important for the agro-based sector which involves cultivation of mulberry and raising of cocoons. Agro-based sericulture at present is the most important cottage industry of the district of Malda where most of the state's mulberry acreage is located (more than 48 %) and North Bengal's share of the state's area was 67.52 per cent in 1986-87. Besides Malda, West

Dinajpur and Darjeeling are two other important districts with 7.70 and 7.20 per cent of the state's area; respectively (IIM, 1988). The fame of Malda as silk rearing centre can be found in records of 11-12th century A.D. and Britishers evinced keen interest in it. However, total area had reduced considerably from 44 sq. km. in 1944-45 to only 12 sq. km. during 1981 (average) (Bagchi and Mukherjee, 1983) but it rose again thereafter. In Malda, highest concentration is found in Kaliachak (55 % of gross cropped area) followed by Englishbazar (25 %), Manikchak (11 %) and Ratua (7 %). Nowhere in India such concentration is seen. The traditional silk worm seeds used in Malda is multivoltine 'nistari' worms and the bivoltine 'Japanese' worm is found important in Darjeeling district for its climatic condition. A sericulture farm of 5000 m^2 could give in 1981-82 an annual return of Rs. 4500 on average keeping aside the annual input cost of Rs. 6000, interests on loan and depreciation on capital goods. Another estimate put the net annual net income from sericulture per family per bigha (one third of an acre) of land at 1984 price index as Rs. 5996 in comparison to Rs. 1550 from mustard, Rs. 935 from aman paddy, Rs. 844 from jute, Rs. 649 from boro paddy and Rs. 379 from wheat (Directorate of Sericulture, 1989). Though acreage has gone down but the production has increased due to better yield following improved techniques, seeds and layers, etc. through training and extension work. The total annual production of raw silk and wastes stood at 2.67 and 1.66 lakh kg. respectively for Malda and 3.93 and 1.66 lakh kg. for the entire North Bengal region, during 1985-86 (Table 4.4). North Bengal's share of raw silk and waste production was about 74.73 per cent of the state in 1985-86 (IIM, 1988). Reeling of yarn has becoming important in Malda. During 1981-82, about 35 thousand families were engaged in cocoon rearing and the industry provided employment to 1.60 lakh persons (Bagchi and Mukherjee, 1983). Large profit is an inducement for increasing popularity of sericulture. Total value of silkworm raised was Rs. 2.77 crore and the output of yarn and wastes was valued Rs. 10.44 crore during 1969-70 which have in all probability been increased to Rs. 3.45 crores and Rs. 12 crores (approximate estimate), respectively in recent years. Coming to the marketing of silk yarn and wastes, almost the entire silk industry is under the control of private traders cum

Table 4.4: Conditions of Sericulture in North Bengal

District	Area (in ha.) on 31.3.87	No.of farmers as on 31.3.86	No. of silk handloom as on 31.3.82	Production		Total production as on 31.3.86 (in kg)
				Raw silk on 31.3.86 (in kg)	Silk wastes on 3.3.86 (in kg)	
Malda	6614.8	33505	36	267562	166330	433892
W.Dinajpur	1055.0	5100	5	74080	N.A.	74080
Kochbehar	251.9	1235	13	N.A.	N.A.	N.A.
Jalpaiguri	332.5	1640	36	N.A.	N.A.	N.A.
Darjeeling	995.1	4914	0	51760	50	51810
North Bengal	9249.3	45394	90	393402	166380	559782

Source: Industrial Development of North Bengal: Some Strategies, IIM, Calcutta, 1988 (unpublished).

money lenders who resort to forward trading. This trading-money lending nexus purchase the silk to be given to the weavers under their control for producing the cloth or sell it to the merchants of outside Bengal, mainly from Benaras. The net loosers are the farmers and weavers and government intervention has made little dent in this nexus (IIM, 1988). A number (12) of co-operatives have come up for organising reelers, rearers, spinners and weavers (UBI, 1971). The industry also suffers from multiplicity of organisational control over different stages of production without striking co-ordination. Moreover, Malda has less number of weaving handlooms that are mostly concentrated in the Murshidabad district or outside Bengal. At present (1985-86) the position of West Bengal is *4th* in All India (though second in earlier years) raw silk production after Karnataka, Andhra and Tamil Nadu. In the last 12 years or so production has more than doubled in Karnataka while in West Bengal it was only 90 per cent (IIM, 1988). The central government has plan to export more silk in coming years through Central Silk Board and though West Bengal received the third largest share of aid (Rs. 498 crore) from World Bank through National Sericulture Project for the increase of silk production (*The Statesman*, 1989) there remains much scope for further increase of silk production in India and unless weaving of silk is developed in Malda, West Bengal may not be able to take advantage of the boom situation prevailing in the world market (IIM, 1988). A spun silk yarn manufacturing unit will shortly be commissioned under private sector by utilising the silk waste byproduct that is available in large quantity in Malda (*The Statesman*, 1990).

Tea

Lastly, we take up the case of the most important foregin exchange earning cash crop of India and West Bengal—Tea. West Bengal rather North Bengal holds the second position after Assam in both area and production of tea in India. The economy of this crop is well-known and, therefore, needs no elaboration. Quality tea means 'Darjeeling tea' whether in India or abroad. Out of the three tea growing areas of the state, Darjeeling area off late has been in grip of some insurmountable problems unlike Terai and Dooars areas. These are— lower yield, decreasing area, increasing cost, 90 per cent of bushes are between 30-50 years old, soil erosion, drought condition, stagnating employment, high cost of essentials and ration to be supplied to the employees, less effort of management in renovating gardens, etc. besides the problems affecting all other areas like high cost of replantation, shift of consumers drinking habit of coffee in the international market, increasing use of tea bags, high tax structure, liquidity crisis, power shortage, etc. The industry as a whole continues to be extractive in nature and has developed a sort of 'enclave' spatial economy having weak linkages with the regional economy of North Bengal as most of the capital, chemicals and fertilizers are imported from outside because headquarters of tea estates are mostly located at Calcutta, thereby benfiting Calcutta traders and suppliers of tea garden requirements. However, NABARD and Tea Board have plans and programmes for rejuvenating the industry.

Conclusion

Though singularly important sub-region within the State for the production of a number of horticultural and cash crops that have both regional, national and even some international importance, the future of the cultivation and processing of products appears to be generally gloomy and discouraging where only tea, tobacco and sericulture could still provide some bright patches though their positions in the competitive commercial markets have been receiving serious threats from both domestic and foreign producers. In the face of this situation the approach and attitude of the state government appear to be lukewarm and very casual and there is serious lack of planning efforts for giving the just thrust and right guidance through research, development, management and setting up of a number of processing complexes with vertical integration of production, processing and marketing of produce.

Notes

1. Mirik Primary Agricultural Co-operative Marketing Society.
2. Interviews with the Commission agents at Siliguri Regulated Market.
3. Mirik Primary Agricultural Co-operative Marketing Society.
4. Informations supplied by commission agents at Siliguri Regulated Market and Mirik Primary Agricultural Co-operative Marketing Society.
5. (i) Annual Plan on Agriculture, Kochbehar (1986-87).
   (ii) Economic Review (Statistical appendix), Govt. of West Bengal, 1988-89.

FIVE

Commercialization of Agriculture and Its Relation with Economic Development in the Ganga Basin of Madhya Pradesh

C.K. JAIN and A.K. JAIN

Commercialization of agriculture is one of the major characteristics of its modernization. With the increasing use of water, and modern yield raising technology, production of crops has increased very fastly. As a consequence of rapid increasing production of foodgrains and pulses, it is expected that area under these crops may be reduced proportionately and may be brought under other commercial crops. Growth of commericial crops can be caused by many other factors also. For example, to meet the cost of agricultural inputs sale of agricultural produces become necessary. Even to meet other social and cultural obligations farmers have to market some of their crops and, from marketing point of view, commerical crops are more profitable than cereals. These commerical crops provide raw materials to many industries and, therefore, industrial growth usually accompany the commercialization of farming (Tiwari and Jain, 1989).

Usually those crops are kept in the class of commerical crops which are transformed into useful products after major processing. Most of the non-food crops come in this group but such a classification of crops is not valid at present. Because most of the food crops particularly wheat and rice are also marketed on large scale and, therefore, exclusion of these crops from the list of commerical crops is not logical. On the other hand, there are many non-food crops which are produced to meet the needs of the producers. Most of the traditional oilseeds are of this nature. Thus, it is not the crop itself but the purpose of its production which places any crop in the class of commerical crops. Hence the concept of commercial crops is not static but a dynamic one and changes with the development of society. However, all oilseeds, cotton, fruits, sugarcane and vegatables and spices and condiments have been treated as commerical crops for the present purpose. The main objectives are to analyse trend and spatial variation in levels of commercialization of agriculture and to present the relationship between commercialization and level of economic development in that part of Madhya Prdesh which falls in the Ganga Basin.

The Region

The catchment areas of the Ganga and Yamuna rivers cover about half of the northern part of Madhya Pradesh. Major rivers of this sub-basins are the Chambal, Betwa, Ken, Tons and Son river basin. They cover 227802 sq. km area and encompass twenty–nine districts of northern half of the state (Fig. 5.1). The sub-basin presents a diversified picture of land and people. Level land is limited in some of the river valleys. But most of the area is the assemblage of hills, uplands and plateaus. The Malwa plateau presents a typical character of Deccan Trap with undulating surface. The Vindhyan country of the Rewa plateau in the east and the Madhya Bharat plateau in the north-west presents level tract marked with scarps. The Bundelkhand upland is a dissected area of ancient rocks. The Baghelkhand plateau is tangled masses of hills and plateaux, highly dissected and widely covered with forest. Similar case with the rainfall and soils. Rainfall varies from more than 150 cms. in eastern part to less than 75 cms in north-western part of the basin. The main soil types found in the basin are black, alluvium, and red and yellow soils. Black and alluvium soils are more suitable for commercial crops in this basin. This region accomodates more than 53.7 per cent of the total population of the state. Despite of recent development of several agriculture-based industries, the basin is basically agricultural with 78 per cent of its population living in rural areas and nearly 73.8 per cent of working population engaged in cultivation.

FIG. 5.1: The Ganga Basin of Madhya Pradesh

Degree of Commercialization

Total area under commercial crops is 2141.8 thousand hectares in 1984-85 which constitutes 17.2 per cent of the total cropped area in the basin. This proportion is much higher than the state average (14.1 %). Proportion of different commercial crops is presented in Table 5.1.

Table 5.1: Trend in Area and Production of Important Commercial Crops

Crops	Area (thousand hect.)		Production (thousand ha)	
	1955-56	1984-85	1955-56	1984-85
Soyabean	12.2+	688.7	40.0*	541.2
Rapeseed & Mustard	85.3	291.8	33.2	217.6
Linseed	250.8	288.6	72.5	80.8
Groundnut	129.9	180.3	79.6	95.5
Sesame	274.2	163.2	73.7	27.0
Total Oilseeds	769.0	1756.5	—	971.9
Sugarcane	31.1	22.9	88.0	65.5
Cotton	613.0	175.1	242.4	102.3
Fruits & Vegetables	29.0	74.5	—	—
Condiments & Spices	57.1	112.8	—	—
Commercial Crops	1499.2	2141.8	—	—

Source: Agricultural Statistics, 1985, Directorate of Agriculture, Bhopal.
* 1977-78;
\+ 1973-74

It is evident from the above Table 5.4 that more than 82.0 per cent of area under commercial crops is constituted by oilseeds in 1984-85 which was 51.3 per cent in 1955-56. Cotton constitutes about 8.2 per cent while other commercial food crops cover only 9.8 per cent of total area under commercial crops. Among oilseeds soyabean is the single major crop, covering more than 688.7 thousand hectares of cropped area. Area under this crop increased phenomenally during last two decades. Other important oilseeds are rapeseed and mustard, linseed, groundnut and sesame. Production of all these commercial crops is very localized phenomenon. At the same time changes in area and production has not been uniform throughout the basin. All commercial crops except sesame, sugarcan and cotton gained in area after 1955-56. Total area under these crops was 1500 thousand hectares in 1955-56 which increased to 2141.8 thousand hectares in 1984-85, recording an increase of 42.8 per cent during this period. Relative significance of this group of crops increased because of increasing area under them. They occupied 16.9 per cent of the total cropped area in the previous year while 17.2 per cent in the latter year.

Oilseeds

Oilseeds were grown on 1756.5 thousand hectares in 1984-85. It constituted 14.1 per cent of the total cropped area of basin and 7.8 per cent of the State. Distribution of area under oilseeds is also far from uniform. Percentage area under oilseed ranges from 5.4 in Vidisha to 41.75 in Morena. Usually western and north-western districts of the basin have comparatively high and very high proportion of area under oilseeds. In contrast to in these areas central and eastern districts have low and very low proportions. (Fig. 5.2).

Soyabean

Soyabean is the first ranking commercial crop in the basin and it occupies 688.7 thousand hectares (5.5% of the total cropped area in 1984-85). Cultivation of soyabean started in this area in 1964-65. Infact its production was started on experimental basis around Indore. Many new varieties of soyabean were invented in later years. Consequently, area under this crop increased very rapidly since 1973-74. It increased from only 12.2 thousand hectares in this year to 688.7 thousand hectares in 1984-85; thus recording an increase by 56 times during this period. No other crop could gain so fastly as soyabean did. Production of this crop increased along with the area. It was only 40 thousand tonnes in 1977-78 which rose to 531.2 thousand tonnes in 1984-85. Thus production increased by 1228 per cent in 7 years which is much faster than the growth of area.

Cultivation of soyabean started in Malwa plateau around Indore and it spread to districts of Indore and Ujjain divisions quickly. Later it reached to other districts of the basin and at present is grown in almost all districts. Though, soyabean has reached in the eastern districts of the basin, the major producers still are the western districts. More than three-fourths of the tota area is concentrated in western districts. These districts are spread over the Malwa plateau. It occupies as high as 26.4 per cent of the total cropped area in Indore and 22.4 per cent in Dewas district. Other important districts are Ujjain, Dhar, Shajapur, Sehore, Rajgarh, Bhopal and Raisen (Fig. 5.2 A). Such a high concentration of soyabean production in western basin is due to several physical, economic and social factors. First of them is the nature of soil. This crop grows well on black soils, which are found in the western part only. From the point of view of the suitability of the soil the Rewa plateau and the Orchha plain have high possibility of expansion of this crop, but due to high pressure of rural population on cropped area not only soyabean but other non-traditional commercial crops could not be popular in these areas.

In production of commercial crops economic considerations are more significant than the physical one. It is because the purpose of production of such crops is to maximise the profit. The margin of profit depends on demand and accessibility to markets to a great extent. Soyabean is such a crop which is produced mainly to provide the raw materials to soyabean processing plants. It is, therefore, more profitable to the producers of this crop in the areas where the processing plants are located. There are more than 40 soyabean processing plants working in this State and mostly these plants are locted in the western basin. Thus, there is a reciprocal relationship between the location of soya plant and concentration of area under soyabean. Further, the western basin is also known for the production of the commercial crops like cotton, groundnut and sugarcane. Therefore, farmers were familiar with the commercial crops, well before the arrival of the soyabean in this area. This is most urbanized and industrialized part of the state which has exerted decisive influence on location of soya plants. Connection of this area with Delhi and Bombay also helped in the distribution of soya products.

Rapeseed and Mustard

This basin is major rape and mustard producing area in the State. Total area under this crop was 291.8 thousand hectares in 1984-85 which is only 2.3 per cent of the total cropped

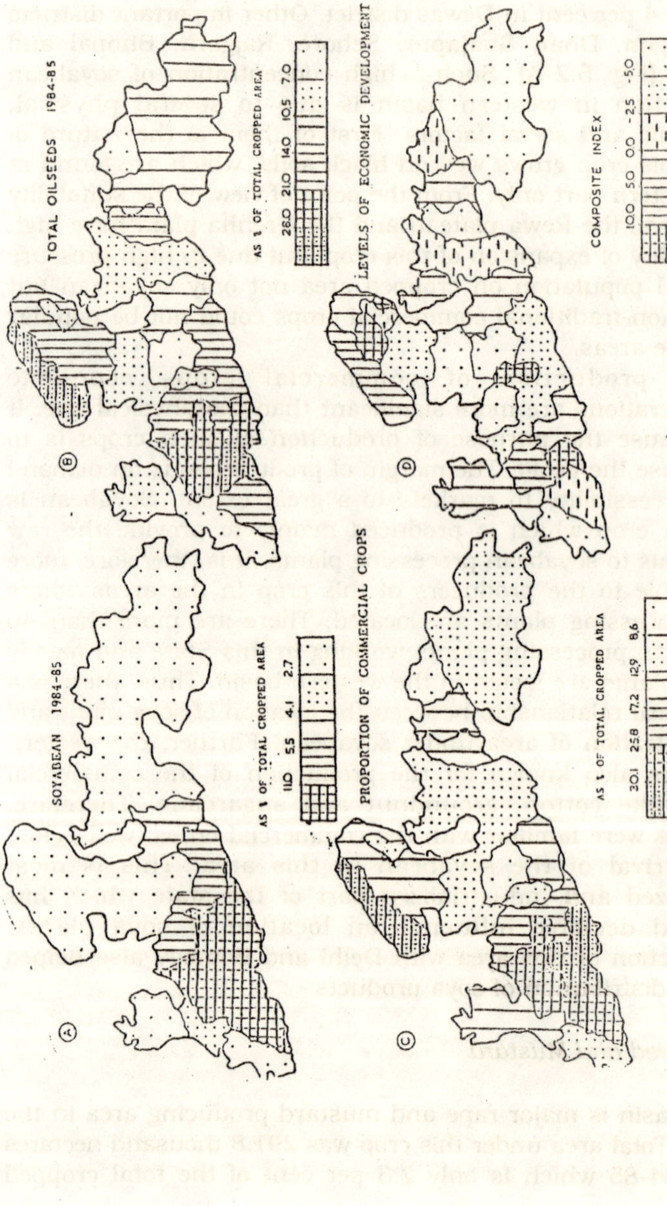

FIG. 5.2: The Ganga Basin of Madhya Pradesh

area. Area under this crop increased by three times during 1955-56 and 1984-85. Total production of rape and mustard was 217.8 thousand tonnes in 1984-85. Gwalior division is the major producer. Percentage area under this crop is as high as 35.4 per cent in Morena and 9.4 per cent in Bhind district. Gwalior, Shivpuri, Shahdol and Surguja are also major producers.

Linseed

Linseed is the third ranking commercial crop in the region. It was grown in 288.6 thousand hectares which constituted 2.3 per cent of the total cropped area in 1984-85. Its total production was 80.8 thousand tonnes in the same year. Linseed is mainly grown in north-eastern part as well as in the central part of the basin. Nevertheless, there are two major areas of linseed production in the basin. One is constituted by the Rewa plateau which extends upto Sagar district. It occupies 9.4 per cent of the total cropped area in the Panna district and 6.1 per cent in Satna district. Second area of concentration of linseed is the central Malwa plateau, where it occupies 3.8 per cent of the total cropped area in Ujjain district. In other districts of this plateau where 2 to 3 per cent of the total cropped area is under this crop are Sehore, Raisen, Indore and Dhar. Besides these two major areas, linseed is also grown in the Gird plain and Madhya Bharat plateau. In fact linseed is one of the traditional oilseeds and its oil has been used since long.

Groundnut

This basin is one of the major groundnut producer in the State. Total area under groundnut cultivation was 180.3 thousand hectares in 1984-85 which is only 1.5 per cent of the total cropped area. Area under this crop increased by 38.8 per cent during 1955-56 to 1984-85. Total production of groundnut was 95.8 thousand tonnes. It has been noticed that before the arrival of soyabean, groundnut was most significant commerical crop used as raw material. Western Malwa is the major producer. Most significant districts are the Mandsaur, Jhabua, Dhar, Shajapur and Rajgarh. Concentration of groundnut production in the western Malwa plateau is also due to suitable soil characteristics and accessibility to urban markets in this area.

Cotton

In this basin, it is concentrated in black cotton soil in western region, where rainfall is low. It is grown on 175.1 thousand hectares. Area under this crop declined by 71.4 per cent from 1955-56 to 1984-85. Total production of cotton was 102.3 thousand bales in 1984-85 and 242.4 thousand bales in 1955-56. Cotton is important in western Malwa, where Dewas and Dhar districts have higher proportion of cotton area. Other important districts are Jhabua, Shajapur and Ujjain.

Fruits, Vegetables, Condiments and Spices

As every farmer tries to grow cereals and pulses to meet his food requirements, similarly each farmer grows some vegetables and spices particularly in rainy season, if not in other seasons. At the same time plantation of mango, guava, banana, lemon etc. are universal. Consequently, these food crops also occupy some cropped area in every district. But their production above subsistence level depends on economic factors, specially on market factor. Since most of these crops are perishable and their production cost is usually high, they are grown near big towns and cities where they can fetch good market. Besides market, cultivation of these crops depend upon availability of irrigation and facility of cheap and easy means of transport. Total area under fruits and vegetables is 74.5 thousand hectares and under condiments and spices 112.8 thousand hectares in this basin. Thus, only 1.5 per cent of total cropped area is under these important crops. Higher percentage area than the regional average (0.50) under fruits and vegetables is in Surguja, Sagar, Damoh, Panna, Tikamgarh, Chhatarpur, Sidhi, Rewa, Satna, Indore, Dewas, Ujjain, Dhar, Gwalior and Bhopal and spices and condiments in Dhar, Ujjain, Mandsaur, Ratlam, Shajapur, Guna and Rajgarh. Most of these districts either support at least one big city or are industrial and mining districts.

Spatial Pattern of Commercialization

Production of commercial crops depends on interaction of several natural, social, economic and cultural factors. Socio-economic factors play important role. Among these factors, availability of marketing facilities, transportation, industrialization, urbanization, low density of population and comparatively large size of holding are important. There is wide variation in these factors in the basin. It causes variation in proportion of area under commercial crops too. This proportion ranges from only 5.8 per cent in Vidisha and 7.9 per cent in Sidhi district to 42.5 per cent of the total cropped area in Morena district (Fig. 5.2C). It is evident from this figure that higher proportion of these crops is in western and northern parts of the basin. Districts in the basin can be divided into six classes on the basis of proportion of area under commercial crops.

Very High

Districts having very high proportion of commercial crops are Morena, Dewas and Indore. This area is covered by fertile alluvial soil (Morena) and black soil (Dewas and Indore). Use of inputs like fertilizers, irrigation and high yielding seeds are more popular in this tract. Soil is also an important factor for significant commercial crops like cotton and oilseeds. Indore and Dewas have become important cotton textile centres because of cotton being grown there extensively. Urbanized population is high. Similar factors together with irrigational facilities help to make the rate of very high in Morena and Indore.

Medium High

Districts having medium high proportion of commercial crops lies mainly in western Malwa plateau—comprising districts of Dhar, Ujjain and Shajapur. This area also covered by black cotton soil. Black soil is the important factor for significant commercial crops like cotton and oilseeds.

High

Only two districts Rajgarh and Sehore belong to high proportion of commercial crops. These districts are also on upper side of adoption of agricultural innovations. In these districts about 17 to 26 per cent area is devoted to commercial crops and oilseeds constitute major commercial crops.

Low and Very Low

Low proportion of commercial crops are found in lower Chambal valley—Mandsaur, Ratlam, eastern Malwa-Shivpuri, Raisen, Gwalior and Bhind of Gird plain, Panna and Satna of Bundelkhand region. Area of very low proportion of commerical crops extends over the Sagar-Damoh plateau, Baghelkhand, Vidisha plateau and Orchha upland of the basin. In these areas there is low and very low proportion of commercial crops due to small holdings, hilly and dissected terrain, high pressure of population in cultivated land, low irrigational facilities except Gird plain, low level of industrialization.

Economic Development

Performance of economic activities should be taken as an index of level of economic development. Probably gross national product may serve this purpose and per capita GNP can offer a rough indication of the degree of inequality among districts of this basin. But at present level of statistical information it is just not possible to compute the district level GNP. Therefore, to meet the need of an aggregate district level index through selective indicators, several studies have been attempted. For instance, Datta (1980) selected twenty five indices to measure the regional variation in level of development, while Agarwal and Khan (1983) selected only nine out of them. Almost indentical indices were used by Sharma (1981) to portray the economic development of the Baghelkhand plateau of Madhya Pradesh. At the same time centre for Monitoring Indian Economy (1982) has selected nine indices to compute the index of level of economic development of districts of entire country.

In the present study, eleven indicators have been used

to measure the level of economic development (Sharma, 1988). They have been selected from all sectors of economy, viz. agriculture, mining, manufacturing, trade and commerce. These indicators are:

1. Value of crops (Rs.) per hectare of net sown area,
2. Proportion of net irrigated area,
3. Use of fertilizers per hectate of cropped area,
4. Percentage area under high yielding variety of seeds,
5. Per capita bank credit for agriculture,
6. Number of factory workers per Lakh population,
7. Number of household workers per lakh population,
8. Length of metalled road per hundred sq.km. area,
9. Per capita bank deposit,
10. Per capita electric consumption, and
11. Proportion of urban population.

Scores of each variable were standardized to zero mean and unit deviation, and these were then summed for each district. On plotting these composite development indices on scatter diagrame the following pattern of economic development emerges clearly (Fig. 5.2D).

Areas of High Development

There are two well marked areas of high economic development. First and foremost region exists in the Malwa piateau and covers two districts viz. Indore and Ujjain. Bhopal in the eastern Malwa is also highly developed. This is urbanized and industrialized belt of the State. Indore, the industrial capital of the state has positive Z scores for all economic activities. Except far household industries and their sum is as high as 19.62. But Ujjain is below regional average in agricultural productivity, household industries and length of the road. This is pertinent of recall here that this region is poor in all natural resources but land; and probably agricultural produces, particularly cotton and soyabean, have been the base of industrial development. Bhopal, an isolated district of high economic development. Its economic status is dependent on manufacturing, trade and commerce. Gwalior and Morena constitute second area of high development. Economic development in Gwalior is based on agriculture, manufacturing, trade and commerce, while Morena is solely dependent on agriculture.

Areas of Medium Development

Moderately developed districts (with scores ranging from 0 to 5) occur in contiguity with highly developed districts. Mandsaur, Ratlam and Dewas districts link Indore-Ujjain belt. Tikamgarh and Sagar form its eastern offshoot. Major component in economy of the districts is agriculture except in Sagar which mainly depends on household industries and tertiary activities. Bhind is contiguous to Gwalior-Morena belt and agin it depends on agriculture. Thus twelve out of twenty nine districts have composite score higher than zero, and only one of them is in the east. Malwa plateau has the largest number followed by Gwalior region.

Areas of Low and Very Low Development

Contrary to its largest block of economically backward districts in the east, it extends from Damoh-Chhatarpur to Surguja. This belt covers seven districts. Only Damoh, Chhatarpur and Rewa could develop household industries to remarkable extent. Sidhi (-9.5), Shahdol (-5.8), Surguja (-5.1) and Panna are most backward districts in the eastern basin. Most of the district of this part are at the bottom level of development in Indian context (Sundaram, 1983, p. 161). Second block of backward districts encircles Bhopal, the capital of the State, and cover eight districts. Guna (-8.2), Rajgarh (-6.3) and Vidisha (-6.0) are most backward among them. These districts are poor as far as resources are concerned. Jhabua (-7.4) in western Malwa also constitute third area of concentration of backward districts.

Correlation of Commercialization with Economic Development and Other Variables

To find out the relationship between the degree of commercialization on one hand and indicators of economic development and aggregated index of development on the other hand, coefficient of correlation is computed. Results are presented in Table 5.2.

Table 5.2: Correlation Matrix

Variables*	1	2	3	4	5	6	7	8	9	10
1	X	0.91	0.65	0.89	0.91	0.88	0.73	0.90	0.83	0.43
2		X	0.72	0.32	0.25	0.35	0.56	0.14	0.17	0.72
3			X	0.55	0.63	0.63	0.91	0.62	0.65	0.63
4				X	0.92	0.93	0.71	0.87	0.80	0.50
5					X	0.93	0.78	0.94	0.87	0.43
6						X	0.76	0.89	0.86	0.55
7							X	0.82	0.83	0.51
8								X	0.93	0.28
9									X	0.26
10										X

* (1) Proportion of Commercial crops, (2) Levels of Economic Development, (3) No. of factory workers per lakh population, (4) Proportion of net irrigated area, (5) Percentage area under high yielding variety of seeds, (6) Use of fertilizers per hectare of cropped area, (7) Proportion of urban population, (8) Value of crops, (9) Length of metalled road, (10) Composite index of Agricultural Modernization.

It is evident from the table that the degree of commercialization has strong correlation with each individual variable as well as with the index of economic development. It indicates that both-commercialization and economic development go hand in hand. It is not possible to encourage the cultivation of commercial crops unless there is no market for them and also provisions of infrastructure. Consequently, most often, it is related with the urbanization. In fact, the Malwa region, which is the major area of concentration of commercial crops, happens to be economically developed part of the state. It is also important urbanized and industrialized part of the state and the footing of industrial development is based on agricultural produces. Cotton attracted several mill in this area and at present soya plants have grown rapidly in the same region. Further, because of high profitability, farmers try to raise yield using modern inputs.

SIX

Food Distribution System in Peri-Urban Space: A Case Study of Urban Fringe of Allahabad Town

V.K. SHRIVASTAVA

Distribution system in peri-urban space is usually controlled by the urban centre in question. With the passage of time the rural areas surrounding the urban centre may develop their own sub-systems around settlements of higher order. These sub-system may strengthen or revive the traditional distribution system operating in rural areas and open new functional linkages with the urban centre in whose fringe they are operating. The entire distribution system can thus be re-organised and strengthened. Such evidences have been noted in the study of geography of marketing in the urban fringe of Allahabad town of Uttar Pradesh.

It has been further noted that food distribution system is a part of the general distribution system. It assumes an important place in the general distribution system because of the dependency of both the urban and the rural areas on food requirements.

The present study identifies the food distribution system and analyses the marketing behaviour of farmers/producers according to their economic status. The socio-economic structure of agrarian production-organization system is reflected in the food distribution system noted in the study region. Four such systems have been identified:

(a) Producer-seller system
(b) Producer-intermediate seller-trader system
(c) Producer-money lender-trader system

(d) Producer-Govt. purchasing centre-Fair price shop system.

The marketing behaviour of farmers/producers has been further examined in context of their economic status. Producers of higher economic status prefer public food distribution system more than the traditional food distribution system. The situation is reversed in case of producers of lower economic status. The importance of middlemen varies. The study is based on primary data.

The identification of food distribution systems has taken into account the status of food crop production in the sample villages of the study area. Out of a total of 241 villages in the urban fringe of Allahabad, 30 villages were surveyed. It has been observed that due to variation in the fertility of soils and use of traditional and modern techniques of cultivation the amount of production varies among the villages. Only a few villages produce surplus food which is salable enough. This situation generates demand of food crops among the villages themselves—leading to horizontal exchange systems.

The Mode of Disposal of Food Crops

The mode of disposal of food crops varies. Nearly half of the farmers dispose of their crops to the local *bania* (trader) who indulges both in horizontal and vertical exchange. The dealings have become monetized. A small quantity of food grains is disposed of more frequently either at the village itself or at the periodic markets involving horizontal exchange. Nearly 1/5th of the producers visit periodic markets and sell to the consumers directly. In some cases the intermediate seller also comes in. He may relieve the farmer/producer of his crops even at the doorsteps, if not at the 'purchasing shops' which operate along the entry/exit points to periodic markets. Nearly 10 per cent of the farmers of the study region indulge in this type of distribution system (Table 6.1). The intermediate seller in turn delivers the goods to the wholesaler. The farmers have also been found to have been tied to the money-lender for keeping the pre-harvest promise of disposal of food crops at his door-steps. The government purchasing centres have also started attracting the farmers and have thus intervened in the food distribution system.

Table 6.1: Marketing Behaviour of Farmer-Producer in Peri-Urban Space of Allahabad Town

Mode of disposal of food crops	% of families involved
Consumers	18
Bania (trader)	50
Intermediate seller	8
Money-lender	5
Govt. Purchasing Centre	19

The Economic Status of Producers and Channels of Food Distribution

The economic status of the farmer also influences the choice of selection of a particular channel of food distribution system. The marginal farmers disposed bulk of their produce to the local trader. Only a small fraction of these poor farmer goes to the periodic market to dispose of their produce directly to the consumer. The intermediate seller, however, claims 1/5th of the produce of poor farmers. The middle-class farmer prefers a variety of options. He is still tied to the local *bania* for disposing of a major part of his food crops, but he is equally aware of the periodic market system and the govt. purchasing centres. The upper class farmers patronise the public distribution system more than any other system prevalent in the area (Table 6.2). They are also tied to the money lender and local *bania*. Direct seller-consumer transaction is less important to them.

Table 6.2: Mode of Food Crop Distribution

Mode of Distribution	High Class farmers %	Middle Class farmers %	Marginal farmers %
Consumer	8.7	28.6	11.4
Bania	21.7	47.6	71.4
Intermediate seller	—	48.0	17.2
Money-lender	17.4	2.4	—
Govt. Purchasing Centre	52.2	16.6	—
	100	100	100

The analysis of data further shows that small farmers are still not out of the traditional, more exploitative distribution system. The middle-class farmers, however, appear to be more conscious of modern, more profitable distribution channels. The public distribution system is benefiting large farmers to a great extent. Thus the socio-economic status of producer-farmers is reflected in the selection of channels of food distribution.

The General Distribution System

The general distribution system in the peri-urban space of Allahabad shows a predominance of the parent town. But it has also given rise to four sub-systems operating within the general distribution systems. The sub-systems are independent insofar as the distribution of food grains, *Kirana* and vegetables is concerned. These are sub-sub-systems within these sub-systems.

The Food Distribution Systems

The study of farmer-producers' preferences insofar as the production and distribution of food crops is concerned has lead to the identification of four systems of food distribution (Fig. 6.1)

Producer-Seller System

This system directly links the producer-seller and the consumer involving horizontal exchange in a limited space (Fig. 6.1A). The patronisers, both the producer and the consumers belong to low socio-economic status. The exchange, however, takes place at periodic markets, thus the probability of vertical functional linkage exists.

Producer-Intermediate Seller-Trader System

Like the farmer, this system is also one of the traditional system in which the intermediate seller relieves the farmer of his produce at his door-steps or at the entry points to periodic markets, thereby reducing his chances for an opportunity of face to face exchange (Fig. 6.1B). The

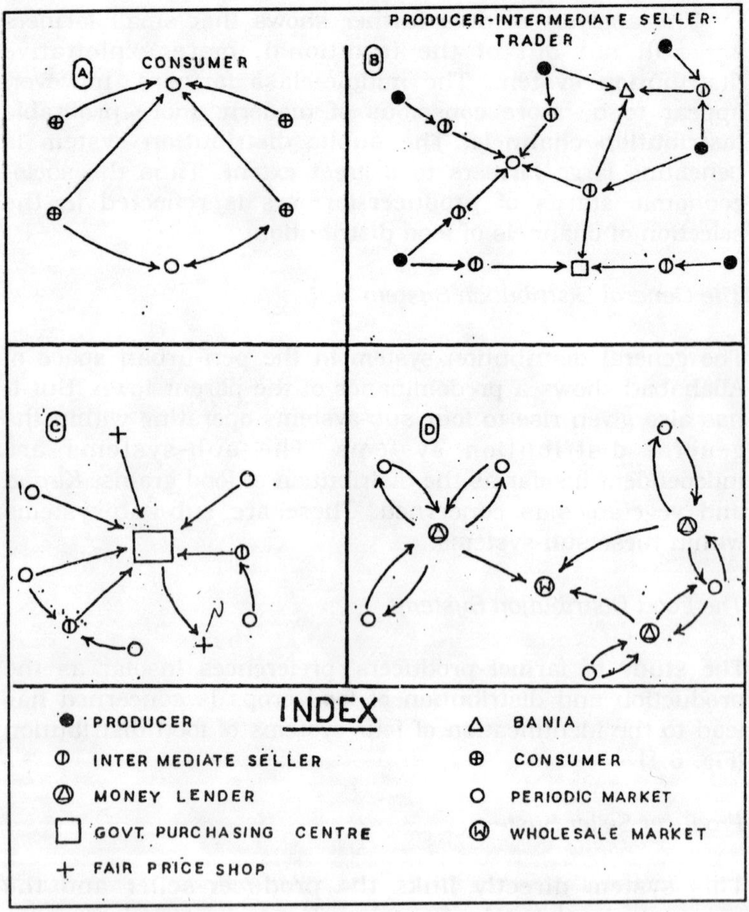

FIG. 6.1 : Urban Fringe of Allahabad: Food Distribution Systems

intermediate seller is, in turn, linked to the periodic market or to the wholesaler. The intermediate seller can also be a local *bania* or an itinerant trader or an agent of the wholesaler.

Producer-Govt. Purchasing Centre-Fair Price Shop System

This may be termed as the public distribution system of food products. As is well known in this system the produce is brought to the regulated market (*mandi*) or to the government purchasing centres established during harvest period. Bulk purchases of food crops at pre-fixed price takes place (Fig. 6.1C). The products so procured are stored and distributed to fair price shops which in turn deliver the goods to the consumers. This system is less complex. The produce changes only a couple of hands so the cost does not multiply. Only the transport cost is added. The final price for the consumers is also fixed. Since bulk purchase of produce is necessary only big farmers are able to patronise this system. The benefits insofar as producer-farmers are concerned, are limited to higher strata of peasant society.

Producer-Money-lender-Trader System

The spatial reach of these system increases from the producer-seller system onwards. The multiplicity of hands in systems B and D makes them much more complex. These systems overlap each other. System A and B are confined to rural areas and the rest are based in urban areas.

This system consists of a two tier functional linkage. On one hand the producer under obligation of age-old ties delivers his produce to the money lender (Fig. 6.1D). This can also be a pre-harvest commitment. The money lender could be the local *bania* or a *sahukar* by profession. The money lender delivers the produce to the wholesaler.

The Future

The existing food distribution systems are likely to be strengthened because the sampled population has a trust in the existing system. Besides, the increasing traffic problems in the parent town are detracting people from making regular and frequent visits to town and as a result the sub-systems are generating more and more business. As food is one of the major important requirements the existing food distribution systems will naturally be strengthened. However, these systems are likely to become integrated in the sense that the existing multiplicity of channels may be reduced. With the shifting of wholesaling of food grains and vegetables in the peri-urban space, the intermediate seller and *bania* will become weaker participants in the distribution systems.

Another important aspect is the increasing milk

production in the peri-urban space. Almost all the 30 families surveyed have shown a surplus of milk production. This means new channels of distribution of milk will enter the existing distribution system and the attention of the farmers now utilising the existing channels of food crop distribution will be diverted to the new channels. It is likely that a new system of milk and milk product distribution will emerge soon.

Theme - II

Agro-Industries and Economic Development

SEVEN

Agro-Industries and Economic Development in Bardhaman: A Case Study in Remote Sensing Technique

ASIT KUMAR SARKAR and NIKHIL KRISHNA DE

Baradhaman, a district situated to the western most part of West Bengal, forms a part of the Lower Ganga Basin. This fertile alluvial plain, excepting the western part, is agriculturally much advanced and is considered as the granary of West Bengal. Various types of agro-based industries have been developed in the district, viz. rice mills, oil mills, cold storages, indigenous sugar manufacturing units, etc. Successful experiments have also been conducted in the district for manufacturing edible oil from rice bran. Yet further scope exists towards economic development of the district based on agro-industries. But to do so, the pre-requisite is to study its agriculture and associated resources properly and throughly. In this connection, application of remote sensing techniques have opened up new vista in respect of resource investigation. The system facilitates collection of large amount of land related resource information witin relatively short time span. The technique also provides with possibilities for repeated collection of information at regular intervals. Hence in the present chapter an attempt has been made to use both aerial photographs as well as satellite imageries to study basic resources of the area under investigation, particularly on the basis of visual interpretation of available photographs/imageries. Field verifications have also been conducted in selected areas as supplementary measure. Information thus collected, has been used to re-delineate the zonal boundaries for different potential land system categories, so that the economy can become more viable. Ultimately, it will also help the planners to formulate the agro-industries for the concerned district, based on revised resource situation.

Introduction

Agriculture is considered as the pivot of Indian economy. This is not only due to the fact that nearly 37 per cent of the Gross National Production (GNP) of the country is derived from agriculture and allied activities and as large as 61 per cent of our work-force is dependent on it and also 75 per cent of the total population sustain their livelihood from this particular sector of economic activity, but also due to dependency of considerable number of industries upon agriculture. Thus development of industries in India is also closely related to the development of agriculture. However, to make agriculture more viable, we are to evolve developmental strategy, the pre-condition of which is assessment of the available land resources in the context of potential landuse. Of course, some academicians as well as some institutions have recently come forward particularly to survey the available land resources so that proper resource planning may be formulated based on survey results. As a continuation to that, in the present chapter, an alternative methodology has been suggested, which is considered to be the best possible solution regarding identification of different categories of land systems, which have been used as basic format for establishing agro-based industries in the concerned area, both in terms of type of the industry and/or the prospective locational site. To complete the exercise, along with other tools, available remote sensing techniques have also been applied, particularly for identification of land systems, because the technique is considered to be quick, scientific as well as dynamic in character.

The Study Area

At the time of evolving the methodology, Bardhaman district of West Bengal was chosen as the field of application. The district forms a part of Lower Ganga Basin. Latitudinally it extends between $22^{0}56'$ north and $23^{0}53$ north and the longitudinal extention of the district is between $86^{0}48'$ east

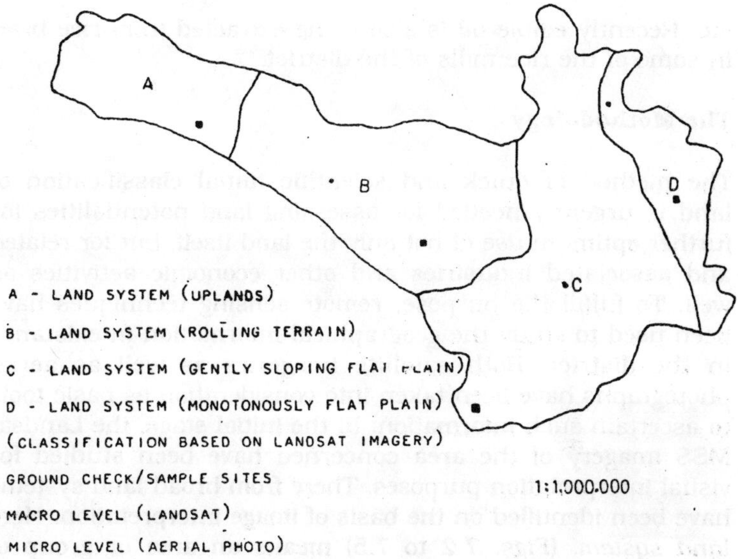

FIG. 7.1: Land Systems of Bhardhaman District
(A Part of Lower Ganga Basin)

and 88°25' east. River Bhagarathi forms the eastern boundary of the district, whereas River Damodr and River Ajoy, two important tributaries, flow through the southern and northern parts of the district respectively. The western part of the district dates to Gondwana era and the famous Raniganj coal fields are located in that part of the district. On the other hand, the eastern part is covered with recent alluvial deposits brought down by Bhagirathi river system. The physiography also coincides more or less with this geological sequence. Agriculturally the western part is less important, though very rich in respect of mineral resources. Excepting that part, the rest of the district is well advanced in agriculture and is known as the granary of West Bengal. But the agriculture of Bardhaman district deserves further improvement and also agro-based industries, although the present industries based on/dependent on agriculture may be listed as rice mills, oil mills, cold storage, indigenous sugar manufacturing units, etc. Recently edible oil is also being extracted from rice bran in some of the rice mills of the district.

The Methodology

The method of quick and scientific initial classification of land is urgently needed for assessing land potentialities for further optimum use of not only the land itself, but for related and associated industries and other economic activities as well. To fulfill the purpose, remote sensing techniques have been used to study the geographical information in existance in the district. Both satellite imageries as well as aerial photographs have been taken into consideration as basic tools to ascertain such information. In the initial stage, the Landsat MSS imagery of the area concerned have been studied for visual interpretation purposes. There from broad land systems have been identified on the basis of image interpretation. Here *land system*. (Figs. 7.2 to 7.5) means an area or group of areas with a recurring pattern of landform, soil, vegetation, climate and also landuse practice. It is to be emphasized that the land system is not just a convenient associaton of land units but a natural aggregation of natural units. However, so called macro land systems identified from satellite imageries (1 :1,000,000), have further been sub-divided into different broad land form units. By availing of complementary tools like Survey of India topographical maps, existing literature, etc. zonal boundaries were further redelineated. Sample field checking have also been conducted to verify the information and also for clarification purposes for doubtful cases.

In the next phase, micro-level land systems have been identified on the basis of aerial photo interpretation (1:60,000). Consultation of topographical sheet, available literature, field verification, etc. were repeated in this case as well.

Each land system, whether macro or micro, has also been illustrated diagramatically (Figs 7.6 to 7.9) so that individual land unit can be visualised. Ultimately the entire landscape, whether present or potential, has been represented in tabular form. The combined information includes landform, soil, vegetation, cropping pattern, etc., which has direct bearing to indicate the sustainable future economy of the area concerned. Basic information thus collected has immense

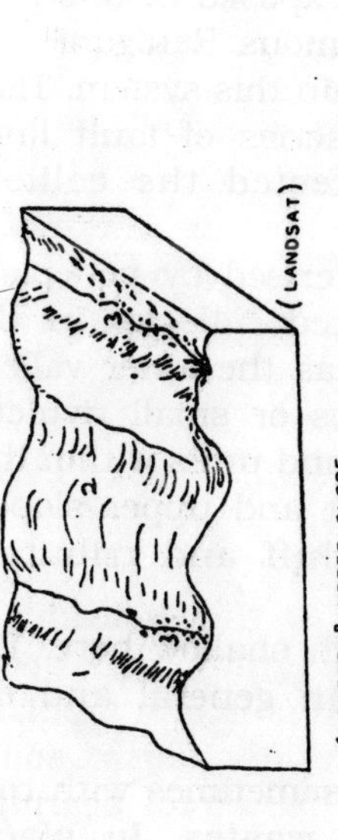

FIG. 7.2: Land System

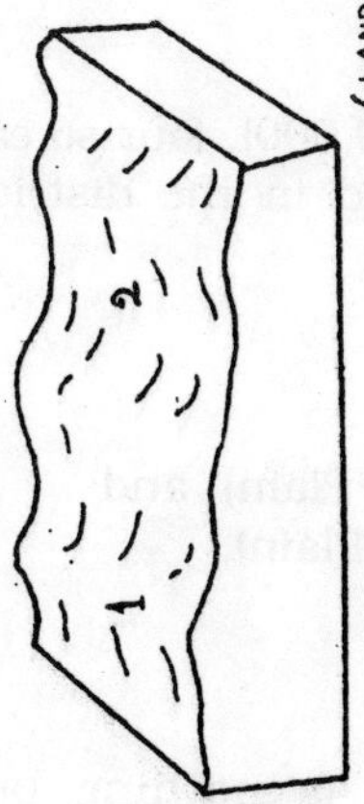

FIG. 7.3: Land System

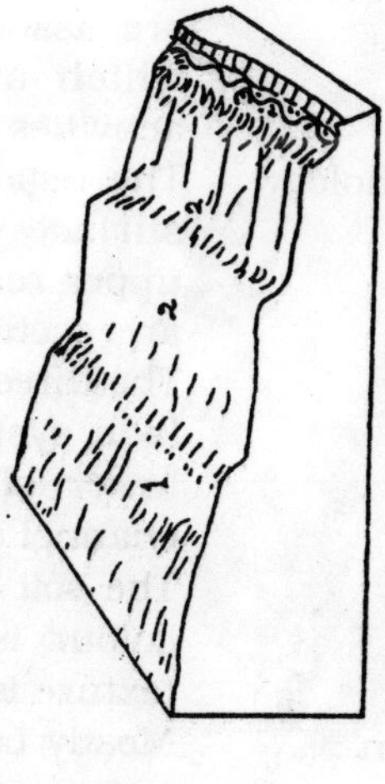

FIG. 7.4: Land System

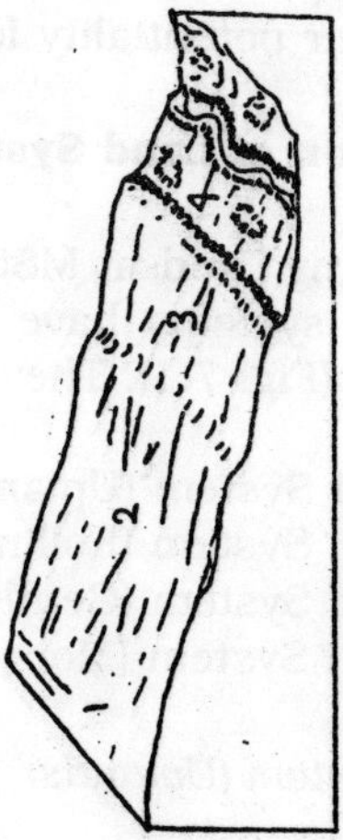

FIG. 7.5: Land System

importance towards formulation for assessing potentiality of each land system identified so far in different scales of working and also for formulating the future landuse planning. This will help to assess the existing agro-based industries and also their potentiality for future development.

Identification of Land Systems

By interpreting Landsat MSS data (1:1,000,000), four so called macro land systems have been identified in the district of Bardhaman (Fig. 7.1). They are:

A - Land System (Uplands),
B - Land System (Rolling Terrain),
C - Land System (Gently Sloping Flat Plain), and
D - Land System (Monotonously Flat Plain).

A—Land System (Uplands)

General :	This plateau region is nothing but a continuation of the Chotanagpur plateau situated further west.
Geology :	Gondwana rocks are exposed in this part of the district. The famous Raniganj coal fields are situated within this system. They are associated with series of fault lines which adversely affected the colliery activities.
Geomorphology :	The region is characterised by peneplain surface with dissected hillocks in the upper reaches, whereas the lower valleys are occupied by rivers or small rivulets. The three distinctive land units within this ladn system are crest and upper slopes, lower slopes and bluff and tributary channel complex.
Soil :	The soil cover is much shallow here. The colour is brownish in general and the texture is coarse.
Vegetation :	Mostly bare surface, sometimes with rock outcrops or stoney wastes. In places scrubs and grasses are grown, whereas some of the valley bottoms are cultivated.

Agricultural Landuse :	The colliery areas are devoid of cultivation. But valley bottoms, depressions and favourable locations are used for cultivating crops like rice, wheat, etc.
Improvement Measures Suggested :	Strict measures are to be taken up for sand stoying of defunct colleries which otherwise cause sinking of cultivated lands and also inviting human hazards.

B—Land System (Rolling Terrain)

General:	This rolling plain region is located to the eastern part of the plateau region. Once a part of *Jungal Mahal*, at present contains the remnants of original forest species in the district.
Geology:	Laterite and older alluvium are two important formations of this part of the district. They are usually composed of massive argillaceous beds of a rather pale reddish-brown hue. Often weathering yellowish, disseminated through which occur kankar and pisolic ferruginous concentrations.
Geomorphology:	This undulating country is interspársed with rocky hillocks and broken up into low ridges and valleys. In places the surface has been denuded leaving in many places hard, bare exposed rocks. The existing landforms belonging to this land system are: undulating upper slope and undulating lower slopes.
Soil:	The soil is mostly medium in depth and reddish in colour. They are coarse-textured.
Vegetation:	Remnants of original sal forests still found in places of this region. Otherwise valley portions are cultivated.
Agricultural Landuse :	Agriculture is practised in valley bottom regions, but the soil is mostly dry and demands irrigation facilities.

Improvement Measures Suggested :	Intensive afforestation schemes should be introduced to bring back forest areas in this once famous part of Jungal Mahal. Extension of irrigation facilities are required to expand agricultural potentials.

C—Land System (Gently Sloping Flat Plain)

General:	The gently sloping territory is the best agrarian part of the district.
Geology:	It is entirely alluvial in origin. Most of the alluvium was brought by Bhagirathi river system assisted by its two important tributaries, viz. River Damodar and River Ajoy.
Geomorphology:	This alluvial plain gently slopes eastward. Successive floods and deposits of silt or sand gradually raised the entire tract permanently above flood level. The upper reaches are characterised by gently sloping surfaces whereas the valley bottoms are occupied by channel complexes. Terraces at different levels are also very distinctive within this land system.
Soil:	The soil cover is comparatively deep and the colour is brownish. The texture is medium in general.
Vegetation:	The territory is mostly cultivated. Sometimes big trees like mango, banyan, palm, etc. are found in different places.
Agricultural Landuse:	The agricultural landuse is dominated by cultivation of rice. Very often multiple cropping is in practice for raising a second and a third crop of mostly rice. Potato, wheat, vegetables, pulses, sugarcane, etc. are other important crops of this area.
Improvement Measures Suggested:	Commercialisation of agricultural activities are to be done in this part of the district. In addition to extension of required inputs in agriculuture, better infrastructural facilities are to be provided with for transportation of rice and potato to rice

mills and cold storages respectively. Necessary finances and entrepreneurships are to be extended for operating such establishment in large numbers.

D—Land System (Monotonously Flat Plain)

General:	Monotonously flat terrain is located to the eastern most part of the district, which also suffers from natural calamity in terms of flood.
Geology:	This land system has been originated due to deposits of young alluvium, mostly brought down by the Bhagirathi River.
Geomorphology:	Here the landscape is monotonously flat and is characterised by the high level formations along the banks of the River Bhagirathi. Numerous swamps in many places show a clear topography of an old delta plain. The micro-relief is characterised by the existence of crest slope and lower slopes of upper terraces, followed by middle terraces, whereas the lower terraces are occupied by meandering channel complex.
Soil:	The soil cover is very deep and is greyish in colour. The texture is very fine. The soil is very moist as well.
Vegetation:	Mainly cultivated crops are found. Aquatic plants like water hyacinth, etc. thrives well in marshy areas.
Agricultural Landuse:	Rice grows abundantly in most of the places. Jute is the other important crop. Vegetables are also grown extensively.
Improvement Measures Suggested:	Proper drainage system should be made into operation to drain out water from depressions. Sand deposits caused by rivers like Ajoy, etc. during flood deteriorates the agricultural land and demands improvemental programmes.

A—Land Systems (Uplands)

Unit	Landform	Soils	Vegetation	Agricultural Landuse		Remarks
				Present	Prospective	
1	Crest and upper slopes: Extensive rounded crests; slopes are more or less rectillinear with broad shallow depressions; the surface is more or less stony; crest slopes- 2° to 3°, upper slopes - 15°.	Shallow and skeletal; texture-coarse locally very stony; well drained; colour - brown	Bare surface without vegetation; locally grass cover	Mostly wastelands; sometimes used for grazing purposes	Woodlands to be created to check soil erosion. General conservation measures to be taken up.	Afforestation scheme should be introduced; proper land-scaping is also to be taken up.
2	Lower slopes and valley depressions: Upper parts are relatively steep; lower portions are comparatively gentle with broad inflexions; slopes- 10° to 12° (lower slopes); 5° to 6° (valley depressions)	moderately deep; medium texture; moderately drained; locally moist; colour-brownish.	Upper parts are covered with scrubs and grasses; lower parts are occupied mostly by grass; locally cultivated in favourable conditions	Rice and wheat are cultivated in valley depressions and upper parts respectively	Multiple cropping by extending minor irri-gation at valley depressions	Crop association to be increased and the land should be devoted to the best possible cropping pattern. Sand stoying in defunct collieries can save collaps-ing of agricultural land.

3.	Bluff and tributary channel: Degraded irrigular surfaces; complex micro-morphology; slope- 30° to 35°; tributary channels are concave in character; channels are mostly dry but contain water during monsoon period; river channels are occupied by cobbles and pebbles	Skeletal with coarse textured soil; brownish in colour on bluff areas but shallow with medium texture & brown colour on channel complex; generally moist	Bluffs are bare though locally grassy; channel complexes are mostly grassy and sandy	Either waste land or grazing land	vegetative cover, woodlands to be grown by adopting afforestation scheme	
B—Land System (Rolling Terrain)						
1	Undulating upper slopes: Rather undulating in character with shallow depressions; strewn with pebbles and cobbles; very extensive; gradually sloping to the east; slope is generally between 10° and 15°.	Shallow to moderately deep; coarse to medium coarse in texture; dark brown to yellowish brown in colour	Partly bare and partly covered with forests (mostly sal species)	Once vast area was covered by forests; at present remnants are only in existence; otherwise scrub covered	Afforestation scheme to be introduced	Deforestation due to industrial/ urban requi-ment. No further deforestation to be allowed.
2	Undulating lower slopes: Very extensive; rectilinear; strewn with finer pebbles and cobbles; gradual slope which is less than 10°.	Mostly deep; yelloish brown in colour; coarse to medium in texture	Partly forested, partly cultivated	Rice is cultivated in favourable places; mostly monoculture	Multiple cropping are to be extended by providing irrigation facilities (minor irrigation)	

C—Land System (Gently Sloping Flat Plain)

1	Gently sloping surface: Very extensive; occasionally minor depressions; micro-relief 10 cm-15 cm with cracks particularly during dry seasons; slopes around 5°.	Very deep; brownish to greyish brown in colour; medium to fine in texture; well-drained; fertile.	Mostly cropland	Extensively cultivated; multiple cropping (mostly rice + potato, linseed; pulses)	Prospect depends upon availability of more inputs	This is the agro-economically most viable part of the district. Better communication system to be developed for carrying agro-products to processing units. New industries like potato chips factory, rice bran oil mill, etc. to be developed; better management and credit facilities to be provided with.
2	Terraces: Very extensive gently sloping towards channel complies with minor depressions; micro-relief 10cm to 15cm with mud cracks; general slope 3°.	Very deep; brown to greyish brown in colour; fine in texture; rather moist; very fertile	Mostly cropland	Extensively cultivated; locally multiple cropping	Extension of multiple cropping areas	– do –

3	Channel complex: Valley sides rather steep; micro relief 5 cm to 15cm; slope around 45°; broad channel floors with meandering channels; occasionally waterlogged; braided channels, ox-bow lakes, etc. are also present.	Deep to very deep; grey in colour finer texture; valley floor is sandy; moist.	Grassy and scruby valley sides.	Wasteland	Afforestation along river bank	
D—Land System (Monotonously Flat Plain)						
1	Upper Terrace crest slope: Convex in form with local undulations; very wide in extension; micro-relief is between 10cm and 15cm; slope around 5°.	Very deep; yellowish brown to greyish brown in colour; medium fine in texture; fertile in character.	Mostly cropland	Extensively cultivated; mostly rice; sometimes multiple cropping + Jute	Extension of multiple cropping areas	It is possible to develop further different agro-based/dependant industries like rice mill/cold storage, etc.
2	Upper Terraces lower slope: Rather rectilinear; locally concave with small shallow depressions; micro-relief 10cm-15cm; slope 3°-5°.	Very deep; matured; light brown in colour; rather medium in texture; well-drained.	Partly cultivated; partly uncultivated	Cultivation of rice, jute, vegeta-bles,etc.	– do –	– do –

3	Middle Terrace: Very extensive with broad undulations; micro-relief between 10cm and 15 cm.	Very deep; dark greyish in colour; medium in texture; relatively moist and fertile.	Mostly cropland	Extensively cultivated	– do – (rice+jute)	– do –
4	Lower terrace with meandering channel complex: Extensive; monotonously flat with very broad depressions and meandering channels; concave-convex form; micro-relief ranges between 10cm and 15cm. slope around 3°-5°.	Very very deep; locally very moist; dark greyish in colour; very fine in texture; channels are sandy; partly water-logged	Mostly cropland	Mostly rice cultivation +Jute; partly water-logged	Extension of agricultural area by draining out water from depressions.	Sometimes arable lands are covered with sand during flood. Extensive embankment for checking flood havoc.

So far as identification of land systems at micro-level (1:60,000) based on aerial photographs is concerned, detail investigations were made in two sample areas one each belonging to B - land system and D-land system which were identified as Durgapur Rolling Plains (Fig. 7.6) and Katoya Plains (Fig. 7.7) respectively. In case of Durgapur Rolling Plains, two broad landforms identified have been termed as Dissected Terrain and Gently sloping Terrain respectively. However, the former has further been subdivided into crest and upper slopes and valley slopes and channel complex, whereas the sub-divisions for later landforms are upper slopes and lower slopes and channel complex. However, in case of Katoya Plains, the two identified landforms are uplands (relatively dry) and lowlands (moist).

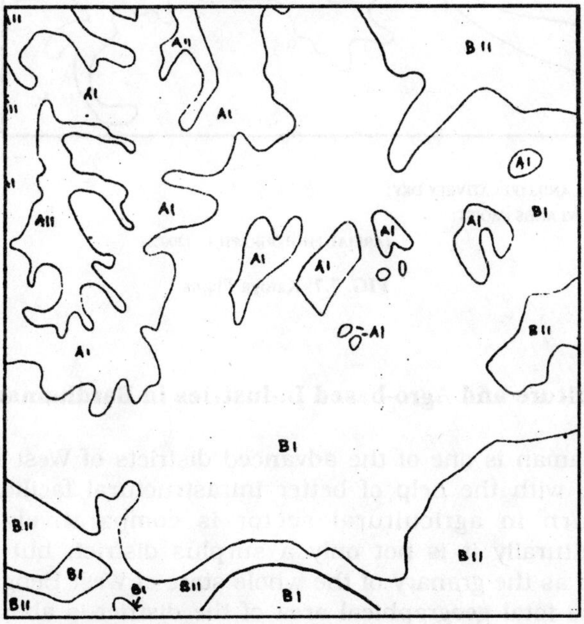

A. DISSECTED TERRAIN
A_I CREST & UPPER SLOPES
A_{II} VALLEY SLOPES & CHANNEL COMPLEX
B. GENTLY SLOPING TERRAIN
B_I UPPER SLOPES
B_{II} LOWER SLOPES & CHANNEL COMPLEXES
(AERIAL PHOTOGRAPH 1 : 120,000)

FIG. 7.6: Durgapur Rolling Plains

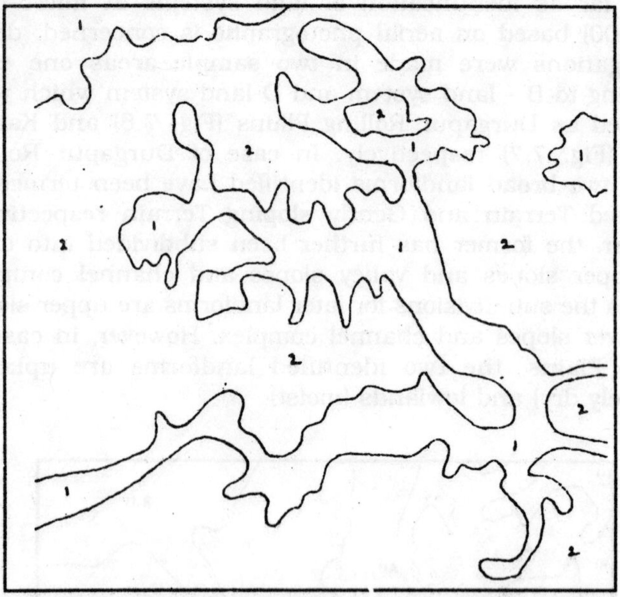

1. UPLANDS (RELATIVELY DRY)
2. LOWLANDS (MOIST)

(AREIAL PHOTOGRAPH 1 : 120000)

FIG. 7.7: Katoya Plains

Agriculture and Agro-based Industries in Bardhaman

Bardhaman is one of the advanced districts of West Bengal, where, with the help of better infrastructural facilities, the out turn in agricultural sector is comparatively more. Agriculturally it is not only a surplus district, but is also known as the granary of the whole state of West Bengal.

The total geographical area of the district is about 7001 thousand hectares. As much as 65 per cent of it is classified as Net Sown Area (NSA). Multiple cropping is practised in 50 per cent of NSA.

Rice is predominently the leading crop of the district, which occupies 85 per cent of the Gross Cropped Area (GCA). Potato (5%) is very important in eastern and southern parts

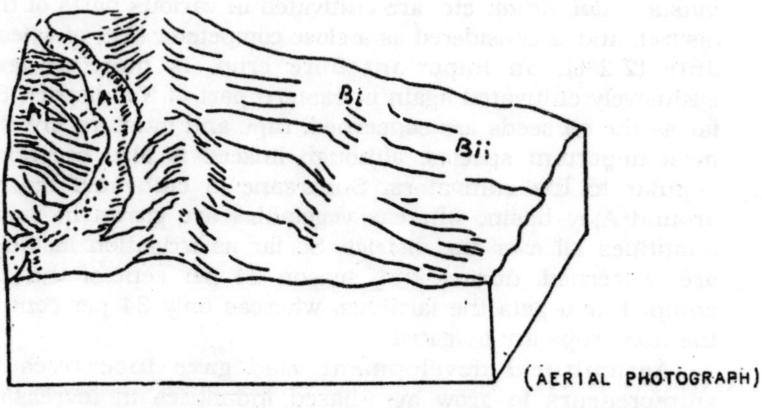

Ai CREST & UPPER SLOPES
Aii VALLEY SLOPES & CHANNEL COMPLEX
Bi UPPER SLOPES
Bii LOWER SLOPES & CHANNEL COMPLEXES

FIG. 7.8: B-Land System

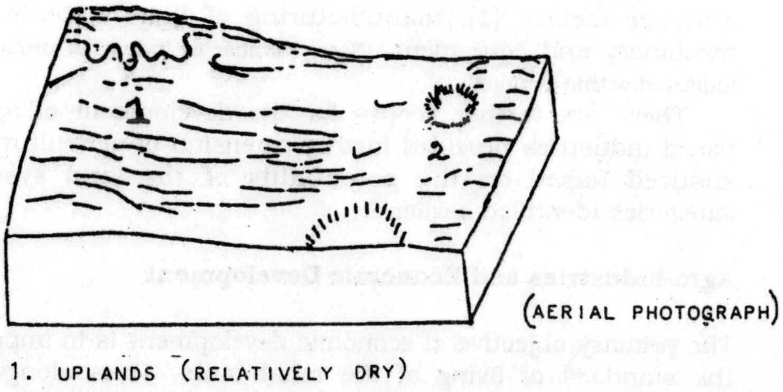

1. UPLANDS (RELATIVELY DRY)
2. LOWLANDS (MOIST)

FIG. 7.9: D-Land System

of the district. Wheat, though stands third, yet covers only 4.4 per cent of the GCA. Different types of pulses like *mung, musur, kalai, arhar*, etc. are cultivated in various parts of the district, and is considered as a close competetor (3%) of wheat. Jute (2.2%), an important fibre crop, is more or less exclusively cultivated again in eastern part of the district. So far as the oil seeds are concerned, rape and mustard are the most important species, although linseed is also becoming popular to the cultivators. Sugarcane is cultivated mostly around Ajoy basin, whereas vegetables are grown in small quantities all over the district. So far as irrigation facilities are concerned, during *khrif* season 74 per cent of the net cropped area gets the facilities, whereas only 34 per cent of the *rabi* crops are irrigated.

Agricultural development also gave incentives to entrepreneurs to grow agro-based industries in increasing order. Thus the district is dotted with rice mills (156) and also locally installed husking machine units. More than a dozen of cold storages have come up, particularly to store potatoes for steady supply to the market during off season period. Other agro-based industries are flour mills (2), indigenous sugar manufacturing unit, bread making, manufacturing of edible oils and fats, e.g. mustard oil, groundnut oil, linseed oil, etc. (15), cotton spinning and weaving (1), weaving of cotton textiles in power looms (4), fertiliser factory (1), manufacturing of light agricultural machinery and equipment. (Note: Number of industrial units are indicated within bracket)

There are further scopes for the development of agro-based industries provided further extension of agriculture is ensured based on the potentiality of the land system categories identified earlier.

Agro-industries and Economic Development

The primary objective of economic development is to improve the standard of living of the inhabitants. Thus alongwith increase of purchasing power, other dimensions of developmental activities like health, shelter, educational facilities, availability of drinking water, etc. are included within the perview of integrated developmental programme.

Our area of investigation is primarily agrarian in nature.

hence its development is also dependent on the development of agriculture. Moreover, agricultural development has also direct bearing on agro-based industries.

To make the economy more viable in the concerned area, the developmental plan may be formulated on the basis of analysis of different land system/units presented earlier. It should take into consideration the assessment of the land potential of each of the land system. The analysis provides information regarding how best the land may be utilised and how to get rid of the inherent problems. The basic information will also indicate the type of re-allocation of agricultural practices and also establishment of agro-based industries by assessing product potentiality and service requirement.

Conclusion

The techniques applied in the present exercise not only help the technician to identify the individual land system alongwith landform units contained therein, but also to map them very precisely, economically and quickly. Moreover, the factual information prvioded against each landform unit will provide ample scope for assessing land potentiality as well. It is also possible to measure the area coverage for each and every land system/landform unit for the purpose of quantification, if necessary. The technique has a universal application and can be applied in varied envirònmental conditions. The technique is dynamic in nature and can be modified depending upon the existing situation. The scale of working can also be changed depending upon unit of study, e.g. macro, meso, micro, etc.

EIGHT

Role of Agro-Industry (Sugarcane) in the Economic Development of Bangladesh

REJUAN HOSSAIN BHUIYAN

Introduction

Sugarcane industry is a 'weight-losing' and raw material based industry. And its sucrose ($C_{12}H_{22}0_{11}$) recovery rate is between 7 to 12 per cent. The sugarcane is very much difficult to trasport, because its sucrose begins to deteriorate after 24 hours of cutting from the fields. It does not form crystals of sugar and passes into molasses. Thus better recovery depends upon the cane being crushed within twenty-four hours of its separation from the root. So sugar factories have to be installed in the areas where sugarcane is cultivated in sufficient quantity, to feed the modern large scale industries. Enough supplies of fresh cane for crushing must be available in the immediate neighbourhood of the factories or within reasonable limits for being transported to factories with the possibility of minimum inversion or dryage. The source of power, i.e, the supply of fuel or electricity always plays an important part in the choice of the location of sugar industries. Though, the sugar industry to a very great extent is independent of the supplies of coal or electricity for running the machinery, because the bagasse obtained as a by-product, which is generally sufficient to meet the requirements of the mills for raising the steam and for heating the juice. Physiography, climate, soil, transportation and communication also play a decisive role for sugarcane production and as well as sucrose recovery rate of the sugar industry. So, all the factors have to be considered for proper development of sugarcane industires.

Study Area

According to river system, Bangladesh is a part of 'Ganga Basin' — stretches latitudinally between 20°30'N and 26°45'N, and longitudinally between 88°E and 92°56' E. It is one of the most crowded rural areas in the world, with 90 million people (1981) in 143,998 sq.km. of land area.

Data Base and Methodology

The analysis has been done on the basis of sugarcane production and sucrose recovery as dependent and physiography, climate, soil, road density, distance of field from the mills, age of industry etc. as independent variables. Five major sugarcane zones have been identified on the basis of physiography, climate and soil (Table 8.1).

Data have been collected both from primary and secondary sources. Primary data were collected through pre-tested standarized questionnaire and secondary data from 'Bangladesh Food Sugar Industries Corporation'.

Regional variation of sugarcane yield and sucrose recovery have been identified through physiographic observation, climatic classification, and soil essential and trace element test analysis. Transportation and communication system also considered for sucrose recovery rate identification.

Simple regression also applied to observe the dependency of sugarcane yield and sucrose recovery rate with the independent variables.

Factors Affecting Sugarcane Yield and Sucrose Recovery

The following factors are affecting in sugarcane yield and sucrose recovery in Bangladesh:

(i) — Physiography (flatplain and well drainage system),
— Soil (structure, texture, chemical elements etc.) and
— Climate (tempurature 20°-25°C, rainfall 2000-2300 mm, humidity more than 80 per cent in growing

time and less than 80 per cent in cutting time and rainless day during the hurvesting time, intensity of sunshine throughout the day),

(ii) Communication and transportation,
(iii) Agro-technological factors,
(iv) Optimum knowledge on sugarcane plantation and hurvesting time,
(v) Administrative and organizational causes,
(vi) Social, cultural and economic causes, and
(vii) Age of Industry.

Results and Discussion

In growing season of 1947-48, sugarcane area was 86,670 hectares (0.65% of total cultivable land) and rose upto 1,67,063 hectares in 1986-87 season (1.25% of total cultivable land) and total production was 32,70,000 tonnes and 70,00,000 tones respectively. Moreover, per hectare yield was 38 tonnes in 1947-48 season and rose upto 50 tonnes in 1986-87 season. Sucrose recovery trends and yield of sugar have been shown in Fig. 8.1.

Before 1947, only 5 sugar industries had been functioning by private ownership in Bangladesh and total capacity of sugar production was 47 thousand tonnes. But during 1947

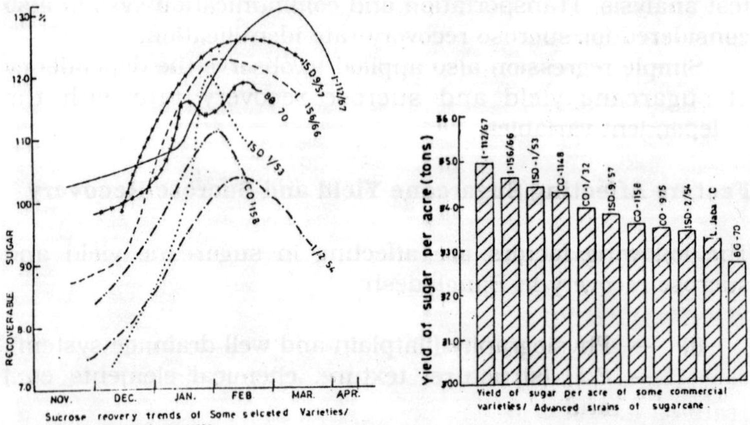

Sucrose reovery trends of Some selceted Varieties/ Advanced strains of sugarcane.

Yield of sugar per acre of some commercial varieties/ Advanced strains of sugarcane.

FIG. 8.1: Sucrose Recovery Trends and Yield of Sugar

to 1970 (Pakistan period) 10 more sugar industries have been setup and sugar production capacity rose upto 1,69,000 tonnes. In 1977-78 season another one sugar mill has been setup with the capacity of 10,000 tonnes and total sugar production capacity rise upto 1,79,000 tonnes.

Table 8.1: Bangladesh—Sugarcane Sub-zones

Sl.	Sugarcane Zones	Name of the sugar mills	Administrative area
1.	Piedmont	PSM, TSM, STSM	Dinajpur
2.	Barind	JSM	Bogra
3.	Tista-Jamuna-Padma floodplain:		
	a. Tista-Jamuna flood-plain	SHSM, RSM	Rangpur
	b. Padma flood-plain	NBSM, RJSM	Rajshahi
4.	Moribund Delta;		
	a. West of Madhumati river	KSM, C&CO, MKSM	Kushtia Jessore
	b. East of Madhumati river	FSM	Faridpur
5.	Jamuna-Old Brahmaputra flood-plain:		
	a. Upper Region	ZBSM	Jamalpur
	b. Lower Region	NSM, KCSM, DSM	Mymensingh Dhaka

Source: Rejuan (1981), *Regional Variation of Sugarcane Yield and Sucrose Recovery in Bangladesh*, M.Sc. Thesis, Delhi University, p. 3.

Table 8.1 shows the sugarcane zones and sub-zones in the sugarcane growing regions of Bangladesh. Name of the sugar mill and their administrative area also can be identified in the same table and Fig. 8.2. The analytical Table 8.2 shows the status of sugarcane growing (both traditonal and modern technology) and sucrose recovery with their factors.

Physical Factors

Good drainage system is one of the prime factors of high rate of sugarcane yield and sucrose recovery of the country. According to Sugarcane Research Institute (SRI), the yield of sugarcane is varying from 1000 *mounds* (36 tonnes) to 800 *mounds* (29 tonnes) and 20 per cent sucrose recovery

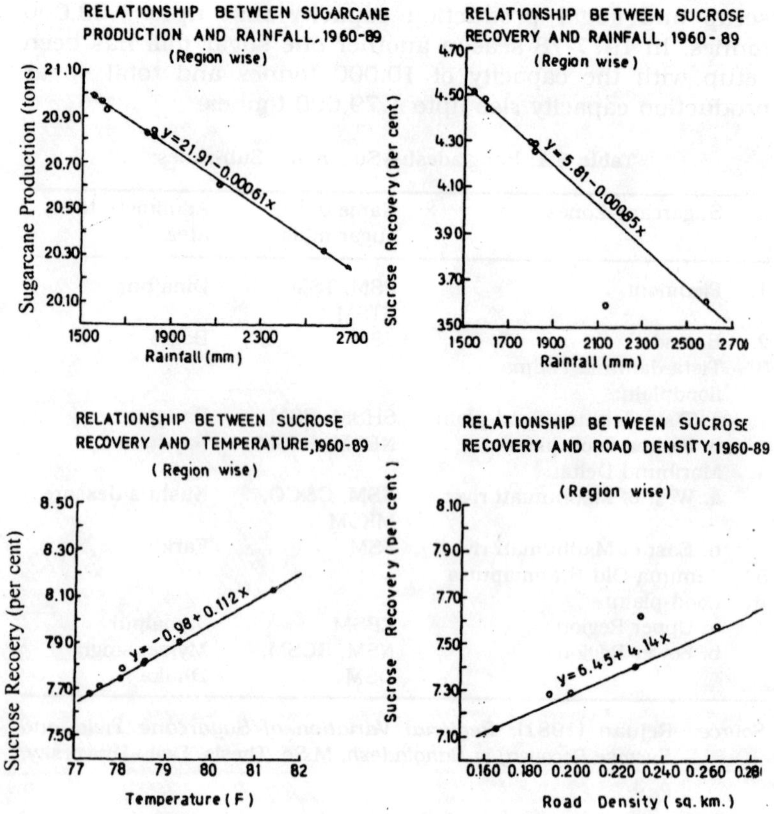

FIG. 8.2: Status of Sugarcane Growing and Sucrose Recovery

deteriorate due to stagnant of water for the good quality of sugarcane. In the light of well drainage system, North-west and western side of Bangladesh (Piedmont Alluvial Plain, Barind, Active and Maribund Delta and Ganges-Padma-Brahmaputra flood-plain) is the best area for sugarcane cultivation (Fig. 8.3 and Table 8.2).

Area under 1-2.5 per cent (minor belt) and area above 2.5 per cent (major belt) of total cultivated land can be shown in Fig. 8.4.

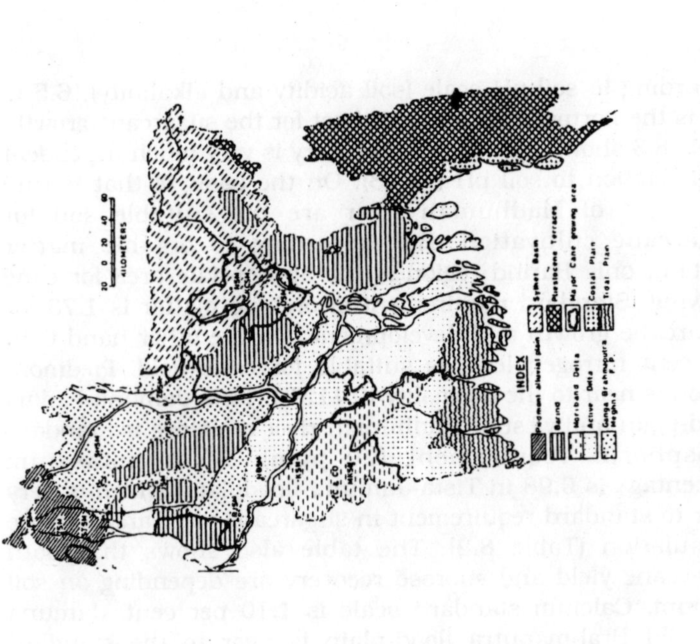

FIG. 8.4: Bangladesh: Physiographic Regions and Sugarcane Belt

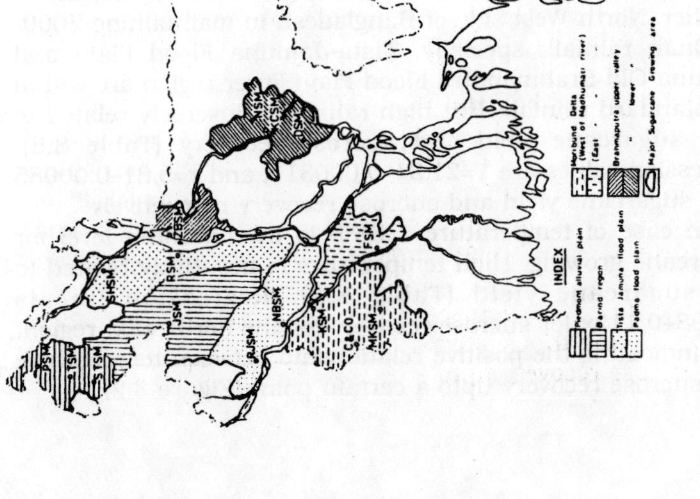

FIG. 8.3: Bangladesh: Sugarcane Sub-Regions

Soil

According to soil pH scale (soil acidity and alkalinity), 6.5 to 7.5 is the normal level and it is best for the sugarcane growth. Table 8.3 shows that sucrose recovery is very much dependent with relation to soil pH (+0.53). On the basis of that Barind and west of Madhumati river are the suitable soil for sugarcane cultivation. But according to organic matter contain, only Barind region is the appropriate area for cane growing. Standard requirement of organic matter is 1.73 for sugarcane growth and development. On the other hand 0.10 per cent nitrogen level is suitable for cane field. Piedmont region is near to the normality (0.112%). Tista-Jamuna-Padma flood-plain and west of Madhumati river are close to standard phosphorus requirement (20 ppm). While potassium percentage is 0.98 in Tista-Jamuna floodplain, which is very near to standard requirement in sugarcane yield and sucrose formulation (Table 8.2). The table also shows that both sugarcane yield and sucrose recovery are depending on soil calcium. Calcium standard scale is 1.10 per cent. Jamuna and Old Brahmaputra flood-plain is near to the standard scale.

Climate

Climate is the very important determinant of sugarcane yield and sucrose recovery. Except rainfall, temperature, humidity and sunshining are not wide difference from one region to another. North-West side of Bangladesh in maintaining 2000-2300mm rainfall; specially, Tista-Jamuna Flood Plain and Jamuna-Old Brahmaputra Flood Plain lower region are within the standard rainfall. But high rainfall is inversely related to both sugarcane yield and sucrose recovery (Table 8.3). Regression values are Y=21.91–0.00081 x and y=5.81–0.00085 x for sugarcane yield and sucrose recovery respectively.

In case of temperature ± 68^{0}F is the optimum level for sugarcane growing. High temperature is negatively related to the sugarcane yield (Table 8.3). Regression line is y=0.98+0.112x for sucrose recovery for the north-west region. It is indicating the positive relationship between temperature and sucrose recovery upto a certain point (Figure 8.2).

Table 8.2: Region-wise Sugar Production, Sucrose Recovery, Rainfall, Temperature, Soil pH, Organic Matter, Nitrogen, Phosphorus, Potassium, Calcium, Road Density, and Age of Industry

Sl.	Region and Sub-regions	Using Modern Technology (Tonnes)	Using Traditional technology (Tonnes)	Avg. sugarcane Technology (Tonnes)	Per Acre sucrose Recovery (Mound)	Sucrose Recovery (per cent)	Rainfall (mm)	Temperature (F)	Soil pH
1.	Piedmond	20.0	9.8	14.9	27.47	7.21	1810	81.3	4.7
2.	Barind	21.8	10.9	16.4	33.53	7.48	1785	79.2	6.9***
3.	Tista-Jamuna-Padma Floodplain:	24.7	14.0	19.4	39.50	7.66	2050***	78.2	—
	(a) Tista-Jamuna F.P.	25.8*	15.6*	20.7*	41.90*	7.28	2575*	78.0***	5.2
	(b) Padma Floodplain	23.6	12.4	18.0	37.08	7.96*	1530	78.3	7.8
4.	Moribund Delta:	24.4	12.2	18.1	36.63	7.85	1695	78.1	—
	(a) West of Madhumati River	25.8	13.1	19.1	38.80	7.91	1580	78.5	7.2***
	(b) East of Madhumati River	22.9	11.3	17.1	34.45	7.33	1810	77.6	7.9
5.	Jamuna-Old Brahmaputra Floodplain:	22.2	10.7	16.4	32.59	6.83	1875	77.7	—
	(a) Upper Region	25.5	13.5	19.5	40.72	7.67	1605	77.3	6.0
	(b) Lower Region	18.9**	9.2**	14.4*	24.45	6.40**	2140***	78.1	5.8
	National Average	23.1	12.0	17.5	33.94	7.69	1840	78.9	
	Standard Requirement						2000-2300	±68	6.5-7.5

Contd.

Table 8.2 (*Contd.*)

Organic matter	Nitrogen (per cent)	Phos-phorus (ppm)	Potassium (per cent)	Calcium (per cent)	Road Density/ Sq.km	Age of Industry
2.22	0.112***	9	0.83	0.14	0.227	STSM-1933
						TSM-1958
1.68***	0.082	40	0.90	0.21	0.197	PSM-1969
						JSM-1962
—	—	—	—	—	—	RSM-1957
1.35	0.069	25***	0.98***	0.25	0.285*	SHSM-1969
						NBSH-1933
1.20	0.064	16***	1.14	0.62	0.263	RJSM-1965
—	—	—	—	—	—	C&CO-1938
						KSM-1965
0.97	0.054	18	1.18	2.68	0.291*	MKSM-1967
						FSM-1977
1.16	0.59	10	1.22	2.54	0.198	
—	—	—	—	—	—	ZBSM-1958
						KCSM-1969
1.04	0.055	38	1.09	0.65	0.200	DSM-1934
						NSM-1937
1.01	0.051	15	0.82	0.38	0.165**	
					0.202	
1.73	0.100	20	1.00	1.10		

* High; ** Low; *** Standard

Table 8.3: Correlates of Dependent of Sugarcane Yield and Sucrose Recovery

Variables x_i	Sugarcane yield Y_1	Sucrose Recovery Y_2
Rainfall	-0.08	-0.81
Temperature	-0.53	-0.09
Soil pH	+0.17	+0.53
Road Density	+0.70*	+0.72*

* Significant at 0.01 level

Communication and Transportation

Communication and transportation is one of the prime important factor for sugar industries. Regular supply of sugarcane is very essential because its sucrose begins to deteriorate after 24 hours of cutting from the field. It does not form crystal of sugar and passes into molasses. The rate of inversion is 0.25-0.50 per cent for every 24 hours after one day (24 hours) of cutting from the field. So better recovery of sucrose depends upon the cane being crushed within twenty-four hours of its separation from the root.

Cart, truck (lorry), tracktor-trolley, railway wagon etc. are being used for sugarcane transportation from the long distance field. From the field experience it has been identified that 4-5 days dumping of sugarcane in cane purchasing centre is a very common phenomenon. Author has observed in Rangpur Sugar Mill (RSM), that only one hour rainfall has stopped the RSM for 12 hours, because the supply of sugarcane has held up for two days for bad communication. Due to that sucrose recovery has fallen from 8.87 to 7.69 per cent. It is very clear that the delay of sugarcane supply reduced 1.14 per cent sucrose recovery. So the good condition of road or accessibility and density of roads are positively related to sugarcane yield and sucrose recovery. Table 8.3 shows the relationship between road density and sugarcane yield and sucrose recovery. Regression line has also shown the positive relationship (y=6.45+4.14x). Table 8.2 shows that the Moribund delta west and Tista-Jamuna Flood Plain areas are the high road density and sucrose recovery is also high i.e., 7.91 and 7.98 respectively, which is higher than any other region. On the other hand lower part of old Brahmaputra region has 0.165 road density per sq.km and sucrose recovery was also very low, which was only 6.68 per cent. It has been observed that distance of field from the sugar mill is inversely proportional to sucrose recovery (Rejuan, 1981). The Fig. 8.6 shows the distance and sucrose recovery relationship. However, an example can be cited—C & CO, NBSM, KSM, ZBSM, RJSM were high percentage of sugarcane supply from the radius of 0-5 miles (8 km) and the percentage of sugarcane supply was 84 per cent, 81 per cent, 71 per cent, 69 and 66 per cent, and sucrose recovery rates were 9.33, 8.30, 8.28 and 8.93 per cent respectively. On the other hand lowest supply of sugarcane has been found from (0-5 miles or 8 km radius) KCSM, DSM, RSM and JSM, and the percentage of cane supply was 23 per cent, 28 per cent, 32 per cent and 36 per cent of total supply, while the rate of sucrose recovery was 7.08, 5.36, 7.79, and 8.14 per cent respectively. It indicates that higher the distance and lower the sucrose recovery.

Agro-Technological Factor

In Bangladesh only 14 per cent of sugarcane area is under modern technology. So it is one of the major factor for high yield of sugarcane production (Rejuan, 1981).

Knowledge on Sugarcane Plantation and Harvesting Time

Both sugarcane yield and sucrose recovery are high in the case of early platation of cane. 25 to 30 per cent of sugarcane yield and 1-2 per cent of sucrose recovery vary from early plantation in October/Noveber (Rejuan, 1981). Early and late plantation status can be shown in Fig. 8.7

Sucrose recovery increase from early harvesting (November) to late harvesting (February) but the sucrose recovery drastically decrease after getting the April monsoon rainfall (Figure 8.8).

Administrative and Organizational Causes

Administrative and organizational lackness has been observed in agro-credit, distribution of fertilizer, pesticides, seed etc.

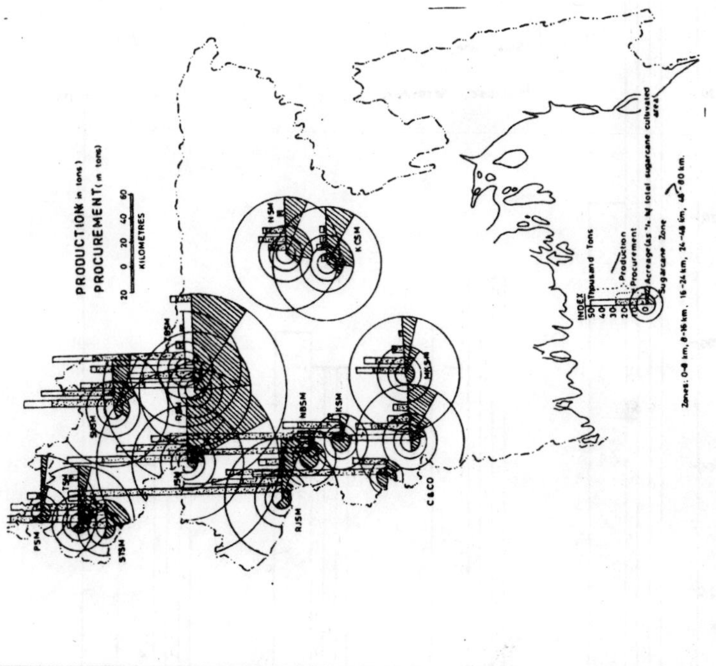

FIG 8.6: Bangladesh: Sugarcane Acreage (As % of total cultivated area)

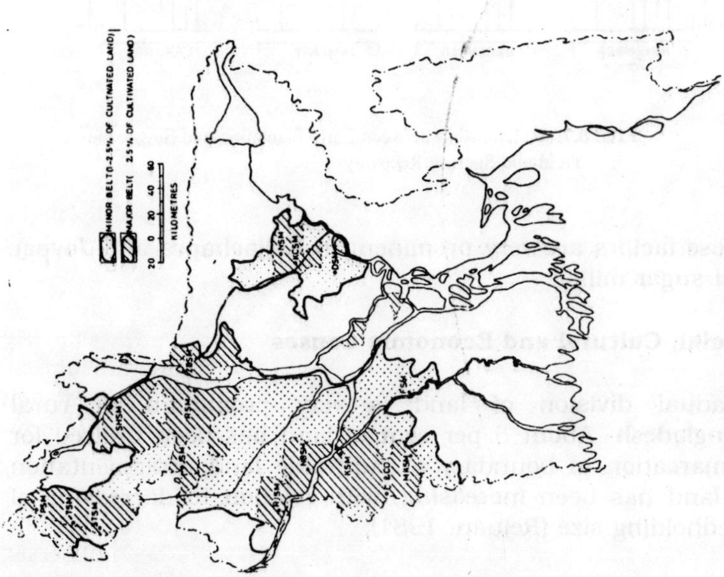

FIG 8.5: Bangladesh: Sugarcane Belts

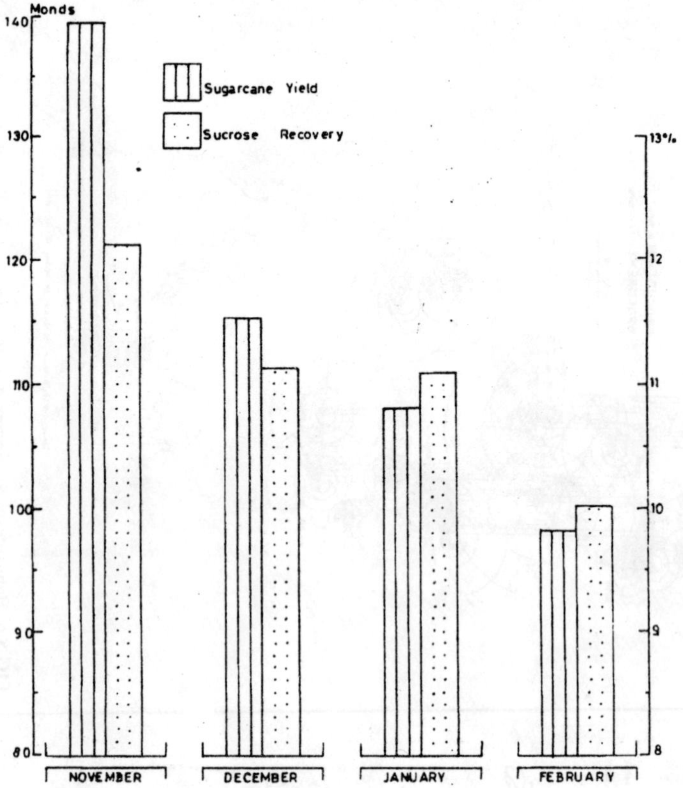

FIG. 8.7: Relationship between Early Plantation and Sugarcane Yield and Sucrose Recovery

These factors are very prominent in Kaliachapra and Joypar Hat sugar mills.

Social, Cultural and Economic Causes

Gradual division of land is very prominant in rural Bangladesh. About 5 per cent of land has been utilized for demarcation of boundary of cultivable land. Fragmentation of land has been increasing, with relation to decreasing of landholding size (Rejuan, 1981).

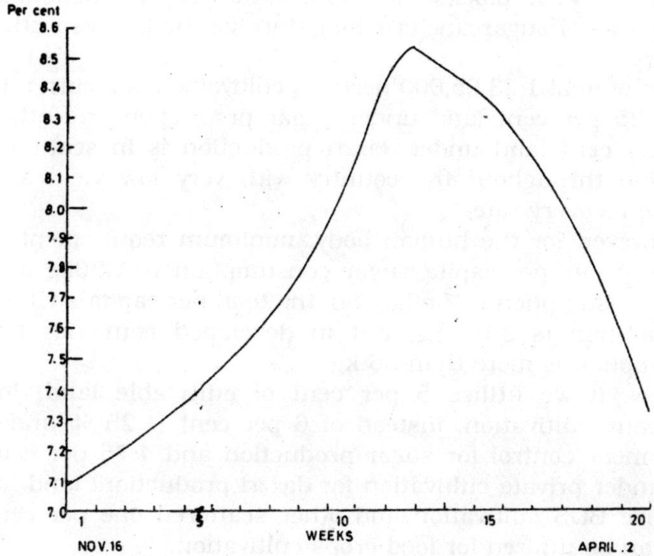

FIG. 8.8: Sucrose Recovery Trend during Crushing Period

Age of Industry

After first five years of installation, every sugar mill reduce their otpimum capacity of sucrose recovery. National Sugar Mill, Deshbondhu Sugar Mill, North Bengal Sugar Mill and C & CO have reduced their 0.5 to 1 per cent sucrose recovery capacity after 20 years of installation of industries. Recently, National and Setabgonj sugar mills stopped function due to the above reason.

However, above discussion indicates that the Tista-Jamuna-Padma flood plain, Barind tract and west of Madhumati river are the suitable zones for sugarcane cultivation.

Conclusion

Block Development System (BDS) is that according to daily consumption (need) of the respective sugarmills, one block will be made within the shortest distance of the sugar mill. In this way +135 blocks will be made for proper functioning of 19 weeks of sugarcane crushing duration by the respective industry.

Out of total 1,33,65,000 hectares cultivable land, currently only 1.25 per cent land under sugar production and other 4.75 per cent land under Jazzri production is in scattered condition throughout the country with very low yield and sucrose recovery rate.

However, for the human body, minimum requirement is 20kg but our per capita sugar consumption is 1.50kg and Jazzri consumption is 7.50kg. So, the total per capita sucrose consumption is 9.00 kg, but in developed countries the consumption is more than 36 kg.

Now, if we utilize 5 per cent of cultivable land, for sugarcane cultivation, instead of 6 per cent (1.25 % under government control for sugar production and 4.75 per cent land under private cultivation for Jazzri production) land for intensive BDS cultivation and other scattered one per cent land can be utilized for food crops cultivation.

However, 40 lakh tonnes of sugar is required for 90 million people. Five per cent land is enough for supplying the required sugarcane. 43 lakh tonnes of sugar can be produced from the 5 per cent land with 9 per cent recovery rate.* After fulfilment of local consumption with the rate of 20kg, we can export the additional 3 lakh tonnes of sugar and earn foreign currency for economic development of the nation. Moreover, other one per cent scattered land can be utilized for other crops. Additional molasses and other byproduct can be utilized in different capital goods forming industry.

* 16,50,000 acres x 29 tonnes sugarcane per acre ÷ 100 × 9 per cent sucrose recovery = 43,06,500 tonnes.

NINE

Agro-processing and Economic Development: Theoretical Underpinning and a Case Study

CHAMPA MITRA

Agro-processing industries have great significance in the economic development of the country. If we look at India's balance of payments position since 1966, there has been a consistent deficit, which was about Rs. 8,000 crores in 1987. To improve the balance of payments position two methods are available: (1) curtailment of import, and (2) boosting of exports. With the constraints existing in our country for expanding technological base, curtailment of import is difficult. The only way left is to boost our export. In the area which has vast and growing export potential, agro-processing industries occupy the foremost position.

A vertical diversification or forward integration in the agricultural sector which implies processing of locally produced agricultural commodities is now universally advocated as a vital aspect of agro-industrial integration. The multiplier effects (including both the direct and indirect employment, and income effects) are significant, and through the creaton of both off-farm and on-farm employment the establishment of agro-processing industires could thus help relieve the problems of low income and of general and seasonal under-employment of rural labour. This also includes women labour which is of profound socio-economic sginificance. In rural areas where agro-processing units are set up, production of suitable agricultural raw materials is obviously encouraged. Whether promotion of agro-processing industries encourages agricultural progress rather being itself the outcome of agricultural development is certainly a debatable question but admittedly the development of one is closely linked with the other.

In view of the relatively slow growth of the organised industrial sector and its employment-generating capacity, the brunt of the edge of the employment problem has to be shouldered by small industries, including the agro-processing industries which are skill-light, without significant economies of scale and allow a wide range of technology with variable capital-labour proportions, Moreover, in the background of rural unemployment-poverty syndrome in our country, the development of agro-processing industries may be conceived as a vital supplement to redistributive land reforms which can not ensure to the large number of landless labourers and small farmers land enough to make them economically self-reliant. In agriculturally advanced Japan, a large percentage of farmers do part-time work outside the farm, including the agro-processing industries.

Altogether then, by stimulating rural income and employment, agro-processing industries could narrow the income gap between the large cities and the countryside and slow down the rate of rural-urban migration by utilizing resource endowments of each region rather than transferring labour force from agricultural to non-agricultural sector. These could also stimualte rural and regional development, and a balanced spatial distribution of industrial and economic activity. It is important to note that some 'value-added' agro-processed items have considerable export opportunities as well. The case for agro-processing industries in India, can, therefore be scarcely over-emphasized.

It must be stressed, however, that a wide network of agro-processing industries requires comprehensive planning and efficient machinery for its implementation to avoid a mushroom growth of non-viable units. There has always been the danger that in a sudden spurt of enthusiasm, a plethora of agro-processing units could be set up without a realistic assessment of resources and without the arrangement of suitable institutional support. A programme of development of mainly rural-based agro-processing industries should form part of a well-thoughtout economic programme rather than a passionate ideological issue. As a result of ideological overtones, very often attention is not paid to their modernization and scientific assessment of their role in development which also accounts for the adoption of several irrational measures of support that merely perpetuate their low-income status, and such additions to employment as are brought about in these industries through essentially short-run measures do not result in conditions favourable to cummulative growth in opportunities for enduring employment in these enterprises.

In the background of the foregoing general discussion, I proceed to analyse briefly, from an empirical angle, the case of a partiuclar agro-processing industry (viz. Paddy processing) with reference to its status in the district of Burdwan in West Bengal.

Paddy processing is not merely one of the major food grain processing industries of India, rice milling is the largest single food industry and the oldest agro-based industry of the country. Rice being the main staple food of the people of West Bengal, has made its processing industry a very integral part of the economic landscape of the almost the entire state. Burdwan district also plays a major part in this sphere.

Milling is the process which involve removel of husk and other layer of bran from paddy to convert it into consumable white rice. The rice milling industry consists of: (i) the large sized and more organised rice mills. In 1988 about 366 mills were working in the state of which 153 are in the Burdwan district — the second largest paddy-producing district in the state following Midnapur. Among the 153 mills, 142 are concentrated in the three sub-divisions of the predominantly agricultural eastern Burdwan, viz, Burdwan Sadar, Katwa and Kalna (almost 95 % of the total paddy production in the district comes from the eastern part). The predominantly industrial Asansol and Raniganj sub-divisions together have only 9 rice mills, (ii) the relatively unorganised husking mills, numbering about 8500 and (iii) the old hand pounding, *dhenkis* which are mainly of a subsistence nature.

Although the eastern part of the Burdwan district is overwhelmingly an agricultural tract, the paddy processing especially the rice milling industry there has to play a vital role in its economy through agro-industrial integration. The most important advantage of husking mills is that they are not under any levy obligation (whereas the mills are compelled to deliver 40 per cent of their production to FCI for meeting requirements of statutory rationing), and even with obsolate and old machineries they are thriving and gradually increasing in number. The mills which also had outdated machineries were declining till late 1970's with their requirements of large number of labourers, as well as more time consuming processing operation, with increasing modernization and introduction of superior technologies, their number and output picked up again. The competition between the rice mills and the husking mills continues, but eventually the rice mills are likely to dominate over the other category because of their higher yield of rice with least brokens and better quality of by-products.

Rice milling is a labour intensive industry, and both male and female labourers are employed in the mill. The workers who are engaged in field operation (mainly drying) are all women. The male workers are appointed for machine operation, packing, official work etc. Most of the mills in Burdwan employ 40 to 50 persons. The total of 153 mills of the district provide employment to 7697 persons. Among them, 7265 are engaged in the rice mills of eastern Burdwan. The density of rural population ensures a large employment of labour.

The location of rice mills is governed significantly by economic factors, as postulated in theory. Like most agro-processing industries rice milling is a more raw material oriented than market oriented industry. A good and regular supply of paddy is essential. Accordingly, most of the mills are located in the proximity of fields from where supply of paddy is assured. Statistically, area under paddy cultivation and production of rice mills in four police stations (Sadar, Memari, Bhatar and Raina) are found to have been directly correlated with each other, the correlation coefficient between these two variables being 0.85.

Linked to the proximity of sources of raw materials is the importance of the transportation factor. Although the rice mills are all located in rural or semi-urban areas, they are at easily accessible points of the transport system, such as on the Grand Trunk Road or along the important roads and railways. River Damodar also helps these rice mills by supplying a large volume of water. And in case of rice mills of Burdwan, road transport is more economic than either rail or water transport. The trucks (usually having a capacity of 100 quintals of rice) are mostly owned by the mill owners themselves. Power is another important infrastructural factor affecting the location of the rice milling industry in Burdwan. Paddy processing requires a good supply of power and captive generation is also resorted to by a few mills to avoid problem of power cuts. Anyway, although mills show a tendency to be located in rural areas, they have not chosen such remote villages where electricity has not yet come.

As rice bran is an important oil bearing material, there is a compelling need for developing an appropriate technology for stabilization of rice bran and increased production of edible oil. Although most of the rice mills in Burdwan now use rubber shellers, quite a few still make use of traditional hullers — the oldest machinery. Normally, the huller mills yield bran having low oil content as it contains appreciable quantity of husk and broken rice mixed in it. The quality of bran coming out of sheller mills equipped with polishers are far better in this respect. Thus a substantial quantity of bran goes waste in the huller process. To stop this waste, measures should be taken promptly to modernize and strengthen the huller mills. The hand pounding units are not cost-efficient (many of them become sick) and hence need not be encouraged. Loans and subsidies should be provided for modernization. For lack of capital even today some of the mills remain totally unmechanized in some remote villages. As early as the 1940's experts had found hullers as being unproductive and wasteful. In 1950 an expert appointed by the Government of India recommended the introduction of paddy separator to improve the yield of rice under the huller system. This was followed by another recommendation that the degree of polish be limited to about 3 per cent with a view to providing increased nutrition. The Rice Milling Committee appointed by the Central Government in 1955 recommended that the huller mills be converted into sheller mills. Based on the Committee's recommendation, the Government of India promulgated the Rice Milling Industry Act and Rules for regulating the industry, but really speaking, before 1964 there was no systematic programme. The Paddy Processing Research Centre at Kharagpur which is engaged in the paddy processing has an important role to play.

Adequate marketing facilities may be provided for the by-products and husk-based industries should be developed.

The improvement of the existing mills in regard to

handling, storage and drying (through mechanical dryers) can yield larger benefits in term of production efficiency and profits. There is no mechanical driver in the whole district because of lack of factory space. However, sweeping modernization of rice mills by means of high capital investment may not lead to substantial increase in efficiency.

Government should take necessary steps for the prompt payment to the millers for levy rice, for at any rate the market prices of rice have generally been higher than the procurement prices fixed by the government.

Basmati (fine) variety has a great potential in overseas markets of U.S.A., Canada, Australia and Gulf States in particular. However, owing to low yield, farmers cultivate less of this variety. The cultivation and milling of basmati which could turn out to be a valuable foreign exchange earner needs support and encouragement. Plant breeders have to assume the responsibility of developing high-yielding varieties of basmati.

Theme-III

Industrialisation and Economic Development

TEN

Industrial Potential and Economic Development in the District of 24-Parganas (N&S), West Bengal

N.K. DE and A.K. MANDAL (BOSE)

Introduction

Industrialisation and economic development in any region is essentially dependent on the availability of supporting infrastructure. The existence of adequate infrastructure plays a catalytic role in the investment process and consequently, accelerates the industrial and commercial development of the region. The pace of greater commercialistion/industrialisation in the district of 24-Parganas took place at a much faster rate upto the end of the sixties. This was particularly due to the better infrastructural facilities, locational advantage, easy availability of industrial raw materials, cheap labour, supply of power and good marketing facilities. The harmonious combination of these factors has enabled the district (N&S) to become the largest industrial district in the state of West Bengal and consequently the economic and commercial activities spread up rapidly in spite of its vast untapped resources. The district of 24-Paragans (N&S) occupies the coveted postion of being the largest district in the state, both in area and population. Being so closely interlinked with advantages of several infrastructural facilities including good market proximity, transport network etc. which have helped to a great extent to attain its present position of being one of the relatively more developed districts of West Bengal. However, the intra-distict industrial structure exhibits stark contrasts in varying degree which are somewhat proportional with the distance from the urban magnet, while the areas in the immediate vicinity of Calcutta and the northern tract covering centres like Baranagar, Khardah, Titagarh, Barrackpore, Jagatdal, Jadavpur, Dum Dum and Budge Budge have a concentration of modern sophisticated industries, both in large and small scale sectors, the southern part continues to be a backward economy primarily based on agriculture and fishery with a sparse growth of small and cottage level units. However, the overall industrial scenario of the district appears to be rather gloomy. This may be attributed to the fact that even in the industrially developed northern 24-Parganas, most of the large industries are traditional—being based on jute, textile and heavy engineering—which have been particularly hard hit in the recent past, resulting in a depressionary state in its industrial economy.

Study Area

The district of 24-Parganas (N&S) is an isosceles trapezium lying between 21^{0}03' and 23^{0}12' North latitudes and between 88^{0}6' and 89^{0}05' East longitudes. The district is 51.49 km broad on its northern boundary, 102.98 km broad on its southern boundary, while the distance between the northern and southern boundary is about 154.46 km. It is flanked by Bangladesh on the east, the district of Nadia on the north, Hooghly and Howrah on the west and the Bay of Bengal on the south (Fig. 10.1).

On economic and geographical considerations the district may be divided into two parts. The northern tract is a fairly well raised delta and the low lying Sundarbans in the south is full of forests with a network of tidal channels, rivers, creeks and islands. The climate is substantially the same as in other parts of the gangetic region of lower Bengal. The climate is sub-tropical with high humidity and high annual rainfall. The seasonal temperature variation is not large, maximum being 36^{0} and minimum 13^{0}C. Average annual rainfall is around 170 cm although wide variation has been observed occasionally.

Population is the most important factor influencing the economic development in the district of 24-Parganas (N&S). Human resources (population) in the economy of the district

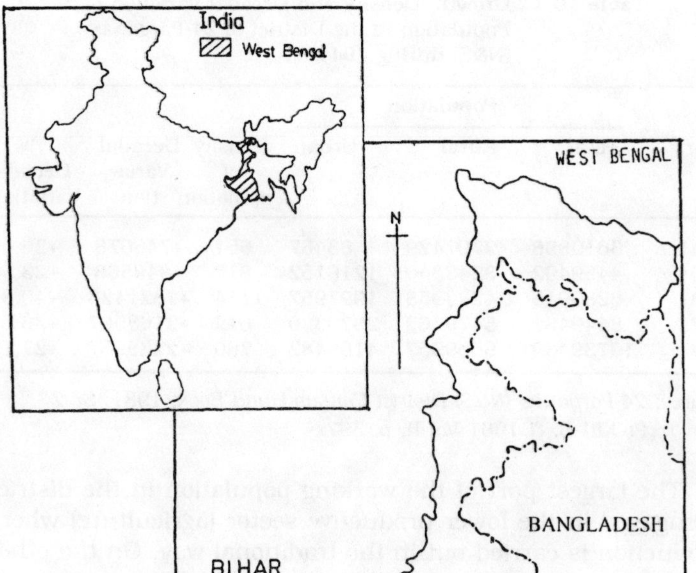

FIG. 10.1: Location of 24-Parganas (North-South) West Bengal

contribute to its commercial and industrial growth in two-fold manner. Labour and entrepreneurship on the one hand constitute important factors of production while, on the other, by floating demand they help in the offtake of goods produced in the economy. The following Table 10.1 shows the population increase in 24-Parganas in some previous decennial counts.

Table 10.1 : Growth, Density and Decadal Variation of Population in the District of 24-Parganas (N&S) during 1941-81

Year	Population			Density of Population	Decadal Variation	% of Decadal Variation
	Total	Rural	Urban			
1941	3610896	2797429	83467	651	+746678	+26.07
1951	4459492	3243340	1216152	817	+848596	+23.50
1961	6280915	4282958	1997957	1114	+1821423	+40.84
1971	8449482	5479162	2970320	612	+2168567	+36.63
1981	10739439	6569957	4169482	760	+2289957	+27.10

Source: *24-Paryanas (N&S) District Census Hand Book*, 1981, Sr-23. Pt-XIII-B; & 1961 Vol-II, p. 387.

The largest part of the working population in the district is engaged in the lower productive sector (agriculture) where production is carried out in the traditional way. On the other hand, a small proportion of the working population is engaged only in the higher productive sector.

Components of Industrial Resources

The industrial economy of a region is dependent on resources like agriculture, forest, marine, livestock and so on. In a developing country like India where the economy is dependent on the flourishing agriculture, the growth of industrial development should also be taken into consideration along with the rapid development of agriculture, forest, marine, livestock and other vital components that are directly or indirectly helping the growth of industry. Some of the important components of industry in the district of 24-Parganas are noted below.

Agriculture

West Bengal is one of the major rice producing states in India—contributing to about 14 per cent of the country's total production having about 14 per cent of the rice area of the country, while the district of 24-Parganas (N&S) contributes to about 13 per cent of the total production of the state

(W.B.). The district is fortunate to have a very fertile land, still it has remained one of the most agriculturally and economically backward area in the country. Agriculture in the district of 24-Parganas (N&S) is mainly dependent on nature which is really a gambling in rain and consequently chances play a pre-dominant role in agricultural production of the region. The available agrarian resources in different parts of the district are as follows:

Rice: Rice is the most popular crop in the district. It has been noted that due to high level of rice production, ample straw and rice bran are avilable here. Special mention may be made of the Canning and Basirhat blocks where these resources may be utilised for industrial purposes. At present, these are used for roofing in house or as cow feed.

Potato: Potato cultivation has been gaining momentum for the last two decades in the district. Attempts may be made to industrially utilise this crop so that the farmers of this region may earn profitable returns.

Sugarcane: Sugarcane is grown here extensively due to favourable soil texture. But the lack of profitable market has compelled the sugarcane growers to resist production at a much lower level. The sugarcane is, however, used mainly for direct consumption as sugarcane juice and as such, the price offered for this product is very unremunerative on the part of the cultivators.

Pineapple: The district also produces pineapple substantially which are marketed in Calcutta, North 24-Parganas and the surrounding districts. It should be noted that this is the most prosperous pineapple growing belt in south Bengal and pineapples produced in this belt can easily compete with those cultivated in Darjeeling and the adjoining areas.

Chillies: Chillies are cultivated extensively in the district, especially in Canning II block and other places of South 24-Parganas. A steady increase in its production has, however, been witnessed in the seventies. It should be noted that dry chillies production in 24-Parganas ranks second only to that in Midnapur.

In addition to these, a number of other agricultural products are also produced here but the levels of their production are much on the lower side. Of these, mention may be made of jute, groundnut, cotton and oilseeds. Mango and guava are also produced in Baruipur area.

Fish: Fishing is one of the oldest occupation of man. Next to agriculture, fishing is the only important source of human food and the most primitive sources of food for man as hunting was no longer of any economic importance due to change of time. The district of 24-Parganas (N&S) is facing a grave food crisis today with the increase in population year after year. Hence, development of fishing industry and fisheries assumes, for all practical purposes today, an integral part of the food production of the district (N&S) as well as the state of West Bengal. There is no doubt that the Sundarbans estuaries abound with valuable food, fish and crustacea and if they are properly worked, they will go a long way in adding to the existing supply of an important article of food. The people interested in fish industry and possessing a moderate capital will also find here a good field for investing their money. A number of marine resources are also available from the sea tract. Of various items, particular mention may be made of fish and oyster cell. Oyster cell is available at the confluence of the river and the sea which numbers more than 15 in this belt. Local poeple lying far below the poverty line are engaged in collecting these cells from the sea shore and river beds. These cells are, at present, grinded locally and transported outside the region for the preparation of poultry feed. Unfortunately, the marine fishery survey in the district is getting its importance only recently. The foundation stone of the Frasergunj Fishing harbour has been laid only during the year 1989. This harbour will provide safe landing and berthing facilities for carrying out fishing operations throughout the fishing season. In recent years, the use of fish meal as a stock and poultry food has grown rapidly in the district. In the district neither the sea fishing has developed nor there is any fish processing industry upto now to offer any wastes for preparation of fish meal. A large tons fish meal is prepared recently in the State Government yard at Frazergunj in the district of South 24-Parganas, which is mainly supplied to the state poultry multiplication farms. The meal is produced from tiny, miscellaneous and unpopular fishes which is used to be previously thrown away as waste by the coastal fisherman during fishing operation.

It is to be noted here that the non-faty, small and partially decomposed fishes, which can't be utilised for fish meal preparation are generally utilised for scrap fertilizer. In this case, fishes are not cooked but simply spread out to dry in the sun. The dried stuff so obtained is pulverised through seive and packed in gunny bags. It is generally used for agriculturists, flower, sugar planters and kitchen garden keepers etc. The organic matters which serves as a carrieer for the nitrogen and phosphoric acid in scrap, is of considerable importance as the organic matter in farm and green manures. Its use has become very popular to the farmers and garden keeprs who prefer unmixed fertilizers.

Forest

The estuarine tracts of Sundarbans supply raw materials to meet the demands of local people and develop industries. Besides vast areas of forests that are sources of timber, firewood, bark of tannin materials, golpata for thatching material, the tract is a potential breeding ground for innumerable species.

The Sundarbans forest is the basis of most of our industrial development. Not only is it necessary for the construction work for non-wood based industry for houses, for many fold domestic uses, but many of our industries, from matchwood to railway coaches, from rayon to newsprint, from incense to essential oils are completely dependent on the wealth of timber and grasses yielded by the Sundarbans forest. The mangrove of Sundarbans is used for various purposes like tannin extraction, paper and pulp, firewood, timber, charcoal, fodder and several other by-products. The mangrove swamps are rich in the larvae of many economically important fishes and prawns, crabs and bivalves. The trees of Sundarbans could not grow to a very big size in view of the locality factors. Consequently, the attempt should be in the sphere of utilization of small wood for industrial purposes. Fortunately some of the mangrove trees are good for the supply of tannin materials and recently they have also been found suitable for pulp making. The other two important forest products of Sundarbans are honey and wax. The wax is sold mainly to the chemical or pharmaceutical firms of the nearby urban centres. The honey is put in labelled bottles or tins and is sold to the general public.

Infrastructural Facilities

There are industrial estates one at Bonhooghly in the North and two in the South located at Behala and Baruipur. The district gets its power supply from WBSEB and CESC. While CESC meets the power requirements of the adjoining areas of Calcutta metropolis as also certain pockets in the North and South 24-Parganas, the blocks like Baruipur, Habra, Barrackpore and Barasat are supplied by WBSEB. Road transport is most important in the northern parts of the district, while in the south, water transport plays a major role in the transport of men and goods. The railway lines also connect different parts of the district with each other, as also with the Calcutta metropolis. The district is widely covered by the post and telegraph offices. All the blocks in the district have commercial banks.

Industrial Impact on Economic Development

The structural superiority of the district of 24-Parganas lies in its square development of indstury and agriculture with inclination towards the former. Its location at the lap of metropolitan magnet (Calcutta) and the consequential prospect of market outlet and the concentraton of skilled hands and brains have formed the corner stone of its industrial upliftment. An analysis of its industrial structure would, however, reveal that alike the other developing economies, a peculiar co-existence of modern and traditional industries are the marketed feature of the industrial economy of 24-Parganas. The most industrialised zone of the district stretches due north through Barrackpore and Naihati. Another development path is seen to run in the north-east direction through Rajarhat and Barasat. At present it is very prospective belt in the northern part of the district where a number of new industires are coming up due to good transport linkage with Calcutta and the availability of cheap industrial land and other allied facilities. In the southern half of the district, however, three distinct paths of industrial growth may be visualised. One is seen to extend due south-east through Jadavpur while the other two take their courses in south western and southern directions respectively (Fig. 10.3).

The present industrial scenario of the district has been

classified as follows:

(a) Traditional Cottage-based Industry
(b) Traditional Large Scale Industry
(c) Modern Industry
(d) Agro-based Industries

Traditional Cottage-based Industry

The district is rich in traditional heritage of industrial culture under the roofs of cottage limits. The important industries which have sprung up at different centres of this district include leather products, gauze and bandage, mat from Kutchaka, hogla and others, batik printing and chikan, oyester cell, etc.

Leather and leather based industries had attained prosperity in the age old days in the northern interiors of the district. Shoes and other leather products produced in these areas contributed a major share of the total supplies in the wholesale market in Calcutta. But in course of time, a number of hurdles began to appear in the vista which even questioned their existences of being viable units. Of various problems, mention, may be made of drain of raw materials into outside regions, lack of proper consciousness as to the changing taste and preference of the consumers, inability to capture large market orbits etc.

Gauze and Bandage industry has flourished in the eastern belt of the district, especially in the Basirhat Block, due to the concentration of skill. The pockets of such industries are found in and around Bhangar, Harishpur, Kamakpur, Madhyamgram etc. Under the present system, weaving is carried out in the cottage level by the weavers who are supplied with raw materials by the primary co-operative societies. They take in turn the finished products from the weavers at a pre-announced rate. At present more than ten thousand weavers are employed in this industry which give them earning in the range of Rs 10 to 15 per day. The main problem that is directly obstructing the smooth flourishment of gauze and bandage industry in this region is the non-availability of raw materials at reasonable prices. Mat industry is clustered in and around Basirhat and Canning blocks. The localy available raw materials are extensively used by the weavers. Weavers in the Canning block, however, use hogla as the raw materials as these may be easily available in those regions. It had been reported that around 300 and 500 families are employed respectively in Basirhat and Canning blocks in this industry. It shoul be noted, however, that the earnings from these activities are not lucrative at present. A weaver could earn only Rs. 5 to 8 per day in this industry. Low return causes mainly from the existence of middlemen who control both the product and market. It may be mentioned here that the district of 24-Parganas, is actively involved in the promotion and development of this industry since it accommodates people belonging to very poor society.

Due to the ample availability of oyster cell, a number of grinding units have sprung up in Canning and its surrounding belts. Almost all the existing units in this region practise primitive method by using traditional tools becuase of the financial and other related problems. The grinded oyester cell is used for the preparation of balanced poultry feed which requires the mixing up of 6 to 10 per cent of grinded power to accommodate calcium content. At present, however, the existing grinding industries supply their products to Hooghly Flour Mills Limited, Hindustan Lever Limited, Intech etc., but the return they receive is very low because of the fact that all the units are operating in an unorganised plane which is exploited suitably by the big industries.

Traditional Large Scale Industries

Jute Industry

Suitable soil texture and the resultant flourishment of Jute production in undivided Bengal had placed the jute industry on wheel in the course of nineteenth and early twentieth centuries.

It has been revealed that the district of 24-Parganas accommodate as much as 8 Jute pressing and baling units, 41 spinning and weaving units, 3 dying, printing and other units. Their respective employment levels are in the order of 193, 127, 440, 2170 and 928. While the main concentration of this industry is seen in and around Titagarh and Jagatdal, a few such units are also seen in Kamarhati, Shyamnagar, Birati, Naihati, and in some other places. The names of major jute mills, their locations and relevant statistics are shown in the Table 10.2

The jute industry is passing through tough phase, due to manufacturing problems from plant operation to market outlets. In case where components are produced in the SSI sector, the quality aspect is very often ignored. The inadequate availability of good quality jute had also been stated to be a glaring problem for this industry. This is mainly due to the inclusion of main jute growing belt in the erstwhile East Pakistan (now Bangladesh). The effort of Jute Research Institute and other related institutions, however, has been improving the situation recently.

Table 10.2: Major Jute Industries in 24-Parganas

Name	Location	Product Mix	Annual Installed Capacity	Production (Tonnes per Annum)
Agarpara Jute Co.	Kamarhati	Jute goods	26,055 tonnes	22,748
Anglo Indian Jute Mills Ltd.	Jagatdal	-do-	50,448 tonnes	43,281
Auckland Jute Co.	Shyamnagar	-do-	25,920 tonnes	10,928
Cheviot Co.	Budge Budge	Gunny	714 Looms	19,283
Kelvin Jute Co.	Titagarh	Jute goods	823 Looms	27,783
Reliance Jute Industries	Bhat Para	-do-	873 Looms	36,000
Hukumchand Jute Mills	Naihati	-do-	140 Broad looms 1356 Narrow looms	—

Source: Industrial Survey on 24-Paraganas; West Bengal Consultancy Organisation Ltd., Calcutta, 1983

The industry's profitability and returns to capital have also been declining owing to the significant escalation in the wages of jute mills workers which increased by 700 per cent between 1960 and 1982 as against 225 per cent in the prices of finished goods. The liquidity of the industry has also been eroded due to the continuous over-prodction which seriously effect the price structure.

Cotton Industry.

Moist climate of riverine region, availability of cheap labour and close proximity to the market centre have caused the cotton industry to grow in the district of 24-Parganas. It has been revealed that the district accommodated as much as 104 units at different stages of the production system which gave employment to around 25,000 persons. The following Table 10.3 emanates the district's importance in cotton industry vis-a-vis in other places of concentration in the state.

Table 10.3: Number of Cotton Industry in 24-Parganas and Other Places of Concentration

Industry	24-Parganas		Howrah		Hooghly		West Bengal	
	No. of Unit	Emp-loyment	No.of Unit	Empl-oyent	No.of Unit	Empl-oyment	Unit	Empl-oyment
Cotton ginning and Baling	1	4	3	33	—	—	4	37
Spinning and Weaving	20	21446	7	8732	9	10137	43	43798
Dyeing cloth and Yarn	7	229	3	17	—	—	11	446
Printing of Cloth and Yarn	1	NA	—	—	—	—	1	NA
Weaving of cotton textile in power	49	414	36	123	3	NA	115	1482
Finishing of Cotton	9	N.A.	3	NA	—	—	16	NA

Source: Review on Industry; Govt. of West Bengal, Calcutta; 1982

N.A.= Not available

Of the different units of this industry, mention may be made of Kesoram Cotton Mills, Hada Textile Industries Corporation, Eastern Spinning Mills, Maharaja Shree Umaid Mills and Basanti Cotton Mills. Availability of raw materials, viz. raw cotton, at competitive prices had been stated to be the cause of main hurdle in the operation way of cotton industry. The following Table 10.4 is the illustrative for these units.

Textile Industry

Textile industry's woes lie in the market outlet. At present, the qualitative deterioration in the pattern of production, occurring as it did in combination with increase in costs and prices, has not been confined to the domestic market. A number of units have been set up in the district to manufacture the machineries of textile industry. Of them the most important unit is TEXMACO which employs more than eight thousand persons in the production system.

Table 10.4: Status of Major Units in Cotton Industry

Name	Location	Product Mix	Annual Installed Capacity	Production/ Annum
Basanti Cotton Mills	Panihati	Cloth Yarn	356 Looms 22,480 Spindles	93 mt. 7 kg.
Hada Textile Industries Corporation	Bishnupur	Yarn	28572 Spindles	26.5 Kg.
Eastern Spinning Mills	Piragachia	Cloth	25,248 Spindles	—
Maharaja Sri Umaid Mills	Shyamnagar	Cloth	1028 Looms 66,740 Spindles	14.7 mt. 133kg.
Kesoram Cotton Mills	Garden Reach	Cloth	—	660mt.

Source: Survey on Cotton Industry, Govt. of West Bengal 1982; and Industrial Survey on 24-Parganas: W.B.C.O. Ltd, Calcutta 1983

Paper Industry

The paper industry has made its head way in the district of 24-Parganas, especially in its traditional industrial belt of Titagarh, Barrackpore, Kankinara. Importance of the district in the field of paper and paper based industries may be apprehended in the following Table 10.5.

The Table 10.5 shows that the paper economy of West Bengal has been localised much in the jurisdiction of 24-Parganas. Titagarh Paper Mill Co. Ltd. is, by far, the most important industry in this region. It has three units of which two are in West Bengal and the rest is in the state of Orissa. During 1986-87, 1987-88, 1988-89 the Titagarh Paper Mills Co. Ltd. has produced 30,205 mt., 27096mt. and 25944 mt. paper respectively. The downward trend in the production of paper has been stated to be due to the shortage of power and coal and the adverse industrial relation. Availability of

Table 10.5: Paper Industry in 24-Parganas and West Bengal

Industry	No of Units		Employment	
	24 PGS	W.B.	24 PGS	W.B.
Manufacture of paper	4	7	7001	11,279
Manufacture of packaging paper (Machine made)	9	13	238	746
Peper board & straw board (Machine made)	24	29	2177	2,821
Paper bag	2	2	104	104
Other paper & paper based articles	15	15	260	286

Source: Survey on Paper Industry, Govt. of West Bengal, Calcutta, 1983

raw materials has been revealed to be the main problem that is eroding the future prospect of paper industry in the country in general and the district of 24-Parganas in particular. Along with the growing problem of raw material availabilities, shortage of power supply, dearth of investment fund, obsoletion of existing machineries flow in water management and the like factors have also put blockade in the growth path of paper industry.

Modern Industry

Engineering Industry

At the core of industrial development of the district, however, the engineering industry had played an important role. The total number of units operating at wide spectrum (engineering industry) had been revealed to be as much as 1171 which provide employment to a large number of persons. The following Table 10.6 represents the important industrial houses in the district.

The Industrial climate in the engineering sector of the district resembles that of the country as a whole which suffers acutely from the recessionary demand, obsolete technology, power deficiency financial constraint and labour unrest.

Pharmaceutical and Chemical Industry

With the establishment of Bengal Chemicals and

Table 10.6 : Important Engineering Units in 24-Parganas and Relevant Satistics

Name	Location	Product Mix	Installed Capacity	Production
TEXMACO	Belghoria Agarpara	Ring frames Doublers and worsted ring frames	900 hos	528 hos
	Sodepur	Wagons	60,000 tonnes	23058 tonnes
Jessop & Co.	Dum Dum	Cranes	7,000 tonnes	3106 tonnes
Hindustan Wires	Sodepur	Steel wares/ Standard wires	71,000 tonnes	19716 tonnes
Bharat Electrical Steel Co.	Baruipur	Binders & additives	1,200 tonnes	60 tonnes

Source: Industrial Survey on 24-Pargana; W.B.C.O. Ltd. Calcutta, 1983

Pharmaceutical works at the advent of the country, this industry had marked its beginning in the district of 24-Parganas. The developed industrial and scientific culture prevalent in and around Calcutta during the first half of the present century and the availability of skilled labour had mainly contributed at the core of its development. At present, a large number of Chemical and Pharmaceutical units, both in medium and small scale sectors have sprung up in the district.

The problems for setting up chemical units in the district were too many and they differed from industry to industry. However, many units complained of problems in getting raw materials, which had to be brought all the way from Western India as local sources were either absent or the supply is irregular. The pharmaceutical industry has also made its head way in the district. Of the major units in this region, mention may be made of Bengal Immunity Company Ltd. and Reckitt and Coalman of India Ltd.

Reckitt and Coalman of India Ltd. having two factory units in 24-Parganas, viz. at Behala and Chetla, are currently engaged in manufacturing and marketing quality consumer and pharmaceutical products, including antiseptics, drugs, shoe and other polishes, cosmetics and food products, particulars of which are given in Table 10.7.

It may be noted that the factory at Behala is the largest

Table 10.7: Installed Capacity and Production Levels of Major Consumer-cum-Pharmaceutical Units

Item Manufactured	Installed Capacity	Actual Production 1980	1981
Liquid Antiseptic	2500 kl	1109 kl	949 kl
Mouth wash & Gargel	120 kl	5.9 kl	5.3 kl
All purpose ointment	30 mt.	12.6 mt.	12.0 mt.
Analgesic Tablets	60 mt.	122.2 mt.	100 mt.
Denture cleanser	36 mt.	5 mt.	1.6 mt.
Food Products	2088 mt.	705 mt.	790 mt.
Polishes and	1297 mt.	952 mt.	1110 mt.
Compositions	474 kl	136 kl	152 kl

Source: Industrial Survey on 24-Parganas; W.B.C.O. Ltd. Calcutta, 1983

producing almost all items except food products like barly which is manufactured at Chetla.

Eclectronic Industry

Insofar as the electronic industry is concerned, West Bengal has been lagging behind some states due to economic and strategic factors. The state government has recently allotted some 100 acres of land for setting up an Electronic Complex at Salt Lake, of which 40 acres will be reserved for private sector entrepreneurs. There is one Electronic test and development centre under the entrepreneurship of State Government which has been set up with the financial support of Govt. of India. Entreprenurs will do well to avail of facilities offered by ETDC at Belghoria.

Agro-based Industries

Due to the availability of raw materials in abundance several fruit and vegetable processing units have been set up in the district. Among the existing units mentioned may be made of Precious Food Industries, Madhyamgram; Jedy's Fruit Processing Co., Madhyamgram, Debpur (P) Ltd., Garia. It may be mentioned that the Kanois, pioneers in the Indian tea industry are diversifying into export based fruit processing unit. The new unit, called Masons Products Ltd. will be a medium size unit proposed to be set up at Bishnupur in 24-Parganas.

Duncan Agro Industries, Agarpara is engaged in the manufacture of cigarettes. It has an installed capacity of 7200 million numbers. The Sundarbans Development Board proposes to set up more than 5000 agro-processing units at various places in Sundarbans.

Conclusion

Economic development of a nation is mainly dependent on its industrial potentiality. It is to be noted that the co-existence of agricultural economy and developing industrial economy are the vital features of economic development of 24-Parganas (N&S). The district has varieties of industrial culture as the district is rich in natural and human resources. Indsutrial growth in the district exhibits a glorious path in the economy of the region. It is second only to Calcutta in magnitude and claims its superiority insofar as the growth quality is taken under purview. The district's industrial performance lags slightly behind the industrial process in Calcutta in general. Certain northern pockets of 24-Parganas demonstrate higher growth rate and brighter future prospect than the industrial heart of Calcutta. This apparent controversey might be enrooted in the lop-sided development of the intra-regional set ups of the district. The contour analysis (Fig. 10.2) may be helpful in analysing the spatial aspects of industrial development in 24-Parganas.

The salient features of spatial industrial development as observed (Fig. 10.2) may be highlighted as follows:

(a) Face contour extending 12.5 km from Calcutta in either side encompasses as much as 60 per cent of total SSI units in the district. This contour covers Dum Dum, Rajarhat, Baranagar, Belgharia and Baguihati in the north and Jadavpur, Garia, Kasba, Behala and Mahestala in the south.

(b) The prospective contour which is located within the kilometers of 12.5 to 25 km from Calcutta accommodates nearly 20 per cent of the total units in the district. This includes Kamarhati, Panihati, Barrackpore, Barasat in the north, and Budge Budge, Amtala, Baruipur, Sonarpur, Narendrapur and Batanagar in the south.

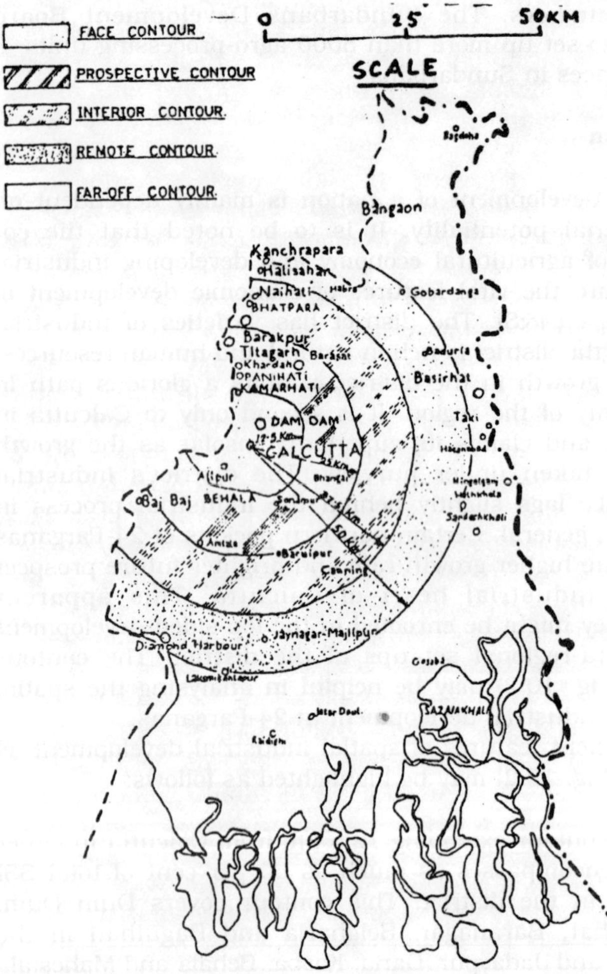

FIG. 10.2: 24-Parganas (North & South) Contour Analysis of Industrial Development

(c) The other three contours, namely, interior contour (within 25 to 37.5 km), remote contour (within 37.5 to 50 km) and far-off contour (from 50 km and above), accommodate only 20 per cent of the total industires in the district.

It should be noted that the above contour analysis has a typical flow as the latter contours of the system do not accommodate regions of equal industrial status. This is mainly because of the fact that after a certain extent, the development process does not follow a circular or semi-circular path. A horizontal path of development is generally seen in the spatial process of industrialization. The diagramatic display of Fig 10.3 shows that the most industrialized zone of the district stretches due north through Barrackpore and Naihati. It now crosses the district boundary at Halisahar to extend

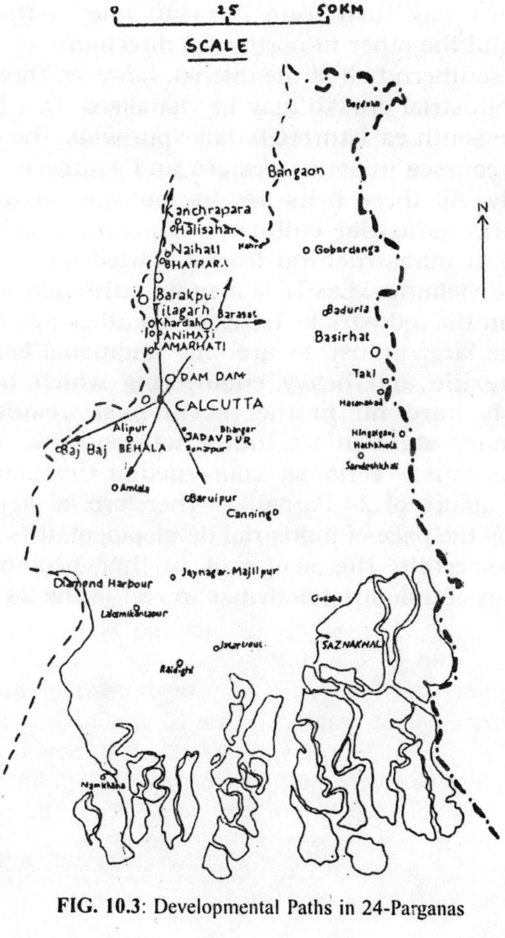

FIG. 10.3: Developmental Paths in 24-Parganas

further into the district of Nadia. It should be noted that this is the oldest industrial belt in the suburban of Calcutta. But, due to the unplanned nature of developmental activities, congestion and the like evils of industrialisation is a fact of life in this belt. In fact, saturation, though at sub-optimal level, has already been reached in this industiral tract of the district.

Another developmental path is seen to run in the north east direction through Rajarhat ad Barasat. At present, it is very prospective belt in the northern part of the district where a number of new industries are coming up due to good transport linkage with Calcutta and the availability of cheap industrial land and other allied facilities. This path has now adopted two way turn from Barasat: one in the eastern direction and the other in north-east direction.

In the southern half of the district, however, three distinct paths of industrial growth may be visualised. One is seen to extend due south east through Jadavpur while the other two take their courses in south-western and southern directions respectively. All these belts are the outcome of the spread effect of the industrial culture of Calcutta which (due to bottleneck in infrastructural fronts) started diffusing in the prospective vicinities. Lastly it may be attributed to the fact that even in the industrially developed northern 24-Parganas, most of the large industries are only traditional being based on jute, textile and heavy engineering which have been particularly hard hit in the recent past, resulting in a depressionary state in its industrial economy. The state government is now seriously concerned at this poor state of industrial affairs of 24-Parganas. Therefore, a step towards accelerating the pace of industrial development, it is an urgent task to ascertain the scope of further promotion and proliferation of industrial activities in rest of the 24-Parganas (N&S).

ELEVEN

Spatio-Temporal Dimensions of Industrialisation: A Case Study of Madhya Pradesh

S.K. SHUKLA and ROLEE SHANKER

The purpose of the present study is to study the development of industries, to identify the areas of temporal change, to analyse the spatial pattern of industries, to analyse the determinants of the continuing concentration and consequent industrial congestion in a few areas.

Madhya Pradesh lies mainly on the table land of Central India. It is the largest state in area in the country with 13.5 per cent (4,43,446 sq. km.) of the country's total land, and is the 6th most populous state with 7.6 per cent (52, 178, 844) of the country's people.

The State of Madhya Pradesh was created on 1 November 1956, out of the former States of Madhya Bharat, Vindhya Pradesh, Bhopal and 14 Mahakoshal districts of old Madhya Pradesh. Administratively the state is divided into 11 commissioners divisions and 45 districts. Madhya Pradesh is one of the few states which have rich forest resources. 21 per cent of the country's area under forests lies in the territories of Madhya Pradesh and 32 per cent of the state's total area is covered with forests, mainly of teak, sal and mixed deciduous trees.

Madhya Pradesh is rich in resource potential, but much of its potential is still unexploited. It ranks 3rd in the country's mineral production; 30 different types of minerals are found in the state. Among them are diamond, coal, iron ore, limestone, rock phosphate, dolomite, bauxite and manganese. In the year 1979, Madhya Pradesh contributed 15 per cent of the value of the principal minerals produced in the country. Again, it ranks 2nd in mineral reserves with 26 per cent next to Bihar. It is the largest producer of diamond, dolomite and limestone and the 2nd largest producer of coal and bauxite (after Bihar), iron ore and rock phosphate (after Rajasthan).

Table 11.1: Mineral Production: State's Share in India

Minerals	Per cent
Coal	22.3
Manganese Ore	16.0
Iron Ore	24.7
Bauxite	23.1
Limestone	23.2
Dolomite	44.6
Fire clay	12.4
Diamond	100.0

Source: Task Force Report on Nucleus Industiral Complexes in District Morena (M.P.), March 1983.

Madhya Pradesh is not only rich in minerals and forests but has 13 per cent of the country's net sown area. The state is an important producer of wheat, jowar, pulses and oil seeds. It produces 9.6 per cent of the country's foodgrains and 8.5 per cent of the cereals.

It is important to note that despite 81.3 per cent (1971) of the total work-force of Madhya Pradesh being engaged in agriculture and its allied activities, its share in the state's total income is only 47.2 per cent. On the other hand, with 8 per cent of the total work-force of the state being engaged in Mining, Manufacturing and Construction, this sector alone contributes 26.1 per cent to the total income of the state.

In spite of the availability of a large variety of industrial raw materials in different parts of the state, still Madhya Pradesh is not considered an industrially developed state of the country like Punjab, Maharashtra, Haryana and Tamil Nadu. Unfortunately, 70 per cent of the state's large and medium scale units are concentrated in 9 districts, while 13 districts of the state have no industry though they are rich in resource potential.

It has been observed that the industries are not only spatially concentrated in the 9 districts but are even temporally concentrated. At the time of the reformation of the states (in 1956) there were 44 large and medium units in Madhya Pradesh, but during the Planwise Development of the state, their number rose to 249 units in 1983. Out of these 148 (60%) units were set up during the fourth (36 units), fifth (42 units) and sixth (70 units) Plans.

Discussing the vast potentialities of the state, the major industries can broadly be classified into the following categories:

1. Mineral-based Industries
2. Forest-based Industries
3. Chemical and allied Industries
4. Agro-based Industries
5. Textiles
6. Animal-based Industries
7. Diamond-based Industries

In 1896, the first unit was set up in the state at Rajnandgaon for the production of cotton cloth and cotton yarn, and with the erection of this industiral unit the industrial era dawned in the state. Since then a number of industrial units have been established, and mainly been producing cotton cloth and yarn, straw and paper-boards, craft paper and vegetabe oil. At the time of the reorganisation of the state, there were 44 large and medium scale units and 84.1 per cent of them were concentrated in the 9 districts. Even after 28 years of planned development 69.5 per cent of the total number of units are concentrated in the same areas. These locations to a greater extent have been influenced by the availability of raw materials. Most of the large and medium scale units in the State have either been raw-material-oriented (Bhilai, Nepanagar or Korba) or demand (market) oriented or somewhere between the two depending upon the availability of the transport facilities to determine the cost of production. The analysis of industrial location in the State indicates that most of the units have developed either in areas of raw materials with developed transport facilities or in market areas where the demand and developed infrastructure have helped to determine the location of industries on the basis of the cost factor. Within the State, the flow of basic raw materials at certain points has been aggregated to develop those points as industrial complexes or industrial hubs. In these areas of the State, the manifold usage of various raw materials decides the complexity of the industrial landscape. The erection of the Bhilai Steel Plant at Bhilai, the Bharat Aluminium Plant at Korba and the Bharat Heavy Electricals at Bhopal indicates the existence of major well planned industrial centres which are also varying in size, character and function.

Temporal Growth of Industries

The analysis of industrial data indicates that the spatio-temporal growth of industries in the State is uneven. At the time of the reorganisation of the States, Madhya Pradesh had only 44 large and medium units. To undertake the temporal analysis, industries established in 1901 have also been included, and to study the temporal growth of industries, the duration of 84 years has been divided into the Pre-Independence Period (1901-1947) and the Post-Independence Period (1948-1984).

In the Pre-Independence Period, 44 large and medium units were established. But these were spatially and temporally concentrated.

The Post-Independence Period is further classifed according to Plans:

1. Pre-Plan Period (1948-1950)
2. First Plan Period (1951-1955)
3. Second Plan Period (1956-1960)
4. Third Plan Period (1961-1965)
5. Annual Plans (1966-1969)
6. Fourth Plan Period (1970-1974)
7. Fifth Plan Period (1975-1979)
8. Sixth Plan Period (1980-1984)

Pre-Independence Period (1901-1947)

Before 1901, there was just one medium scale unit in the State, which had been established in 1896 at Rajnandgaon with an investment of Rs. 143 lakh, and it provided employment to about 4800 persons. The industry was engaged in the production of cotton cloth. The second unit was set up at Burhanpur (Khandwa) in 1906-1907 to produce cotton cloth and yarn to meet the increasing demand. The first cement unit in the State was set up in 1913 at Katni to utilise the locally available limestone deposits and to meet the needs of the construction works. (Fig. 11.1)

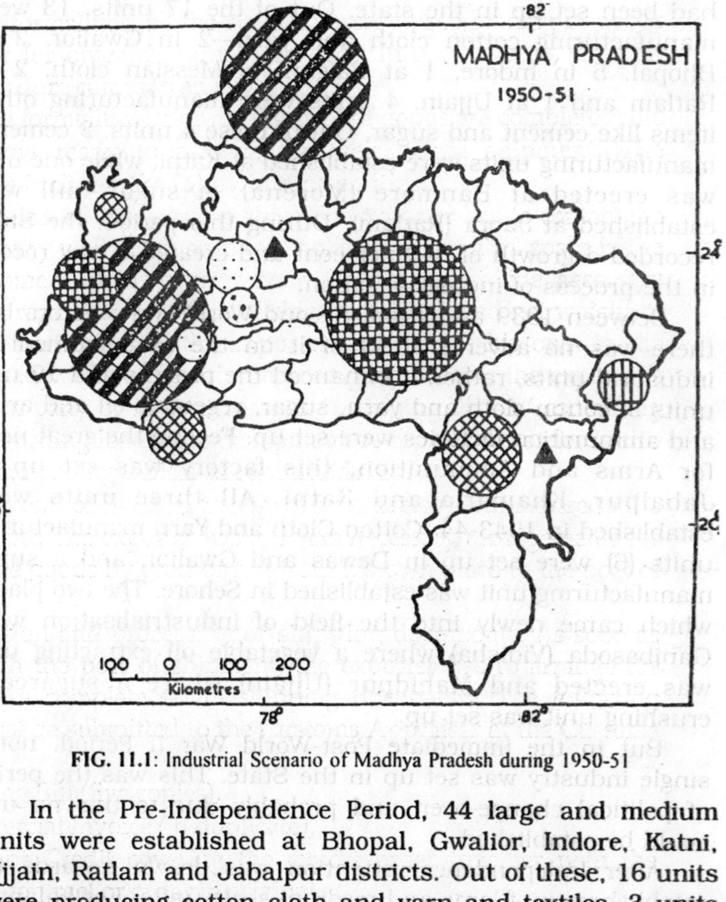

FIG. 11.1: Industrial Scenario of Madhya Pradesh during 1950-51

In the Pre-Independence Period, 44 large and medium units were established at Bhopal, Gwalior, Indore, Katni, Ujjain, Ratlam and Jabalpur districts. Out of these, 16 units were producing cotton cloth and yarn and textiles, 3 units were producing cement and 5 units were engaged in sugar production. The remaining 20 industrial units established were the craft paper, vegetable oil, textile machinery, ammunition and telegraph and telephone components units.

Between 1914 and 1918, because of the outbreak of World War I, only one unit could be established for the production of cotton cloth. The investment in this unit was Rs. 762 lakh and it provided employment to about 500 people.

Due to the problems of short supply and transport during the war, the demand of goods increased in the Post-World War I Period and by 1938, 17 new large and medium units had been set up in the state. Out of the 17 units, 13 were manufacturing cotton cloth and yarn—2 in Gwalior, 2 at Bhopal, 5 in Indore, 1 at Rajgarh of Messian cloth, 2 at Ratlam and 1 at Ujjain. 4 units were manufacturing other items like cement and sugar. Out of these 4 units, 2 cement-manufacturing units were established at Katni, while one unit was erected at Banmore (Morena). A sugar mill was established at Jaora (Ratlam). During this period, the State recorded a growth of 340 per cent and created a new record in the process of industrialisation.

Between 1939 and 1945, Second World War was on, but there was no adverse affect of it on the establishment of industiral units, rather, it enhanced the process and 12 new units of cotton cloth and yarn, sugar, vegetable oil and arms and ammunition factories were set up. Feeling the great need for Arms and Ammunition, this factory was set up at Jabalpur, Khamaria and Katni. All three units were established in 1943-44. Cotton Cloth and Yarn manufacturing units (6) were set up in Dewas and Gwalior, and a sugar manufacturing unit was established in Sehore. The two places which came newly into the field of industrialisation were Ganjbasoda (Vidisha) where a vegetable oil extracting unit was erected and Mahidpur (Ujjain) where a sugarcane crushing unit was set up.

But in the immediate Post-World War II Period, not a single industry was set up in the State. This was the period of political change-over, and probably due to this no unit could be established.

After Independence, attention was drawn towards the establishment of large and medium scale units. For balanced development and for minimising the gap between the developed and backward areas, Five-Years Plans were initiated.

Post-Independence Period (1948-1984)

After Independence, the Government of India paid special

attention to the all-round development of the country. India is an agricultural country and, in order to raise the per capita production, scientific means were to be adopted. For this too, industries were to be established considering the multi-sectoral demands and resource exploitation. To achieve balanced regional development, the Government of India, on the recommendation of the Planning Commission, initiated a development process under Five-Year Plans with fixed targets and definite objectives. To evaluate the achievements, the state governments were also advised to follow the recommendations suggested by the Planning Commission for their respective states.

Pre-Plan Period (1948-1950)

During this period 7 units were established, 2 units were erected in Indore, 1 unit each of vanaspati and flates, rounds. Together they accounted for Rs. 246 lakhs of investment and gave employment to 470 people. During this period, a fireclay brick manufacturing unit was established at Niwar (Jabalpur) in 1950-51. A vanaspati extraction unit, with Rs. 57.74 lakh investment was erected at Khandwa and it provided employment to 436 persons. An Art silk cloth manufacturing unit was set up in Gwalior (Rs. 548 lakh investment and 1650 workers). Dalauda (Mandsaur) had sugar manufacturing unit. Rs. 147.84 lakh was invested in the unit and 600 people were employed. A MS Bar rods and angles unit was established in 1947-48 at Bangrod (Ratlam) which employed about 1700 people. The aforesaid 7 units had investment of Rs. 1024.58 lakh and employed 5206 persons.

First Plan Period (1951-1955)

During the first Plan period, only 3 large and medium units—Biscuit Confectionery at Gwalior, Straw Board at Ratlam and Silk Manufacturing at Nagda, were established with an investment of Rs. 1409 lakhs and provided employment to 5787 persons. The Biscuit and Confectionery making unit was the first of its kind. Till then textiles, sugar and cement were, the main items being manufactured in the State (Fig. 11.2).

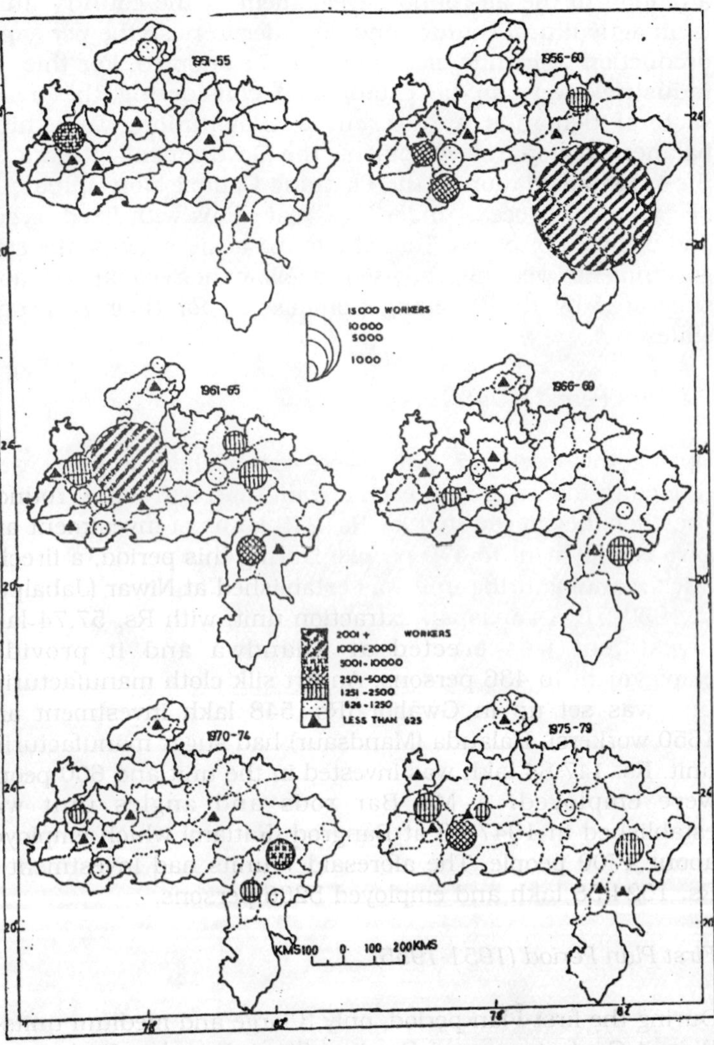

FIG. 11.2: Madhya Pradesh: Industrial Growth

Second Plan Period (1956-1960)

The Second Plan Period made important strides in the field of industrial development. Three important units— BHEL, Bhilai Steel Plant and the Newsprint factory at Nepanagar were erected due to which the investment grew.

During the Second Plan, 10 large and medium units were established. The main industrial unit which was set up was a Steel Plant at Bhilai. The BHEL at Bhopal established in 1960 was also a large scale unit with an investment of Rs. 8906 lakhs and provided employment for 19298 persons. Wheat Products (Bhopal), Deoiled Cakes (Dewas), Cotton Yarn (Indore) and Newsprint (Nepanagar-Khandwa) were the other units established during the Second Plan period. The first unit of the Satna District was of steel castings, established in 1958, and the next one erected there was a cement unit in 1959. A staple and synthetic yarn manufacturing unit was set up at Birlagram (Ujjain).

Third Plan Period (1961-1965)

During this plan period 28 units were established and accounted for Rs. 8439.66 lakhs and provided employment to 17752 persons. They recorded an increase of 51.8 per cent in the number of units and 10.1 per cent in employment over the second plan. Out of these, 12 units were established at Bhopal (3), Dewas (3) and Durg (6) already known as the centres of maximum industrial concentration. Units producing valves for Combustion Engines, Densified Wood and Glass Fibre and Oxygen, Nitrogen and Acetylene were erected at Bhopal and were the first of their types in the State. Three units were established at Dewas in 1962 for the production of Automobile Gears, Power-Driven Pumps and Cast Iron Castings. At the same time Oxygen, and Acetylene, Chemicals and Steel casting units were set up at Kumhari (Durg). A CI Casting and Machine Spares Equipment Manufacturing unit was also set up at Durg. Portland Cement Manufacturing Unit of the State was started in 1964-65 at Jamul (Durg).

The remaining 8 units were established at Gwalior, Itarsi (Hoshangabad), Khandwa, Raipur, Ratlam, Sehore, Satna and Khargone. Vicky Moped, an important transport industry, was set up at Gwalior in 1964-65. Particle Board was the first unit to be set up at Itarsi in the Hosangabad district. Cotton Yarn and Steel Casting Units were set up at Indore. Fireclay Bricks and Refractory Material Units were established at Jabalpur. Cotton Yarn manufacturing units were established at Khandwa (1) and Sanawad (1, Khargone). The first industrial unit producing Arc Welding Electrodes was erected at the Raipur district in 1962. A Denatured spirt and alcohol manufacturing unit was started at Ratlam. The other units established during this period were Power Cables at Satna, Chemicals, Writing and Printing Paper at Sohagpur (Shahdol) and Nutrition Products, Cotton Textile and Equipment for Rayon Pulp in Ujjain District.

Annual Plans (1966-1969)

During these three Annual Plans, 19 Units were established at Lalkhadon (Bilaspur), Sawar (Indore), Mahasamud (Raipur) and started producing cotton, synthetic and staple yarn, wheat products and rice bran oil respectively. With the erection of these units, three new places were added on the industrial map of the State.

The remaining 16 units were set up at the existing industrial centres like Bhopal, Bilaspur, Bhilai, Gwalior, Indore, Jabalpur, Ujjain and Vidisha. These units related to steel forging, pesticides formulation, solvent extraction conductors, currency paper, tungsten filament, woolen yarn, gelatine, wagon repair workshop, straw/grey board and cast iron pipes. During this period Rs. 4532.12 lakhs were invested and 6999 persons were employed. The period recorded an increase of 23.2 per cent in the number of units and 3.6 per cent in employment. The difference in the growth of units and employment was mainly because medium scale units were erected during this period which employed fewer people.

Fourth Plan (1970-1974)

There was a tremendous growth of large and medium scale units during the fourth plan period, 36 units were set up during this period and a resultant growth of 35.6 per cent was recorded. Three-fourths of the units established during this plan period were added to the existing Industiral complexes like Bhopal (2), Dewas (4), Gwalior (3), Indore (6), Jablapur (2), Raipur (5) and Ratlam (2), the Beer manufacturing unit established at Bhopal in 1971-72 was the first of its kind in the State. Bharat Aluminium Company, the largest public sector enterprise was established in 1973 at Korba with an investment of Rs. 32000 lakhs and provided employment to about 6000 persons.

The 3 units set up at Dewas in 1974 were of currency printing, crown wheel and vegetable oil. In 1971-72, a unit of Ferrous Forge Components was erected at Durg. Manufacturing of all types of steel wires was started in the Bhilai Steel Plant under the expansion plan from 1973. The other industries established in Durg were of Rice Bran Oil, Synthetic Resins and Carbon and Alloy Steel Castings. Gwalior started manufacturing of Oxygen, Maida, Sooji and Transformers during this period. A wooden furniture manufacturing unit was started at Hoshangabad. The 5 units established at Indore were of Plastic products, steel tubes and pipes, barrels, steel billet, chemicals and beer. A unit for manufacturing Transmission tower and line parts was started at Deori (Jabalpur). MS Ingots was another unit established during this period in Jabalpur. A sugar manufacturing unit was set up at Banmore (Morena) in 1971-72.

Portland Cement, Steel Ingots, Jute Twine, Rice bran oil, Soya seed oil and sal seed oil was started being manufactured in Raipur district during the fourth plan. Chemicals and Vitamins at Ratlam, Steel Ingots at Shajapur and Grey Cloth at Ujjain were the other products started being manufactured during this period.

Rs. 57178.47 lakhs was invested in the 36 units, and 16939 people were employed by these units.

Fifth Plan (1975-1979)

The growth rate during this period was 30.6 per cent. Forty two industrial units were established with an investment of Rs. 11066.67 lakhs and provided employment to 12063 persons. Of the 42 units, 19 units (45.2%) were erected in Dewas. Of these, 8 units were manufacturing synthetic fabres, readymade garments, leather garments, Art silk fabrics and Non-worsted Yarn. Four units were at Bhopal producing Copper conductor strips, Dry cell batteries, Pesticides and Oxygen. A Bread and Vegetable oil extraction unit was set up at Indore. Alkaloid and high Alloy units were set up at Neemuch and Mandsaur respectively. The first large scale unit of Raisen District was established at Mandideep in 1977 with an investment of Rs. 2133.55 lakhs and provided employment to 892 persons. This unit is producing Graphite Electrodes, Nipples and Anodes. A Motor/transformer lamination unit was set up at Rewa, the first industry of this district.

Sixth Plan (1980-1984)

The number of industries steadily grew during the plan periods. Their number rose to 70 during the Sixth Plan. The growth rate during the Plan, was 39.1 per cent. Jagdalpur, Betul, Akaltara (Bilaspur), Narsingarh (Damoh), Barlai, Mangliya and Chanda (Indore), Nayagaon (Mandsaur), Goharganj and Salamatpur (Raisen), Sagar, Maihar (Satna), Bundi and Pachama (Sehore), Sapkheda and Maksi (Shajapur) and Waidhan (Sidhi) were the new places where the industrial units were erected. On the other hand, the existing industrial centres like Bilaspur (3), Dewas (15), Dhar (3), Bhilai (3), Indore (3), Banmore-Morena (5), Raipur (3), Rewa (2) and Ujjain (1) also recorded continuous growth.

Reviewing the growth of industries, according to Table 11.2 in the Pre-Independence Era and the Post-Independence Era, one can confidently say that the number of industries continuously rose during the Five-Year Plans. This indicates that during the fourth, fifth and sixth plans greater attempts were made to accentuate the process of industrialisation in the State and to maintain the increasing trend.

The growth of the industrial units was highest (340%) between 1919-1938 in the Post-World War I period. This was probably because the industries could not be established during the War. But the demand grew and in order to fulfil this growing demand of the people, a number of industries had to be set up after the war. The industrial investment recorded an increase of 300 per cent while the increase in employment was only 240 per cent.

During the Second Plan Period (1956-1960), the investment growth was highest and recorded an increase of 720 per cent. Three large scale public sector units Bharat Heavy Electricals, Steel Plant and Newsprint Paper Manufacturing units were established at Bhopal, Bhilai (Durg) and Nepanagar (Khandwa) respectively. As these units were based on modern scientific technology, the employment position did not improve significantly.

Table 11.2: M.P.: Spatio-Temporal Distributions of Industrial Units

Districts	Pre-Independence period till 1947	Pre-Plan period 1948-1950	First Plan period 1951-1955	Second Plan period 1956-1960	Third Plan period 1961-1966	Annual Plan period 1966-1969	Fourth Plan period 1970-1974	Fifth Plan period 1975-1979	Sixth Plan period 1980-1984	Total
Dewas	1	—	—	1	3	—	4	19	16	43
Indore	6	2	—	1	2	5	6	2	6	30
Bhopal	2	—	—	2	3	2	2	4	1	16
Jabalpur	8	1	—	—	2	1	2	2	—	16
Raipur	—	—	—	—	1	3	5	3	3	16
Durg	—	—	—	2	5	1	4	—	3	15
Ujjain	3	—	1	1	3	1	2	1	1	13
Ratlam	4	—	1	—	1	—	2	2	2	12
Gwalior	4	1	1	—	1	1	3	1	—	12
Bilaspur	—	—	—	—	—	2	2	2	3	9
Morena	1	—	—	—	—	—	1	1	5	8
Khandwa	1	1	—	1	1	1	1	—	—	6
Mandsaur	2	—	—	—	—	—	—	2	2	6
Hosangabad	—	—	—	—	1	1	1	1	1	5
Sehore	1	—	—	—	1	—	—	—	3	5
Shajapur	—	—	—	—	—	—	1	—	4	5
Others	3	—	—	2	4	1	—	2	20	32
M.P.	36	5	3	10	28	19	36	42	70	249

Source: Directory of Existing Medium/Large Units of Madhya Pradesh (as on 31.3.83) Audyogik Vikas Nigam, Bhopal.

Except for the major breaks, one during the Pre-Independence Period and the other in the Post-Independence Period, a uniform upward trend is noticeable in the growth of industiral units, investment and employment in the state.

Spatial Distribution of Large/Medium Units in Madhya Pradesh

The spatial distribution of industrial units in the State is very uneven. This can be confirmed by the very fact that 69.5 per cent of the large and medium units are concentrated only in a few districts, that is, Indore, Dewas, Gwalior, Ujjain, Durg, Bhopal, Raipur and Jabalpur. Considering the industrial imbalances and in order to achieve the balanced development, a planned development was initiated. As per the strategy, the districts of the State were divided into Advanced and Backward Districts. The former consists of Bhopal, Durg, Gwalior, Indore and Jabalpur. Looking to the large number of backward districts and the varying degree of backwardness, the Backward districts were further divided into category 'A', category 'B' and category'C'.

The industrially developed districts— Bohpal, Durg, Gwalior, Indore and Jabalpur, account for about 54.6 per cent (136 units) of the total number of units. Five districts which are included in category 'A' of the Backward class — Bilaspur, Dewas, Raipur, Ratlam and Ujjain have 54 units (21.7%). Thus we can say that more than three-fourth (76.3%) of the industries are concentrated in the eleven districts of the State. On the other hand, 13 districts, i.e. Balaghat, Chhindwara, Mandla, Surguja, Narsinghpur, Panna, Chhattarpur, Tikamgarh, Bhind, Datia, Shivpuri, Guna and Jhabua are among the no industry districts.

Looking to the wide spatial variation, the districts can be divided into different categories according to the number of industries:

1. Districts of Conspicuously High Concentration
2. Districts of High Concentration
3. Districts of Medium Concentration
4. Districts of Low Concentration
5. No Industry Districts.

Districts of Conspicuously High Concentration

Dewas with 43 units has the largest concentration of industries. It accounts for about 17.6 per cent of the total number of units in the State. Though the process of industrialisation started as early as 1941 with the establishment of a cotton cloth and yarn unit but in more than three decades (upto 1975) only 8 units were added in the district. The process of industrialisation accelerated during the fifth and the sixth plans when 14 and 20 units were established in the district.The concentration of the units in the Dewas district was due to the increasing congestion at Indore while Dewas being just about 40 km away from Indore also has an advantage of its location on National Highway No.3—Bombay-Agra. Besides, nearness to the Indore, since Dewas has been included in the 'A' category of Backward districts in the State has been provided special concessions and facilities. Due to these facts private enterpreneurs started establishing their units at Dewas.

Most of these units are basically infrastructure and market oriented and cover a wide range of products — from cotton cloth and yarn, tractor to engineering items.

Districts of High Concentration

Indore ranks next to Dewas and has 30 units. Unlike Dewas, the development of industries in the Indore district was continuous since the Independence of the country. The growth of industries was steady and from amongst the Princely States in India, Holkar state (Indore) was one of the most progressive and adaptable in administration.

On the eve of Independence Indore had only 6 units while the remaining 24 units have been added during various plans. Except for the First Plan period (1951-55) when no large and medium scale unit was erected in the district the growth was continuous. About 1/3 of the units of the Indore district are engaged in producing cotton cloth, yarn and synthetic cloth the remaining 21 units manufacture a wide variety of goods i.e. soft drinks, steel casting, wheat products, plastic products etc.

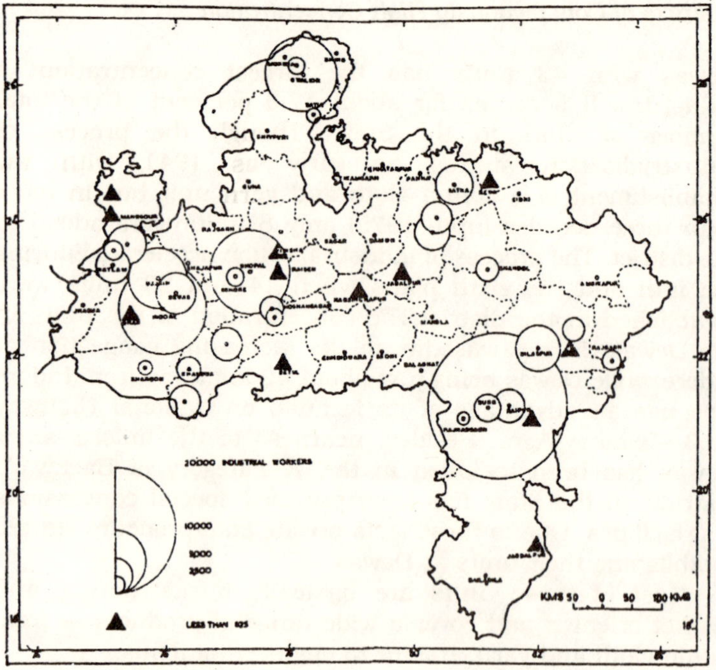

Fig. 11.3: Madhya Pradesh Industrial Centre

Districts of Medium Concentration

Bhopal, Jabalpur, Raipur, Durg, Ujjain, Ratlam, Gwalior, Bilaspur, Morena, Khandwa and Mandsaur are the districts which have medium concentration. The upper limit of this group is 19 units and the lower limit is 6 units. Jabalpur, Raipur and Bhopal districts with 16 units each belong to the upper limit of the category. As Table 11.2 shows, Jablapur has a different trend of growth from Raipur and Bhopal. In Jabalpur district 9 units were established before 1956 and just 7 have been set up after the reogranisation of the State. On the other hand, there was no unit in Raipur, and there were only 2 in Bhopal, before 1956. BHEL is the major large scale unit of Bhopal erected in 1960. Oil solvents, steel and cement are the main items being manufactured in Raipur. This infrastructure has been developed alongwith the establishment of Steel Plant in Bhilai (Durg) in 1959. Jabalpur has two large defence units which have made it an important industrial centre of Madhya Pradesh.

Durg, having 15 large and medium units, ranks 6th in the State. Bhilai Steel Plant was set up in collaboration with the Russians in 1959 with an investment of Rs. 60057.47 lakhs and provided employment to 63291 persons. A number of industries are manufacturing items like different types of steel wire, cast iron castings and cement, which are needed in this huge establishment.

Ujjain (13 units), Ratlam (12 units) and Gwalior (12 units) mainly manufacture cotton cloth and yarn. Ujjain and Gwalior have been developed from very early times due to the patronage given by the rulers like Holkars and the Scindias respectively.

Bilaspur (6 units), Morena (8 units), Khandwa (6 units) and Mandsaur (6 units) belong to the lower group of the category. Bilaspur and Morena are the developing districts, where 9 and 7 industries have been established after the third plan. Bilaspur has rich deposits of limestone and bauxite, and most of the units erected here are resource-based. Bharat Aluminium Company erected in Korba in 1973 is an important large-scale public sector unit of the district. Two Cement units were also established in 1981 and 1982. In Morena district, Banmore is an important town where all the 7 units of the district are located. After 1922-23, the next unit in the district was established as late as in 1971-72. Since then the growth has been continuous. A wide range of industries are found here — Sugar, Barley Malt, Filter Papers, Oxygen, Iron Castings and Steel Ingots and other products.

Districts of Low Concentration

The districts having units between 5 and 1 are included in this category, Shajapur, Sehore, Betul, Hoshangabad, Damoh, Satna, Sagar, Vidisha, Dhar, Khargone, Rajgarh, Rewa, Shahdol, Raigarh, Rajnandgaon, Bastar, Raisen, Seoni and Didhi are in this category. These districts have resource potential, which has not been exploited. The state government is giving attention to these districts and so industries have begun to be established after second Plan. These districts are socially backward and do not provide market and infrastructure.

No Industry Districts

Balaghat, Chhindwara, Mandla, Narsinghpur, Surguja, Panna, Chhattarpur, Tikamgarh, Bhind, Satna, Shivpuri, Guna and Jhabua districts do not have even a single large and medium scale units and have been grouped into the 'No Industry Districts' in the State. These districts surprisingly are known for variety of raw materials like coal, iron, limestone, forest produces and agricultural produces. Considering the potentiality of these districts extractive industry has been developed. Unfortunately, these areas have been identified as the resource areas from where the resources are exported to other parts as has been the system during the colonial period. Raipur, Durg and Korba (Bilaspur) have developed as industrial centres on the resource potential of the Balaghat, Chhindwara and Mandla districts where no industry is established except for the extraction of minerals. It is the only economic activity carried on in these districts.

Panna is an important diamond mining district of the country but no diamond cutting unit has been established in the district, the whole of the uncut diamond is exported. Another group of districts — Bhind, Tikamgarh, Datia, Shivpuri and Chhattarpur have rich forest resources but they are also not utilised in the respective districts.

Apart from the backwardness of the people, poverty, illiteracy and lack of political patronage also has enhanced the backwardness of these districts.

Conclusion

Indstrial development in Madhya Pradesh is greatly hampered due to the non-availability of adequate means of communications, local capital, resources and technical personnel. As it is noticed in the above discussion that the process of industrialisation has been greatly enhanced after the reorganisation of the state. At this time (Nov. 1956) there were 44 large and medium units in the State mainly concentrated in Indore, Jabalpur, Ratlam, Gwalior and Ujjain Districts. After the reorganisation of the States, Madhya Pradesh Government along with the Government of India paid special attention towards the industrial development of the State and the number of units rose to 249 in 1983. Alongwith the old centres, new centres like Dewas, Raipur, Durg, Bilaspur, Morena, Khandwa, Mandsaur, Hoshangabad, Sehore and Shajapur were added in the industrial map of State.

But in spite of the rapid industrialisation still there is a wide gap between the advanced and the backward districts. Dewas with 43 units has the highest number of industries in the State followed by Indore with 30 units. On the other hand Balaghat, Chhindwara, Mandla, Narsinghpur, Surguja, Panna, Chhattarpur, Tikamgarh, Bhind, Datia, Shivpuri, Guna and Jhabua have no industries. The backwardness of these districts is not because of lack of required resources but because of the lack of local skilled labour, initiative of the local people, political patronage and so on.

The study shows that though efforts have been made by the State Government to narrow the gap between the advanced and the backward districts and could not achieve great success. Even after the planned development, still 69.5 per cent of the total large scale units are concentrated only in the 9 districts. Looking to the uneven spatial and temporal distribution of industries the government should try to establish industries in the backward districts and to ensure that the process of industrial development already being initiated in newly developed districts, must keep on without a sad back. The industrial units should be established after considering and assessing the local resources, market and infrastructure, various types of concessions and facilities should be provided to the enterpreneurs to establish industries in the backward areas. In due course it should be ensured that the concessions announced are being properly utilised and have generated the process of industrial development. An important thing which should be done to minimise the gap between the advanced and the backward districts is to create social conciousness in the local people which is greatly lacking. Apart from this private sector should not only be encouraged to start the industrial units but be convinced that all facilities and protection required will be provided as has been done by the princely states like Gwalior and Indore in our own State. Normally the resources of the State are being used in the colonial pattern, where administration was not interested in the region but only in the resources. This practice must be stopped and a definite part of the revenue earned out of the resource must be spent on the region's development. Apart from the old industrial centres, a set of new centres with public and private investment should also be developed possibly with a combination of heavy and ancillary industries to avoid the past experience where public sector has failed to affect the neighbourhood substantially.

TWELVE

Rural Industrialization: A Case Study of Tahsil Amethi District-Sultanpur (U.P.)*

S.C. SHARMA, D.N. TRIPATHI and O.P. MISRA

In a developing country like India, where more than 75 per cent population lives in the villages, which are still faced with the problems of chronic poverty, large scale unemployment or under-employment and economic disparities in levels of development. Agriculture alone cannot guarantee the solution of these problems and ensure the sustainable development of rural masses. It is only the rural industrialization which refers to the setting up of wide range of agro-based, forest based, animal-baded, and other cottage and small scale industries for utilization of local material and human resources, can help removal of poverty and bring about an all round development by reducing regional disparities, increasing employment opportunities, providing useful outlet for many of the raw materials and waste materials of agriculture, providing the farmers and their families an additional source of income which is needed to raise their status and to help them in the times of crop failure, establishing backward and forward linkages with other sectors to maximise the inter-sectoral pay offs, meeting the internal demands in particular and external ones in general and attracting the flow of labour and capital from bigger areas to smaller service centres and villages so on and so forth. In short, rural industrialization is a strategy for formulating schemes for rural development which will promote agricultural productivity together with setting up a host of labour intensive smaller and medium scale industries using modern techniques on the outskirts of a cluster of villages on decentralised bases for boosting up village economy and thus providing a basis for sound balanced development.

Decentralised industrialization, besides developing rural areas, will lessen the problems of urban migration, slum dwellings, urban congestion and pollution and increase the agricultural productivity.

There is, thus, an immediate need of country-wide rural industrialization on micro-level, for which there are great potentials. The present chapter attempts to suggest a suitable and pragmatic plan for the rural industrialization for economic development of Amethi Tahsil of District Sultanpur (U.P.) after analysing its existing position and potentials for future development.

Study Region

The tahsil Amethi is situated between 26⁰-01'-30" to 26⁰-17' -30" N latitude and 81⁰ -40' -50" to 82⁰ -04' -25" E longitude in southern part of Sultanpur district covering an area of 586.26 km^2. Its population is 244216 (1981) of which 237084 is rural living in 290 inhabited revenue villages (orgaised in 4 development blocks i.e. Amethi, Bhadar, Bhetuwa and Sangrampur) and 7132 is urban living in one Urban centre i.e. Amethi. The literacy in the tahsil is 21.92 per cent and the working population is 30.86 per cent. Thus, it is an under-developed and backward area which is characterized by mass unemployment and poverty, low levels of agricultural development and standard of living, lack of adequate capital and wide dispartiies in the level of socio-economic development.

Methodology

For the present study, the study area has been divided into 27 basic planning units on the basis of spatio-functional organisation. (Tripathi, 1988). These units have been further reorganised into 29 units on the basis of spatio-functional and hierarchic gaps in the study area (Appendix-I) of the chapter. The industrial potentialities have been analysed planning units wise and the establishment of industrial units has been recommended service centre wise.

Existing Industral Structure

Since the study area is basically agrarian and agriculture is the backbone of its economy, it is backward as regards the industrial development. It has been declared as "industrially zero" area and recently, particularly after 1980, the efforts have been made here to develop small scale and cottage industries on modern lines.

Table 12.1 and Fig. 12.1 which depict the industrial structure of the area, show that except one large scale unit named as Hindustan Aeronautic Ltd. which is being established on Gauriganj-Sultanpur road at a distance of 6 km from Amethi with an estimated cost of Rs. 500 crores, destined to manufacture the parts of an aeroplane and give employment to 1500 persons, almost all the industrial units are related to the small scale and cottage industries. There is one rice mill located at a distance of one kilometer from Amethi, which has started functioning after 1986 and has a capacity of dehusking 10,000 metric tonnes paddy per year, while the number of the rice hullers is 131 and that of the

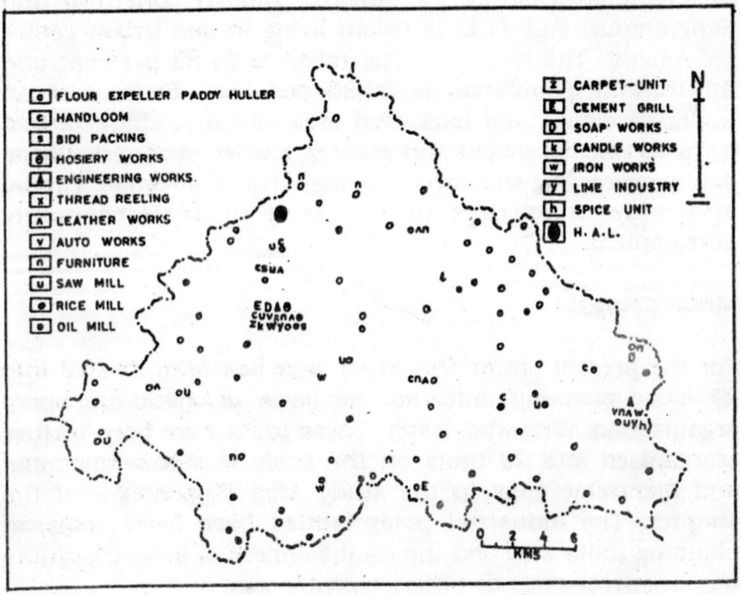

FIG. 12.1: Existing Industrial Units in Amethi, 1987

oil expellers, flour-mills and *Tat Patti* and Rope making units respectively is 135, 200 and 133. These units are widely distributed in the study area but the distribution of other units is uneven. Most of these other units are concentrated in Amethi and Ramnagar clusters. The hosiery, Wax candle, Ice candy, automobile reparis, steel furnitures, Bidi packing units are absolutely concentrated at these places. Ramganj is another centre where seven industrial units are located. Resha Udyog which includes the *Tat Patti* and rope making units are concentrated in the southern part of the blocks Sangrampur and Bhadar. These units are almost negligible in Amethi and Bhetua blocks.

Table 12.1: Existing Industrial Structure (1987)

Name of Industry	No. of units	Persons engaged
A. Large Scale Industry-		
Hindustan Aeronautics Ltd.	1	1500
B. Medium Scale Industry-		
Rice mill	1	29
C. Cottage Industry-		
Flour mills	200	200
Rice hullers	131	131
Saw milling	16	78
Oil Expellers	135	155
Brick making	8	N.A.
Kiln and Surkhi Industry	3	17
Tat Patti and rope making	153	N.A.
Wooden Furniture	10	20
Handloom Industry	18	N.A.
Hosiery	1	6
Carpet works	8	36
Light Engineering Works	8	34
Printing press	6	23
Soap works	6	18
Leather works	8	16
Candle works	1	3
Paper works	1	3
Ice candy	2	8
Auto works	1	3
Readymade works	1	6
Steel furniture works	1	6
Ink Industry	2	2

Potential for Industrial Development

The foregoing discussion discerns that the industrial sector contributes but quite insignificantly to the economy of the region and very small part of its population is provided employment by it, although the region is endowed with adequate potentialities for developing agro-based, animal based, forest based and demand based industries. There is a need to encourage entrepreneurs to establish industrial units and to make available adequate capital and infrastructures and to develop industries in accordance with the local resources and local needs. Keeping this in view, a ten years perspective plan in two phases has been proposed here for the development of the small scale and cottage industries in the region.

Agro-based Industries

These units may be classified into agricultural products processing units, viz., rice-mill, dal-mill, oil-mill and seed processing units etc., and the agricultural products manufacturing units, viz., handloom industry, *Gur* and *Khandsari* units etc.

Rice-mill

Rice is the main food stuff consumed in the study area, which is obtained from paddy by dehusking the same. Rice dehusking is an important industry which employs from hand implements to rice hullers and rice mills. As already mentioned there is only one sheller rice-mill, but the number of rice hullers is 127.

Table 12.2: Estimated Production of Rice

(Metric Tonnes)

	1995-96	2000-01
Production of Rice Total	37,055	55,865
Quantity available for extraction (80% of the total)	29,644	44,708
Quantity available for hand pounding	5,929	8,942
Quantity available for milling		
Capacity of existing mills and hullers	15,715	23,715
Surplus quantity of paddy	8,000	12,051
Proposed mills (Annual capacity 4000 metric tonnes)	2	3

Table 12.2 shows that the estimated productionof rice in the study area is 37,055 and 55,865 metric tonnes for the years 1995-96 and 2000-01. After deducting 20 per cent of the production reserved for seeds and export, and the same quantity that is processed manually paddy available for processing by rice mills and rice hullers is estimated to be 23,715 metric tonnes in 1995-96 and 35,766 metric tonnes in 2000-01. Paddy required by existing rice hullers (the existing capacity of a rice huller has been estimated 0.5 metric tonne paddy for 90 days and that of the rice mill 10,000 metric tonnes per annum) is 15,715 metric tonnes. Thus, the paddy available for further processing will amount to 8000 metric tonnes in 1995-96 and 12,051 metric tonnes in 2000-01. As such one rice mill each with a capacity of 4000 metric tonnes is proposed to be established at Ramganj and Sheoganj by 1995-96. Three more mills will be needed by 2000-01 which are proposed to be established at Bhadar, Bhimi and Bishesharganj.

Rice Bran Oil Mill

Rice bran which is a by-product of rice milling industry is a powder type of material obtained during the process of dehusking paddy. This bears oil contents which are extracted in the extraction plants of the rice mill. Bran is processed by oil solvent extraction plants which produces the following (Sen, L.K., 1975):

Raw bran oil	15 per cent
De-oiled bran	70 per cent
Wax and sugar	15 per cent

De-oiled bran is highly nutritive and digestive even for human consumption and when mixed with wheat flour, makes good ingredient for biscuits, bread and other confectionary. Washing soap can be manufactured from rice bran oil which is also used for splitting fat. Since refined oil has lower content of saturated fatty acids in it, it is superior to other cooking oils. Rice sugar contains succrose and glucose. The sugar is edible and rich in B-vitamins. The wax is suitable for making polishes and emulsifiers.

There is no rice bran oil mill at present in the study

area. Therefore, it is proposed to install three rice bran oil mills two in the first phase (one each at Amethi and Ramganj) and at Bhimi in the second phase.

Pulp and Board Factory

Pulp and board can be manufactured by utilizing paddy husk. The foregoing discussion reveals that different rice mills and hullers will produce 4077 metric tonnes paddy husk by 1995-96 and 6038 metric tonnes by 2000-01, which can sustain one pulp and board factory unit each in the first and second phase, which are proposed to be established at Amethi in the first and at Ramganj in the second phase.

Dal Mills

There is no *dal* mill in the study area at present. The local demand in the rural areas is met by the pulses prepared manually in a traditional manner. The estimated production of the pulses for the year 1995-96 is 15,170 metric tonnes and for the year 2000-01, 19,921 metric tonnes. It is assumed that only 40 per cent of these quantities will be available for milling, as the remaining will either be processed by manual labour by traditional method or will be reserved for seed etc. The quantities available for *dal* milling will be 6308 and 7968 metric tonnes respectively for which three *dal* mills with installed capacity of 2000 metric tonnes per year are required to be established in the first phase and one more in the second phase. They are proposed to be installed at Amethi, Ramganj and Kalyanpur in first and Bisheshargani in the second phase.

Oil Mill

There are 135 oil expellers and oil mill in the study area, which have limited capacity. Traditional *ghanies* are also used in some villages for oil crushing. In view of the increased production of oil seeds, it is proposed to establish one mill each with an anual capacity of 500 metric tonnes at Ramganj by 1995-96 and at Tikar by 2000-01.

Flour Mills

There are 20 small size flour mills at present but no big size roller mill. There is no maida/suzi mill in the region. It is estimated that the region will produce 32,046 and 45,365 metric tonnes of wheat by 1995-96 and 2000-01 respectively. About 15 per cent of this amount may be used for making maida/suzi, i.e. 4807 and 6805 metric tonnes of wheat will be available for making maida and suzi. This will require the establishment of two roller mills in the first (one each at Amethi and Ramganj) and one more in the second phase (at Sheoganj) with a capacity of 2400 metric tonnes per year.

Gur and Khandsari Units

There is no *Gur* and *Khandsari* unit, nor a sugar mill at present in the region, as the sugarcane produced locally is used for making *gur* by traditional cane crushers. Therefore, it is proposed to establish *Gur* and *Khandsari* units at all the service centres in the region and one sugar mill with an installed capacity of 1,50,000 metric tonnes per annum at Amethi in the second phase.

Tat Patti Manufacturing Units

Tat Patti is made up of sanai and jute. This work is done mainly in the southern part of the region, offering great potentialities for the development of the *Tat Patti* manufacturing units. There is no organized unit at present in the region. This work is done by the families of the backward and scheduled castes in the old traditional manner. There is a need of new technology and qualitative improvement in this industry. It is proposed to establish these units on modern lines in the clusters— Bisheshargani, Sangrampur, Sheetalganj, Bargaon, Dhema, Dhaurahara, Bhadar etc. providing employment to the unemployed poor. Rope making and *Resha* making units may be developed as co-industrial units.

Forest Based Industries

There is a lack of Sheesham, Teak and Sal trees, but there

is abundance of Neem, Mahua, Jamun, Mango, Babool etc. which are popular timber trees. The important forest-based industries in the region are as follows—

Saw Mills

There are only 16 saw mills at present which are unevenly distributed in the region. Nine saw mills are located at Amethi and in its environs (Fig. 12.2). The result is that the people have to travel a distance of 8 to 10 km to avail the services of the saw mills. It is, therefore, proposed to establish saw mills at every central village in the region.

Wooden Furniture Units

There is now great demand of the wooden furnitures in the rural areas also. In order to meet this demand, it is proposed that wooden furniture units should be established at all service points by 1995-96 and at all central villages by 2000-01.

Bamboo and Cane Units

These units are proposed to be established at all the central villages.

Bidi Packing Units

At present these units are working at Amethi and Ramnagar. Keeping in view the increasing demand for *Bidi*, it is proposed to establish such units at all the service points by 1995-96 and at all the central villages by 2000-01.

Animal Based Industries

Dairy Unit

The study area has adequate potentials for the development of dairy industry, as there is great demand for dairy products and milk which is not met adequately due to low yield of milk from the indigeneous cows and buffalos. There is no

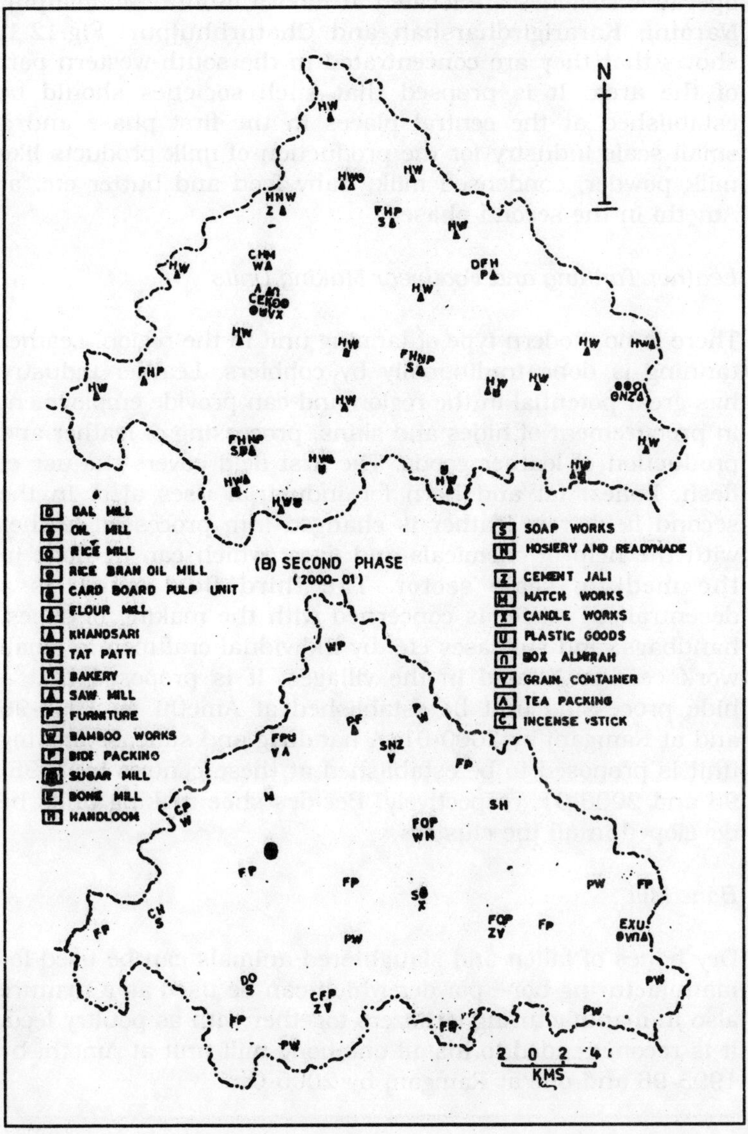

FIG. 12.2: Proposed Industrial Units in the First Phase (1995-96), Amethi

dairy unit at present in the study area. Seven diary co-operative societies are located at Kakwa, Kohra, Mahmatpur, Naraini, Kararigirdharshah and Chaturbhujpur. Fig.12.1, shows that they are concentrated in the south-western part of the area. It is propsed that such societies should be established at the central places in the first phase and a small scale industry for the production of milk products like milk powder, condensed milk, baby food and butter etc. at Amethi in the second phase.

Leather Tanning and Footwear Making Units

There is no modern type of tanning unit in the region. Leather tanning is done traditionally by cobblers. Leather industry has great potential in the region and can provide employment in procurement of hides and skins, processing of leather and production of leather goods. The first field covers the use of flesh, bones, fat and horn for industrial uses also. In the second field, raw leather is changed into processed leather with the help of chemicals and dyes, which can be done in the medium scale sector. The third field which is a decentralized sector is concerned with the making of shoes, handbags, and suitcases etc. by individual craftmen in small work centres located in the villages. It is proposed that a hide processing unit be established at Amethi by 1995-96 and at Ramganj by 2000-01. A handbag and suitcase making unit is proposed to be established at these centres by 1995-96 and 2000-01, respectively. Besides shoe making units be developed in all the clusters.

Bone Mill

Dry bones of fallen and slaughtered animals can be used for manufacturing bone powder which can be used as a manure also in manufacturing fertilizers together with as poultry feed. It is recommended to install one bone mill unit at Amethi by 1995-96 and one at Ramganj by 2000-01.

Demand Based Industries

Agricultural Implements Manufacturing and Repairing Units

The demand for improved agricultural implements is on an increase as a result of the recent advances in farming practices. At present, it is only at Amethi that the manufacturing and repairing of the light agricultural implements is being done. It is proposed that plants manufacturing improved agricultural implement be established at Ramganj by 1995-96 and by 2000-01 at all service points. The repairing workshops should be established at all the central villages. Blacksmith and carpenters should be trained in modern technical know-how and they should be provided with accessories and financial assistance for manufacturing agricultural implements.

Soap Making Industry

The main raw materials utilized in soap industry are rice bran oil, neem, castor, mahua, linseed, soda ash etc. Most of them are available in the study area. The existing six soap making units (4 of which are located at Amethi and one each at Ramganj and Sonapur) are not adequate enough to meet the rising demand of detergents which have become an integral item of daily use even in the rural areas. It is recommended to extend these units to centres like Bisheshargani, Navgirwa, and Tikar by 1995-96 and by 2000-01 at all the service points.

Handloom Units

The handloom industry which has a long tradition of excellence and a living legacy of unrivalled craftmanship possesses large avenues for employment in the rural areas. It has the advantages of being a labour intensive and capital saving industry. The is why it has been given a prominent place in the 20-points programme. More and more stress is being laid on setting up handlooms in the rural areas.

These units at present, are located at Tikar, Sonari Kalan, Peeparpur, Ramnagar, Benipur, Manapatti Sakar, Amethi, Amaye Maffi, Pindaria, Rajgarh, Dhaurahara etc. where spinning of yarn and weaving of cloths are carried out. The production capacity of these units is low. It is recommended that these units should be set up at all the central villages and liberal loans and aid grants together with the working space for setting up these units and modern technology be provided. Regular and adequate supply of yards at reasonable price should also be made. Credit at subsidised rates and marketing facilities should be made available.

Carpet Making Units

Carpet and *Daree* making industries is allied with the handloom industry hence it should be developed in the same way as the latter. At present, there is only one carpet making unit at Amethi. Such units should be established at all the central villages in the region.

Readymade Garments Units

These days, there is a great demand for readymade garments in the society. There exist two units at present in the study area (one each at Amethi and Bhadar). It is recommended that one unit each should be installed at Ramganj, Tikar, Bisheshargani by 1995-96 and at Navgirwa, Kalyanpur, Bhimi and Maharapur by 2000-01.

Kiln and Surkhi Industry

These units are located in Ramganj, Amethi and Karariheershah. Brick kiln are wide spread in the region. There is great potential to develop these industries, particularly when there is rising need of building construction. Raw materials used in these industries is thick mud clay and Kanker. Surkhi making units are proposed to be established at Ramnagar, Bhadar, and Sarai Khema. Brick kilns have to be established in every cluster.

Cement Zali Making Units

There is one unit each at Amethi and Jogapur preparing cement zalies. It is recommended that one unit each should be established at Ramganj and Munshiganj by 1995-96 and one each at Sangrampur, Bhadar and Navgirwa by 2000-01 in order to meet the rising demands.

Other Demand Based Industries

The following is the list of other proposed industrial units:

Match Industry
Ayurvedic Medicines
Wax candle
Ice candy
Plastic Industry
Box-Almirah Making Units
Grain Tea Packing
Pin Manufacturing
Perfume
Balpen and Refil Manufacturing
Nail Polish
Fountain pen
Plastic button
Chalk Making Units.

These industrial units like Ayurvedic medicines, tea packing, pin, Ballpen, Nail polish, plastic button and fountain pen manufacturing units will provide employment opportunities to rural folk. This will augment the monthly income by Rs. 500 to 2000. These industries require less capital and the markets for manufactured goods are also available easily.

Organizational and Infrastructural Planning for Industrial Development

The implementation of the above proposals for the establishment of different industrial units warrants proper organizational and infrastructural planning on the following lines—

(1) In order to speed up the industrialization the enterpreneurs should be encouraged to establish industries by providing adequate financial assistance and Technical know-how under IRDP. During the field

study, it has been observed that not only unnecessary delay is caused in making available the government financial assistance to the needy persons but only a fraction of it reaches the beneficiaries and a larger part of it is taken away by the commission agents and middle men or given in liberity. It is suggested that unnecessary formalities should be avoided and there should be simple and straight forward procedures for giving financial assistance and licenses. There should not be any differentiation on the basis of caste, creed and religion. A co-ordination Committee is also recommended to be constituted in every clusters, 50 per cent members of which should be from entrepreneurs.

(2) It has been observed that the entrepreneurs engaged in small and cottage industries lack confidence and enterprise which are an essential input in terms of management skills consequently, the trained personnels prefer service to installing their own units. As such, the essential qualities of entrepreneurship have to be developed and liberal financial assistance has to be made available on priority basis. For this financial institutions are recommended to be established at all the service points.

(3) The success of rural industrialization, to a greater extent, depends on the quality of the products and their marketing procedure. This needs a proper publicity and advertisement of the products and their proepr marketing.

The government may think in terms of setting up marketing co-operatives, public sector marketing institutions and make the initial investment on publicity and transport. Marketing guidance and marketing intelligence cells should be made available in the tahsil indudstiral centres proposed to be set up for promotional measures for indsutry in the rural areas.

(4) Co-operative societies should be established and through them all purchase of raw material and sale of manufactured goods should be done.

(5) The bases of rural industrialization programme should be socio-economic and beneficiaries selected should

be from the poorest families. The indigeneous industries of which should be given priority.

(6) Appropriate training in recent innovations and techniques related to the rural industries should be imparted to the entrepreneurs. In this connection, it is recommended that display and information cells should be set up, levels of technology used in rural industrialization should be shown, design and development facilities for re-saling of technology for transfer should be established, regional trade fairs spot lighting development of technology in selected industries should be held, buyers and sellers meet on technology should be arranged, panorama of available technology for diffusion and consultancy services to the entrepreneurs should be provided. The institutions like Small Industries Service Institutions, National Small Scale Industries Corporation and Deen Dayal Research Institute can play an important role in providing this type of technical assistance.

(7) There should be an adequate arrangement of physical infra-structures required for industrial development, viz., road, transportation and electricity etc.

It may be concluded that if keeping in mind the principles of horizontal and vertical integration and adopting the strategies already narrated the industrial development in the area is carried out it will definitely attain its objectives of offering better opportunities for encouraging the use of local agricultural and other resources in the national interest, providing additional sources of income to the target groups, particularly small and marginal farmers, controlling the incessantly growing pressure of population on land resources, raising the standard of living and thus narrowing down the disparities in the income of rural people, increasing an attraction for the rural areas thus checking the out migration to the urban areas, and bringing about a balanced, integrated and comprehensive development of the area, provided, of course, if the people's participation and the co-operation from the government are obtained.

APPENDIX-I

A. Growth point
   1. Amethi

B. Service Centre
   1. Ramganj

C. Service Points
   1. Tikar
   2. Bisheshargani
   3. Maharajpur
   4. Navgirwa
   5. Kalyanpur

D. Central Villages
   1. Ramnagar
   2. Bhadar
   3. Durgapur
   4. Munshiganj
   5. Peeparpur
   6. Shitalaganj
   7. Sangrampur
   8. Kakwa
   9. Ayodhyanagar
   10. Sheoganj
   11. Thengha
   12. Dhema
   13. Bargaon
   14. Hathkila
   15. Bhimi
   16. Tala
   17. Karariheershah
   18. Kararigirdharshah
   19. Sandha
   20. May
   21. Daurahara
   22. Trisundi.

Theme-IV

Infrastructure and Economic Development

THIRTEEN

Geographical Analysis of Rural Markets—Satkhira Upazila

RAZIA SULTANA

Introduction

The chapter is a generalised study of the market centers of Satkhira Upazila. Objective is to analyse some geographical aspects of market places of the study area, which focuses its attention on the initial market evolvement impulse, hierarchy, spatial distribution pattern, periodicity characterisitcs, spatio-temporal synchronization and development of market rings or cycles of the market centers. Methodology adopted is based on some nominal statistical analysis which are done on the primary data collected during the field work in February, 1989. Findings reveal that, markets developed without any well thought planning resulting to a random spatial distribution pattern, but these are well synchronized in time and space. Market rings are more or less well developed. It is hoped that this sort of study may help in future planning of the commercial activities of the area as well as of the country.

Economy of the rural landscape is reflected in its marketing activities. In less developed countries rural market centre held a prime position in overall controlling of developmental activities in rural area, so research on this field of study is gradually gaining importance.

Objective of the study is to reveal some geographical aspects of rural markets of Satkhira Upazila which is located in the lower Ganga Basin. Methodology adopted in the study includes analytical discussion based on primary data obtained from the questionnaire survey done in February, 1989.

Study Area

Satkhira Upazila formerly called Thana was first created in 1923. It is the headquarter of the Satkhira subdivision now Satkhira district which is in the lower Ganga Basin (Fig 13.1) and located in between 22°37' to 22°50' north latitude and 88°55' to 89°5' east longitude. It has got an area of 145 square miles. Physiographically Satkhira Upazila lies in the delta plain build up the river Ganga. The area mostly lie above the flood level. Rivers are almost dry most of the year with slightly entrenched characteristics. Ichamati, Betna, Kholpetua and Sonai are notable rivers. The climate of the Upazila is generally subtropical monsoon type with the influence of salt-laden air throughout the year. Soil has the

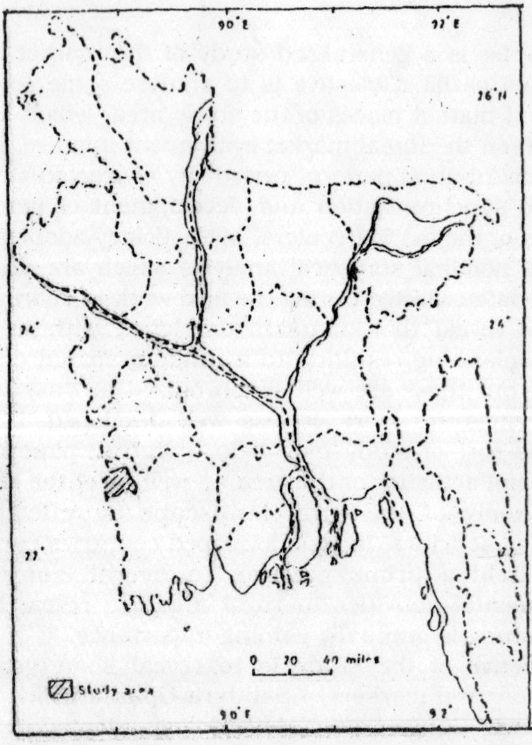

FIG. 13.1: Bangladesh and Location of the Study Area

uniform charactersitcs, varied mainly by a greater admixture of sand. The Upazila is inhabitated by 245645 persons (Census. 1981) with a density of population of 1694 per square mile. The economy of the region is agricultural as like total situation of Bangladesh. The agricultural goods are the main items of transaction, so all the markets of this area are treated as rural markets.

Initial Market Evolvement Impulse

Location of market like other economic activities on geographic space is the result of combined effect of both physical and human factors. In this study, initial market evolvement impulse indicates the very first factor which is responsible for the starting of market operation on specific site and exclude other factors which combinedly help to run the establishment permanently. Satkhira has got 26 market centres locally called *Hat* and *Bazar*. Bazar means daily market and *Hat* periodic market. *Bazars* are held to permit the functioning of local exchange only, existence of internal trade and central place functions are very little, normally do not affect the regional exchange pattern. *Hats* are important for a wider area exchange, normally perform three functions, local exchange, internal trade and central place services. In Satkhira Upazila, there are four factors, such as personal influence, surplus production, population pressure and communication facilities are responsible for the selection of very first site of the market activities, shown in Table 13.1. Major share of personal influence for the initiation of the market centers, indicates that influential persons served their own interest by virtue of their strength.

Hierarchy of Market Centre

Hierarchy of markets means ranking of markets into successive groups (Gedam, 1980). Hierarchy may be sorted out in different ways. In this study it has been done on the basis of following six variables, such as area, income earned by the Government, market population, monthly duration of market hours, infrastructural facilities and the number of open shop on market days. These variables are selected as indicators to find out the hierarchical order of the market

Table 13.1: Market Centres along with their Evolvement Impulse

Initial Market Evolvement impulse	Name and number of the market	Percentage
Personal influence	1. Puratan Satkhira	46.2
	2. Dhuliar hat	
	3. Binerpota	
	4. Shakra	
	5. Bashdaha	
	6. Mirzanagar	
	7. Varkhali	
	8. Mahmudpur	
	9. Bhomra	
	10. Khuskhali	
	11. Babulia	
	12. Alipur	
Surplus Production	1. Satkhira	19.2
	2. Sreerampur	
	3. Dhuliar bazar	
	4. Boikari	
	5. Kaṭhanda	
Population Pressure	1. Machkhola	19.2
	2. Madhabkati	
	3. Katia bazar	
	4. Itagacha	
	5. Ghona	
Communication facilities/ Transport connection	1. Abder hat	15.4
	2. Jhowdanga	
	3. Kadomtala	
	4. Akrakhola	

centre. Market are ranked separately for each indicator mentioned above, each indicator for each rank has been given points on the basis of its respective rank order position. Table 13.2 shows the six indicators, in point position. Finally to get the final rank order position, all the points are summed up and then the average situation for the six indicators have been calculated out. To find out the hierarchical order of different group of market centres, the average point gained per market centre has been used which is illustrated in Table 13.3, the range of the average points has been divided into three equal parts as upazila contains lower three hierarchical tier of administrative units of the total seven tier hierarchical order administrative units of the country. The market centre spacing and number of markets in different hierarchical group

Table 13.2: Hierarchical Position of the Individual Market Centre of Satkhira Upazila

Rank order of the market centres	Area Point	Income (Yearly) Point	Market Population Point	Monthly Market Hours Point	Infrastructure Point	Open Shop on market day Point	Total of all indicators Point	Average per indicator Point
1. Jhowdanga	18	21	26	13	2	25	105	17.50
2. Abder hat	17	22	23	15	3	22	99	16.50
3. Satkhira	15	20	14	15	4	23	91	15.16
4. Akrakhola	10	18	22	14	3	20	87	14.50
5. Bashdaha	16	11	25	5	3	26	86	14.33
6. Kadomtala	12	19	17	12	4	21	85	14.16
7. Dhuliar hat	17	14	12	9	3	18	73	12.16
8. Varkhali	11	9	24	7	2	16	69	11.50
9. Puratan Satkhira	13	15	10	10	1	17	66	11.00
10. Itagacha	7	16	12	13	4	13	64	10.66
11. Katia bazar	2	17	19	9	3	14	64	10.66
12. Shakara	6	12	14	6	1	24	62	10.33
13. Boikari	6	10	20	11	4	9	60	10.00
14. Kathanda	8	6	21	5	1	19	60	10.00
15. Ghona	6	7	18	9	2	15	57	9.50
16. Kushkhali	9	4	16	4	2	12	47	7.83
17. Machkhola	8	8	9	5	2	11	43	7.16
18. Madhabkhati	1	6	7	12	2	10	38	6.33
19. Binerpota	6	13	5	6	—	7	37	6.16
20. Dhuliar bazar	5	10	3	8	1	5	32	5.33
21. Mirzanagar	6	6	8	3	1	8	32	5.33
22. Mahmudpur	3	3	15	1	3	6	31	5.16
23. Sreerampur	6	1	6	9	1	4	27	4.50
24. Alipur	3	2	1	12	2	2	22	3.66
25. Babulia	3	5	2	2	2	3	17	2.83
26. Bhomra	4	1	4	2	2	1	14	2.33

in the study area follow the general proposition of Christaller (Christaller, 1933) very loosely, reflecting a haphazard, backward and unplanned economic space organization in this area.

Table 13.3: Hierarchical Order of the Markets-with Average Intercentre Distance

Hierarchical order of the market centres	Name & number of the market centres	Percentage	Average distance between the nearest neighbour (in mile)
1.	1. Jhowdanga	23.07	2.50
	2. Abder hat		
	3. Satkhira		
	4. Akrakhola		
	5. Bashdaha		
	6. Kadomtala		
2.	1. Dhuliar hat	38.46	2.05
	2. Varkhali		
	3. Puratan Satkhira		
	4. Katiabazar		
	5. Itagacha		
	6. Shakra		
	7. Boikari		
	8. Kathanda		
	9. Ghona		
	10. Kushkhali		
3.	1. Machkhola	38.46	2.00
	2. Madhabkhati		
	3. Binerpota		
	4. Dhuliar bazar		
	5. Mirzanagar		
	6. Mahmudpur		
	7. Sreerampur		
	8. Alipur		
	9. Babulia		
	10. Bhomra		

Spatial Distribution of the Market Centres

The spatial distribution pattern of the markets of Satkhira Upazila have been determined by applying the widely used statistical technique, Nearest Neighbour Analysis. The Table 13.4 illustrates distribution pattern of the market centres. As in the area, number of daily bazar, bi-weekly and tri-weekly *hat* with daily bazar and only *hat* which includes weekly, bi-weekly and tri-weekly account for a quite significant number, so situation for different types have been separately described. Considering all the *hats* and *bazars* combinedly, the 'R' value is 1.31, which denotes a random distribution pattern, quite similar to that of total Bangladesh which is 1.17 and in Savar it is 1.23 (Sultana, 1982; Sultana, 1985-86). Random distribution pattern of rural market is a common picture of underdeveloped economy, similar other studies in Dhaka and Kanpur confirms this (Baquee, 1980; Dixit, 1983). Facts revealed in Table 13.4 regarding spatial organisation of market centre of different catagories jointly and independently, lead to the conclusion that market centres of the upazila are the creation of chance, not a planned and well thought one.

Table 13.4: Spatial Distribution of Different Types of Market Centres

Types of Markets	Percentage	'R' value
All markets	100.00	1.31
Hat	38.46	1.14
Bi-weekly hat with bazar	38.46	1.06
Bazar	23.07	.89

Temporal Distribution of the Market Centres

Limited economic demand in the underdeveloped economy compelled the rural markets to be temporally bounded up or periodic in nature. Periodicity has three types of temporal attributes or characteristics, (i) frequency of occurrence in a certain time span, normally in a week, (ii) dirunal fixation of the market activities, and (iii) the very day or days of the week on which market activities occur.

Frequency of Market Occurrence

Frequency of occurrence of market activities in a certain time denote to the total number of market meeting during a specific lenght of time. In a week in Satkhira 26 market centers are furnished with 133 market meeting which includes 92 *bazar* days and 41 *hat* days. There are five types of frequency of occurrence observed in the study area, Table 13.5 shows the situation.

Table 13.5: Frequency of Occurrence of Market Centres

Nature of weekly periodicity	Number of market centres	Weekly frequency	Percentage
Daily	6	42	23.07
Weekly	1	1	3.84
Bi-weekly	7	14	26.92
Tri-weekly	2	6	7.69
Bi-weekly *hat* with *bazar*	10	70	38.46

Dirunal Fixation of Market Centres

Dirunal fixation of market centres denote to the spacific time of a day which is fixed up for market activities. Six types of dirunally fixed up market centres have been recognized in the study area, such as morning till evening, late morning till afternoon, morning till noon, noon till evening, afternoon till evening and morning till noon with bi-weekly morning till evening surge. These are shown in the Table 13.6.

Table 13.6: Dirunal Characteristics of Market Centres

Nature of dirunal fixation	Name and number of market centers	Percentage
Morning till evening	1. Puratan Satkhira	7.691
	2. Akrakhola	
Late morning till afternoon	1. Satkhira	3.841
Morning till noon	1. Binerpota	26.920
	2, Shakra	
	3. Alipur	
	4. Katiabazar	
	5. Dhuliar bazar	
	6. Varkhali	
	7. Bhomra	
Noon till evening	1. Machkhola	19.230
	2. Dhuliar hat	
	3. Bashdaha	
	4. Mirzanagar	
	5. Abder hat	
Afternoon till evening	1. Sreerampur	38.360
	2. Itagacha	

	3. Kadomtala	
	4. Mahmudpur	
	5. Kushkhali	
	6. Babulia	
	7. Kathenda	
	8. Boikari	
	9. Ghona	
	10. Madhabkati	
Morning till noon with Bi-weekly morning till evening surge	1. Jhowdanga	3.840

Daywise Market Frequency

Daywise frequency of market centers denote to the number of occurrence of market meeting on a specific day. The frequency picture regarding the market meeting of days of the week along with average distance and 'R' value has been projected in the Table 13.7 and graphical representation of which has been shown in the Fig 13.2. Illustration for *hat*

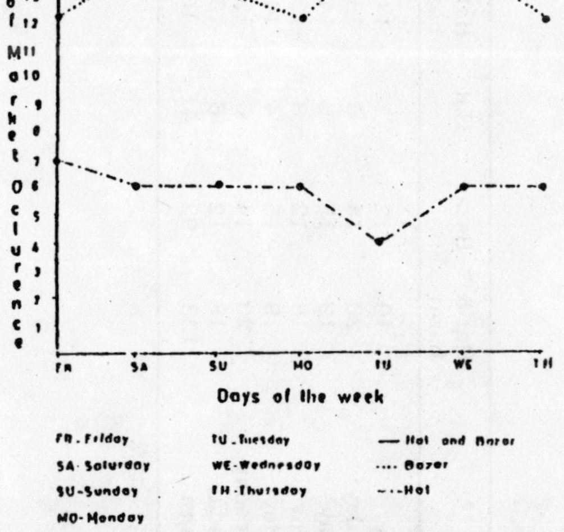

FIG. 13.2: Daywise Frequency of Market Occurrence

Table 13.7: Daywise Frequency of Market Meeting

Market day	Frequency			Percentage			Average distance between nearest neighbour Market centres			'R' value		
	Hat & bazar	Bazar	Hat	Hat & bazar	Bazar	Hat	Hat & bazar	Bazar	Hat	Hat & bazar	Bazar	Hat
Friday	19	12	7	14.2	13.0	17.0	1.7	1.7	3.3	1.2	1.0	1.4
Saturday	20	14	6	15.0	15.2	14.6	1.7	1.8	3.5	1.2	1.2	1.4
Sunday	19	13	6	14.2	14.1	14.6	1.5	1.9	1.5	1.4	1.1	1.8
Monday	18	12	6	13.5	13.0	14.6	1.7	1.8	3.7	1.2	1.0	1.5
Tuesday	19	15	4	14.2	16.3	9.7	1.5	1.6	4.2	1.1	1.0	1.4
Wednesday	20	14	6	15.0	15.2	14.6	1.9	1.9	3.1	1.4	1.2	1.2
Thursday	18	12	6	13.5	13.0	14.6	1.5	1.9	4.6	1.1	1.1	1.8
Satkhira	133	92	41	100	100	100	1.6	1,8	3.8	1.2	1.1	1.5

and bazar have been combinedly and separately given here. It may be commented from the 'R' value shown in column no. 5 of the Table 13.7 that *Hats* are temporally quite uniformly distributed and higher frequency of market occurence is observed not on adjacent day but on either one or two days gap to provide uniformity service, all the week around. In Satkhira number of Friday *Hat* is highest, which is in conformation with other muslim dominated area (Hill & Smith, 1972; Sultana 1985-86). The spatial distribution of markets on geographic space as independent point is random, but when considered in terms of spatio-temporal situation, picture is quite different for the seven days of the week for three separate cases, such as *Hat* and *Bazar* combinedly and separately. The 'R' value revealed in the Table 13.7 help to conclude that the temporal placing of *Hat*, the most important centre of rural market activities are more or less evenly distributed on space to provide service to all. Beside, Friday, described as the popular day of the muslim world for both praying and marketing activities.

Spatio-Temporal Synchronization of Market Centres

Spato-temporal synchronization of market centres denote to the coordinating relationship of market places between time and space in connection with the location of markets (Fig. 13.3). Location on space as point is refered as spatial location. The distance between spatial location of market is measured with distance unit, here it is in mile. Fixation of a certain day of the week is termed as temporal location. Temporal separation is measured by the gap between the established sequential order of seven days of the week on which markets are held, thus four types of temporally fixed up market groups are recognized—same day, adjacent day, one day separated and two days separated markets.

Spatio-temporal synchronization characteristics of the market centres of the Satkhira Upazila have been shown in the Table 13.8. Spatial placing and temporal placing are inversely related as is also found by Fagerlund & Smith and Sultana (Fagerlund & Smith, 1970; Sultana 1985-86). In Satkhira in most of the cases; spatial and temporal placing of *Hats* are inversely related and that for *Hat* and *Bazar* combinedly and *Bazar* separately is very negligible still the

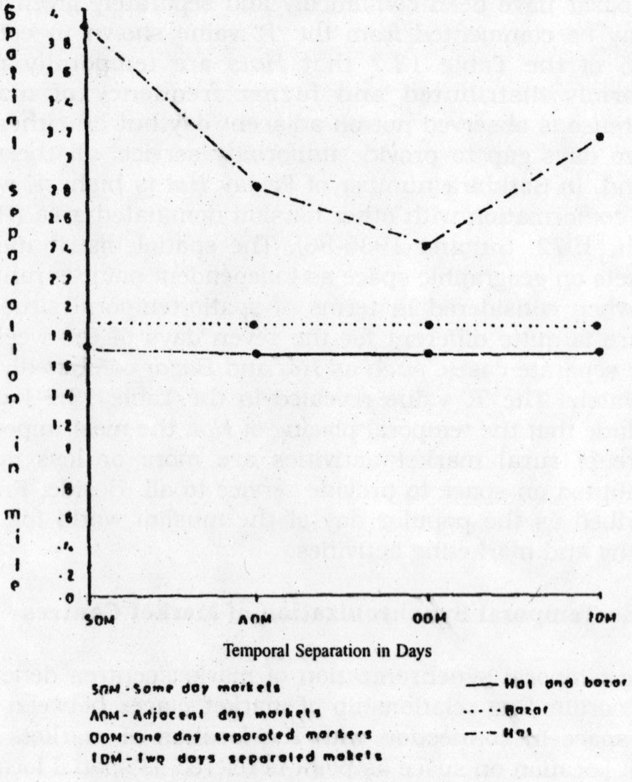

FIG. 13.3: Market Synchronization Pattren

Table 13.8: Spatio-Temporal Characteristics of Market Centres

Temporal separation (in day)	Spatial separation (in mile)			'R' value		
	Hat & Bazar	Bazar	Hat	Hat & Bazar	Bazar	Hat
Same day market	1.67	1.85	3.88	1.21	1.11	1.54
Adjacent day market	1.64	1.84	2.77	1.67	1.53	1.34
1 day separated market	1.64	1.83	2.37	1.68	1.56	1.55
2 day separated market	1.64	1.81	3.32	1.68	1.57	1.89

trend is in inverse position. The Fig. 13.3, represents graphically the situation of inverse relationship of spatial separation and temporal separation of the market centres of Satkhira Upazila.

Market Cycle/Ring of the Study Area

Market centres operating on a sequential order in a compact area, more or less within walking distance is termed as market ring or market cycle. Symanski defined market ring as "interrelated group of neighbouring periodic markets taking place on different days" (Symanski, 1971). Dixit describes it

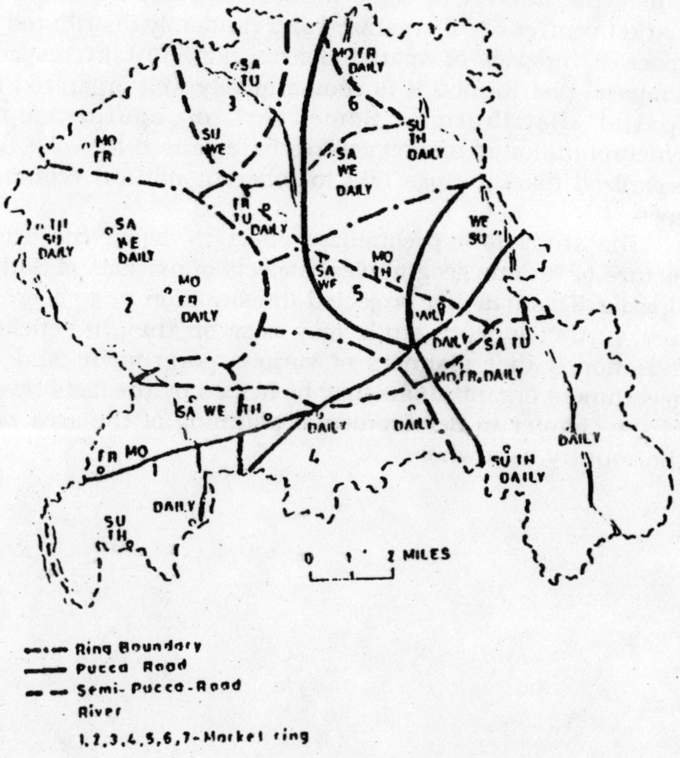

FIG. 13.4: Market Ring of Satkhira Upazila

as "a wholly indigenous phenomena expressing an intelligent mutual self interest among neighbouring village chiefs" (Dixit, 1984). Market meeting on all the seven days of the week on geographic space within a limited distance makes a complete market ring. In Satkhira Upazila six complete and one incomplete market rings are in existence. These rings are shown on the Fig. 13.4.

Conclusion

Market centres of the Satkhira Upazila, from the very begining have developed not in accordance with the need and demand of the people of the region concerned, but it has emerged to satisfy the interest of some influencial persons. As a result market centres are illorganized and randomly distributed over space in respect of spatial distribution. But in respect of temporal distribution it is comparatively well organized than spatial distribution. Some sort of spatio-temporal synchronization of market centres have caused to evolve better organized market rings due to inherent natural econmomic laws.

The study is a preliminary effort to depict the existing picture of various geographical aspects of markets of Satkhira Upazila. This has just projected the situation in a generalised way, further indepth study may base on this. In conclusion it is hoped that planners of various government and non-government organizations may be helped by the facts revealed in the chapter in developmental planning of the area rather the country as a whole.

FOURTEEN

Regulated Agricultural Markets and Rural Development: A Case Study of Eastern Uttar Pradesh

P.R. CHAUHAN and R.S. SINGH

The present chapter deals with the role of regulated agricultural markets (agricultural *mandis*) in promoting the rural economy of Eastern Uttar Pradesh, a fertile and densely populated segment of the Ganga Basin. It has been analysed with the help of sample *mandi* centres that these are the exchange points in economic space which connect the rural production areas to the distribution and consumption areas. The *mandi* centres operate not only like an exchange centres but also provide market infrastructures at site and diffuse the agricultural innovations and its spatio-functional integration with the marketing network of the area in question.

Introduction

Rural development, primarily based on agricultural economy, comprises three basic components—production, distribution and consumption. The regulated agricultural markets being as an exchange centres operate these three components. Firstly, these centres work like a collection points of surplus agricultural commodities and promote the agricultural productivity at one hand and disposes the surplus commodities for consumption to remote areas. In doing, so, a variety of functions i.e. collection and distribution of agricultural commodities, diffusion of innovations, provisions of infrastructures at site and trading facilities like grading and fair price selling of commodities etc. are performed.

A well developed marketing network with functional integration and spatio-temporal synchronization is the vital aspect for rural development in the region. Infact, regulated markets are like a nuclei with which the surrounding rural markets and villages of their influence area are economically integrated with each other. Therefore, this well developed network of settlements helps the process of rural develoment.

Objectives of the Study

The important objectives of the present study are—

(i) To analyse the spatial distribution of *mandis* in the study region.

(ii) To evaluate the functional characteristics of mandis.

(iii) To analyse the role of *mandis* in rural development with the help of sampled *mandi* centres.

Data Base

The study is based on the primary and secondary data. Primary data have been collected in case of sampled centres by interview and lay outs and shop structures are made by the authors.

Spatial Pattern of Agricultural *Mandis*

The study of the spatial distribution of agricultural *mandis* can help to understand the devleoped and undeveloped network of market centres causing the imbalance in the process of rual development. The spatial pattern has been analysed with the help of nearest neighbour analysis. The regional significance is expressed in the 'R' values. It is 1.757 for the whole region which shows the random to regular pattern. Geographically, a slight variation is noted in almost all the areas. (Fig. 14.1).

It is noted that Ganga-Yamuna Doab (Allahabad) indicates very regular pattern while Saryupar and Ganga Saryu Doab have random to regular distribution (Table 14.1). However, the analysis concludes that there are random to regular patterns of agricultural *mandis* in Eastern Uttar Pradesh. Geographically, the regions of Ganga-Yamuna Doab and

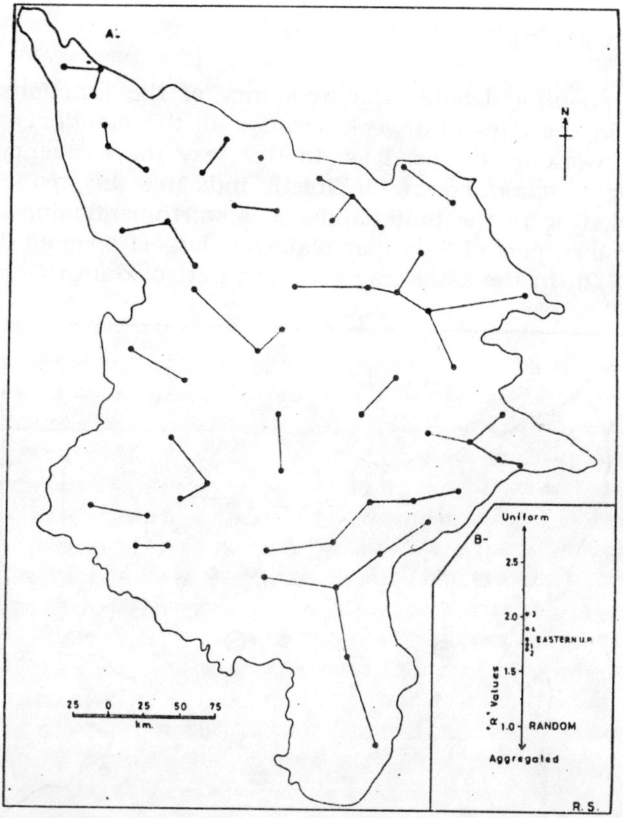

FIG. 14.1: Eastern Uttar Pradesh—Nearest Neighbour Analysis

southern part of Ganga Ghagra Doab have comparatively more *mandi* centres with frequent transportation while north-western Ganga Ghagra Doab, tarai tract of Saryupar plain and Gangapar, though having satisfactory *mandi* centres, yet, these are the regions of poor transportation network.

Table 14.1: R. Values

	Regions	R. Values
(i)	Saryupar plain	1.725
(ii)	Ganga-Saryu Doab	1.724
(iii)	Ganga-Yamuna Doab	2.092
(iv)	Gangapar	1.757

Mandi Openings

Mandi opening denotes the frequency of the functions of *mandi* in the days of a week because all the *mandi* centres do not work in all the days. In this way the frequency of opening of *mandi* centres indirectly indicates the frequency of marketing in the hinterlands. It is worthmentioning that the western part of Saryupar plain has largest opening days (Fig. 14.2). In the same way southern part of Ganga Ghagra

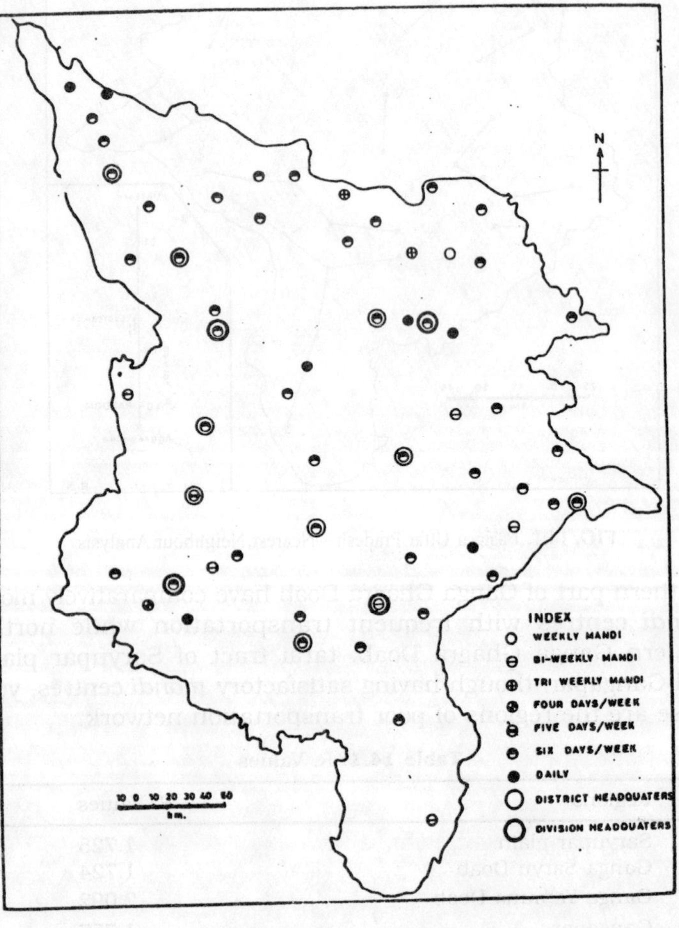

FIG. 14.2: Eastern Uttar Pradesh: Frequency and Distribution of Mandi Centres

Doab and Gorakhpur district of Saryupar plain have medium opening days while western part of Ganga Saryu Doab and Gangapar Region have least opening days. In this way the opening of *mandi* centres indicates that western part of Saryupar plain, southern part of Ganga Ghagra Doab have comparatively efficient marketing network which can affect the agricultural productivity of the region. The frequency and distribution of market centres and opening of *mandi* centres clearly indicates that large opening days of *mandis* are influenced by the densiest daily markets in the region.

Socio-economic Integration of *Mandi* Centres

Socio-economic integration means the interrelationship of socio-economic structures and *mandi* centres in the region. The *mandi* centres develop socio-economic integration with the collection of foodgrains and its interregional distribution. The rural population satisfy their necessity through sale of surplus grains at *mandi* centres and also achieve the new agricultural innovations. In the same way rural markets also supply surplus production to *mandis*. All these functions ultimately develop a spatial socio-economic network among *mandi* centres and rural markets and population.

In this way *mandi* centres are established on the basis of cotemporary economic conditions of the region. It is hereby clear to analyse the following infrastructural elements.

Population

The distribution of population is the important factor which affect the locations of *mandi* cnetres and also its grading. Generally, the Saryupar plain and litteral areas of Ganga river possess dense population, hence dense distribution of *mandi* centres and high frequency of opening are found there. Instead of this, western part of Ganga Ghagra doab and Gangapar region have even distribution of population and *mandi* centres.

Agricultural Production

The regional pattern of agricultural production affect the distribution of *mandi* centres. In the study region Gorakhpur,

Basti, Gonda and Bahraich districts have large number of *mandi* centres due to high quantity of production. The districts of Pratapgarh, Sultanpur etc. have less number of *mandis* because of the less quantity of agricultural production.

Transportation Network

The transportation network indicates the interconnectivity of *mandi* centres to other market and settlement centres of the region. A well developed network helps the *mandis* to create the spatio-economic integration with the hinterland. It is seen in the distribution of *mandi* centres which are estalbished through railway or road axises. This fact is also analysed with the help of *mandi* accessibility. The study of accessibility indicates that 47 per cent of total *mandis* is located upto 1 km from nearest bus station. This type of regions are eastern part of Saryupar plain and eastern Ganga Ghagra doab. In the same way, 35.5 per cent *mandis* are 1-2 km away (Gonda, Basti, Varanasi) and 8.5 per cent are 2 to 3 km from nearest bus stations (Fig. 14.3).

In the same way nearabout 80 per cent of total *mandis* is between 2 km from the railway line.

Administrative Centres

It is worthmentioning that 80 per cent of *mandis* are located at the districts or Tahsil headquarters becuase of the convergence of surrounding population at administrative centres. Actually these centres are not only administrative centres but these are the control points of economic functions of the surrounding region and provide multipurpose facilities to the population. Hence, the exchange of commercial functions naturally takes place there.

Religious and Cultural Centres

Traditionally, the religious and cultural centres attract a large number of population. Hence, there a large variety of commercial activities develop. Therefore, the agricultural *mandis* are located there in reference to the nodal evolutions of infrastructures and other business activities. In the study region Allahabad, Varanasi, Ayodhya, Bahraich and

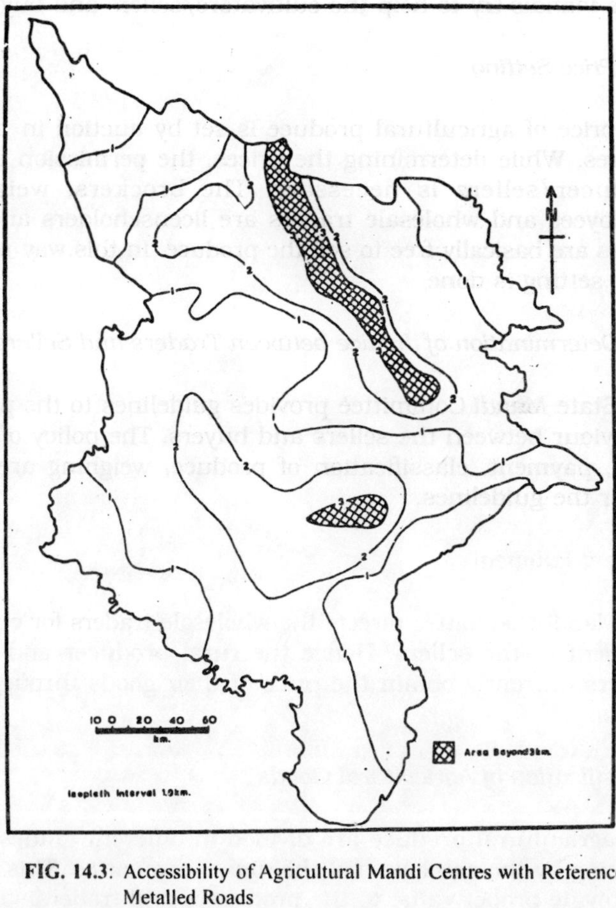

FIG. 14.3: Accessibility of Agricultural Mandi Centres with Reference to Metalled Roads

Gorakhpur are like such centres which posses 'A' grade *mandi* centres.

Functions of Agricultural *Mandis*

The agricultural *mandis* or regulated agricultural markets are different from rural markets where no guiding principle operates in commercial process. In stead of this, agricultural *mandis* are directed by 'State Mandi Committee' which prevents the presence of mediators and unfair pricing. The following are the important functions of *mandis* through which these *mandis* try to help the cultivators/sellers and buyers.

Fair Price Setting

The price of agricultural produce is set by auction in *mandi* centres. While determining the prices, the permission of the producer/sellers is necessary. The brockers, weighing employees and wholesale traders are licenseholders and the sellers are basically free to sell the produce. In this way proper price setting is done.

The Determination of Justice between Traders and Sellers

The State *Mandi* Committee provides guidelines to the proper behaviour between the sellers and buyers. The policy of sale, price, payment, classification of produce, weighing are also under the guidelines.

Current Payment

The Mandi Committee directs the wholesale traders for current payment to the sellers. Hence the rural producer and rural traders currently obtain the price of their goods through the banks.

Classification of Agricultural Goods

The agricultural produce are divided in different grades after cleaning by the employees of the *mandi* committee. This helps to provide proper value to the producers and traders.

Collection of Information and Diffusion of Innovations

The mandi centres always collect the agricultural and trading informations. These centres also diffuse the various agricultural innovations. In the study region Varanasi, Allahabad, Gorakhpur etc. are the centres which provide different innovative programmes and facilities.

The Provision of Public Facilities

The public facilities at *mandi* centres attract the sellers and buyers both. These are worthmentioning — drinking water supply, banks, post offices, electricity, the facilities provided to the animal, labourers, cleaning and lavotary etc.

The Storage Facilities

The *mandi* committee also provide storage to the sellers and buyers both at minimum cost.

Sample Study

There are 59 regulated agricultural markets in the study region. Only two *mandis*— Varanasi and Bahraich belong to special grade and for the purpose of the study, these are selected to study the various roles played by *mandi* centres for rural development.

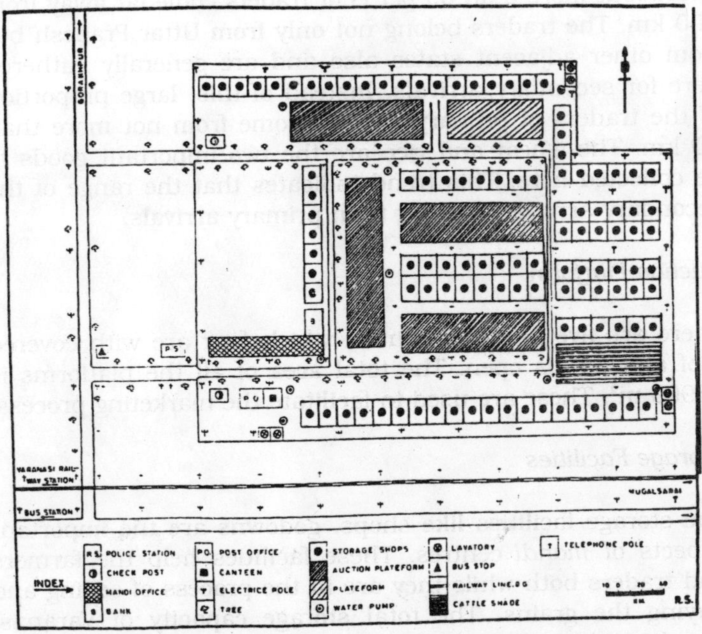

FIG. 14.4: Morphology of Agricultural Mandi Centre, Varanasi

Varanasi Mandi

Location

Varanasi *Mandi* is situated along the Varanasi-Gorakhpur national highway No. 29. This is connected with all the important towns of Eastern Uttar Pradesh and with some major towns of Bihar and Madhya Pradesh.

Public Facilities

Varanasi Mandi is of special class and has bus service, post office, telephone office, banks, canteen, checkposts, rest houses and other infrastructures regarding marketing.

Traders Behaviour

The hinterland of Varanasi *mandi* is very much extensive as it is clear from the interview of traders at *mandi* centre. Nearabout more than 50 per cent traders come far away from 100 km. The traders belong not only from Uttar Pradesh but from other adjacent states also and are generally gathered here for secondary arrivals. Instead of this, large proportion of the traders of primary arrivals come from not more than 40 km. The wheat and rice are the two important goods to be collected here. This trend indicates that the range of the secondary arrivals is larger than primary arrivals.

Auction Platform

There are five platforms out of which four are with covered roof and one is open. The total area of all the platforms is 16900 m^2. These are used to facilitate the marketing process.

Storage Facilities

The storage facilities like shops, godowns are the important aspects of *mandi* centres. These facilities help the farmers and traders both while they are in the process of selling and buying the grains. The total storage capacity of Varanasi *Mandi* is 1427 tonnes. Only storage facilities are provided to licenseholders. There are 110 godowns of which 26 'A' class with capacity of 520 tonnes, 26 'B' class with a capacity of 370 tonnes and also 26 'C' class with capacity of 260 tonnes. There are 32 'D' class godowns with the capacity of 256 tonnes. These godowns are constructed around the *mandi* platforms.

In this way it is clear that Varanasi *Mandi* has a vast influence area due to large proportion of secondary arrivals.

Bahraich Mandi Centre

This is located at the crossing of Bhinga and Kakarahi roads with Dargah road 3 km north from the town. It is connected with the surrounding towns by roads.

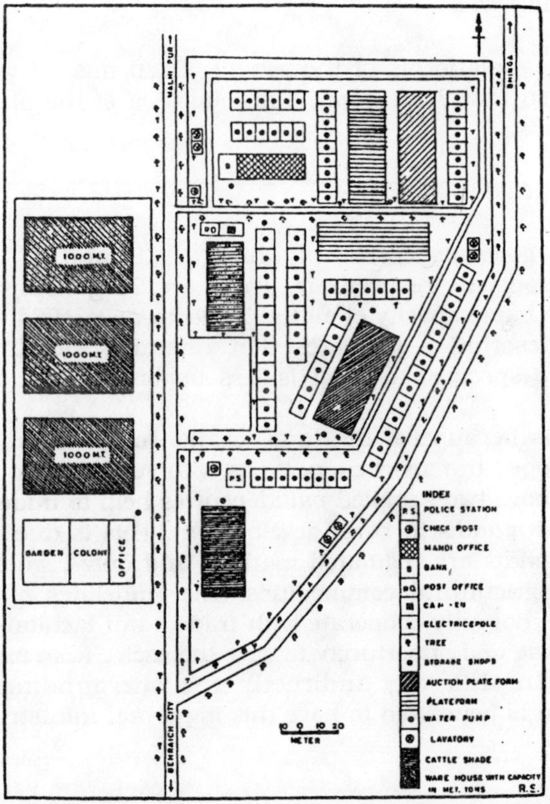

FIG. 14.5: Morphology of Agricultural Mandi Centre, Bahraich

Traders Behaviour

The major goods coming to this *mandi* are wheat, rice, pulses and oilseeds. More than 55 per cent traders come from less than 10 km distance. Only one third part of the traders belong to the distance of 30 km. This is specially due to the northern international border of Nepal and southern Rapti river.

Public Facilities

The infrastructural facilities like check post, post office, telephones, storage, animals house, banks and rest houses are constructed here.

Auction Platforms

There are 4 platforms of the size of 60x20 mts. of which 2 are covered and 2 are open. The total area of the platforms is 4800 m^2.

Storage Facilities

The total godowns are 83 of which 'A', 'B' and 'C' classes have 20 godowns respectively. There are 23 godowns in 'D' class. The total capacity of all the 20 godowns is 1084 tonnes.

The description indicates that Bharaich *mandi* centre belongs to special class but is less important than that of Varanasi.

This is because of the tarai location of this *mandi* and less developed transport connections with surrounding region.

The above two sampled *mandi* centres help to understand the role of *mandis* in rural development. This is due to that all the *mandis* are regulated markets and only regulate the trade of agricultural commodities. The guidelines of *mandi* committee not only cooperate with traders but facilitate them for fair trade and opportunity to save themselve from improper traders. In this way indirectly the surrounding farm population is benefitted to have this important infrastructure.

FIFTEEN

Regulated Market as a Focal Point of Economic Development: A Case Study of Mohibullapur Mandi, Lucknow

O.P. SHARMA

The chapter deals with the case study of a regulated agricultural market, Mohibullapur, located in the northern periphery of Lucknow metropolis. It is the cardinal point in the marketing channel connecting rural production centres with urban distribution and consumption centre. The development of ancillary facilities and market infrastructure at *Mandi* site, fair price regulation, quality control, construction of rural link roads, diffusion of agricultural innovations and its spatio-functional integration with marketing structure of the area, are some of the factors which help in raising agricultural production and rural income, leading to the socio-economic transformation of the surrounding area.

Introduction

The development process aims at transforming the efficiency level of the three basic components of the economy, i.e. the production, distribution and consumption; the regulated market, being the focal point of the distribution network of surplus agricultural commodities, infuses agricultural growth and raises the level of productivity at one hand, and with the help of efficient transport system collects and disposes the commodities for ultimate consumption at the reasonable price on the other. It is, therefore, a well planned meeting place for buyers and sellers to conduct wholesale business of agricultural commodities covered by government regulations.

Objectives of the Study

The main objectives of the study are:

(i) To deal with the genesis of establishment of Mohibullapur *mandi*, its location, morphological pattern, role of market committee, market-functionaries and marketing process of the commodities.
(ii) To examine the modes of transport and spatial linkages with its hinterland, traders' behavioural and visit patterns, *mandi*'s spatio-functinal integration with the marketing structure of the area and process of economic development through this market.

Data Base

The study is based on primary and secondary data collected from the market-yard by interviewing all categories of market participants and seeking verbal and documentary evidences from the office of the market-committee during the peak and slack seasons of the market arrivals.

Statement of the Problem

During the last few decades, the rapid industrial growth followed by high degree of urbanization has resulted in organizing large scale movement of foodgrains and other agricultural produce from rural areas in densely populated urban agglomerations. Therefore, the establishment of a regulated agricultural market in the periphery of major metropolitan centres is viewed not only as means of encouraging the local farmers, but also as an instrument of reducing the overall costs of the retail distribution of agricultural commodities. In the metropolitan city of Lucknow with more than 1.2 million population, the existing facilities for marketing agricultural commodities are located in Pandeyganj and Daliganj wholesale grain markets and other retail markets of Rakabganj, Fatehganj and Murlinagar. But these markets are located in highly congested localities surrounded by narrow streets and multi-storeyed buildings with chaotic jams throughout the day. Moreover, these markets are neglected, devoid of basic amenities with no place for further expansion and also inhospitable to producers and consumers.

Thus under U.P. Krishi Utpadan Mandi Adhiniyam, 1964, the present *mandi* was established by Rajya Krishi Utpadan Mandi Parishad and started functioning with effect from 28th Sept., 1978. The main objectives of its establishment are:

(i) to meet out ever-increasing demand of food grains for Lucknow urban agglomeration and its suburbs,
(ii) to reduce overall cost of commodities in retail markets,
(iii) to shift wholesale foodgrain trade from congested city markets to *mandi* site,
(iv) to eradicate mal-practices of the trade ensuring fair price-setting,
(v) to enfuse agricultural growth in the surrounding region,
(vi) to develop rural link-roads and effective channels of transportation, and
(vii) to develop agro-based industrial units in the area.

Location

This is an 'A' grade *mandi* located on the left side of Lucknow-Sitapur road (N.H.-24) covering an area of 31.31 acres of Mohibullapur and Purania villages in the Chinhat *Vikaskhand* of Lucknow tahsil (Fig. 15.1A). The site is free from water-logging and threat of floods with sufficient open space for future expansion of the market yard. Its surrounding hinterland is very fertile. The Mandi's sub-market yards have been established at Malihabad (29 km), Amaniganj (29 km), Mal (38 km), Itaunja (21 km) and Kakori (13 km).

Morphological Pattern and Functional Structure

The market yard is rectangular in shape (Fig. 15.2). The entry to the market yard is controlled from the main approach road by a guard room. The morphology of the *Mandi* can be explained by categorizing the premises of the yard into three parts, i.e. trading, ancillary and infrastructural ones.

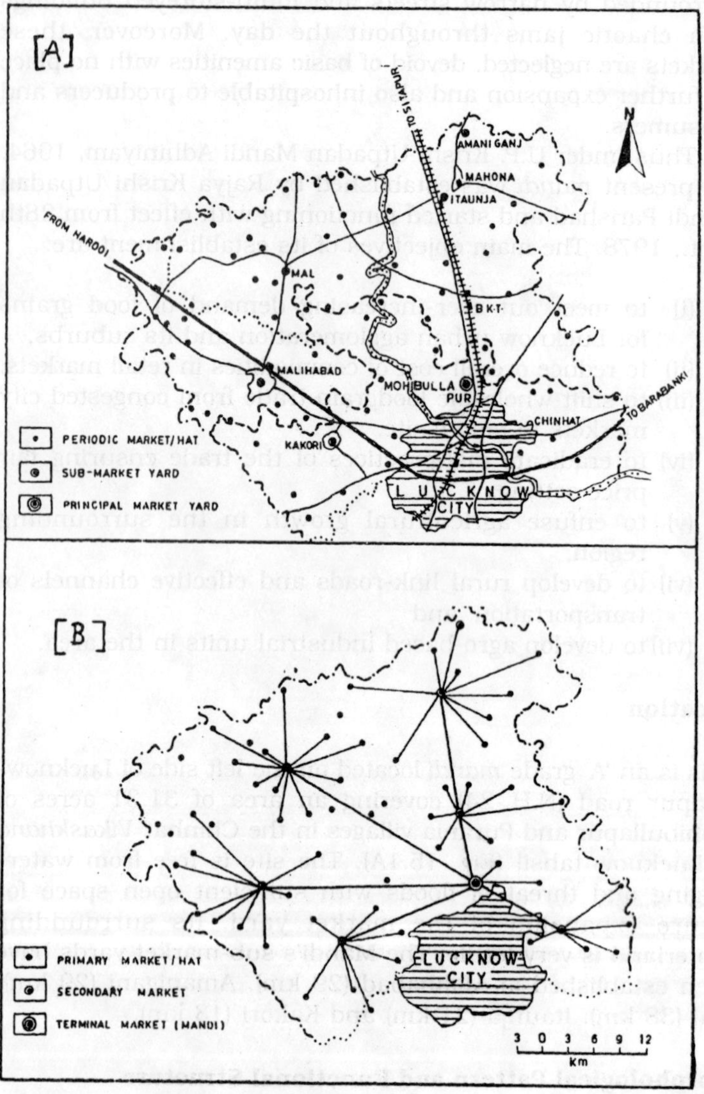

FIG. 15.1(A) : Mohibullapur: A Regulated Market
FIG. 15.1(B) : Pattern of Market Organisation in Hinterland of Mohibullapur (Based on Johnson's Method)

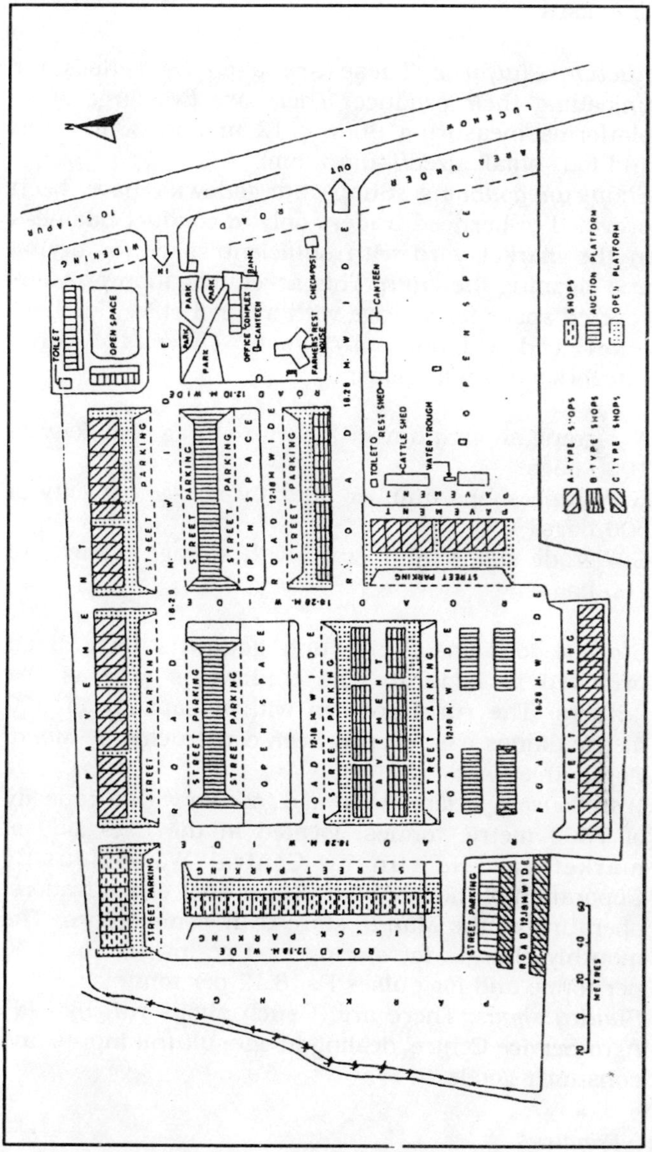

FIG. 15.2 : Market Morphology of Mohibullapur, 1986

Trading Premises

(a) *Auction Platform*: These are used by sellers for unloading their produce. There are two large sized platforms measuring 90m × 12 m and 88m × 9m and four small sized (40m × 8m).

(b) *Shop-cum-godowns*: Shop-cum-godowns have been provided to licenced traders only to conduct business in the market yard with sufficient space for drying and cleaning the grain. This accommodation provides covered space for storage with a small office, kitchen, toilet and a back court-yard. There are three categories of such shops:

(i) A = grade shops number 46 with storage capacity of 1000 bags.

(ii) B = grade shops number 30 with storage capacity of 500 bags.

(iii) C = grade shops number 10 with storage capacity of 100 bags.

(c) *Storage-godowns*: Ten such godowns have been provided to facilitate the traders as well as the farmers. The rural godown with a capacity of 500 metric tonnes has recently been constructed by *Mandi* Committee.

(d) *Warehousing facility*: A storage godown with a capacity of 7500 metric tonnes, located in the back-side of market yard is run by Central Ware Housing Coporation of India. About 60 per cent of the traders, operating at the *Mandi*, store their commodities. The monthly charges for storing food grains are Rs. 6.90 per tonne and for pulses Rs. 8.12 per tonne.

(e) *Sundry shops*: There are 3 such shops run by 'U.P. Agro Service Centre' dealing in agricultural inputs and consumer goods.

Ancillary Premises

Some of the ancillary facilities available in the market are check-post, administrative building, guest house, farmers' rest house, police post, Bank, Post office, canteen and public toilets.

Infrastructure

(a) Internal roads (18.28 m wide) have been provided.
(b) Parking space for trucks, tractors and other vehicles has been provided in the back side of the exit gate.
(c) Drinking water is supplied from Mandi's own overhead tank.
(d) Other amenities like electric supply, resting park, radio, television, newspapers, drainage, sanitation and first aid are also available in the market yard.

The Market Committee (*Mandi Samiti*)

It is named as *Krishi Utpadan Manaı Samiti*, Lucknow, and consists of 25 members, out of which 15 are farmers' representatives, 5 traders' representatives, one each from cooperative, warehouse, Senior Marketing Inspector, *Mandi Sachiv* and its President (District Magistrate of Lucknow). The main functions of the committee are:

(i) To ensure fair dealing between the producers/sellers and purchasers/traders and efficient marketing of the produce,
(ii) to ensure promopt and ready payment to the sellers,
(iii) to manage for grading, standardisation and auction of the produce,
(iv) to check the weights and meausres used by the traders,
(v) to provide better facilities in the yard and also to accelerate rural development programmes in the area,
(vi) to collect and provide upto date and reliable market information to the participants, and
(vii) to act as mediator in case of disputes between the parties.

Market Functionaries

Market functionaries consists of producers/farmers, traders (buyers and sellers), commission agents/brokers, employees for weighing, cleaning, bagging, loading, unloading and grading and 37 employees of Mandi Samiti's office. The peak-season daily number of participants during the months of

Table 15.1: Licence Holder Trader - 1985-86

Sl.No.	Licenced Traders	Number	Percentage
1.	The wholesalers cum commission agents	320	13.09
2.	The wholesalers	239	9.77
3.	Commission agents	191	7.81
4.	Retailers	743	30.39
5.	Mill owners	200	8.18
6.	Flour millers	64	2.61
7.	Brokers	19	0.78
8.	Truckers	626	25.61
9.	Oil Millers	18	0.74
10.	Others	25	1.02
	Total	2545	100.00

Source: Records of Market Committee.

November to January, and May and June was roughly estimated to be between 6000 to 10,000; and during the slack season participants during July to October and February to April were assessed to be between 3000 to 5000. Table 15.1 denotes that during 1985-86 the total number of licence holding traders of this *mandi* was to be 2445, out of which retail traders are the largest, i.e. 743 (30.39%).

Commodity Arrival

The agricultural commodities sold in the market consist of cereals, pulses etc., which fall under 24 commodities regulated by U.P. Mandi Parishad. Among the cereals paddy, wheat, maize, gram, barley are prominant; whereas pulses and oilseeds consists of 'arhar', 'masur', gram, mustard and linseeds etc. During the peak season of May and June, the daily arrival of the commodities range between 5000 to 6000 quintals whereas off-season arrivals fall to about 2000 quintals. During 1985-86 season the total annual arrivals were recorded to be 264409.2 metric tonnes with an increase of 36.22 per cent. The arrivals in the market may be categorized into primary and secondary:

(a) *Primary arrival* — It is mainly brought by the farmers and itinerant traders who frequent the market from nearby areas and periodic markets. Such arrivals constitute 70 to 75 per cent of the total commodities brought.

(b) *Secondary arrival* — Brought about by the wholesalers, it shares 25 to 30 per cent of the total. During 1985-86 it was 30630.7 metric tonnes.

Marketing Process

Here both types of trading, i.e. wholesaling and retailing, are undertaken during the week except weekly off on Sunday. First the produce is weighed in the yard and then brought to wholesale agent and graded. The role of auction takes place on the covered auction platform, where buyers and sellers negotiate openly. The market price is determined by the price mechanism of demand and supply and affected by prevalent market prices in other cities. The market fee is paid to the market committee on the value of the commodity sold. If the produce is not sold fully or partially due to unfavourable price offered on that date, the produce is kept in the storage godown maintained by the Market Committee.

Taxes

(i) *Mandi Shulk* (market fee) is leveyed on selling party at the rate of 1 per cent by the Market Committee.
(ii) Sales Tax at the rate of 4 per cent is charged from the buying traders.
(iii) Weighing and unloading charges are Rs. 0.70 per bag.
(iv) Commission at the rate of 1.5 per cent is charged from the retail traders (buyers) by the wholesalers.

Income of Market Committee

The income of the market committee falls under four categories:

(a) Market fee realized on the produce entering the market yard.
(b) Licence fee collected from the traders, commission agents etc.
(c) Miscellaneous charges consist of weighing, cleaning

fee and interest on surplus funds.

(d) The rent from shops and godowns, i.e. 'A' type shop is rented for Rs. 300 per month, 'B' type for Rs. 180 and 'C' type for Rs. 90, 'D' type and godowns for Rs. 90 per month.

Table 15.2 denotes that income of market committee is steadily increasing during the last five years except in 1983-84. The total income has registered an increase of 152.6 per cent during the last two years' period. Out of the total income of 40.62 lacs during 1985-86, about 90 per cent is received from market fee. With the full occupation of shops, godowns, increase in additional market arrivals and higher realization from cleaning, weighing charges, the income may become further substantial in the later years (i.e. atleast 25 to 30 per cent of the total income). Expenditure during 1985-86 amounted to be 31.58 lacs recording a net saving of Rs. 9.04 lacs (22.25%), which may be utilized for the extension of storage facilities, providing amenities in the yard and construction of rural roads linking primary and secondary markets to the *Mandi*. (Table 15.2)

Table 15.2: Income of Market Committee

(in Lakh Rs.)

Year	Total income	Increase %	Market fee	Licence fee	Misc. charges	Rent
1980-81	16.80		15.13	1.02	.50	.16
1981-82	20.27	20.00	18.62	.83	.10	.72
1982-83	22.33	10.16	17.36	.73	.08	2.16
1983-84	16.08	-27.98	14.90	.52	.04	0.62
1985-86	40.63	152.61	36.52	1.04	1.46	1.60

Source: Records of Market Committee.

Hinterland of the Market

This regulated market located in such a primate city, may also be termed as terminal market, where the agricultural commodities arrive not only from the immediate hinterland but also from its regional hinterland. The immediate hinterland consits of Lucknow urban agglomeration and the rural areas falling in development blocks of B.K.T., *Mal*,

Malihabad (Malihabad tahsil), Kakori and Chinhat blocks of Lucknow tahsil. The regional hinterland consists of Sitapur, Barabanki, Hardoi and Raebarely districts. It was revealed from the field investigations that most of the farmer-sellers and full time traders come from Itaunja, Mahona, Amaniganj, Kakori, Malihabad, Mal Chinhat (Lucknow district), Barabanki, Dewa, Kursi (Barabanki district), Sindhauli, Kanilapur, Barai, Jalalpur, Maschheta, Khairabad, Kuraura (Sitapur district), Sandila (Hardoi district), Bachhrawan (Raebarely district) and some parts of Unnao district. Therefore, the effective trade area of this *mandi* is stretched between 40 to 60 km in the north and north-western direction, 30 to 40 km in the east and 50 km in south and south-east direction.

Means of Transport and Spatial Linkages

Means for transporting the agricultural produce in the market are the trucks, tractor-trollies, horse-carts, tempo etc. All the means of transportation are available near the market yard. Most of the traders and producer-sellers (about 60%) use the trucks for transporting their commodity to the market. Sometimes a batch of 10 to 15 small farmers may hire a truck to the *mandi*. About 95 per cent of the sellers belonging to far and wide areas of Lucknow, Barabanki, Hardoi and Sitapur districts ranging between 15 to 60 km use the trucks; whereas, the small farmer-sellers covering the distance below 15 km, use the tractor-trollies. Since the creation and development of wholesale market well depend on roads and highways, Lucknow city is linked with all the surrounding towns and district headquarter thorugh national highways, state highways and district roads. The secondary markets (sub-market yards and daily markets) of the district are linked with all weather roads, while the primary markets (periodic *hats*) have also been linked with the former through semi-metalled roads. 'Under the Food for Work Scheme' following link roads, joining the prospective villages with main roads, have also been constructed by the Mandi Committee (Table 15.3).

Traders' Spatial Visit Patterns

The traders in the market yard can be categorized as (1) fixed buying traders, (2) visiting selling traders and farmers and (3) retail traders cum distributors and consumers.

Table 15.3: Village Link-roads Constructed by Mandi Committee

Sl. No.	Name of the Road	Length (in km)	No. of Bridges
1,	From Salempur Pataura to Lucknow-Mohan road	1.00	3
2.	From Qula-Mohamdi village to Lucknow-Bijnaur Road	1.00	3
3.	From Aurangabad village to Lucknow-Bijnaur Road	2.50	2
4.	From Ahibullapur to Malihabad	5.00	8
5.	From Mandwana to Mal	1.06	8
6.	From Mampur-Bana to Bakshi Ka Talab	1.06	9
7.	Mohibullapur village to Sitapur road	.55	2

Fixed Buying Traders

These are the registered wholesalers, commission agents and millers (Table 15.1), which are allottees of various types of shops in the market. Out of total wholesalers and commission agents about 25 per cent have occupied the shops and remaining still continue their trading activity in Pandeyganj, Daliganj and Murlinagar grain markets. About 90 per cent of the fixed traders reside in Daliganj, Chowk, Pandeyganj, Murlinagar, Naka and Aliganj localities. The distance travelled from their residence to the *Mandi* ranges between 3 to 7 km Their total investment in the trade averages between Rs. 50,000 to 5 lakh; and income is 1.5 per cent of the amount of the daily sales. It was revealed from the respondents interviewed in the market yard, that the traders operating in city's old wholesale markets earn more than 3 per cent profit. Some of the fixed traders, who are millers, purchase paddy, pulses, wheat and oilseeds for their processing mills.

Visiting-selling-traders and Farmers

The number of such traders was estimated to be 400 per day in the peak season and 200 during slack season. Out of visiting traders about 10 per cent are permanent traders, 60 per cent part-time traders and 30 per cent are the farmer-sellers. The permanent traders are mostly based in the periodic and daily market centres of the hinterland.

Retail Traders cum Distributors and Consumers

The number of these traders averaged about 500 per day during peak season and about 275 during slack season. They function as link between the wholesalers and the consumers. 95 per cent of them transact their retail business in different local (Lucknow city) markets, i.e., Chowk, Nakkhas, Rakabganj, Murlinagar, Sadar, Aliganj, Saadatganj, Alambagh etc. The consumers (5 % of the total purchasers) come from surrounding localities of the *Mandi.*

Mandi's Spatio-functional Integration

Functionally integrated and spatio-temporally synchronized marketing system, being the component of hierarchically organized settlement system in an area, 'is vital aspect for economic development, because this system will carry the impulsives of change' (Riddell, 1974). Johnson (1965, 70) has stated that wholesale markets (*mandis*) should be the nuclei with which the clusters of nearby villages should be economicaly integrated in such a way as to bring the adjacent villages within the region of influence of one other. In view of the above statement it has been observed that existing marketing structure of Lucknow district consists of the primary markets (periodic *hats*) at the central village level, secondary on assembling markets (permanent markets) at block and tahsil headquarters and the terminal or wholesale market at Mohibullapur, Lucknow (Fig. 15.1 B). In terms of hierarchical structure, villages are linked with small markets (primary markets) at lower level, where small and marginal farmers bring in the small quantities of agricultural produce for sale, and itinerant traders, petty merchants and agents of wholesalers/processers purchase and constitute the produce into sizeable units and the same is carried for further sale to the secondary markets, where wholesale merchants or the agents of sub-market yards make purchases. Itaunja, Mahona, B.K.T., Amaniganj, Mal, Malihabad, Kakori,

Banthara, Mohanlalganj and Gosaiganj are some of the secondary markets from where the traded commodity is brought to and disposed off in Mohibullapur *Mandi* or to some big traders and processers located in other parts of Lucknow city.

Impact on Economic Development

Regulated market is cardinal point in the nation's system of distribution of surplus agricultural produce. Though the development of efficient agricultural marketing system is an important part of agricultural development process, but it also transmits gradual transforming impact on the rural society.

The process of economic development in rural areas, through regulated market is illustrated with the help of a model (Fig. 15.3). It envisages that the surplus agricultural

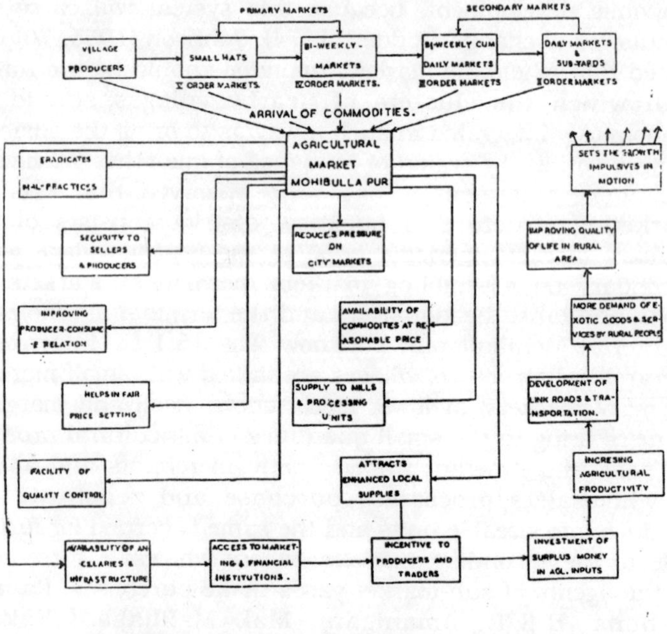

FIG. 15.3: Regulated Market and Economic Development

produce arrives at this wholesale terminal market, directly through the village producers or through primary and secondary markets in hierarchical pattern. Regulated market in turn ensures security to sellers by fair price setting and removing the mal-practices of under weight, unauthorized deductions etc. Further, grading, standardization and quality-control measures, availability of ancillary facilities and infrastructure, credit and banking facility, construction of rural link roads, diffusion of agricultural innovations, agricultural research facility etc. give impetus for increasing the agricultural productivity. Consequently, more surplus income is generated, which may be reinvested in agricultural inputs and may place more demands for exotic goods and services in rural area. Improvement in the farmers' quality of life i.e. the higher socio-economic and cultural needs, thus sets the growth impulses in motion.

On the other hand, the *mandi* reduces pressure on congested city markets, as most of the wholesalers of other markets have shifted their transaction to *mandi* site. It also makes available the commodities to consumers at reasonable prices and has also given incentive to agro-based processing units located in Daliganj area and other markets, by supplying the needed commodities. Therefore, it is obvious that regulated market has immense potential to help not only the rural people but also the entire spectrum of market users in both rural and urban centres.

SIXTEEN

Role of Commercial Activities and Development in the Ganga Basin: A Case of Pokhara City — Nepal

M.P. TRIPATHI and P.C. POUDEL

The lakes, snowy peaks of Annapurna, Dhaulagiri and Machhapuchre Himalayas, picturseqe natural scenes and scenaries, caves other spots have made the city an important tourist centre of the kingdom of Nepal. This has also been a major Himalayan trading centre in the past. It has an area of 52 sq. km. and population of nearly 80,000 at present (67521 in 1987). The meeting of several highways and routes from the sorrounding hills, helped in providing the basic needs of the city and it has also affected the general layout of the town. Till 1953 (with the development of Airport), it was connected by hill trails only, from all sides (East, West, North and South). It was inaccessible and its social and economic development has been more or less developed independently.

Pokhara, the zonal and regional headquarters is situated at the junction of three high ways — Prithwi, Siddhartha and Baglung in the central hill region of Nepal. The Seti River divides the city into two parts—west and east. It is located between 28° N.L. and 84°5' E.L. It is connected by Air from Kathmandu, Bhairawa and Baglung. It is about 200 km west from Kathmandu, the capital city of Nepal. It is nearly straight located in the north at the distance of 300 km from Gorakhpur city, the important commercial and administrative centré of the State of Uttar Pradesh, in India. The average height of the city is 3000 ft. from the sea level. Pokhara is the inter mountain city bounded by the hills of Mahabharat ranges. Therefore, this is a beautiful city of Himalayan region.

The whole city is drained by Seti River, tributary of Gandaki River (Fig. 16.1).

> "Being an intermountain city, it has remained cut off from the rest of the country and world till recently (1953) and its habitat economy and social structure have grown more or less independently having a little influence of the out side world. But now Pokhara city has experienced much change in all aspects within two and half decades."

Historical Development of Commercial Activities

Till the close of 18th century, development of commercial activities was negligible and insignificant. It was not a town,

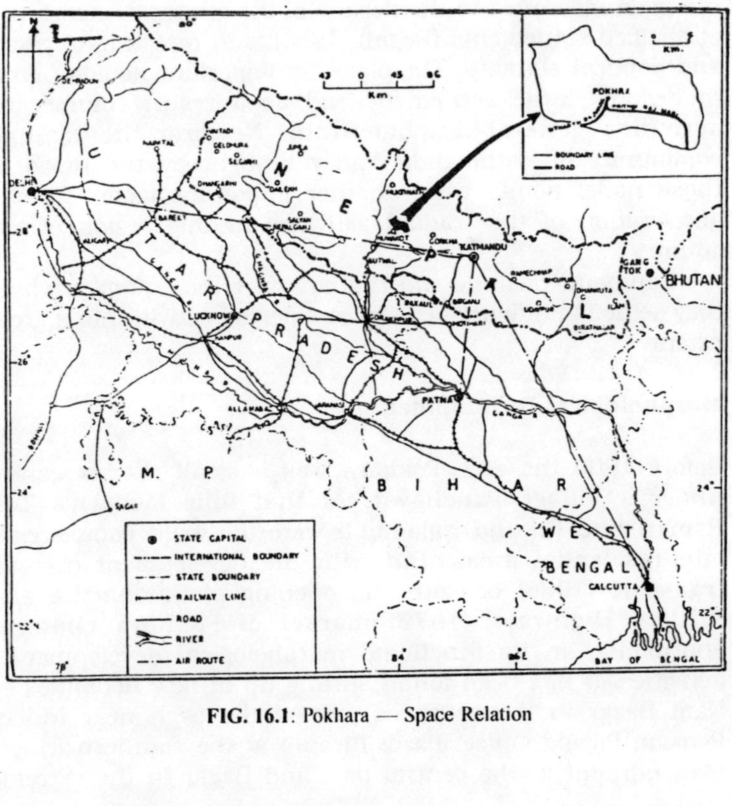

FIG. 16.1: Pokhara — Space Relation

but a small rural village. In 18th century the country was divided into many principalities controlled by the *Baise* (22) and Choubise (24) Rajas. Kaskikot, 3 hours walking distance from the present Pokhara City was only the capital town of Kaski King. Kaskikot is located on the south-eastern part of Kaski Ridge (1600m). All the major settlements were fortified on hills (*Kots*) and the lower places were used for cultivation due to unsuitable climatic condition and their weak strategies. Gorkha, Tanahum, Syangja, Kaski and Lamjung were the main settlements at that time. These settlements were generated as Military centres to serve the military and administrative needs commercial activities coming out of the principalities.

Thus, it may be said that town in this region came into existance only after the conquest of western Nepal by Gorkha dynasty to the close of 18th century and foundations of one strong kingdom led to the decline of the strategic importance of fortified settlements (Regmi, 1956) with restoring of peace and political stability. The places of important nodality grew to become large settlement and as a result commercial activities generated momentum. Newars, the trading community of Kathmandu Valley brought by the Rajas at those nodel points were another important factor for the acceleration of the trading activities in this region of the country.

Bandipur, Baglung and Pokhara were the examples where they settled and flourished the commercial activities to a great extent.

Morphological Development

Before 1960 the city, Pokhara was a small market centre under a Village Panchayat. At that time Mohoriya Tol, Ramkrishne Tol and Nalamukh were the main commercial-cum-residential areas. But with the development of road transport (1968) or with the opening of Siddhartha and Prithwi Highways (1972) market of Pokhara changed enormously in its functional morphological developmental activities. It has been found sprung up in new nodalities — Ram Bazar in the southern part of the twon near Indian Pension Paying Office, Pardi Birauta at the southern fringe, Mahendrapul in the central part and Bagar in the extreme north of the city. All these centres have developed in the different nodialities away from the old market centres.

Medium and small industries have sprung in the out skirt of the city's industrial estate. Besides, many small scale industries like ice factory, soda water, drinks, sweets, rice amd flour mill and several other industries have also came into existence. The introduction of land and air transport have now brought the modern phase of development of the city. So far as the educational functions are concerned the city has grown considerably. It has a University Campuses, Engineering, Medicine, Forestry, Education, Humanity and Social Sciences, Science and Technology, Law and Management.

Commercial Functions in the City

The nature of commercial functions in Pokhara is different from the commercial functions of the Tarai Towns of Nepal. As the economy of the hinterland is poor and purchasing capacity of the people is low, the commercial function in general is of low level. For the purpose of this study various functions have been identified and grouped in order to their local importance. Functions of Banks, Electric works, Veterinary services are of secondary importance in the developed zone but here these functions are of prime importance.

Retailing is one of the most common function in the city. Most nodality of the city have retail shops dealing mainly convenience retail goods. Grocery, cigarettes and country liquors are found the dominant commercial activities. Medical shops, provision shops, books shops, stationary are found in centres and these things do not get in small places. Meat and vegatables are found in open space. However, treaking route consume a good amount of cold drinks and provision goods.

A detail land use survey of Pokhara City reveals that ther is no market system of specialised commercial activities. Majority shops in the cicy are of mixed nature e.g. a portion of the shops is used for grocery and other for clothes. Whole-saling is also practiced along with retail activity. Functions belonging to catering includes restaurants, hotels and *bhatti*. *Bhatti* are gradually replaced by hotels and restaurants.

Table 16.1: Nature of Commercial Activities in Pokhara, 1981-1989

(In percentage)

No	Nature	Before 1966	1966-74	1975-80	1981-84	1985-89	Total in 1989
1.	Medical	12 (7.9)	4 (1.8)	12 (3.3)	16 (2.3)	3 (0.41)	47 (2.17)
2.	Clothes	29 (19.2)	57 (25.5)	36 (9.9)	41 (5.8)	84 (11.5)	247 (11.39)
3.	Hotel/ Restaurant	13 (8.6)	16 (7.1)	10 (2.8)	27 (3.8)	8 (1 1)	74 (3.42)
4.	Hardware/Construction Materials	1 (0.7)	5 (2.2)	5 (1.4)	8 (1.1)	12 (1.7)	31 (1.43)
5.	Tourist Industry	—	2 (0.9)	3 (0.8)	14 (2.0)	26 (3.6)	45 (2.08)
6.	Petrol Pump	—	1 (0.5)	2 (0.6)	6 (0.85)	4 (0.6)	13 (0.60)
7.	Electrical Goods	—	1 (0.5)	2 (0.6)	8 (1.1)	5 (0.7)	16 (0.74)
8.	Grocery/General Store	37 (24.5)	37 (16.6)	46 (12.8)	142 (20)	150 (20.7)	412 (19.0)
9.	Printing Press/ Typing	—	2 (0.9)	3 (0.8)	6 (0.9)	11 (1.5)	22 (1.02)
10.	Provision shop	2 (1.3)	2 (0.9)	6 (1.7)	12 (1.7)	45 (6.2)	67 (3.09)
11.	Photo Studio	2 (1.3)	1 (0.5)	2 (0.6)	11 (1.6)	9 (1.2)	25 (1.15)
12.	Metal Works	4 (2.7)	2 (0.9)	10 (2.8)	21 (3.0)	20 (2.7)	57 (2.63)
13.	Service Industry	—	2 (0.9)	4 (1.1)	29 (4.1)	30 (4.1)	65 (3.0)
14.	Jewlery/ Goldsmith	5 (3.3)	3 (1.3)	2 (0.6)	4 (0.6)	10 (1.4)	24 (1.10)
15.	Stationary/ Books	2 (1.3)	2 (0.9)	3 (0.8)	13 (1.8)	7 (0.96)	27 (1.24)
16.	Industries/Cottage Medium	15 (9.9)	14 (6.3)	47 (13.0)	52 (7.4)	39 (5.4)	167 (7.70)
17.	Tea Stall	20 (13.3)	40 (18.0)	101 (28.0)	138 (19.5)	147 (20.2)	446 (20.57)
18.	Cold/Soft Drinks	—	10 (4.5)	33 (9.1)	45 (6.4)	32 (4.4)	120 (5.54)
19.	Others	9 (6.0)	22 (9.9)	34 (9.4)	112 (15.0)	86 (11.8)	263 (12.13)
	Total	151 (100)	223 (100)	361 (100)	705 (100)	728 (100)	2168 (100)

Note - Figures in bracket indicate the percentage of the total.

Source : A.R. Mulmi, *Prithwinarayan Campus Journal*, 035/36, p. 4. Town Panchayat Office, P.C. Poudel, *Urbal Land Use of Pokhara Town (1981/82)*: A Project Report. Field Work 1989.

Old market of Pokhara is mainly associated with goods of daily uses—Grocery and other essential goods like clothing, food items etc. But the situation is different in new market complex of Mahendrapul. Here catering, fancy goods and garments, provision stores etc. associated with modern urban life dominates the commercial activities (Fig. 16.2). The

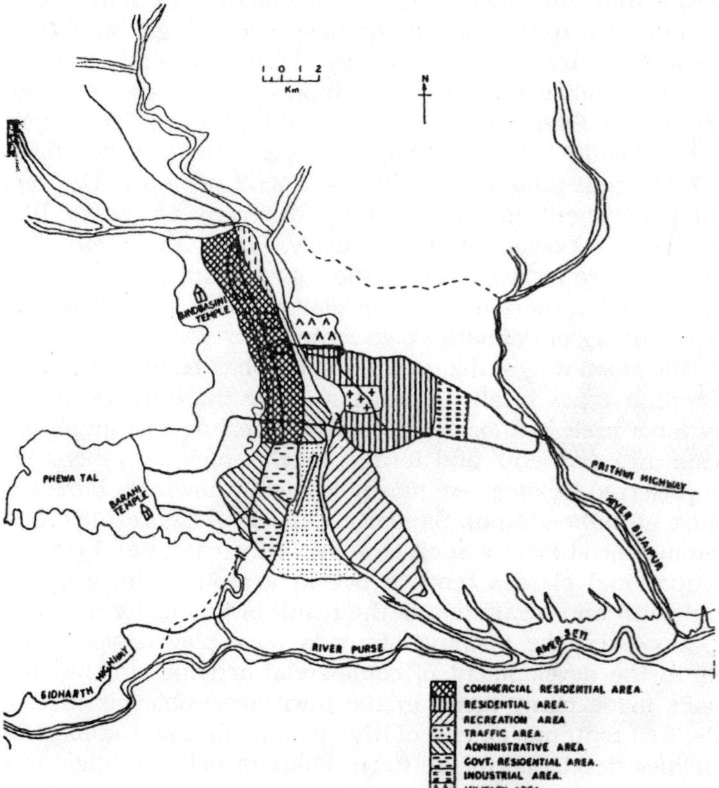

FIG. 16.2: Pokhara Town: Land Use

unplanned lay out of the street, traditional type of the buildings and geographical location are the main reasons for the more concentration of traditional type of business activities in the old section of Pokhara Town. Whereas planned layout of the street, modern designed building etc. have attracted the business activities mainly associated with modern amenities in new market complex of Pokhara.

It is obvious that there are different retail shops characterised by a large variation in the number of shopping unit as well as in the number of retail function. Table 16.1 reveals that out of the total major commercial activities of Pokhara Town (1989) the highest percentage (20.57) is occupied by tea stall followed by Grocery+general store 19 per cent, Clothes 11.39 per cent, Industries Cottage + medium 7.7 per cent, Cold + soft drinks 5.54 per cent, Hotel + Resturant 3.42 per cent, Provision Shop 3.09 per cent, Medical stores 2.17 per cent, and Tourist Industry 2.08 per cent. The rest 25.04 per cent is occupied by different activities like Stationary + Books, Service Industry, Photo Studio etc. One medium wave broadcasting station, two hydro electric power houses and airport are the special function located within the boundary of Pokhara Town Panchayat.

The clustering of the urban function has resulted because of certain types of shops can pay more than others in the city for a preferred location. So shops dealing with imported goods and garments and tourist hotel, which can afford for the preferred locatioin are mostly located in the main business centre at Mahendrapul. Similarly, clustering has resulted due to some social factors such as most of the castes and certain occupational classes tend to live in a group. Clustering of Goldsmith and meat shop is the result of this factor.

Moreover, the opening of roads have played significant role in the development of commercial activities in the city. Roads made many areas in the town accessible because of this frequent movement of the people to the commercial activities developed in the town. Pokhara being a single city is performing a central functions to the surrounding rural areas. It is said that roads have brought market, markets have given birth to commercial activities and the latter subsequently have caused urban development. In other words opening of roads seems to be the first stage in the rapid development of marketing activities in Pokhara.

Before the construction of the two highways — Siddhartha and Prithwi (between 1968-72) commercial activities were very limited in different localities of Pokhara. But soon after the construction of two highways and with the declaration of Pokhara as a regional administration centre, series of commercial complexes have been developed in different localities — Mahendrapul, Chipledhunga, Prithwi Chowk, Bagar, Tersapathi, Ratnapuri, Pardi, Birauta, Ram Bazar, Pokhara Hospital Complex, Kundher, and Phewa lake side area of the city. Now the city has an opportunity of enjoying all regional services and inter-wening opportunities. Several commercial activities of high orders have been sprung creating an organised marketing system especially in the central business district area of Mahendrapul. Now the newly constructed Mahendrapul Bridge (20 tonnes capacity) has also enhanced the capacity of commercial and industrial establishment of the city. The under construction of Pokhara Baglung Highway has also added the further developmnt of the town recently.

Thus the retail structure of Pokhara city has developed rapidly and systematically within two and half decades. The population in 1954 was 3755 which increased to 67500 in 1987 and 80000 at present. During 1961 commercial activities in Pokhara town were very limited and insignificant. It was limited in old town area of Bagar, Terchapatti, Bhimsen Tole, Nalamukh and Bhairab Tole. But after two and half decades the pattern has enormously changed (Table 16.1). Business complexes have expanded through all the existing shoping centres. One of the trend results is that some new centres of commercial activities have been emerged recently in the town. The development of the commercial activities in the city has maintained a continuity along with development of the city. It shows the linear development along both side of the road. Further it will serve as an important service centre to the rich agricultural region of Hill and Tarai region of Ganga Basin.

SEVENTEEN

Periodic Markets in Million Cities of Ganga Basin: A Case Study of Kanpur Metropolis

R.C. SRIVASTAVA

Beyond peasant socities periodic markets not only continue to flourish in cities but also play a significant role in their retail trade. This chapter aims to (i) trace out the evolution of periodic markets, (ii) focuss light on spatio-temporal visit patterns of traders and consumers, (iii) analyse their role in the retail trade of Kanpur metropolis, (iv) identify their problems and suggest a plan for their survival and development. Study is based on intensive field surveys. Five per cent of consumers and 10 per cent of traders of six selected markets have been covered by schedules implying stratified random sample technique.

Periodic markets in Kanpur metropolis came into existence during different stages of its growth. As the average intermarket distance is 5.5 km there is a good spatio-temporal synchronization among them. Periodic markets in all have 6200 shops (under 38 functions) but the outstanding feature is the concentration of the shops of low-order convenience goods. As the traders give preference to the nearest markets a strong correlation (-.62 to -.87) has been observed between the numbers of traders and travel distances. The local traders patronize those markets where they get some cultural affinity and homogenity. Ninety per cent traders visit a respective market on all market days. Periodic markets of this city, in real sense, are the market of low-income population group whose attachment is still towards rural culture. They satisfy themselves on poor-quality low-order convenience goods and give much stress on the price of the commodity.

These markets, though, deal a small percentage of city's retail business but the role they play in fulfilling the requirements of low-income population, is immense. These markets are facing a lot of problems for their survival. Since these markets are unplanned and lack basic amenities, they deserve patronization and improvements by civic authorties.

Beyond peasant societies periodic markets not only continue to flourish in cities but also play a significant role in their commercial structure. Moreover, the intineracy of stall holders is more fundamental than the periodicity in metropolitan cities (Scott, 1970). Periodic markets are still surviving in all million cities of the Ganga Basin, i.e. Delhi, Kanpur, Lucknow, Calcutta and Dhaka because they have maintained their indigenous character. Kanpur, an industrial city of the Ganga basin, still maintains nine periodic markets which attract consumers of all walks of life as the existence of periodic market is closely related to the needs of the society and not just the exchange of goods (Symansky, 1973). It is striking that such markets are surviving in the areas of well-established retail markets and the of CBD Kanpur. Periodic markets of Kanpur metropolis not only play a dominant role in its retail trade but also, indirectly, control the expenditure budget of its consumers.

Objectives

The objectives of this study are:

(i) trace out the evolution of periodic markets which survived under different conditions,
(ii) focuss light on spatio-temporal visit patterns of traders and consumers,
(iii) analyse the role of such markets in the retail trade of this metropolis, and
(iv) identify their problems and suggest a plan for their survival and development.

Methodology

The present study is based on intensive field surveys carried during the period of 1976 to 1986. Data regarding consumer and traders travel patterns, consumers' buying behaviour, existing and changing functional structure and problems of periodic markets have been collected with the help of interview schedules prepared seperately for consumer and trader. Ten per cent of traders (both local and farmer sellers) representing only cloth, apparel-cum-hosiery, vegetables, grains and *kabar*[1] items (reprsenting more than 75 per cent total traders) were covered on the basis of stratified random sampling technique. 5 to 10 per cent of the consumers (purchasers of vegetables, grains, *kirana*[2] cloth, apparel and *kabar* representing about 90 per cent) were covered randomly. Out of nine periodic market only six markets[3] have been selected for this study on the basis of their location, functions, and size. Some of the hypotheses related to trader and consumer travel patterns have been tested. A spatio-temporal shopping trip model has been developed to show the interrelationship of various factors affecting their mobility and trip decisions.

Evolution and Characteristics

Periodic markets in Kanpur metropolis came into existence during the different stages of its growth. Parade, the largest periodic market, ows its inception from the year of the First War of Independence, i.e. 1857. Five hundred acres of land (adjoining to Mestan road and Parade) along with a garden was given to Salar Bux, the then *Kotwal* of the city on February, 1962 for his meritorious services to the British Government in the year 1857 by Queen Victoria. Later on the request of the then influential persons of the city Salar Bux permitted this land for holding open free market in the name of 'Salar Ganj'. Kanpur Municipal Board made attempts to acquire a considerable part of this land under 'Civil Improvement Act'. Since 1951 the 'Parade Market Committee' is managing this market.

Kanpur Improvement Trust, which was established in 1919, took up the work of the construction of *ahatas*[4] and workmen's quarters (Bhatnagar, 1965) to provide residences to factory labourers who were growing day by day. Darshanpurwa and Dwarikapuri, the two small periodic markets, situated within *ahatas*, were started by the *ahata* owners near factory area in the 3rd decade of this century to fulfill the requirements of low-order convenience goods for labour population. Sisamau, Beconganj and Faithfulganj markets came into existence later on due to expansion of the city and unending flow of rural immigrants as Majumdar (1960) has rightly remarked "about the persistant rustic aspects of its especialized (periodic) markets which is due to the flow of rural immigrants who continue to nurse their old culture". Jajmau and Lal Banglow which are located in the east of Cantonment area in the outer zone of the city (Fig 17.1) are the old village periodic markets but at present are owned by urban lanlords. Bakerganj market was started after the construction of Babupurwa Labour Colony (during Sixties) in the south of G.T. road to cover the shopping needs of the people inhabiting in nearby old villages and labours residing in this area.

The characteristics of periodic markets of this city are quite different to the other metropolises of the Ganga Basin where such markets have been included in the category of specialized markets, particularly dealing with vegatables, fruits and second hand goods. These markets are also different than the permanent daily retail markets of the city. The rural immigrants and labours who reside in slums, labour colonies and old villages of the city continue to nurse their old culture, need typical market. These markets have still maintained their indigenous character. In real sense, such markets are the market of low-income group population who depend upon periodic markets and not only visit them for low-order convenience goods but also for a few high-order shopping goods. These markets, except Parade, are managed by urban landlords who collect *tahbazari* (rent) from shopkeepers on each market day. Schedule of the markets are in such a way that the traders can easily dispose off their goods during the weekend. Except Jajmau, all are tri-weekly market. There is a good spatio-temporal synchronization among the markets. Retail traders of new and second hand goods gather two or three times a week on fixed days at these places and spread their goods for sale (Bhatnagar, 1965). These markets, being unplanned, have haphazardly developed and formed typical shapes. Their poor physical condition gives a rustic appearance. Consumer behaviour differs as compared to daily retail market goers as majority of its consumers give stress on the price of the commodity rather than their quality. The functional structure and morphology of some of these markets are under gradual change.

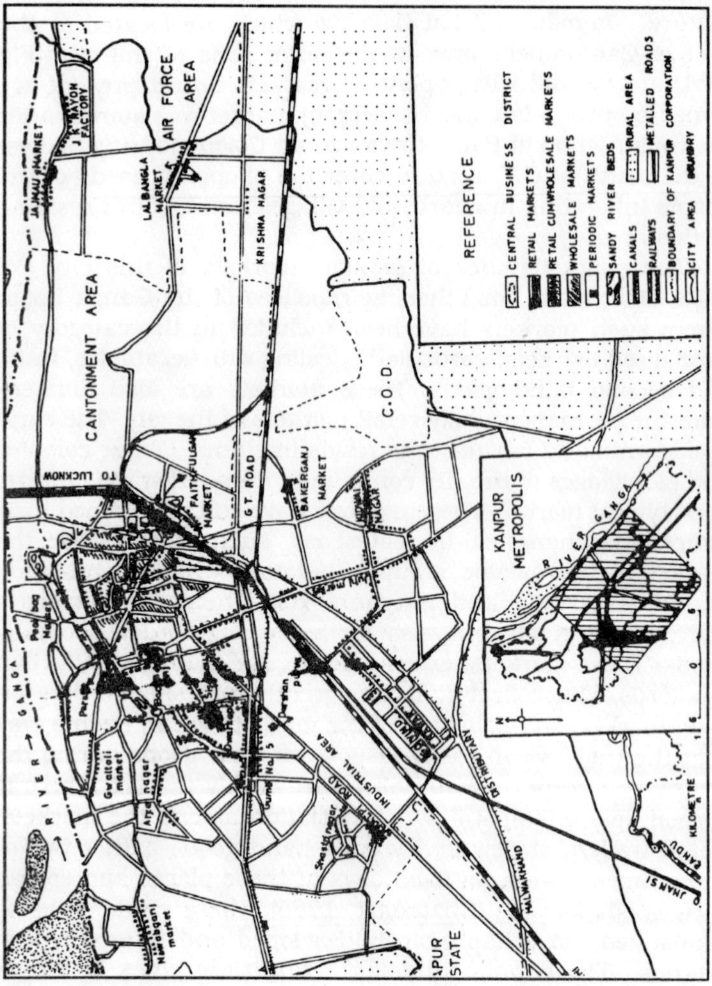

FIG. 17.1: Distribution of Markets

Retail Trade and Periodic Markets

The retail structure of this city has developed in phases but it has maintained a continuity along with its expansion, though the previous development is haphazard. Initially the city grew around the business district and later the business district expanded and encroached upon the open lands. It has developed a specialized nature of retail trading. More than 50 per cent of the especialized area is located in CBD. About 75 per cent of the commercial establishments of the city are found here, attracting large number of buyers and sellers, which swell to several lakh at times. Most of the regional shopping areas fall in CBD which lies in the heart of inner core of the city. Retail markets of CBD constitute a lower percentage of total trade in comparison to its wholesale trade. Though the intensity of business activity gradually declines towards the edge of CBD and more sharply towards the east and north but in the west several planned markets, such as Gumti No. 5 market, P. Road market, Eighty Feet Road market and Aryanagar market which primarily deal with retail trade, have also developed. In the southern and eastern parts of the city some commercial ribbons and small shopping centres have been added in the newly developed residential areas during the last two decades.

In the presence of different types of commercial ribbons, arteries, main business thorough fares and regional shopping areas the traditional and indigenous character of shopping is well marked in this metropolis on account of the existence of periodic markets. Retailing is the main characteristic of periodic markets existing in cities whether it is in European countries or in India. Most metropolitan markets exhibit fluctuation in trading and not all are daily market (Fig. 17.2). All the nine periodic markets of this metropolis perform a good deal of retail business. Periodic markets, in all, have about 6200 shops but this number fluctuates season to season. Thirty-eight functions have been identified but the outstanding feature is the concentration of shops of low-order convenience goods, such as vegetables, fruits, grains, fish and meat, grocery, other edibles and domestic goods. Among high-order shopping goods cloth, apparel, hosiery, footwear, cosmetic and utensils represent a good percentage. Almost all markets have service shops among which repair shops dominate. Some of the markets (Parade and Beconganj) are

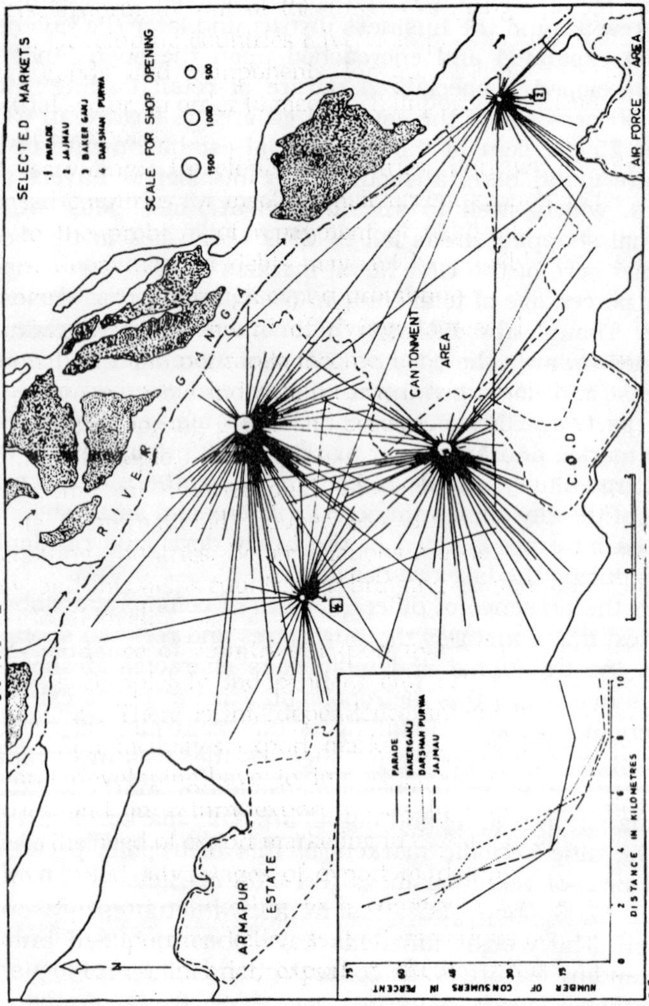

FIG. 17.2: Consumer Travel Patterns

popular for secondhand goods and *Kabar* items which are purchased by low-income and middle-income group population.

Parade, the biggest market, having 1500 shops is extended in a rectangular shape (Fig. 17.1). It is primarily a market of cloth-cum-apparel and *kabar* items which share 59 and 16 per cent of the total shops respectively. It is the only market which especializes in *kabar* goods for which the customers come from all walks of life both from the city and nearby villages and towns. Among *kabar* items; military disposal goods, secondhand garments, clothes, machinery parts, old shoes, equipments, tyres and books are sold. The shops in front of M.G. Road deal with only footwear and perhapes give the highest sale in the city. Its eastern sector adjoining U.H.M. Hospital accommodates only readymade garments. Bakerganj, the second biggest market, with 1300 shops mainly deals with vegetables, grocery items, grains, cloth and apparel. This market had a cattle sale space but due to encroachment by the shopkeepers it gradually disappeared. Beconganj, located in a Muslim locality, is the market of cloth, apparel and *kabar* like Parade but the number of shops is about 900. Sisamau is again a planned periodic market and deals with cloth, readymade garments and vegetables. Jajmau and Bakerganj are the two markets in which farmer sellers percentage is very high and they deal in grains and vegetables. Dwarikapur, Darshanpurwa and Lalbanglow, smaller in size, are the market of low-order convenience goods and cheap quality of high-order shopping goods.

Since the periodic markets of this metropolis provide retail business their contribution in the retail trade of the city is significant and valuable too. If the sale of cloth-cum-apparel items is taken into consideration during the weekend period this sale of all small and big markets is in no way lesser than permanent retail markets because the major trade of cloth and hosiery items in Kanpur city is handled by wholesale markets. The next item which dominates the retail business is the *kabar* items as no other daily market deals such items. These markets are also known as 'vegetable markets'. Retail trading of vegetables handled by these periodic markets is more than three fourth of all retail trade because the price of different items is found much lower than permanent isolated vegetable shops. Retail trade of other articles, such as grocery, cosmetics, utensils, footwear and ready garments is not significant as these items have to face a tough competition to permanent retail markets. In fact it is a great legacy of the old inhabitants of the place who created such markets, the commodities of which reflect various needs of almost all levels of population, rich and poor, urban and rural, culturally advanced and backward, sophisticated high officials and poor labours, etc. (Suresh, 1971).

Spatio-Temporal Visit Patterns of Traders and Consumers

Periodic markets of this metropolis deal with only horizontal trade which is shared by local traders (residing in the city) and farmer-sellers. The question of itinerant trader does not arise as intermarket distances are small and all the traders are home-base trader. Farmer-sellers who represent only 12 per cent of the total sampled sellers of selected markets, deal in grain, pulses, vegetables, fruit and fish and a few other agricultural produce. The spatio-temporal travel purpose model indicates that the visit pattern of traders is influenced by goals, poisitional utilities, physical and cultural barriers, value system, style of life and cultural determinants (Fig. 17.3). Accessibility or proximity of periodic makets influeneces the visit patterns of traders to a great extent. Traders actually visit that market which is closest to them on a given day. This hypothesis seems to be correct in the present context as there is strong corrletaion between the number of traders and their travel distances (*r* values in reference to Bakerganj, Parade, Jajmau and Dwarikapuri markets come to -.62, .87, -.81 and -.71 respectively (Srivastava & Gupta, 1978).

Distance above 10 km is covered by one per cent traders. Moreover, the mean walking distances covered by five categories of traders in four selected markets i.e. Parade (2.40 km), Bakerganj (1.60 km), Jajmau (2.10 km) and Dwarikapuri (1.80 km) also supports the said hypothesis that traders give preference to the nearest centre. Cultural barriers of the city obstruct their mobility to some extent as they have to follow much circutious and longer routes. Value system, life style and socio-economic and cultural determinants influence the visit pattern of traders to a great extent. Traders sometimes patronize those markets where they get some cultural affinity and homogenity as Beconganj and Sisamau are patronized by 72.5 per cent Muslim and 85 per cent Hindu traders

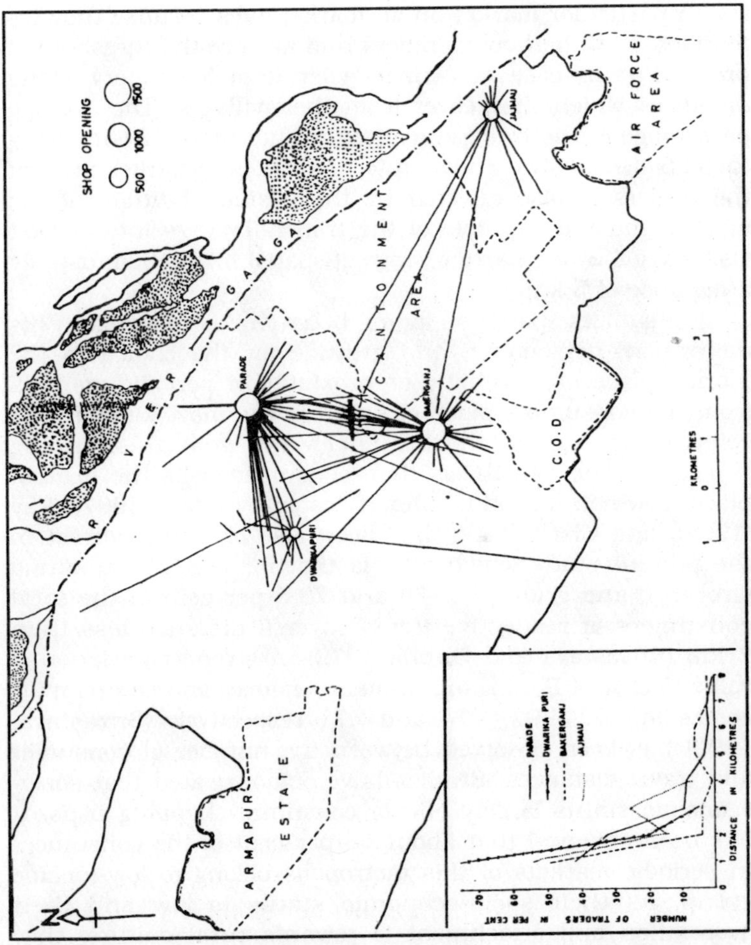

FIG. 17.3: Trader Travel Patterns

respectively.

Traders temporal travel pattern is decided by their frequency of visit to a particular market and also by intermarket visits. Traders frequency of visit to the selected markets is very high as more than 90 per cent of the traders visit a particular market on all market days because they try to dispose off their consignment and achieve the threshold of profit. But in case of farmer-seller it is low due to long distances which they cover from their villages. The average percentage of the traders involved in intermarket visit comes to 63.5 (Srivastava and Gupta, 1978). Intermarket visit of the traders is also affected by the positional utility of the market and the life style of the trader. Traders intermarket visit reveals a very narrow range of spatial interaction, usually a distance of 5 km.

Consumers spatial shopping behaviour is reflected in his motivation, personality, and attitude for the choice in the market place. Accessibility or proximity of periodic markets from the consumers place of origin is the most forecful and relevant factor which influences his spatial shopping behaviour. The hypothesis that 'consumer visits the nearest place at which a good is offered' tested by Berry (1967), Ray (1968), and Clark (1968) has been also observed correct in the present study which reveals that for vegetables, *kirana* (grocery), and grains 76, 75 and 73.5 per cent of the total consumers of respective items cover a distance less than 2 km (Srivastava and Gupta, 1979). A strong correlation (*r* value in case of Beconganj, Sisamau, Jajmau and Dwarikapuri comes to -.67, -.92, -.74 and -.71 respectively (Srivastava, 1990) has been observed between the number of consumer and travel distances. Studies have demonstrated that socio-economic status largely affects consumer shopping trips. It has been observed that about 66 per cent of the consumers in periodic markets of this metropolis belong to low-income group. As their socio-economic status is low and their association and attachment is towards rural culture, they satisfy themselves on poor quality cheap goods and give preference to these traditional markets (Srivastava and Gupta, 1979). Dwarikapuri and Jajmau, in real sense, are the market of 'low-income group population' as 70.8 per cent and 85 per cent of the total sampled consumers visiting these two markets, belong to this group.

Consumers of these markets seldom visit high-order business centres for more specialized goods. Consumers shopping trip is also controlled by the physical and cultural barriers existing in and around the city, particularly the river Ganga which forms the northeastern boundary of this city. Analysis of the data also reveals that the consumers visiting such markets prefer to indulge in minimum transport, cost and time. Murdie's (1965) statement that "There is decrease in the number of shopping trip as the distance to a centre increase" has been tested in the present context and was found correct as there is a high correlation between the consmers' frequency of visit to a market (once in a week) and travel distances in case of the selectd markets (*r* value for Sisamau -.91, Jajmau -.78, Beconganj –.73 and Dwarikapuri -.85) (Fig. 17.2). As these markets have narrow locational spacing, consumers attempt to cover more periodic markets on different days of the week. 78.6 per cent of the consumers, who gave stress on the price of the article rather their quality, were found indulged in bargaining which is profitable to the seller in every case and stage (Srivastava, 1982)

Problems of Periodic Markets

The problems faced by these markets are varied. These markets, at present are facing the problem of their survival though it is a unique characteristic of the retail business of this metropolis. Such markets are loosing their hold day-by-day even on low-income group population because the purchasing capacity of the low-income group has also increased. As the wages and salary of factory workers, daily-wage earners and low-paid government employees are increasing gradually they have started to prefer the shops of high-order business ribbons and those markets where they get wide choice of the article and satisfy their brand preference. The next significant problem is the gradual encroachment by permanent retail shopkeepers due to negligence and connaivance of the officials of Municipal Corporation. Encroachment is taking place in the vicinity of these markets. Parade and Bakerganj have been badly affected due to this phenomenon which is injurious to their existence. The space infront of U.H.M. hospital has recently been converted into a permanent retail market by stall holders who sale their article on all days of the week. Darshanpurwa and Dwarikapuri markets, situated in *ahatas*, have been reduced to simply a vegetable market. Darshanpurwa market is being badly affected due to stall holders who arrange their articles, particularly cloth, readymade garments, hosiery items, utensils and plastic footwears. Shopkeepers dealing with such items in this market have stopped to visit it. Bakerganj is also facing the same problem. It is gradually loosing its periodic nature and taking a form of permanent retail market of high-order shopping goods.

Moreover, these markets lack basic civic amenities. There is complete absence of proper drainage, toilet facility, drinking water tap, bricked or metalled lane/paths. Except a few, majority of the shopkeepers arrange their article under open sky and face an odd situation during the days of scorching heat and rains. The cover (shade) which they arrange, are totally temporary. Moreover, underweighing, quoting high prices and pick-pocketting are the three notorious characteristics of these markets and each of these features discourages gentry of high staus from attending these periodic markets. Since these markets, except Parade, are unorganised the traders are harassed by the owners of these markets. On account of these problems and drawbacks the consumers of middle and high-income class hestiate to visit. On the whole these problems have largely affected their retail trade.

Planning Strategy

In spite of various problems which they, at present, are facing they still attract a huge number of consumers of all walks of life. Since these markets form an integral part of the commercial structure of this important metropolis of Ganga Basin, it is, therefore, highly desireable that such markets are rescued from the pitiable plight. In order to maintain their periodicity, improve their internal structure and management, and to make them worthvisiting, following strategies have been recommended.

(1) Physically these markets need proper planning for allocation of space for shopkeepers so that shopkeepers may arrange their articles on the alloted space and consumer may also move coveniently.

(2) Kanpur Development Authority (KDA) and Municipal Corporation must come to their rescue for solving the problem of basic civic amenities. They should construct proper roads and atleast bricked footpath, toilets, *pucca* drains and shades for deserving shopkeepers.

(3) Management of these markets should either be done by Municipal Corporation or on the lines Parade Market Committee, a registerad body, so that the exploitation of shopkeepers by their owners may not be done in future.

(4) Such types of improvement is being hampered at present by the legal suit, pending in court, especially in the case of Parade market. In the interest of the city as a whole the suits should be vocated as early as possible and the right administration be given to civic authorities who may be in a position to chalk out and execute development plan in coordination with the master plan of the city (Suresh, 1971).

(5) Encroachment by the permanent daily shopkeepers and stall holders with the connaivance of municipal corporation officials (which is transofrming the nature of these markets), must be stopped by the intervention of the State Government authorities so that the significance and usefulness of these periodic markets may not be marred. Some rules should be strictly imposed to check the encroachments in these markets.

(6) Periodic markets being an organ of the city should function efficiently. This can be achieved by the cooperation of civic authorities on one hand and traders and consumers on the other hand.

Notes

1. The word *Kabar* is used for old, broken and used articles.
2. The word *Kirana* stands for grocery items.
3. Sampled Periodic Markets of Kanpur Metropolis : (1) Parade, (2) Bakerganj, (3) Beconganj, (4) Sisamau, (5) Faithfulganj, (6) Jajmau, (7) Lalbanglow (8) Darshanpurwa, and (9) Dwarikapuri.
4. The word *Ahata* is used for big enclosures consisting of a group of tenants with one or two rooms intended for human need.

EIGHTEEN

Problems and Prospects of Mandis in Ajoy-Kopai Inter-riverine Tract of Birbhum District

DEBASHIS DAS

Introduction

Human habitat is not a self-sufficient and self-contained entity, but an interdependant unit that must exchange ideas and products with other human habitats (Ramachandran, 1982: 15). The society is not selfsufficient in the production of all commodities which are needed by the inhabitants. So the exchange of commodities becomes one of the important functions that the societies of the region perform for meeting their demands. The development is accompanied initially by production specialisation and consequently each centre exhibits its own distinct products mix. On the other hand there is a trend towards similar consumption patterns with each income group of population in various centres give rise to intricate functional interaction between settlements in an economy. The functional and spatial integration processes of settlements can be analysed through interaction, through the pattern of exchange of goods, people and ideas, between settlements and communities that define a complex web of territorial interconnections. This process gives birth to economic development of a region.

Objective

The objectives of the present study are as follows:

(a) to study the structure and characters of the *mandis*.

(b) to uncover the real problems of the *mandis*.
(c) to suggest policy measures to control the problems of *mandis*.

Analytical Procedure

The facilities and infrastructures of the mandis have been collected, whose weightages are found out with the help of following formulla:

$$W_i = \frac{N}{F_i}$$

W_i = Weightage of the *i*th subfunction.
N = Total number of *mandis*
F_i = Number of *mandis* where *i*th facility occurs.

Then the weightages are multiplied by the number of individual facility. The multiplied figures of each facility is added together to get composite centrality score.

The formulla is:

$$I = \sum_{i=1}^{K} W_i X_{ij}$$

K = Total number of sub-functions under a given function
X_{ij} = value of the *i*th sub-function in *j*th settlement.

Location of the Study Area

The Ajoy-Kopai inter-riverine tract of Birbhum district is a part of lower Ganga plain, is located at the southern part of the district and western part of West Bengal. It is bordered on the north and south by two perennial rivers. The Ajoy makes its southern boundary whereas the Kopai forms its northern. The total area of the region is 1169 km^2 where 4,84,536 population reside (Fig. 18.1).

The average height of this region is 195 feet. The region is covered by sandy loam, sandy clay, loam and clay soils. Red, laterite and older alluvium soils are the two important

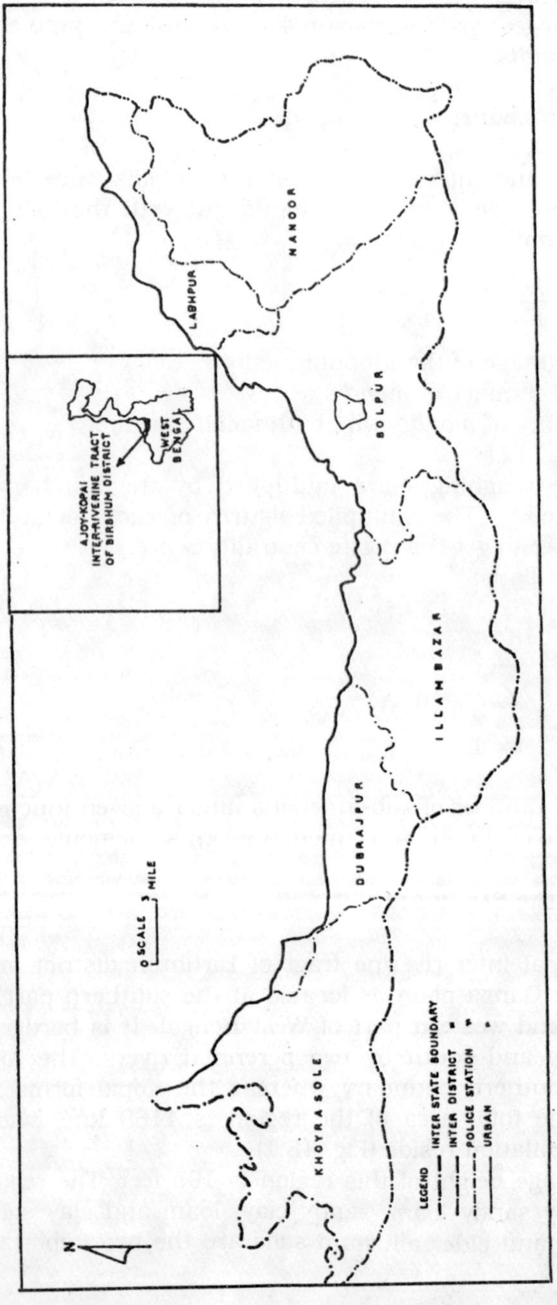

FIG. 18.1: Ajoy-Kopai Inter-riverine Tract of Birbhum District, 1971

soil groups of the region. The region has 1,93,593 acres of land or 58.11 per cent of the net sown area as net irrigated area. Agriculture is the major occupation of the region. Paddy is the main crop grown in the region, followed by potato, vegetables, wheat, sugarcane, mustard etc. crops, and in summer season paddy is cultivated where irrigation is assured, besides til, pulses etc. crops are grown in other areas.

Distribution of Mandi

There are twenty *mandis* in the study area, out of which 35 per cent are located at the western fringe area, 20 per cent are located at eastern fringe area, and remaining 45 per cent of the markets are located at the central part of the region, where Bolpur town—the highest node of the region—is situated (Fig. 18.2).

The *mandis* are haphazardly distributed over the region and are mostly located at the big, medium sized settlements, where different infrastructures and facilities are agglomerated and which are located at the centre of the productive areas (Table 18.1).

Table 18.1: Distribution of Mandis

Area under police station	No. of mandi	Per cent to total
Khoyrasol	6	30.00
Dubrajpur	1	5.00
Illambazar	5	25.00
Bolpur	4	20.00
Nanoor	4	20.00
Labpur	0	00.00
Total	20	100.00

Source: Market Directory, Department. of Marketing, Bolpur.

These *mandis* are the places where population interaction takes place. This interaction can be measured with the help of the volume of daily market participants (Table 18.2), which include cultivator buyers and sellers, non-cultivator buyers and sellers and consumers. These *mandis*, with different number of participants, have been divided into four orders by the quartile method which represent different levels of nodes of the region.

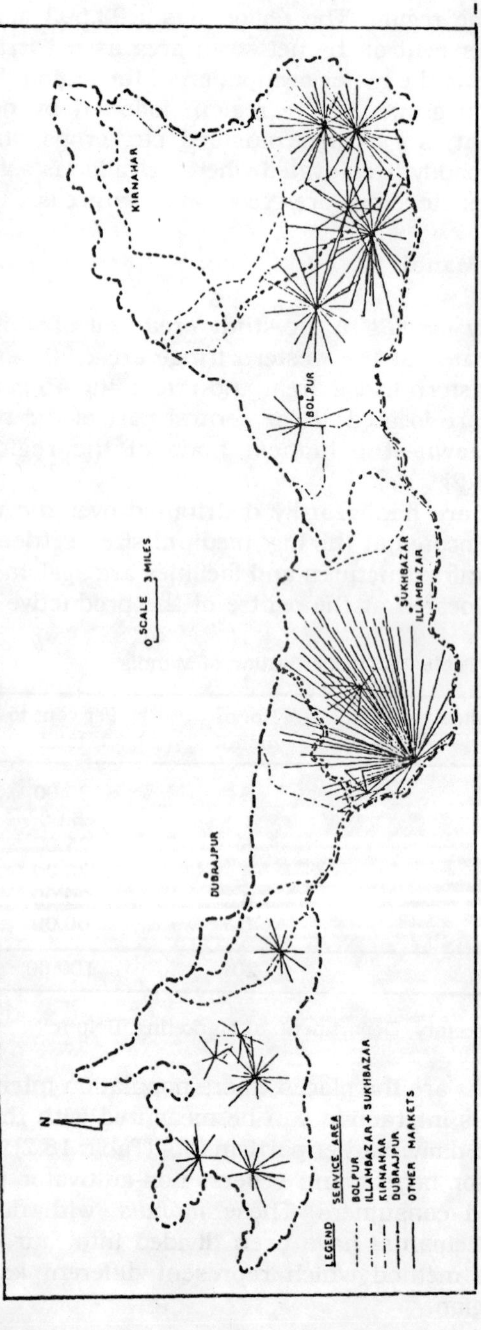

FIG. 18.2: Location of Markets (Mandi) and their Service Area, 1983

Table 18.2: Distribution of Daily Mandi Participants

No.of participants	Order of mandi	Order of node
1721-3500	First	High
651-1720	Second	Middle
361-650	Third	Low middle
111-360	Fourth	Low

Source: Field investigation.

The large number of participants are found in the *mandis* where the size of population of the mouza, in which the *mandi* is located, is large, and distance between the *mandis* and the town/head-quarter of the P.S. is considerably less.

Most of the *mandis*, including all the first and second orders, had been introduced during the colonial period and as low as 20 per cent of the *mandis* have been established after Independance. Apart from that five markets of area under Bolpur, Nanoor and Labpur P.S. have already been closed down, because the *mandis* lost their importance under the adverse influence of first and second order *mandis* and some of the thrid and fourth order *mandis* are already in moribund condition. This is due to increasing dependance of the participants on the first and second level *mandis*, which causes the decline of the importance of lower order *mandis* gradually.

Working Days and Hours of the Mandis

The nature of population interaction depends on the distribution of working days of the *mandis* and on their span of working hours (Table 18.3). The present study reveals that, there is no overlapping of the working days in the same level of *mandis*, but some overlapping of working days takes place between the higher and lower order *mandis* of the study area.

This means, the participants have large number of choices to visit different higher order *mandis* throughout the week, but they have limited choices to visit the higher and lower order *mandis* in a week. In that case, a large number of participants prefer to visit higher order *mandis*, whereas the poor villagers mainly satisfy themselves by purchasing commodities from the lower order *mandis* only.

Table 18.3: Working Hours of the Mandis

Mandis with no. of daily participants	Average working hours
1721-3500	8
651-1720	5
361-650	5
111-360	3

Source: Field investigation

Most of the *mandis* are the property of high caste Hindu population. Some times, the religious organisations or trustees have become the owner of the *mandis*, which are administered by the members belonging to higher caste Hindu population. Besides, very few *mandis* are owned and managed by the Muslims or by the Department of Market, Government of West Bengal.

Distribution of Daily Participants of the Mandis

The daily participants of the *mandis* include: (a) the cultivator buyers and sellers, (b) non-cultivator buyers and sellers, (c) other consumers. The number of participants and their different categories tend to decline from the higher order to the lower order *mandis*. Besides, large number of consumers also visit the *mandis* of the region. Followed by them, relatively small number of cultivator buyers/sellers and small number of non-cultivator buyers/seller also visit different *mandis*.

The consumer category of market participants are primarily service holders, who rarely depend upon agriculture. So, they have to depend entirely upon the *mandis* to get their daily requirements. The cultivators category of participants own land, and most of their daily requirements are supplied from agriculture, whereas the non-cultivator category of participants are very poor and they cannot afford to purchase their requirements from the *mandi* frequently. Rather they procure the commodities from here and there for maintaining their livelihood.

The study further reveals that most of the sellers of all the *mandis* sell mainly vegetables. In higher order markets, the large proportion of sellers sell vegetables, foodgrains, oil seeds, fish, egg, poultry and livestock, etc. and conversely the sellers of lower order markets sell mainly the vegetables.

Apart from the above, a large proportion of sellers in the first order *mandis*, sell vegetables, and oilseeds. Their proportion is low in the second order *mandis*. On the other hand, small proportion of shopkeepers of first order markets sell cereals and *gur*, while their proportion increases in the second order *mandis* (Appendix-I).

Commodities Dealt with in the *Mandis*

A variety of commodities are sold in the markets of the study area. The important commodities that are sold are vegetable, foodgrain, oilseed, *gur*, fish, egg, fowls, mutton, livestock, bamboo basket, earthern ware, textiles, dresses, etc.

The above mentioned commodities are sold in the higher order *mandis*, whereas in the lower order *mandis* vegetables are the main commodities, that are sold there.

The consumers can satisfy their multiple needs by purchasing different commodities in the higher order markets, whereas the consumers' choice is limited in the lower order *mandis*. The sellers of the higher order markets sell comparatively larger number of commodities, than the same of lower order *mandis*. However, the case is different in case of vegetables. The sellers of the second order markets sell larger quantities of vegetables than the first order *mandis* but that oradually declines to further lower order *mandis*.

The stalls of careals and oilseeds are virtually absent in the lower order *mandis*.

Infrastructures and Facilities of the *Mandis*: Identification of Centrality

In general, availability of infrastructures and facilities in the *mandis* is another ingradient that identify the levels of the nodes in the nested hierarchy of settlements of the region. The study observes that a large number of higher and low level infrastructures and facilities are agglomerated in the higher order nodes; while a small number of low level facilitie are available in the small sized settlements.

The study area has on the whole 72 link roads, whose total length is 672 km. Among them 59.72 per cent are all weather metalled roads, and remaining 40.28 per cent are unmetailed road which are damaged by drained water during the time of the excessive rainfall.

The first order *mandis* have 25 link roads, whose total length is 305 km. Among them 80 per cent are metalled, whereas small proportion of metalled link road is found in the lower order *mandis*. The total length of link roads of the fourth order *mandi* is as low as 63 km only.

Among the first order *mandis*, Bolpur and Dubrajpur towns have extensive link roads around them, which indicates that these two towns link up larger number of settlements of the region, than the other *mandis*. So, these two towns have larger tributary areas than the next order *mandis*. Likewise, the second order *mandis* link up larger number of settlements than the lower order *mandis* and so on.

The magnitude of centrality of the *mandis* have been computed with the help of the infrastructures and service facilities that are located at or near the *mandis*. These include: (a) shed, (b) bathroom, (c) drinking water facilities, (d) godowns, (e) cold storages, (f) Bank, (g) proximity to railway station, (h) highway, (i) bus stop, (j) link road.

The composite centrality scores have been worked out to find out the aggregate functions that are performed in the *mandis*.

The study reveals that most of the high and low level infrastructures and facilities are located at the higher order *mandis*, whereas the lower order *mandis* have very few low level facilities. Moreover, a wide gap prevails between the higher and lower order *mandis* in respect of the location of infrastructures and facilities.

The study further reveals that the composite centrality scores decline from the higher order *mandis* to the lower order *mandis* in area under every P.S. of the study area except in Bolpur P.S. Although the composite centrality score of high order *mandis* in Bolpur P.S. is quite high (442.38) but at the same time, the composite scores of second (9.44) and third order (10.58) *mandis* are smaller than that in the fourth order *mandis* (19.35). The fourth order *mandi* (Sriniketan) of Bolpur P.S. is located very close to Bolpur town, so some facilities have been installed there, which are not present in other markets at all. However, after considering the number of participants, Sriniketan has to be ranked as fourth order *mandis* (Appendix - II).

Service Area, Served Villages and Served Population of the Mandis

The service area of the first order *mandis* is quite extensive. Large numbers of high level infrastructures and facilities are located at first order *mandis*, which are rarely available in lower order *mandis*. Moreover, these first order *mandis* sell huge amount and variety of commodities, that are also rarely provided in the lower order *mandis*. These infrastructures, service facilities, and the commodities have larger ranges. That means that the inhabitants from distant regions come to the first order *mandis* to get the service.

In this manner the second order *mandis* have infrastructures, facilities and commodities of the next spatial range, which serve the inhabitants of much lesser area than the first order *mandis*. These second order *mandis* are located around the first order *mandis*.

The third order *mandis* are located around the second order *mandis*, which provide infrastructure, facilities and commodities of the next spatial range and served relatively lesser number of population and villages. This ordering of *mandis* continues until the infrastructures, facilities, and commodities of the lowest spatial range are taken into account (Appendix-III).

The study further reveals that, the service area of first order *mandis* is more than six times larger than the second order *mandis*, but the service area of second and thrid order *mandis* are more or less same in size, which Christaller did not postulate, and the service area of fourth order *mandis* is two and half times or three times less than the former orders of *mandis*.

Problems of the Mandis

The problems, that the participants of the *mandis* face while transacting commodities in the *mandis*, can be grouped into four types: (a) physical, (b) socio-economic, (c) infrastructural, and (d) administrative.

Physcial Problems

(i) Some of the *mandis* are located at very close to the bus stand. So, often and on the crowd of the market is mixed up with the crowd of the bus stand. Thus, the huge crowd obstruct the proper functioning of the *mandis*.

(ii) Despite the availability of different sources of irrigation, the existing water resources are not fully utilised in the study region. So, the diversification of crops is at a low level which restricts the intensification of crops. This constraint becomes an impediment to the cultivation of commercialized, market oriented crops extensively over the study area. Therefore, inadequate amount and less variety of crops are brought by the seller to the markets for sale.

(iii) The agricultural economy is affected by the frequent attack of flood and droughts. These constraints disturb the cropping pattern of the area and causes a decline in the production of crops. So, the total arrival of commodities in the *mandis* fluctuates considerably which influences the price structure of commodities adversely.

(iv) The yards of all the markets are dirty and have become unhygienic due to the prevailing under drainage condition. Maintenance works are rarely practised to solve the above problem.

Socio-economic Problems

(i) The sellers, belonging to strong socio-economic class of the society, manage to sit in the favourable position of the *mandi* yards from where they can easily attract large number of consumers, whereas the poor sellers are forced to sell their commodities in the outer parts of the *mandi* yards, where the number of consumers is much less.

(ii) The *mandis* do not have adequate number of rooms for the stalls. Moreover, the nouveauriche sellers have occupied most of these rooms, so the poor sellers cannot avail them.

(iii) Due to non-availability of the store rooms, the sellers, particularly the poor, cannot store the unsold commodities in the markets. So, they have to keep their commodities in the *mandi* yards under the open sky, which is unsafe because often these commodities are either stolen by thieves or are eaten up by animals. This difficulty compels the sellers to sell their commodities at a low price, which reduces the amount of their net income.

(iv) Sometimes, the supply of commodities is much less than the total demand of the market. This is due to the fact that the middle-man marchants often purchase fresh commodities from the poor farmers at a low price, and then sell them in the *mandis* of Durgapur, Asansol and other industrial towns, where the per capita purchasing power of the consumers is comparatively higher than the consumers of the study area.

(v) The poor sellers cannot accumulate adequate amount of capital to purchase sufficient amount of commodities. Moreover, these sellers cannot predict the total supply of commodities in the *mandis*, which fluctuates considerably and become uncertain.

(vi) The socio-cultural festivals of the region bring huge number of observers from outside in the region. This increases the volume of demand for commodities in the *hat*, but generally the supply of commodities is much less than the demand, which increases the price of commodities, hence the common people face problem to purchase goods which are needed daily. The smaller order *mandis* face this crisis more strongly than the larger order because there will be a inflow of commodities from smaller order *mandis* to larger order. Larger order *mandis* also depend upon for the commodities either from Bihar state or from Burdwan and Hooghly district, alongwith the local production. So, the *mandis* of the region are not self sufficient in respect to bring adequate commodities from local areas, but have to depend considerably for outside commodities.

(vii) Sometimes the vegetables, that are brought from Bihar, are available in large number whose price is lesser than the local vegetables. In that case local vegetable sellers face difficulty to sell their product in higher price and in this way the outflow of money takes place from the region to either Bihar or to outside part of the region.

Infrastructural Problems

(i) Except in the first order *mandis*, the infrastructures, facilities are rarely located at different orders of *mandis*. So, these *mandis* cannot become a centre where people can meet their multiferious needs. Therefore, the *mandis* cannot serve a large number of population of the area.

(ii) Inadequate number of link roads and other transport problems cannot connect the large number of villages, specially the small sized remote villages, to the *mandis*.

(iii) Most of the small sized villages are connected to each other and to the *mandis* with the footpaths. These foot paths are often damaged by flood and overland flow during the mansoon season. The repair works are performed in delay and consequantly, the bullock carts of the farmers are damaged severely.

(iv) The drinking water facilities, storage facilities, sheds, bathrooms, lavatory, and other facilities are located at the higher order *mandis* only, but these facilities are not available in 75 per cent of the *mandis* which exist at the low level of market (*mandi*) hierarchy. This problem gives rise to discomfort to the *mandi* participants to a large extent.

(v) Cheap hotel or alike places for overnight stay are rarely available even in the higher order *mandis*, but these are not at all available in the lower order *mandis*. So the sellers cannot stay for some days in the *mandis* and sell their commodities there. Sometimes rooms are available, but the poor sellers cannot afford to pay the rent of the room, because it is very high.

(vi) The *mandi* yards are very small in regard to the influx of *mandi* participants. So, huge crowds gather in the *mandis*, and hinder the transactions of business and sale of commodities.

(vii) The Ajoy and Kopai rivers stand as natural barrier in the district, that limit the interaction of population and flow of commodities in the *mandis* of the region. The culvert, bridge and relevant transport facilities are lacking in this region, which are by and large responsible for the above problem.

Administrative Problems

(i) The transaction of most of the *mandis* are carried on in only two days in a week, which seems to be inadequate to serve a large number of population of the respective hinterlands of the *mandis*. Moreover, the transaction of commodities takes place for only two to three hours in the lower order *mandis*. It appears that, this small span of time is also quite insufficient to serve a large population. The selection of *mandi* days has not been done properly in different *mandis* of the region. So, that ristricts the scope of interaction of population and limits the flow of commodities of the study area. Besides, the random distribution of *mandi* also increases the spatial conflict in the region.

Prospects

(1) The markets of different orders should be located at appropriate places of the region, from where services can be rendered to different corners of it. Besides, all the necessary infrastructures and facilitiers with their distinct spatial ranges should be located at different orders of *mandis*. Then, the functional links should be strengthened between the *mandis* of the nested hierarchy in order to provide services of the integrated marketing system, to the population of the entire region.

(2) The different orders of *mandis*, in the nested hierarchy, must specialise in the production of goods with respective spatial ranges and must exhibit their own distinct product mix. Besides, the per capita income of population of the region should be raised through the development of the economy of the region. This will give rise to reasonably similar consumption pattern with each income group of population in the region. These spatial trends increase the volume of interaction of population between the settlement in an

economy. The integration of space economy through such kinds of interactions of population define a complex web of territorial interconnections.

(3) The economy of different settlements should be intricately knit and strongly connected to each other. At the same time, the time-space convergence of settlements should be made in the region with amazing variety and density interconnections between the communities and among territorial sub-units (Ramchandran, 1982:1).

(4) Along with the trades, the socio-cultural, religious and other non-trading activities should also be practised in the *mandis*, which will attract a large number of population of the region to these *mandis*, and hence will increase the volume of population inter-action in those *mandis*.

(5) The temporal distance of *mandi* days between the *mandis* can be expressed as the number of days separating any two *mandi* days of the interval of the *mandis*. On the other hand, the spatial location of a mandi relative to another *mandi* is concerned with the geographical distance between the two *mandis*. The space-time arrangement of the *mandis* should be made optimal by reducing the geographical distance between two *mandis* to the minimum and by increasing the temporal separation of *mandi* days between them. This kind of space-time arrangements of *mandis* must encourage the weaker strata of the community to vist the *mandis* frequently. This process should be followed for increasing the number of participants of the markets in one hand and for increasing the volume of population interaction on the other. In this way, the spatial conflict can be reduced to the minimum.

Conclusion

Different order of *mandis* of this region are located haphazardly over the region, where inadequats infrastructures are available. This inadequacy limits huge population interaction mainly in the higher order *mandis*. The higher order *mandis* perform scoio-cultural functions along with their economic activities, whereas these activities are almost absent in smaller order *mandis*. The space-time arrangements of different orders *mandis* are done in inappropriate and unscientific manner which cause a decline of the total volume of population interaction, hence increase the spatial conflict. All these problems should be tackled priority-wise in order to attend Economic developoment of the region.

APPENDIX-I

Average Number of Daily Market Participants

Name of P.S.	1721-3500			651-1720			361-650			111-360		
	a	b	c	a	b	c	a	b	c	a	b	c
Khyorasol	—	—	—	225 (450)	62 (125)	750 (1500)	162 (324)	27 (54)	350 (700)	70 (140)	10 (20)	125 (250)
Dubrajpur	400 (400)	150 (150)	1600 (1800)	—	—	—	—	—	—	—	—	—
Illambazar	410 (820)	127 (254)	2100 (4200)	125 (125)	42 (42)	1500 (1500)	—	—	—	17 (34)	0	110 (200)
Bolpur	280 (280)	71 (71)	2500 (2500)	120 (120)	41 (41)	600 (600)	64 (64)	6 (6)	350 (350)	40 (40)	10 (10)	250 (250)
Nanoor	500 (500)	100 (100)	2000 (2000)	75 (75)	40 (40)	600 (600)	52 (105)	22 (44)	450 (900)	—	—	—
Total	397 (2000)	122 (576)	2100 (10500)	136 (700)	46 (248)	863 (4200)	93 (494)	18 (106)	383 (1950)	42 (215)	10 (30)	162 (720)

Source: Field Investigation

Note: (1) Figures inside the bracket indicate absolute number.
(2) (a) Cultivator buyer/seller, (b) non-cultivator buyer/seller, (c) other consumers.

APPENDIX-II

Distribution of Composite Centrality Scores of the Mandis

Names of P.S.	Number of participants			
	1721-3500	651-1720	361-650	111-360
Khoyrasol	—	15.00	15.00	10.22
Dubrajpur	443.96	—	—	—
Illambazar	29.39	10.78	—	10.00
Bolpur	442.38	9.44	10.58	19.35
Nanoor	276.25	24.76	16.91	—
Labpur	—	—	—	—
Region	244.27	14.85	15.02	11.96

Source: Field investigation.

APPENDIX-III

Average Service Area and Served Population

Name of P.S.	1721-3500			651-1720			361-650			111-360		
	a	b	c	a	b	c	a	b	c	a	b	c
Khoyrasol	—	—	—	11 (22)	2314 (4628)	9533 (19066)	18 (36)	2782 (5564)	13929 (27858)	9 (18)	2082 (4165)	7951 (15902)
Dubrajpur	198 (198)	38596 (38596)	167637 (167637)	—	—	—	—	—	—	—	—	—
Illambazar	190 (380)	32909 (65818)	160663 (321326)	80 (80)	13894 (13894)	51779 (51779)	—	—	—	7 (14)	2637 (5274)	9304 (18608)
Bolpur	200 (200)	42883 (42883)	171897 (171897)	25 (25)	7660 (7660)	25034 (25034)	40 (40)	10994 (10994)	39798 (39798)	15 (15)	4775 (4775)	17715 (17715)
Nanoor	199 (199)	36590 (36590)	165906 (165906)	30 (30)	7184 (7184)	22659 (22659)	24 (48)	5434 (11468)	24383 (48767)	—	—	—
Labpur	—	—	—	—	—	—	—	—	—	—	—	—
Region	195 (971)	36777 (183887)	165353 (826766)	31 (157)	6673 (33366)	23707 (118538)	24 (122)	5604 (28022)	23284 (116423)	9 (45)	2842 (4214)	10445 (52225)

Source: Field investigation.

Note: Figures inside the bracket indicate total number.
(a) = Served villages.
(b) = Service area in hectare
(c) = Population served.

NINTEEN

Anatomy of the Betel Leaf Marketing in Mahoba (U.P.): A Case Study

R.S. DIXIT

Mahoba is the biggest town of its district, Hamirpur (U.P.). It is also the biggest trade centre of the dirstrict. Despite the fact that daily marketing is a rule in the town, the periodic marketing in Mahoba is very specific in several perspectives amongst which the betel leaf marketing is the most significant one. Mahoba is the only place in the district, which has thrice a week periodic marketing (i.e. on Monday, Friday, and Saturday). The betel leaf market in Mahoba is held on Monday and it is a very specialized market in the sense that it is a commodity oriented market (Dixit, 1984b). Mahoba and betel leaf are the two synonyms well known to the Bundelkhand region of Uttar Pradesh. The present endeavour is based on the results of an empirical study completed by the author in the study area. It analyses the basic elements of betel leaf marketing such as market place location, day and time, sellers, volume of trade, purchasers, middle-men, betel flow etc. It, thus, attempts to present an anatomy of the betel leaf marketing in Mahoba.

Selection of the Case — The Rationale

There are certain factors behind the selection of the case study in hand. The author hails from the district of Hamirpur in which the town is located. Besides, he completed three research projects in which he studied this town. The first project encompasses the study of a major functional zone of a metropolis and Mahoba is one of its towns/trade centres, while the second one is based on the district level of which Mahoba is the biggest town/trade centre. The third, however, is based on the town i.e. Mahoba itself and analyses the various periodic marketing activities of the same. Hence, the author has selected this case for the present study.

Mahoba — The Locale

Mahoba is located on 25° 18'N and 79° 53'E. It lies in the southern part of Uttar Pradesh known as Bundelkhand of U.P. It is a tahsil headquarter of its district within the Jhansi administrative division of the state. Lucknow (the state's capital city), Kanpur (the first largest city as well as the only industrial metropolis of U.P.), and Hamirpur (the district headquarter) are located towards north at the distances of 241 km, 168 km, and 85 km respectively. Jhansi, the divisional headquarter is 165 km away towards west. Khajuraho (the temple city of the Chandel rulers), and Chhatarpur, both in Madhya Pradesh, are 65 km and 48 km respectively towards south from Mahoba.

The twon is located on state highway (S.H.) No. 4. The state highway No. 17 starts from Mahoba and leads to Kanpur (via Hamirpur) in the north. A section of the Central Railway (broad gauge line) between Jhansi in the west and Manikpur in the east passes through Mahoba.

The township of Mahoba spreads over an area of 7.47 km^2 (which excludes the entire Railway land). The municipal limits of the town roughly assume a triangular shape with its base in the north and the apex in the south (Dixit, 1988).

Betel Leaf (i.e. 'PAN') Marketing — The Anatomy

Betel Leaf — A Way of Life

Betel leaf or *pan* is a way of life in Mahoba. It is a commodity of multi-dimensional significance for the entire populace of a country like India. It has social, cultural, religious, economic, medicinal, and emotional importance (Yusami, 1989). It is considered as an essential article in various activities — right from personal or individual acts (specifically relating to romance/love, and beauty) to religious acts (relating to prayer/worship of gods).

Betel leaf is taken as a symbol or a token by individuals for taking a specific oath relating to do a challenging job or an act of bravery/gallantry more particularly in Rajasthan. Among the Chandel kings of Mahoba also *pan* had the same high esteem as it was brought by them from Rajasthan. The importance of betel leaf, especially in the cultural life of India, is well known. All over the country, it is used in worship of gods. It is used as an aide in beautifying face, particularly adding beauty to mouth and lips.

For a number of diseases, betel leaf is used as a mother remedy in the Indian country-side. It is known as an aphrodisiac, a carminative, and is used as a stimulant. It is a cure for snake-bite and its essential oil is used in respiratory catarrhs and as an antiseptic. The juice of the betel leaf is used as eye-drop and it cures painful infections and night blindness. For millions of Indian, the daily routine remains incomplete without chewing betel leaves. On various social/family occasions, *pan* is presented to elders as a symbol of respect while it is presented to friends in love and affection as well as to one's beloved, especially, in romance. It is considered as a pious thing and hence in prayer/worship, it is offered to gods.

The importance of betel leaf, more particularly in view of its medicinal use, is clearly explained in various works such as *Charak Samhita, Sushrat Samhita, Prabandh Kosh, Katha Sarit Sagar, Braht Katha* etc. Various Hindu writings read that the king of *Patal* (Pluton), Raja Nag Vasuki, offered four precious presentations, as dowry on the occasion of his daughter's marriage including betelvine to a king on earth, King Udayan of Kaushambi.

As a matter of fact, betel leaf has a great significance to both the individuals as well as society not only in Mahoba, rather, over entire India. The betel leaf of Mahoba is, especially, known for its crispness and it dilutes easily in mouth as also it gives a good taste. Betel leaf, thus, is a way of life.

Market Place Location

The betel leaf market of Mahoba is a very old market. The site for betel leaf trade, presently, is located between the Police Out Post and the Raikot hill on the Kulpahar Road, almost opposite to the Rang Mahal Cinema. It lies to the southern side of the road. It is known as *Pan Mandi* or the *Somwari Bazar* (The Monday Market). It is significant to note that, primarily, the wholesale activities take place in betel-leaf here. There is a specific platform, the *chabutara* on which the sellers sit with their betel leaf baskets. The platform is, rather of a defined shape and size. The entire platform is divided into two parts by a passage which makes the way for purchasers to enter the market from the main road. The size of the platform is 60' x 100'. The width runs along the main road while the length of the area is perpendicular to the road, i.e. towards south. Thus, the market place spreads over an area of 6000 sq. ft. with its dimensions as east-west (width) and north-south (length). It is, actually, a *nazul* land and it is in possession of a person on lease basis. Here, nearly all transactions on Monday take place in the form of wholesale trade. This area, the *Mandi* place, is private in terms of its possession but no kind of tax is realized either from the sellers or from the purchasers.

There is, however, a proposal to shift the present site to a bigger plot of land of about 2 acre area as the present site is too small, especially, to hold heavy marketing on Monday.

Marketing Day and Time

Primarily, Monday is the marketing day for betel leaf trade in Mahoba. It is the peak day of the week in this reference.

It is important to note that the periodic marketing in the context of wholesale betel leaf trade is related to Monday marketing while the retail marketing takes place at the same place everyday. 'Sunday' however, is the weekly closure in this respect. Hence, marketing on Monday is really, very very brisk. Earlier, only Monday marketing used to take place here while on other days at the conservatories, the *barejas* only as all such transactions used to be small. With the passage of time the volume of transactions has increased and hence daily trading in this commodity is taking up its shape with Monday as the busiest day. Sometimes, the congregation of sellers and buyers on Monday is as large as 10,000.

As far as it is related to timing for *pan* marketing, seasonal variations are too common. During the summer season, the trading hours are 6.00 a.m. to 11.00 a.m. on

Monday while on other days these are 6 a.m. to 10 a.m. In case of winter season, however, marketing takes place from 7 a.m. to 12 noon on Monday and 7 a.m. to 11 a.m. on other days.

The peak hours on peak day are 7 a.m. to 9 a.m. during the summer season while 8 a.m. to 10 a.m. during the winter season.

Betel Leaf Varieties

The scientists have collected about 80 varieties of the vine in the country. In Mahoba, however, the *Deshi/Deshavari* varieties of the vine are mostly grown in the conservatories. The Mahoba betel leaf is known for its softness, fibre-lessness, and taste and it is very much popular in foreign countries, particularly the countries of West Asia (Roy, 1984).

The National Botanical Research Institute, Lucknow has taken up a tremendous work in this direction in Mahoba as the betelvine cultivation had been showing a downward trend, more particularly, after 1955. Under this project, an area of 5 acre land of the local Gram Samaj has been converted/ developed into an experimental conservatory of 40 rows since April 1986. This conservatory is making experiments on the *Deshi/Deshavari* varieties of betel leaf, especially, the one, female variety got from Bangladesh border area (Das and Banerjee, 1984; NBRI, 1987).

In the market of Mahoba, four major types of betel leaves are brought for trade. These are; Desh/Deshavari, Bangla, Bengali, and Golta Kapoori (Vijayavada, A.P.). Bengali, is particularly demanded by traders from Kanpur, Varanasi, and Allahabad. The mature and old leaves are rich in several qualities and characteristics. Both ends of the leaves are cut before these are actually eaten.

Sellers and Volume of Trade

Hundreds of sellers who come to the betel leaf market place, are actually, not traders but they are farmers, the growers or the cultivators of betelvine. There are both big and small sellers in the town. About 800 growers bring betel leaves to the market site as per their need and convenience. On Monday, generally, big farmers bring their produce as wholesaling takes place in large quantities. On other days, however, retailing and small scale wholesaling is done.

On Monday, during winter season approximately 100 big and small sellers collect at the market place while during summer season the number is as high as 250 (Table 19.1). On other days, on the other hand, the number stands around 50 during winter while that during summer season stands around 100. It is important to note that many of the sellers do not come to the marketing site, rather, they sell their produce at their conservatories only. Hence, the number of those actually present in the market is so small while the actual number of sellers is as high as 1500, and they cannot be accommodated in the market place, in case, all of them come.

Table 19.1: Mahoba Betel Leaf Marketing on Monday

Sl. No.	Hindi Month Name	English Month Sl. No.	English Month Name	Average Number Sellers	Average Number Buyers	Baskets	Specification
1	Chaitra	3-4	March-April	200	300	500	Dry Summer
2	Baisakh	4-5	April-May	200	300	500	
3	Jyeshtha	5-6	May-June	250	350	600	
4	Ashadh	4-6	June-July	250	350	600	Wet Summer
5	Shravan	7-81	July-August	200	300	600	
6	Bhadra	8-9	Aug-Sep.	200	300	500	
7	Ashwin	9-10	Sep.-Oct.	150	200	300	Less Cold Winter
8	Kartik	10-11	Oct.-Nov.	150	200	300	
9	Margshirsh	11-12	Nov.-Dec.	100	150	200	
10	Paush	12-1	Dec.-Jan.	75	150	150	Severe Cold Winter
11	Magh	1-2	Jan.-Feb.	50	150	150	
12	Falgun	2-3	Feb.-March	75	150	150	

Almost every betel leaf seller comes with his family members — wife and/or children — to this market. The male members and/or the head of the family sells the betel leaves while other members sell the vegetables brought with them. These vegetables are fresh and green and are grown by them as a side or supplementary business. The vegetable marketing takes place on both sides of the main road to the north of the betel leaf market.

On Monday 500 to 600 baskets of betel leaves are sold here for further sale outside the twon as well as within the town in both forms — retail and wholesale — during the summer season while during winter season, 150 to 300 baskets are sold (Table 19.4).

Sixty baskets of betel-leaves are sent out of the town daily. Each basket contains 100 bundles, *dholis*, of betel leaves. Thus, about 2000 bundles of leaves are exported daily from Mahoba these days. Generally, each *dholi* contains about 100 betel leaves. Baskets, also are of different sizes — both the small and the big ones. Besides, there used to be a *deshi-pan-dholi* containing 200 betel-leaves. But now the size of the bundle, too, is getting smaller with the passage of time. It has also been observed that sometimes the bundles are as small as the one containing about 15 leaves only. Earler, either two bundles of 100 leaves each or 4 bundles of 50 leaves each used to be arranged in each *dholi*. These days a very common practice followed in this area is that the betel leaves of uniform size are not arranged in the smaller bundles rather some leaves are of good quality and good size while most of them are smaller and inferior. The *dholis* are bigger, however, in winter season as against their sizes during summer season when the leaves are fully mature.

Every seller sells at least one basket of betel leaves daily. The producer-seller, thus, earns at least Rs. 1500 per month from the same. He receives approximately Rs. 2000-3000 per year from each row or *pari*. The growers have a number of *paris* or rows with them ranging from 10 to 100. Each conservatory or *baroj* has 100 rows and it is, generally, shared by 10 growers who have 10 rows each. Each grower earns approximately Rs. 20,000 from 10 rows during a year. These small or marginal sellers, generally, sell their leaves to local traders only for further retail sale. Some big farmers, although they are only a few in number, have large number of rows of betel leaves ranging from 100 to 200 each. They, normally, export their produce in large quantities. However, the commodity is perishable one and has a very short span of life—hardly one/two days after separating it from its vine—in case it is not chemically treated before keeping it in the *dholi*. After chemical treatment, however, it may be kept fresh for several days — more or less 8 days.

Purchasers

It is a very important as well as a very unique feature of

betel-leaf trade that the actual consumer does not appear in the scene in the *Mandi* place. All the purchasers at *Mandi* place are the traders — both big and small — only and not the consumers. The actual consumer appears in the scene at the end of the retail chain only (Dixit, 1989b, 1990). The all purchasers, thus, in the *mandi* are the wholesale or retail traders only. Dozens of the purchasers are big wholesalers while hundreds of retailers also make purchasing in the same market. The Monday market is actually, known for wholesale trade in betel leaf but the local retail traders also make purchasing here for further retail sale.

The purchasers belong to Mahoba itself as well as the surrounding areas located on Kulpahar Road, Charkhari Road, Banda Road, and Hamirpur Road. These purchasers sell their commodity further to other areas like Kanpur, Jhansi, Allahabad etc. The purchasing take place in large quantities on Monday rather than other days. Likewise, large scale transactions take place on summer days as against the winter season too. The number of buyers on a summer Monday is 300 to 350 while that during winter Monday is 150 to 200. (Table 19.1).

Commission Agents/Middlemen

The commission agents play a very significant role as mediators (*bichaulias*) in the entire marketing activities in this area of trade. As a matter of fact, the large scale transactions are done through the mediators only. Generally, the *dholis* are sold on credit, that is to say, no immediate payments are made to the sellers. In case, however, the immediate payments are made, the rates or the prices of the commodity are considerably lesser — 6 to 10 per cent — than those for the sales on credit. The commission agents earn large profits from growers/farmers, particularly the marginal ones. The betel leaf reaches the actual consumer after going through several hands in between. The entire betel leaf market of Mahoba is controlled by a few middle-men in case of wholesale trading activities. The sellers have to depend upon them as their product is highly perishable. At times, the prices of betel leaves are very high when the sellers are less and the commodity is less in the market while the purchasers are large in number collected from Mahoba itself as well as its surrounding areas. On the other hand, however, if the purchasers are comparatively less and the sellers have considerably large volume of the commodity, the prices, consequently, are comparatively lower. Both the big farmers as well as traders send their commodity in bulk to big cities and thus they earn good profits.

Betel Leaf Flow

Mahoba is, characteristically, known for both the inflow as well as the outflow in betel leaf. Here, large demands are made for *pan* and hence its inflow takes place in considerable quantity. On the other hand, the outflow of betel leaf from Mahoba is also equally important as it is related to export of the commodity. There is much demand for Mahoba *pan* and hence attractive prices are offered for the same. The traders (as well as some farmers too), therefore, export their produce to outstations through various means of transportation.

(i) *Inflow*: The fresh commodity used to come over to Mahoba from a distance of about 10 to 35 kilometers and a large area of adjacent Madhya Pradesh also used to supply betel leaf to Mahoba for further sale.

At present, there are 1500 betelvine growers in the town but 60 per cent of the growers are only the small and marginal farmers and are not in a position to grow betelvine on modern guidelines for want of necessary funds and facilities. In view of their economic status, only 10 to 15 per cent of the farmers are big ones and about 30 per cent farmers are middle class farmers.

It is also equally important to mention that the Uttar Pradesh Government Betelvine Conservatories meant for production and sale on large scale (commercial level) absolutely produced nothing over several years. The entire product, thus, came from the private growers of Mahoba and its surrounding areas.

Besides Mahoba, there are as many as 16 villages in the sourrounding area which produce betel leaves. Some vilalges of Madhya Pradesh also have been supplying betel leaves to Mahoba. The most important places from where the sellers used to bring their commodity for sale to Mahoba are: Malahara, Maharajpur, Lauri, Didwara, and Baldeogarah (located to the east of Tikamgarh). Amongst the most important places located in Uttar Pradesh supplying betel leaves to Mahoba in the vicinity are Barigarh and Chandera. However, Malahara, and Maharajpur also directly export their produce to Delhi adversely affecting the trade of Mahoba to a considerable extent.

(ii) *Outflow*: The production on large scale started in Mahoba when the betel-vine was brought from Banswara, Udaipur, Rajasthan. It is already mentioned that the Mahoba betel leaf is, especially, known for its taste and crispness.

In India, Mahoba has been well known for betel leaf export in large quantities to other cities of the country as well as foreign countries too. Even upto 1950s, the town exported 2-3 wagons - luggage vans - of betel leaves daily. Each wagon contained a large number of baskets, about 400, of betel leaves and each of these baskets used to have a weight ranging from 20 to 80 kg.

Due to the cold wave of 1962, large scale devastation of betel leaves took place and the goods were sent out of Mahoba thrice a week only. The total export was only 5 to 6 truck load of the commodity (per week). The most important destinations used to be the cities of Uttar Pradesh such as: Agra, Meerut, Bulandshahr, Pilibhit, Nanital, Delhi, Aligarh, Moradabad, Rampur and Bareilly.

Besides, large quantities of the commodity were sent regularly to Bombay as well as Calcutta. The deliveries to all these cities used to be given by Mahoba within 24 hours of their demand. Through the movement of a large quantity of betel leaves, the Railway Department also received a considerable amount of income. But later, however, due to negligence of this very Department, the bundles of betel leaves at the intermediary stations like Banda, Kanpur, Lucknow, Jhansi, etc. could not be re-loaded on time and with proper care. Hence, large quanities of the commodity were destroyed in transit only. It is important to note that despite the clear instructions of the Railway authorities to give top priority to betel leaves under perishable goods for sending the bundles through the express or mail trains, no care was taken under several pretexts compelling the grower/trader to offer undue and illegal gratification to railway employees.

It is also noted that the Madhya Pradesh produce is generally, directly exported to Delhi and hence it does not come to Mahoba for sale. Thus, the outflow of betel leaves from Mahoba to Delhi has been affected adversely. Malahara of Madhya Pradesh has particularly captured the export trade of Mahoba to a considerable extent. In view of sellers, in Uttar Pradesh, the sales tax rates are very high on betel leaf while according to them, there is no tax at all on this commodity in Madhya Pradesh. Hence, as against Mahoba in this respect Maharajpur and Malahara have been more successful.

Presently, about 60 baskets of betel leaves are sent out from Mahoba daily to Rath, Panwari, Kupahar, Lucknow, Kanpur, and Jhansi in particular through railway or road transport. Only through road transport, Mahoba exports about 20 baskets of betel leaves daily to Kanpur and Lucknow cities. Likewise large quantities are sent to Rath through road transport. Some growers/traders arrange the daily deliveries by hand to the traders of Banda, Karwi, Atarra, Kulpahar, etc. Monthly railway passes are used for such services and business transactions, more particularly, to deliver the goods at the door of the traders/purchasers themselves.

The volume of export varies through season to season during the year. It is at its lowest during winter, while maximum during summer season.

The Bangali variety is largely exported to Kanpur, Allahabad, and Varanasi. Due to its taste and fibrelessness characteristics, the betel leaf of Mahoba is loved over a large area in the country and the foreign countries. Now-a-days, in the name of Mahoba betel leaf, the leaves of Balamau — the cheap ones — are also sold in large quantities.

An important feature noted in the outflow of betel-leaf from Mahoba is that, physically, entire volume of the commodity does not move from the *Mandi* place rather a diversified trend has come-up. From different points — conservatories etc. — the commodity is directly moved out of Mahoba. Had the entire volume of the commodity collected at *Mandi* for transactions the *Mandi* place would have been totally unable to handle the same for want of space and other facilities.

Besides, it is also observed that instead of exporting betel leaves directly from Mahoba to Delhi and other centres in north-western part of India, the large quantities are sent from Mahoba to Maharajpur and/or Malhara during night time. These quantities are, later, sent from Madhya Pradesh to other areas of the country. By road, Maharajpur and Malahara had been sending their commodity to Kanpur etc. only 3 days a week but now about 200 baskets i.e. two truck loads of betel leaves are daily exported from these places. To promote the export trade of betel leaf from Madhya Pradesh, sometime back, the King of Chhatarpur made unsuccessful efforts to establish a *pan Mandi* at Chhatarpur. The wholesale traders from Mahoba also were attracted by Chhatarpur for trade in this commodity. However, due to lack of railway facilities the Chhatarpur *Mandi* could not flourish as desired. Thus, the *Mandi*, ultimately, stopped functioning. It is already noted that the winter is the starting season, and the marketing activities are at their lowest during this season. During the summer seasons, however, the activities are at peak. Large quantities of Mahoba betel leaves are sent to the north-western part of the country from Lucknow, Kanpur, and Delhi. Further export is made to Pakistan, and West Asian countries. To boost the export trade, the special varieties prepared in the research centres at Mahoba would be sent in near future.

Transport Problem

Betel leaf is a perishable commodity. The quick means of transportation — both roads and railways — have a great role to play in the movement of this commodity. It is observed that the trains get, generally, delayed and hence large quantities of goods are destroyed in transit. The railways also charge higher rates of transportation in case of betel leaf as it is considered perishable. And yet, no special care is taken in movement of this commodity by the railways. At times the bundles keep lying carelessly at stations causing heavy losses to the traders. Also, in case the trader makes a claim for his perished goods due to undue delays by the railway authorities in handling etc., the trader himself has to suffer for one reason or the other in a long run.

The Uttar Pradesh Government has stopped the booking of betel leaves by bus all over the state due to some diseases common to this commodity. Later, several efforts had been made to revive the booking but just in vain. Although, the transport ministry of the Government of Uttar Pradesh has also been approached several times but with no results. For transportation of betel leaves by trucks, only the large quantities are preferred by the transporters meaning thereby that the small quantities of this commodity are not accepted for transportation hence these are sent by trucks generally, at higher cost. However, the small vans are becoming more popular these days for transportation of small quantities of this commodity as compared against the trucks. By these vans, a load of about 25 baskets is easily transported.

TWENTY

Role of Periodic Markets in Agricultural Marketing System in North India: A Case Study of Faizabad District

NIZAMUDDIN KHAN

After the introduction of 'Green Revolution' during the late sixties and early seventies in India a considerable break through has been recorded in term of foodgrain production. Thus now the farmers are changing their altitude from subsistence agriculture to commercial agriculture. For such type of agriculture an efficient, convenient and renumerative marketing system is needed.

Generally agricultural products are marketed through mainly two agencies, i.e. government and private agencies in the country and especailly in the study area. The government agencies purchase the agricultural commodities under the auspices of support or procurement price in order to maintain the buffer stock. While the private agencies, which include all village traders, commission agents, wholesaler and so on, purchase the commodities at open or free market rate. This market rate varies from person to person and from place to place and agent to agent. Such type of trade or transaction are made, generally, in village periodic markets, town markets and regulated markets.

The periodic market, are main centres for transaction of agricultural products. The producer, generally small and marginal farmers, dispose of their surpluses in such markets on account of small size of surplus and inaccessibility to regulated or town markets. Almost all surplus of perishable products like vegetables and fruits are being marketed in periodic markets in rural areas of the northern India.

The present study is mainly based on primary as well as secondary data. The primary data on marketed surplus of different commodities in periodic markets, percentage of marketed surplus through the different marketing agencies, price system and problem faced by producers-sellers in marketing of their commodities are collected through field survey. The markets were selected on sample basis. 5 per cent villages were also selected for the survey purpose. The secondary data were aslo collected from office record or published bulletin.

A genuine breakthrough in Indian agricultural production, especially in food grains, has raised the hope of not only meeting the domestic needs satisfactarily, but also exporting the products to a considerable extent (Jaiswal, 1988 p. 23). After the advent of green revolution during the late sixties and early seventies, the production of foodgrains increased from 72.35 million tonnes in 1965-66 to 150.47 million, tonne in 1985-86. Such success in boosting agricultural production has been made on account of institutional reform, technological change and industrial support.

The increasing use and price of modern inputs, like fertilizer, irrigation, insecticides, seeds, implements and so on, requires much capital for investment. The cost of these inputs have been increasing year after year. While the price of agricultural output is not increasing at the same ratio. Thus the under pricing of farm products, perhaps, tend to affect the optimum use of inputs. One of the main constraints on increasing productivity is the price that producers get for their output in relation the price paid for input. Therefore, the market price of output is crucial for providing adequate incentive to producers which induce them to make greater investment for raising yield. Therefore, the success of any agricultural development programme rests ultimately on the efficiency of marketing system. The increase in agricultural production in the absence of efficient market support may adversely affect the welfare of agricultural class itself (Mishra, 1987, p. 10).

Faizabad district lies between 26°9'N and 26°50'N latitudes and 81°41'E and 83°8'E longitudes, located in the middle part of the Ganga plain in the state of Uttar Pradesh which is one of leading foodgrain producing area of the country

(Fig. 20.1). The district has 227 periodic markets spread over 18 development blocks.

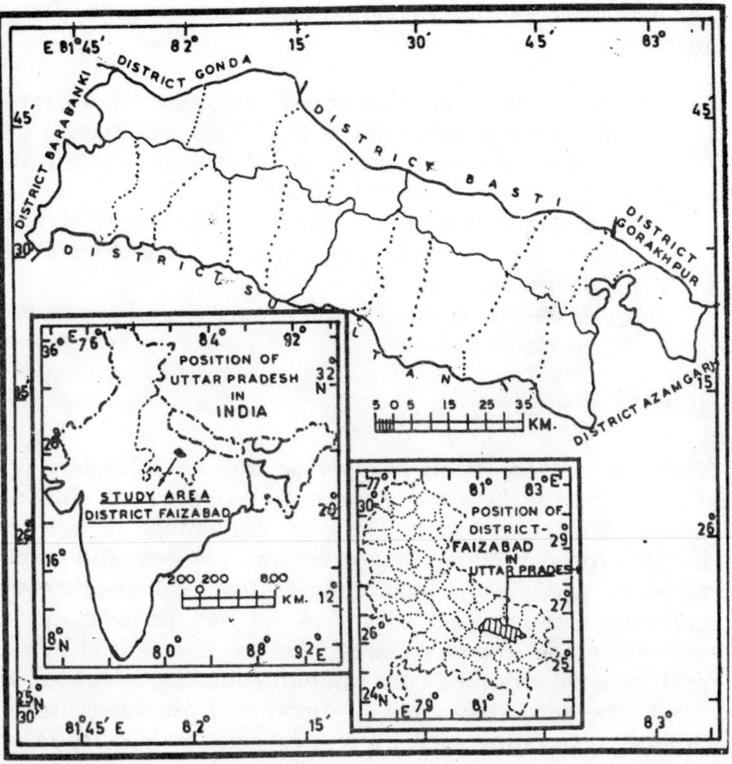

FIG. 20.1: Location Map of District Faizabad

Objective of the Study

Periodic markets is one of the important agency in which the producers directly or indirectly sell their agricultural surpluses. Generally, villages are not linked with specialized or town markets through all weather roads. Majority of producers have small amount of surplus which is uneconomical to be transported to distant *mandis* for sale and the perishable nature of commodities like vegetables restrict the long distance movement. Under such circumstances, the periodic markets are the only places where producers sell their surplus. Keeping in view, the importance of periodic markets in the marketing of agricultural commodities, the present study has been undertaken with the following aspects of agricultural marketing in periodic markets:

(i) Proportion of marketed surplus of different agricultural commodities in periodic markets.
(ii) Proportion of traders dealing with agricultural commodities in periodic markets.
(iii) Comparative study of price structure of different agricultural commodities in periodic markets and near by town markets.
(iv) Problems in the marketing of agricultural commodities in periodic markets.

Method of Study

The Study is based on primary as well as secondary data. The primary data on marketed surplus of different commodities in periodic markets, percentage of marketed surplus through different agencies, price system and problem faced by producer in marketing of their commodities were collected through field survey of selected periodic markets and villages in the study area. For the selection of markets and villages, stratified-cum-random sampling technique was used. The secondary data on amount of purchase made by different marketing agencies was collected from office records of different marketing agencies. The analysis of the data was made by calculating the percentage of marketed surplus purchased by different agencies. The percentage was calculated regarding the presence of traders dealing with agricultural commodities.

Result of Discussion

On the basis of the data analysis the following results were obtained.

Proportion of Marketed Surplus in Periodic Markets

In the study area the agricultural products are marketed through different agencies. It requires a channel through which the commodities are moved from farmer's home to ultimate consumers. The agricultural surpluses are sold through the following main agencies:

(i) Formal Agencies
(ii) Informal Agencies

Formal agencies include the government purchase centres, semi-government agencies like Food Corporation of India, State Food Corporation, Regulated Markets, co-operative societies, State Agro, Purvanchal Vikas Nigam and Marketing. These agencies purchase only some specific agricultural commodities like paddy and wheat under the scheme of minimum support price.* The informal agencies are concerned with private trading system. They are private mills, Periodic Markets and Direct Farm gate sale.

Periodic market is one of the most important agencies of agricultural marketing system. Table 20.1 gives the details of marketed surplus of different commodities through various agencies.

It was found that during 1985-86, 33610 tonnes wheat, 16596 tonnes paddy, 4538 tonnes rice, 1463.60 tonnes pulses and 34463 tonnes vegetables were marketed in the periodic markets. The Regulated Markets accounted for 57486 tonnes wheat, 81263 tonnes paddy, 4538 tonnes rice, 565.50 tonnes pulses and 17335.30 tonnes vegetables. Other government agencies like P.C.F., U.P. Agro, and F.C.I. purchased only wheat and paddy. They purchased 9551, 5914 and 10726 tonnes wheat, and 516,435 and 16084 tonnes paddy respectively during same period. Mill's purchase was confined only to paddy. They purchased 4636.40 tonnes paddy during 1985-86.

---

* Among the formal agencies the "Regulated Markets" is exceptionally transacting all type of commodities.
The price of out-let (heaps of commodities) is decided on the basis of auction by licencee traders.

Table 20.1: Purchase of Agricultural Commodities by Different Agencies in District of Faizabad (1985)

(Weight in tonnes)

Agencies	Wheat	Paddy	Rice	Pulses	Vegetables
1. Formal Agencies					
a. PCF	9551	516	—	—	—
b. UP Agro	5914	435	—	—	—
c. FCI	10726	16084	—	—	—
d. SFC	—	—	—	—	—
e. Marketing	5237	—	21681.80	—	—
f. PVN	—	—	—	—	—
g. Regulated Market	57486	81263	4538	565.50	17335.30
2. Informal Agencies					
a. Mills	—	46364.40	—	—	—
b. Private Trader	NA	NA	NA	NA	NA
c. Periodic Market	33610	16596	—	1463	34463
d. At home by consumer	NA	NA	NA	NA	NA

Source: RFC Faizabad, Mandi Samiti, Faizabad, Tanda and Akbarpur, and Assessment based on field survey in the case of Periodic Market.

PCF- Provincial Co-operative Federation
FCI- Food Corporation of India
SFC- State Food Corporation
PVN- Purvanchal Vikas Nigam

Table 20.2: Proportion of Agricultural Produce Marketed at Different Stages During 1985-86 in Faizabad District

Market Agencies	Wheat	Paddy	Rice	Pulses	Vegetables	Oilseeds
1. Direct Consumer at home	5	10	30	7	10	3
2. Village Trader	60	50	30	73	5	90
3. Village Market (Periodic markets)	10	15	20	8	80	—
4. Whole sale market	5	8	—	—	—	—
5. Regulated market	3	5	8	2	4	—
6. Government Agencies	10	1	—	—	—	—
7. Town Markets	6	7.5	7	10	1	7
8. Mills	—	3	—	—	—	—
9. Village shop	1	0.60	5	—	—	—
Total	100	100	100	100	100	100

Table 20.2 indicates the proportion or share of different marketing agencies in marketing of agricultural commodities in Faizabad district. The share of periodic markets in the sale of different agricultural commodities varied with the nature and demand of the articles. The non-perishable commodities like wheat, rice/paddy and pulses were transacted in low proportion. Only 10 per cent wheat, 20 per cent rice and 8 per cent pulses of marketed surplus were disposed of in periodic markets for sale. In the marketing of perishable commodities like vegetables including chilli, vegetable nursery etc. the periodic markets had a lion's share. About 80 per cent of marketed vegetables were sold in such markets.

The share of village traders was 60 per cent for wheat, 50 per cent for paddy, 30 per cent for rice, 73 per cent for pulses, 5 per cent for vegetables and 90 per cent for oil seeds. The whole sale market accounted for 5 per cent wheat, 8 per cent paddy of total marketed surplus. The proportion of marketed surplus of different commodities exchanged through regulated markets was 3 per cent for wheat, 5 per cent for paddy, 8 per cent for rice and 4 per cent for vegetables. In the town markets 6 per cent wheat, 7.5 per cent paddy, 7 per cent rice, 10 per cent pulses, 1 per cent vegetables and 7 per cent oil seeds were marketed. The government purchase centres, including all agencies like P.C.F., S.F.C., U.P. Agro, marketing and co-operatives, accounted for 10 per cent wheat and 1 per cent paddy. Moreover, through direct marketing, where consumers purchase directly from producer, the proportion of marketed surplus of wheat, paddy, rice, vegetables, pulses and oil seeds was 5, 10, 30, 20, 7 and 3 per cent respectively. Besides a very insignificant percentage of marketed surplus reached to village shoppers.

Proportion of Traders Dealing with Agricultural Commodities in Periodic Markets

The study revealed that the majority of traders in the periodic markets were dealing with agricultural commodities. Their percentage of total traders in the markets varied from market to market and from commodity to commodity. It ranged from 41.75 per cent in Toron Muafi to 92.46 per cent in Ashrafpur Kicchauccha among 27 selected periodic markets. Such variations were due to the different size and dimension of markets. The urban and rural nature of the settlements, in which markets are held, also influenced the distribution of agricultural traders. The urban periodic markets had, generally, larger proportion of agricultural traders than those in rural peridoic markets done to the fact that the urban population had larger demand for agricultural commodities.

However, the variation in percentage of traders dealing with different commodities also varied. Durability and demand of commodities had much contributed in such variation. The vegetables traders had dominant share in all periodic markets on account of their perishable nature and daily demand. It varied between 29.41 per cent in Ajrauli and 79.36 per cent in Partappur Chamarkha. The paddy and wheat traders were in low proportion on account of relatively lesser demand in the markets. The percentage of wheat and paddy traders ranged between zero and 16.47, and between zero and 17.04 respectively among the sampled periodic markets.

Price-structure of Agricultural Commodities in Periodic Markets

There are several determinants which control the price of a commodity in any market. Some of the important factors are — trends of demand and supply, trader's travel cost and profit, durability of the items, security and storage facilities. The relative prices of different commodities in both periodic markets and near-by town markets are given in Tables 20.3 and 20.4. It was found that there was significant variation in prices of different commodities in all sampled periodic markets.

Table 20.3: Proportion of Traders Dealing in Agricultural Commodities to Total Traders in Selected Periodic Markets in Faizabad District

Sampled Periodic Market	Paddy	Wheat	Pulses	Vegetables	Total
1. Mahauli Uprahar	7.40	6.17	2.46	49.38	65.11
2. Raunahi Uprahar	8.42	4.67	1.86	56.07	71.01
3. Maujadubans pur	12.95	9.06	2.07	33.67	57.75
4. Jalaluddin Nagar Uparahar	8.59	8.59	1.03	48.10	66.31
5. Bhadarsa	6.56	4.63	3.86	54.05	69.10
6. Gosainganj	1.48	2.19	4.46	52.08	60.21
7. Barun (Deoria)	2.99	2.02	2.02	57.88	64.81
8. Toron Muafi	2.73	3.42	1.36	34.24	41.75
9. Ajrauli	7.35	5.88	5.89	29.41	48.53
10. Mohammadpur	2.71	2.26	3.38	67.87	76.23
11. Hatihigaon	6.66	4.94	—	66.66	77.76
12. Bhiti	—	—	4.61	76.92	81.53
13. Ariya	—	—	2.00	75.00	77.00
14. Bariyawan	2.02	2.42	3.23	60.62	68.29
15. Sultangarh	3.75	2.52	0.80	62.52	69.59
16. Kasian pur	2.09	1.57	6.25	68.02	77.90
17. Rafiganj	1.42	1.18	3.66	65.32	71.58
18. Jalalpur	13.88	15.88	3.56	55.01	87.88
19. P.Chamarkha	1.58	1.98	2.77	79.36	85.69
20. Iltifatganj	17.81	16.70	4.76	50.11	89.38
21. Mubarakpur	17.04	14.20	2.89	56.81	90.94
22. Hanswar	6.41	9.61	5.68	51.28	72.98
23. Indaipur	—	—	0.38	59.52	60.00
24. A.Kichhanchha	5.85	4.68	3.90	78.00	92.46
25. Jahangirganj	13.28	12.91	3.69	59.04	88.92
26. Deorila Buzurg	—	—	1.47	66.17	67.64
27. Kamalpur	1.57	6.29	—	49.30	57.16

Table 20.4: Wholesale and Retail Price (Rs.) of Different Commodities in Selected Periodic Markets (Feb. 1985)

S.No.	Market	Wheat		Rice		Pulses		Potato		Cabbage		Chilli		Tomato	
		Whole sale	Retail	Whole sale	Retail	Whole sale	Retail	Whole sale	Retail	Whole sale	Retail	Whole sale	Retail	Whole sal	Re-teail
1.	Mohauli Uprahar	2.00	2.10	—	4.50	—	8.10	0.90	0.75	1.70	1.75	—	2.00	—	1.75
2.	Raunahi Uprahar	—	2.00	—	4.45	—	8.00	—	0.80	—	1.70	—	2.05	—	1.80
3.	Maujadubanspur	—	2.05	—	4.50	—	8.00	0.90	1.00	—	1.80	—	2.10	1.80	1.85
4.	Jalaluddin Nagar	—	1.95	4.30	4.40	—	8.05	0.95	1.00	—	1.90	—	2.00	—	2.00
5.	Bhadarsa	2.10	2.15	—	4.50	—	7.95	0.90	1.00	1.97	2.00	—	2.20	2.07	2.10
6.	Gosainganj	2.13	2.15	4.30	4.40	8.00	8.10	1.00	1.05	2.00	2.10	.05	2.10	2.00	2.05
7.	Barun	1.95	2.00	—	4.35	—	7.90	—	1.00	—	2.00	—	2.00	—	1.90
8.	Tarun Muafi	—	2.00	—	4.40	—	7.50	—	0.90	—	1.90	—	—	—	1.90
9.	Ajrauli	1.90	1.95	4.40	4.45	7.15	7.25	0.85	0.90	1.80	1.85	—	2.10	1.90	2.00
10.	Mohammadpur	1.92	1.95	4.35	4.45	7.80	7.90	0.80	0.90	1.80	1.90	—	2.20	1.90	2.00
11.	Hathigaon	—	1.80	—	4.50	—	7.30	—	0.85	—	1.90	—	—	—	1.95
12.	Bhiti	—	2.00	—	—	—	—	—	0.40	—	1.85	—	—	—	2.00
13.	Ariya	—	—	—	—	—	—	—	0.95	—	1.90	—	2.00	—	1.80
14.	Bariyawan	2.00	2.05	—	3.90	—	7.85	0.80	0.40	1.85	1.95	—	2.15	1.95	2.00
15.	Sultangarh	1.90	2.00	—	3.95	—	7.80	—	0.95	1.85	1.90	—	2.20	—	2.10
16.	Kasianpur	—	1.90	4.00	4.00	—	7.50	—	1.00	—	1.95	—	1.50	—	2.00
17.	Rafiganj	—	2.10	4.25	4.30	—	7.85	0.95	1.00	—	1.75	—	1.75	—	2.00
18	Jalalpur	2.10	2.20	4.15	4.60	8.15	8.20	1.00	1.05	2.10	2.10	—	1.20	2.10	2.15
19.	Katehri	2.00	2.10	4.45	4.50	7.90	7.95	1.00	1.00	2.00	2.05	—	1.70	2.00	2.05
20.	Iltifatganj	2.00	2.15	4.30	4.40	8.05	8.10	0.95	1.00	1.95	2.00	—	1.30	2.05	2.10
21.	Mubarakpur	2.05	2.10	—	4.50	7.98	8.10	1.00	1.05	2.00	2.05	—	1.10	2.00	2.15
22.	Hanswar	2.00	2.10	4.40	4.55	7.95	8.05	1.05	1.10	1.85	1.95	0.50	0.75	1.95	2.00
23.	Indaipur	—	—	—	—	—	—	0.85	0.90	—	2.00	—	0.80	—	2.00
24.	A. Kichhanchha	1.95	2.10	—	4.50	—	8.10	1.05	1.10	1.90	2.00	—	1.00	1.85	1.90
25.	Jahangirganj	2.00	2.05	4.20	4.45	7.75	7.90	0.80	0.90	1.80	1.95	0.60	0.85	1.90	2.00
26.	Deoria Buzurg	—	—	—	—	—	—	—	1.00	—	1.80	—	—	—	2.00
27.	Kamalpur	—	—	—	—	—	—	—	1.00	—	1.75	—	—	—	2.10

Source: Field Survey.

The retail price (in rupees per kg.) varied between 1.80 (Hathigaon) and 2.20 (Jalalpur) for wheat, 3.90 (Bariyawan) and 4.45 (Hanswar) for rice, 7.90 (Jahangirganj) and 8.20 (Jalalpur) for pulses, 0.75 (Mahauli Uprahar) and 1.10 (Hanswar) for potato, 1.70 (Raunahi Uprahar) and 2.10 (Gosaingang) for Cabbage and 1.75 (Mahauli Uprahar) and 2.15 (Jalalpur) for tomato. Similarly the wholesale price for the same commodities also varied from market to market as evident from the Table 20.5.

The analysis and comparative study of retail and whole-sale prices of different commodities in periodic markets and near by town market revealed same important facts which are given below:

(i) The producer-sellers sell their commodities to wholesaler at rather lower price than retail price prevailing in the same markets.

(ii) The price system in the periodic markets, generally, is influenced by prices prevailing in near by town markets and is always lower than prices in town market for the same commodities.

(iii) The direct trading (Stone 1975) which is common in periodic markets, is beneficial for both sellers and consumers. It is because the producer sellers realize all middle men's share to consumer's price and recieve more price in periodic markets than offered by village traders at farm gate. But this price is always lower than the price exists in the town markets for the same item. On the other hand the consumers have to pay lesser price in comparison to price in twon markets.

Problems in the Marketing of Agricultural Commodities in Periodic Markets

Periodic markets are, generally, held in remote rural areas to cater on local daily needs of different commodities.

Undoubtedly, these markets contribute a significant share in the marketing of agricultural commodities brought from neighbouring and distant villages for sale. There are a number of difficulties which are to be faced by the producer-sellers in disposing off and transacting their surpluses in periodic markets.

Table 20.5: Wholesale and Retail Price (Rs.) of Agricultural Commodities in Some Town Markets in Faizabad District (Feb. 1985)

Market	Foodgrains						Vegetables							
	Wheat		Rice		Pulses		Potato		Cabbage		Chilli		Tomato	
	Whole sale	Retail	Whole sale	Retail	Whole sale	Retail	Whole sale	Retail	Whole sale	Retail	Whole sale	Retail	Whole sale	Re-tail
Faizabad	2.20	2.30	4.38	4.50	8.10	8.25	1.40	1.50	2.00	2.25	1.85	2.10	2.40	2.70
Bhadarsa	2.05	2.20	4.40	4.45	8.05	8.30	1.35	1.40	1.95	2.00	1.80	2.15	2.40	2.60
Gosainganj	2.10	2.20	4.40	4.45	8.00	8.25	1.35	1.45	2.05	2.10	1.85	2.00	2.45	2.65
Tanda	2.10	2.30	4.55	4.60	7.95	8.35	1.35	1.50	2.10	2.15	1.75	2.10	2.25	2.50
Jalalpur	2.10	2.25	4.50	4.65	8.05	8.30	1.40	1.45	2.10	2.20	1.70	1.75	2.30	2.55
Akbarpur	2.15	2.27	4.50	4.60	8.00	8.35	1.45	1.55	2.00	2.05	1.80	2.00	2.55	2.75
Baskhari	2.05	2.15	4.45	4.55	8.00	8.30	1.45	1.50	2.00	2.10	0.60	0.75	2.45	2.50
Kichauchha	2.13	2.15	4.45	4.50	8.10	8.40	1.50	1.55	2.05	2.10	0.70	0.80	2.45	2.50

Source: Field Survey

Inaccessibility of periodic markets, from neighbouring villages is a very important constraint in the marketing of agricultural commodities. Farmers are unable to visit the rural markets in order to sell the surplus on account of bad roads. They are bound to sell the commodities at distress rate in the villages.

Shortage of space for loading and unloading of vehicles is another problem in the periodic markets. Such problems are very common in urban periodic markets where shops are set along the roads or street on both sides. Because of this constraint the whole selling practices on large scale appears impracticable.

Moreover, uncertainty of prices and taxes (collected by market management) discourage the farmers to dispose off their commodities in periodic markets. Market prices of different commodities vary from market to market and even within the markets. Lack of storage facilities compel the sellers to sell their products at relatively lower price at the evening when the markets, generally, set off. Besides, lack of standard weights and measures, grading and standardization and registered traders and other functionaries had many deplorable effects. There are greater opportunities for cheating the ignorant farmers and they give rise to needless complications in practice between one market and the other.

Conclusion and Suggestion

The present study shows that the periodic markets contribute 10 per cent for wheat, 15 per cent for paddy, 20 per cent for rice and 8 per cent for pulses marketing of agricultural commodities in the study area.

Vegetables are such agricultural commodities which are sold mainly in periodic markets. These markets help the farmers in increasing their income by providing opportunities for sale of agricultural surplus especially during the sowing period when there is immediate need of money for investment in inputs.

Taking into consideration the welfare of farmers and role of periodic markets in marketing and agricultural commodities, some important measures may be suggested as under.

Regulation of all periodic markets is urgently needed to

remove the imperfection that exists among them. All inaccessible markets should be linked by metalled roads to important *mandis* and market centres in the region. A scientific approach to price structure, might be the parity approach. There should be a price list of all commodities prepared by price committee, of different markets on different days and it should be released and distributed at every village.

The periodic markets should be held in open space out of settlements. They should have separate place for loading and unloading of the vehicles, auction, storage and parking. Govt. purchase centre should be set up at such markets. Co-operative marketing system is also needed. Agricultural inputs like fertilizer, pesticides, insecticides, seeds and implements should be distributed through periodic markets.

TWENTY-ONE

The Socio-economic Structure of Shopowners in Peppeganj (U.P.): A Marketing Town

MAHATAM PRASAD and S.P.L. SRIVASTAVA

Methodology

This study is based on primary data. The collection of data is based on field survey with the help of questionnaire and interview method. About 58 per cent of the total of 642 shops of the town have been taken into account. These shops are randomly sampled from all 9 municipal wards of the town. On the basis of the data so collected, the socio-economic characteristics of the shop owners have been illuminated. After evaluating the participation of various castes in the marketing function of the town, six major castes—*Baniya*, Backward, Muslim, Scheduled Caste, Goldsmith and Brahmin, have been recognised on the basis of their strength in total sampled shops. Afterwards the age of their establishments and occupational mobility have been highlighted to mark the gradual increase of shop owners. In addition to educational status of shopowners their age structure has also been taken into account to focus on the social composition of major business castes. In order to present the economic aspect, the ownership of shops, shopstructure, the average income per shop as well as per caste has also been discussed with help of maps and diagrams. Thus the study identifies the participation of major castes in marketing activities of the town and the emerging features thereon.

Locational Aspects

Peppeganj (26° 55' N Lat. & 83° 17' E Long. approx.) having an area of 0.31 sq km with a population of 6160 person (1981) is a town of Campierganj Development Block of Gorakhpur district of Uttar Pradesh. The town is located in Rapti-Rohin Doab, a part of the Saryupar plain of the Middle Ganga Valley. Rapti and Rohin flowing the west and east of the town respectively have deposited alluvial deposits in this locality and formed a monotonous plain.

The town is located just 24 km from the district headquarters Gorakhpur. The town does not possess any administrative status. In spite of the absence of administrative offices the town has emerged as a marketing and rural service centre and has attracted larger population than nearby block headquarters. It is most remarkable that on the basis of population engaged in business activities Peppeganj has third place in whole of the Pharenda tahsil. Business is the main stay of the inhabitants of the town as about 60 per cent working population is engaged in activities related to business.

The town has about hundred years span of development. Formerly it was just a village with weekly market known as Sahibganj. Later it was named as Peppeganj in 1885 when Gorakhpur-Gonda Railway line was constructed and it became a railway station. Prior to this it was connected to Gorakhpur with an unmetalled road which later developed as international highway connecting the Nepal border. Besides marketing it provides Bank, Medical and educational (including one Degree College) facilities to its service area. Now it has acquired the status of 'Town Area' since 1979. More than six hundred shops are functioning with a shop-population ratio of 1:10.

Spatial Distribution of the Shopowners

Prima facie, shop distribution of the town is lineated along differant roads but on the basis of concentration of shops the town may be divided into four shop areas Fig (21.1A).

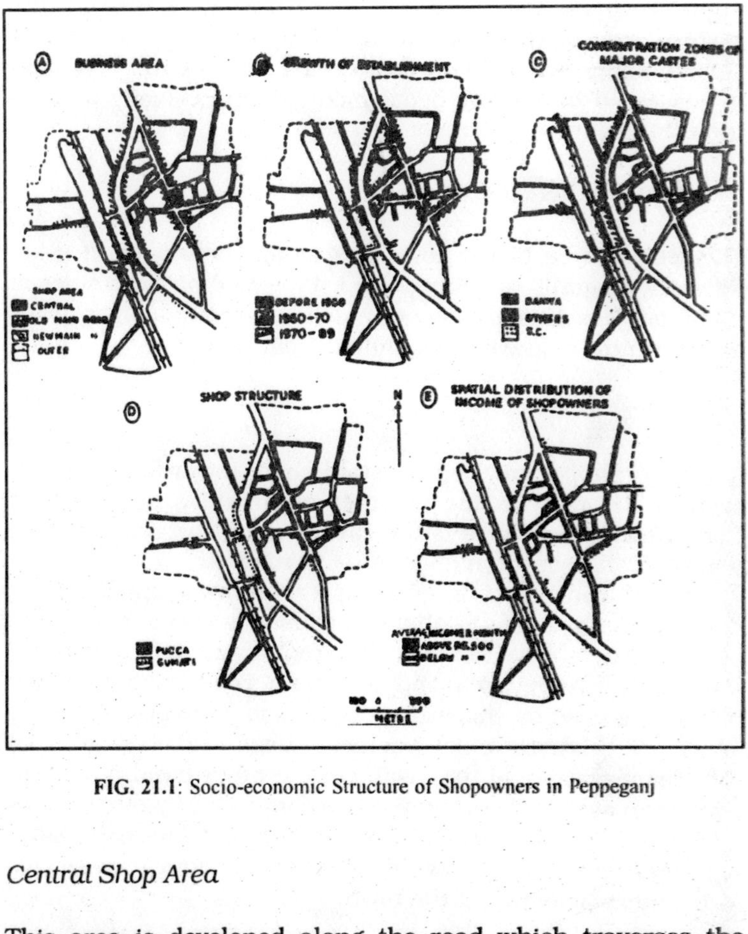

FIG. 21.1: Socio-economic Structure of Shopowners in Peppeganj

Central Shop Area

This area is developed along the road which traverses the central part of the town. This road has an east-west orientation and connects the railway station and the new main road with the old main road. This area attracts majority of shops due to its favourable location and intense marketing interaction. This area is accessible for most of the consumers either of the town itself or of the influence area of the town.

New Main Road Shop Area

This area lies along both sides on the new main road elongated north to south near railway station. It is second in importance on the basis of concentration of shops. The eastern side of this road is full of *pucca* shops while only *Gumati* shops are seen on its western side because the land is possessed by railway department which normally permits the establishment of temporary shops.

Old Main Road Shop Area

This oldest area of the town lies along the old main road. Formerly majority of shops were established on both sides of this road. Now this area is not much important comparatively as the centre of gravity has shifted from here.

Outer Shop Area

Recently shops are being established towards the west, accross the railway line in other outer areas of the town. Concentration of shops is increasing along the Barhya road, northern and southern ends of main road etc.

As the concentration of shops varies markedly along the different roads due to locational factors, castewise distribution of shopowners also varies in different localities. It is noted that central shop area and old main road shop area are mainly occupied by shopowners of *Baniya* caste because these areas are relatively older business areas and *Baniya* is an old business caste of the town. On the other hand new main road shop area and outer areas are dominated by other castes due to late development of these areas and late indulgence of other castes (viz. Backward caste and scheduled caste etc.) in business activities of the town.

Social Composition of Shopowners

Caste Pattern

From the very beginning, caste system has been one of the major determinants of individual's ocupation and it is still effective. But recently many multipliers of development have tended to arise non-traditional castes in business activities. Therefore, virtually shopowners of different castes are engaged in business activities of the town. There are mainly six major castes/sub-castes which represent 95 per cent shopowners of the town. *Baniya* caste is especially noticeable among these as 44 per cent shopowners of the town belong to this caste. Remaining shopowners are related to Backward caste (27%), Muslim (13%), Scheduled caste (5%), Goldsmith and Brahmin (each 3%). In the caste structure of whole town, share of these castes is 36, 22, 17, 14, 3 and 3 per cent respectively. It may also be noted that caste pattern of the shopowners is not in accordance with the caste pattern of the town.

Fig, 21.2A reveals that the percentage of *Baniya* and Backward caste shopowners is exceeding than their actual share in population of the town, while Muslim and Scheduled castes are less than their percentage share of population. Goldsmith and Brahmins are engaged in this activity in accordance to the caste pattern of the town. It is to be noted

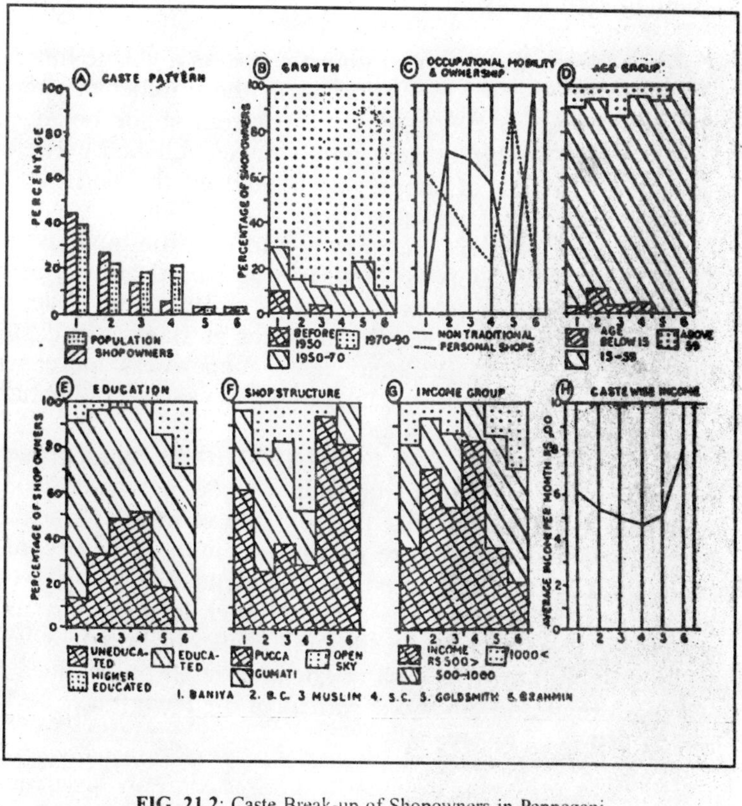

FIG. 21.2: Caste Break-up of Shopowners in Peppeganj

that the caste pattern of the shopowners is much affected by a number of shopowners coming to the town daily from adjacent villages to participate in the business activity. Muslim and Scheduled castes are trailing because of economic limitations and engagement in other activities.

On the basis of concentration of major business castes of the town, zones of concentration have been identified. It is marked that old and central shop areas are dominated by *Baniya* shopwners. Shops in new main road area and outer shop area are mostly operated by other castes, though *Baniya* shopowners are found in these areas also. Some shopowners of Scheduled caste are operating on footpath in the central shop area also (Fig 21,1C).

Growth of Establishment

As aforesaid, the town came into existence as a village having a few retail shops. Further addition in the number of shops was negligible upto 1950 as only 5 per cent shops belonged to Baniya and Muslim shopowners, were established between this period. Growth of shops was limited on the both sides of central part of the old main road.

Another 15 per cent shops were added in the business of the town between 1950 to 1970. In this period growth area of shops prolonged towards railway station and covered central shop area. Non-traditional castes as Backward caste, Scheduled caste and Brahmin caste shopowners increased in this period. Even increase in traditional castes—Goldsmith was higher followed by *Baniya*.

In the next span of 20 years (1970-1989) rapid growth took place in development of shops as 80 per cent shops came into existence in this period. This is most noticeable that 48 per cent shops were established after 1980 because the town became upgraded and organised authoritative development arose with the help of other facilities. In this period, the growth of non-traditional castes in business was dominating and growth area of shops covered outer sides of new main road and other outer areas of the town (Figs. 21.1B and 21.2B).

Occupational Mobility

Convergence of occupation is recognised as occupational mobility. In this town it is seen that only 40 per cent shopowners are identified as traditional. The remaining 60 per cent shopowners belong to non-traditional castes. It is very low in traditional castes such as *Baniya* and Goldsmith while in other castes viz. Backward, Muslim, Scheduled caste and Brahmins occupational mobility has been very high (Fig. 21.2C)

Age Structure

Since labour force is determined by age-structure of workers therefore age is one of the very important aspects which affects the ability, capacity and performence of shopowners in business activities. Thus the age-structure of shopowners of the town has influenced the working setup and interactions of them. This is very important that 87 per cent shopowners of the town belong to effective age group (15 to 59 years). In this group Brahmins are leading. The strength of such shopowners is slightly less in other castes while Muslim castes has lowest strength of shopowners in this group comparatively.

Child shopowners (upto 14 years age) being immature and shopowners above 60 years due to old age belong to non-effective age group. Remaining 13 per cent shopowners of the town represent this group. These persons are forced to enter in business due to their poor economic conditions, Muslim shopowners are leading in non-effective age group followed by Backward and Scheduled caste shopowners (Fig. 21.2D).

Education

Education strengthens the capacity and helps in deciding the occupation of persons. It may be noted that 76 per cent shopowners of the town are literate. It may be pointed out that nearly 40 per cent population of the town is literate. Brahmins are leading in literate shopowners followed by Goldsmith and *Baniya* respectively and only these have got higher education also. Remaining 24 per cent shopowners of the town are identified as unschooled. In this respect about 50 per cent shopowners of Scheduled caste and Muslim belong to the category of illiterate followed by Backward (30%), Goldsmith (15%), and *Baniya* (12%) respectively. (Fig 21.2E)

Economic Composition of Shopowners

Shop Structure

There are three main types of shop structure in the town—*Pucca* shops, *Gumati* shops and open sky shops. The shop structure represents the status of shopowners.

It may be noted that 48 per cent shopowners of the town are operating in *Pucca* shops which are housed in permanent structure. This type of shops are wide spread along the road sides in the whole town, but their main concentration lies in central shop area along both sides of old main road and on the east side of new main road. According to caste-breakup of shopowners Goldsmith, Brahmin and Baniya are important in operating *Pucca* shops (more than 60%).

45 per cent shopowners of the town are operating in *Gumati* shops which are made of wooden structure. This type of shops are concentrated on the western side of the new main road and in outer shop areas. The land on the western side of the new main road is under the possession of railway department where shopowners operate their shops on lease basis and are not authorised to construct permanent structures. In this category shopowners of Backward caste (50%), Muslim (45%) and Scheduled caste (25%) are more numerous. It may be noted that 5 per cent shopowners of *Baniya* caste are also operating in *Gumati* shops.

It has been observed that 7 per cent shopowners of the town operate their business activities under open sky. These are distributed in limited parts of footpath in the central shop area and in new main road area. Shopowners of Scheleduled caste (50%), Backward caste (25%) and Muslim (18%) are respectively important in this category (Fig 21.1D and 21.2F).

Ownership of Shops

Though the town has emerged mainly as a marketing town

yet business activities prevail mostly in tenant shops. 71 per cent shopowners of the town do not own their shops and are operating as tenant shopowners. Mostly Backward, Scheduled caste and Brahmin shopowners are tenant shopowners. Even some Baniya shopowners also pay rent for their shops. The remaining 29 per cent shopowners have their own shops. In this category Goldsmith and *Baniya* shopowners are important (Fig. 21.2C).

Income

Income is the real economic index of any establishment or household. On the basis of average income (Fig. 21.2H), shopowners of Brahmin caste are leading followed by Goldsmith, *Baniya* and Muslim respectively by earning a profit of more than Rs. 500 per month. While shopowners of Backward and scheduled caste belong to weak economic status as they are trailing by earning a profit less than Rs. 500 per month.

On the basis of average income shopowners of the town have been grouped in three income groups—

(i) Lower, (ii) Medium, (iii) Higher.

It is noted that 49 per cent shopowners of the town belong to lower income group of profit below Rs. 500 per month. Shops of this category are spread in the outer shop area and limited parts of central shop area and new main road shop area (Fig 21.1E). Shopowners of Scheduled caste, Backward caste and Muslim are much important in lower income group by sharing 83 per cent, 71 per cent and 50 per cent of shopowners of their respective castes. It is noticeable that more than 20 per cent shopowners of other major business castes are also earning below Rs. 500 per month. All such shopowners are influenced by either weak economic status or by less marketing interaction (in outer areas) of their shop areas.

Forty-two per cent shopowners of the town belong to medium income group of profit ranging between Rs. 500 – Rs. 1000 per month. Especially these shopowners are distributed in central shop area and old main road area. Shopowners of Goldsmith, *Baniya* and Brahmin are much important in this group by sharing more than 50 per cent while shopowners of Muslim, Backward and Scheduled caste are trailing in this group by sharing 35 per cent, 23 per cent and 17 per cent respectively.

Few shopowners (9%) of the town belong to higher income group of profit above Rs. 1000 per month. Among such shopowners Brahmins are leading (30%) followed by *Baniya* (19%), Goldsmith (15%) and Muslim (14%). This is noticeable that only 6 per cent shopowners of Backwards caste are earning above Rs. 1000 per month while shopowners of scheduled caste are nil in this category.

Conclusion

It is concluded by this analysis that the participation of various castes in the marketing activities of the town is varied. Though in the town *Baniya* shopowners are comparatively much developed due to their traditional base yet Brahmins, Goldsmith and even Backward caste shopowners are developing in all respects very rapidly in spite of their late engagement in these activities. Now providing of some financial and other facilities is enevitable for upliftment of the weaker shopowners of the town.

Some raised platform type temporary shops may be built on footpath of central shop area and these should be alloted to weaker shopowners. On the other hand some permanent/ *Gumati* shops may be built near railway crossing on the southern side of the Barhya road because this area is gradually attracting much marketing interaction.

TWENTY-TWO

Spatial Pattern and Types of Market Centres of Awadh Plain (North)

VISHWA NATH and J.S. VERMA

This chapter attempts an analysis of the spatial pattern of market centres of the Awadh Plain (North) which is followed by the types of market centres into seven categories.

Awadh plain is a distinct historical and cultural region of the upper Ganga Plain. It extends from 26°53'N. to 28°53' N. latitude and 79°37'E to 81°24' E. longitude over an area of 24 thousand km^2. Population of this region according to the 1981 census, was 7.77 million. This region comprises of fourteen Tahsils and forty-seven development blocks of the five districts viz. Pilibhit, Shahjahanpur, Hardoi, Kheri and Sitapur of Uttar Pradesh. The economy of this region is based on subsistence agriculture. Therefore majority of the population fulfils its needs through periodic market centres.

Spatial Pattern

Awadh Plain has a total of 722 market centres (Fig. 22.2). These market centres are not uniformally distributed. The regional distributional pattern shows a great disparity. Lakhimpur Tahsil of Kheri district possesses 10 per cent of the total market centres of the region, while Puranpur (Pilibhit) and Shahjahanpur Tahsils comprise 2.8 per cent and 2.6 per cent of the total market centres respectively. Nearly 1/3 of the total market centres of the region lie in Sitapur district. Hardoi district has 28 per cent market centres and Kheri district posseses about 25 per cent of the total market centres of this region. (Table 22.1).

Nearest Neighbour Analysis method has been applied to

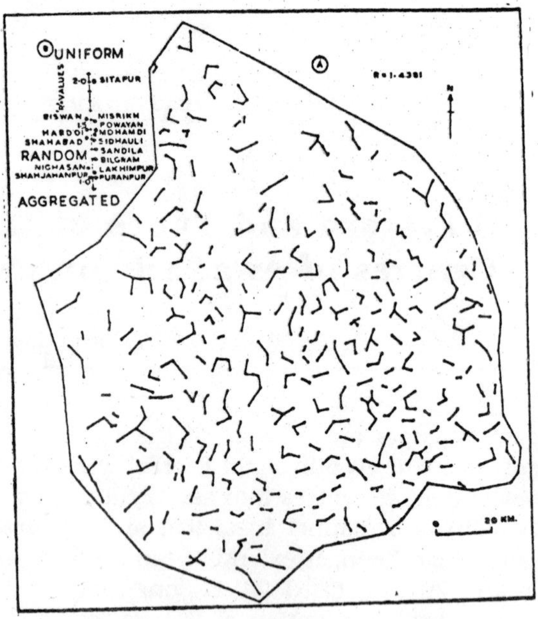

FIG. 22.1: Nearest Neighbour Analysis

identify the spatial pattern of market centres in Awadh Plain (Fig. 22.1A). This method has been helpful in the study of spatial pattern of elements in question.

Using the formula* 'R' values of the tahsil-wise spatial pattern have been obtained (Fig 22.1B) for the region.

Forumla

(1) $r_A = \frac{\Sigma r}{N}$

(2) $r_E = \frac{1}{2\sqrt{P}}$

(3) $R = \frac{r_A}{r_E}$

Here:

$r =$ Distance from one point to other nearest point.
$r_A =$ Mean of Range of distance from nearest neighbour point.
$N =$ No. of distance in a measure of a particular area.
$\Sigma r =$ Total distance of a nearest point.
$r_E =$ Mean expected distance from nearest neighbour point.
$P =$ Density of mean observed distance of particular unit.
$R =$ Measurement of deviation from Randomness.

Table 22.1: Awadh Plain: Distribution of Market Centres

Sl. No.	Tahsil/District	No. of Market Centres	Percentage
1.	Purnapur	21	2.9
2.	Powayan	55	7.6
3.	Shahjahanpur	20	2.8
	Powayan and Shahjahanpur	75	10.4
4.	Nighasan	47	6.5
5.	Lakhimpur	76	10.5
6.	Mohammadi	64	8.9
	Kheri	187	25.9
7.	Misrikh	55	7.6
8.	Sitapur	68	9.4
9.	Biswan	59	8.2
10.	Sidhauli	52	7.3
	Sitapur	234	32.5
11.	Shahabad	43	5.9
12.	Hardoi	66	9.2
13.	Bilgram	36	4.9
14.	Sandila	60	8.3
	Hardoi	205	28.3
	Awadh Plain (North)	722	100.0

As a whole 'R' value comes to 1.291 which shows that the spatial pattern is moving towards uniformity. It is not worthy that of all the fourteen tahsils of the region, twelve have an 'R' value indicating uniform spatial distribution of market centres. Only in two tahsils, i.e. Puranpur and Powayan, the spatial pattern is found to be random (Table 22.2).

Types of Market Centres

The types of market centres may be attempted in several ways. For example, according to periodicity, the following types of market centres are distinguished: (1) Daily markets, (2) Periodic markets, and (3) Daily-cum-periodic markets. Skinner, on the basis of his empirical study, classified the market centres of rural China. The main basis of his

Table 22.2: Nearest Neighbour Analysis Indices

Sl. No.	Tahsil	Area (sq. km.)	No. of Villages		N.	P.			R.
1.	Purnapur	1697.2	393	20.0	17	0.2315	1.1294	1.0390	1.0869
2.	Powayan	1553.0	810	58.15	55	0.5215	1.0572	0.6924	1.5269
3.	Shahjahanpur	1022.3	540	21.0	14	0.5282	1.5	1.4535	1.03119
4.	Nighasan	3281.0	420	58.0	37	0.1280	1.5675	1.3976	1.1216
5.	Lakhimpur	2806.5	690	80.0	77	0.2458	1.0389	0.9916	1.0475
6.	Mohammadi	1844.6	661	79.0	64	0.3583	1.2343	0.8353	1.477
7.	Misrikh	1557.6	657	66.0	53	0.4218	1.2452	0.7698	1.6176
8.	Sitapur	1324.8	586	71.5	46	0.4423	1.5543	0.7518	2.0675
9.	Biswan	1479.9	513	95.3	68	0.3466	1.4014	0.8493	1.6501
10.	Sidhauli	1437.2	605	60.5	55	0.4209	1.1	0.7707	1.4272
11.	Shahabad	1397.3	562	47.7	42	0.4022	1.1357	0.7884	1.4405
12.	Hardoi	1642.4	492	90.8	64	0.2993	1.4187	0.9137	1.5524
13.	Bilgram	1534.3	512	34.3	32	0.3337	1.0718	0.8655	1.2384
14.	Sandila	1461.5	417	70.6	55	0.2853	1.2836	0.9361	1.3712
	Awadh Plain (North)	24040.6	7858	852.85	679	0.3268	1.25603	0.8745	1.4363

classification were means of transport, status of a market place, local agricultural product etc. India too, like China is a traditional agricultural country. Therefore, Skinner's scheme of types of market centres can be applied in classifying the market centres of the study region.

The market centres of the Awadh Plain have been classified on the basis of their functional forms, economic activities, transport facilities and other empirical evidences into the following categories (Fig 22.2), starting from the lowest level, i.e. *Hat* to the regional city:

1. Hat;
2. Minor Market Centres,
3. Standard Market Centres,
4. Intermediate Market Centres.

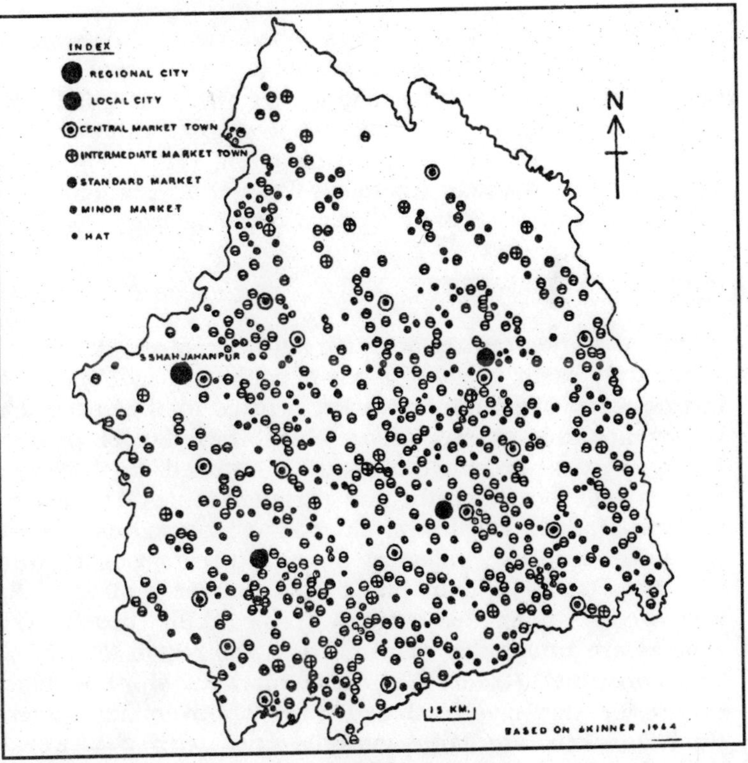

FIG. 22.2: Market Classification

5. Central Market,
6. Local City,
7. Regional City.

Hat

Hats are centres where horizontal exchange of commodities takes place. These chiefly consist of perishable goods and articles of daily use. Their functions are restricted in type and number both. In the study region nearly 12 per cent market centres come under the category of *Hats* (Table 22.3). Vegetables and *kirana* shops are common in *hats*. These market lie in inacessible places of the region, i.e. Saraiyan Abad, Bhojipur, Pathra, Muradpur etc.

Minor Market Centres

Minor market centres are centres, where goods of daily needs are made available. Horizontal exchange of goods and services takes place. Horizontal exchange means that goods are exchanged among the local population groups. There are 222 minor market centres in the region (Fig. 22.2). These are purely periodic markets generally with once a week frequency, i.e. Jamunia Khas, Roshan Nagar, Govindnagar etc.

Standard Market Centres

Standard market centres are such market centres where rural community easily avails of goods of common need. These are distinguished from minor market centres in the sense that sellers are able to buy goods which they do not produce locally. Vertical exchange of goods is initiated. Such centres are generally located on the transportation routes. The farmers dispose of their surplus production, which moves towards the towns and the inflow of manufactured goods to rural areas starts. More than half of the market centres of the region come under this category (Table 22.3). These market centres are uniformaly distributed in the region (Fig. 22.2). The consumers/traders of these markets show a mixed nature, i.e. they may combine the role of buyers and traders. Such markets are large periodic ones with a bi-weekly component.

Intermediate Market Centres

Intermediate market centres collect the manufactured goods and distribute them to standard market centres. These centres are located along main highways and have a higher level of accessibility. Most of the shops are permanent and the mixed nature of consumers and traders observed above disappears. These markets control the vertical flow of goods and services. Intermediate market centres are directly related with their higher counterparts. Intermediate market centres are generally located in small towns.

Neraly 3 per cent of the total market centres of the region come under this category (Fig. 22.2).

Central Market

Central markets are situtated in large urban centres. These centres supply higher order goods to lower order centres. Such centres are located at transportation nodes. Secondary activities are also present in such type of market centres. A greater veriety of goods and services is also noted. Nearly 3 per cent of the total market centres of this region come in this category (Table 22.3).

Table 22.3: Types of Market Centres

Sl. No.	Types of Market Centres	Number	Percentage
1.	*Hat*	84	11.6
2.	Minor Market Centres	222	30.8
3.	Standard Market Centres	372	51.6
4.	Intermediate Market Centres	21	2.9
5.	Central Market	19	2.6
6.	Local City	3	0.4
7.	Regional City	1	0.1
	Total	722	100.0

Local City

These centres import goods for rural areas from the outer productive area. Later on the goods are distributed to various categories of market centres. Almost all shops in a local city are permanent and wholesaling of goods emerges. Such activities accelerate the complex functional forces, which in turn generate intra-regional and inter-regional trade.

In such centres big merchants control the economic activity of the city. Banks, Co-operative Societies, godowns, cold storage facilities, quick and easy means of transport make the process of exchange comfortable at such centres. There are three local cities in Awadh Plain i.e. Sitapur (Pop. 98270), Hardoi (82617) and Lakhimpur (60110).

Regional City

A regional city is a big market centre. Here wholesale and retail business go together. It has a wider area of service. Distributors and agents of various companies are found in a large number. Besides, these are also centres of production of different goods. In the study region only Shahjahanpur is classified as regional city.

It may thus be seen that more than half (51.0%) of the total market centres of Awadh Plain come under the category of standard market centres. Minor market centres form 31 per cent of the total market centres. *Hats* constitute only 12 per cent of the total market centres (Table 22.3).

Conclusion

It may thus be seen that the market centres of Awadh Plain show a tendency of uniform spatial pattern. This is in contrast to the Saryupar plain and the lower Ganga-Ghagra doab regions of the Ganga plain, where random spatial pattern predominates. The study shows that Skineer's scheme of types of market centres can be usefully employed in the Ganga Plain with little modification.

TWENTY-THREE

Spatio-Temporal Organisation of Tertiary Economic Sector: A Meso Regional Study

A.K. JAIN and C.K. JAIN

Introduction

In the rural resource based economy the periodic market centres are, perhaps the world over, the best instruments of spatial organisation of people and space. Thus most of the rural people cater their demands of daily routine through periodic markets. They (periodic markets) are also fore-runner of latter urban developments. Further periodic markets signify the most rational attempts of a society to overcome the need for sufficiently close spacing of marekt centres, even though the economic demand and level of transport development are much too inadequate to support trading/marketing function economically at so closely spaced places. Along with this, these periodic market centres in larger villages and small towns are also the points of social change, modernisation and diffusion of modernisation.

Periodic market system attempts to explain some of its characteristics on the basis of types of traders, the cost of trading operations and on the basis of the pattern of spatial behaviour of traders (Wanmali, 1981). In terms of periodic market system the itinerancy is genuine skill of traders which consumates, from the angle of traders, the indigenious traders' wisdom of periodic markets, providing them with almost daily business on different days of the week at different places. Thus the itinerancy greatly augments the trading scope for traders, who with this economic interest, the traders move around an available set of market centres. With the change in modes of transportation the pattern of movement of traders has also transformed and is manifested in quite different form. This pattern of movement is the focal theme of the present chapter taking the example from Vidisha Plateau region of Madhya Pradesh (Jain, 1987).

The Region: Locational Context and Geographical Backdrops

The macro region called Ganga Basin is par excellance and extensive agricultural region settled since very long. In the comparatively backward State of Madhya Pradesh have hardly any region match with Ganga Basin per say however certain small pockets in the State are fairly rich tract in an agriculture. One such small region of Madhya Pradesh lies in the upper Betwa Basin which at least remotely forms a part of Ganga Basin i.e. via media of Chambal and Yamuna Basin. The region broadly recognised as eastern Malwa Plateau and Vidisha Plateau as a meso region.

Vidisha Plateau region of Madhya Pradesh extends over 13000 sq. km. of the plain of upper Betwa Basin. The major right hand tributory— the Bina river is surrounded by hill ranges on nearly all sides. Thus it forms the part of Yamuna sub-basin of the Ganga Basin. It entails two rather distinct terrain types — the river plain and the hilly tracts — with pertinent difference between them with respect to land use development status of agriculture, distribution of population and characteristics of settlements, and commercialisation. These elements are found to have significant bearings on the periodic market system of the region. Thus while the plains of Betwa and Bina rivers have a good development of agriculture, fairly dense distribution of population and of periodic markets. The surrounding hilly areas are either under forest or poor stoney soils and bushy vegetation, have but a meagrely developed agriculture and sparse populaton in the form of small settlements. Periodic markets also poor and far-flung here. The population of the region is approximately 1.4 million. The region gives the gross density of 109 person per sq. km. very poor indeed as compare to other part of the Ganga Basin. Though many lineaments of the physical and human landscape trend in an essentially north-south direction including the Bina-Bhopal section of the central railway almost along Bina river, the two important roads across the region run in east-west direction. They join Bhopal on the west and Sagar on the east of the region — one via Vidisha and another via Raisen (Fig. 23.1). The region is also recognised as eastern Malwa Plateau.

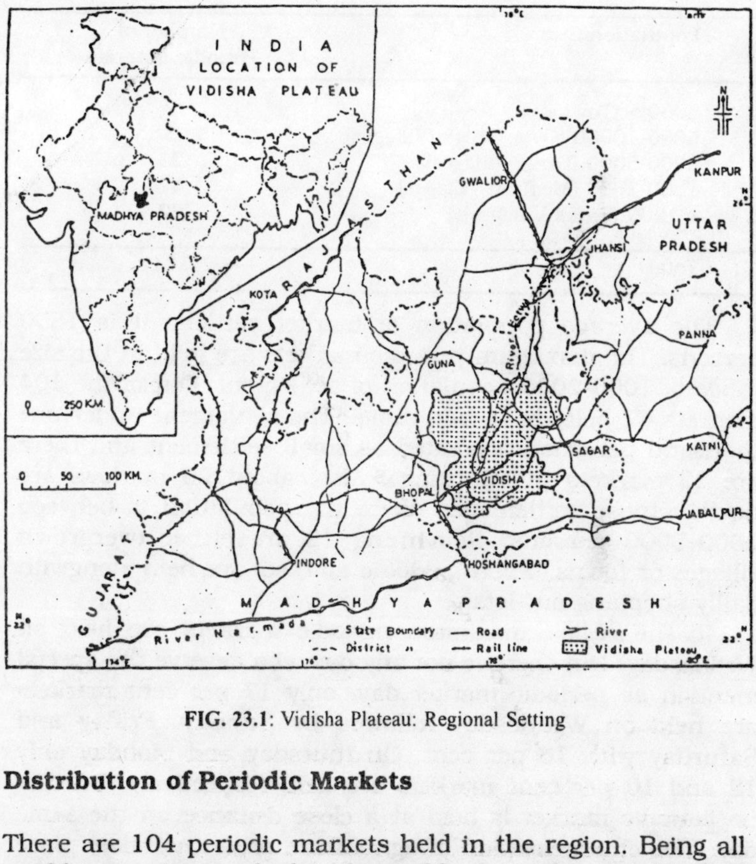

FIG. 23.1: Vidisha Plateau: Regional Setting

Distribution of Periodic Markets

There are 104 periodic markets held in the region. Being all weekly except one which is bi-weekly. It is also notable that varigating the distribution of markets is the location of very big market centre, around which no small centre could grow as periodic market for quite some distance. Sironj town, in the north western part has a radius of 15 km or more of no market, where after there is nearly a ring of periodic market centres. Here, combined with the overshawing effect of Sironj town, thin density of population and lack of large enough villages to support a periodic markets are other factors.

The population size and market centre is given in the following Table 23.1.

Table 23.1: Periodic Markets and Population Size of Settlements in Vidisha Plateau

	Population Size	Number of Periodic Markets
1.	5000 > (Towns)	9
2.	5000-10000 (Over Grown Villages)	3
3.	2000-5000 (Large Villages)	23
4.	1000-2000 (Medium Villages)	47
5.	< 1000 (Small Villages)	22
	Total	104

The average population of market settlement is 1800 persons. The maximum periodic markets are held in the size range of 1000-2000 population of settlement. Out of the 104 markets 47 belongs to this range. The settlement under one thousand persons are treated as small settlement and there are 22 markets in this range. Also, about 23 markets are held in those settlements where the population is between 2000-5000 persons. Remaining 12 are either overgrown villages or towns, where periodic markets are held alongwith dailly shopping out-lets.

In the region maximum periodic markets are held on Wednesday. But there is not any day who deserve the special mention as periodic market day, only 17 per cent markets are held on Wednesday followed by Sunday, Friday and Saturday with 16 per cent. On thursday and Monday only 12 and 10 per cent markets are held respectively. Further no periodic market is held at a close distance on the same day. The channelisation of agriculture produces takes place through mandi-centres which is twelve in numbers and the wheat and gram are the important commodities for sale. Among total arrivals to *mandis* the share of wheat and gram is 37 to 40 per cent. Since 80's the soyabean has also become important crop and commodity for sale and the production of soyabean is growing fastly at the cost of other crops.

It is also notable fact that besides *mandis* there are some periodic markets grown as specialised markets as collection centres of agriculture produces.

Methodology

Out of 104 periodic markets in the region 47 centres were selected for direct field survey such that every part of the region and all size classes of market were properly represented. Accordingly visiting pattern of itinerant traders has been presented and different pattern of market cycle such as radial, cyclic or composit identified. Similarly, the means of transport adopted by traders and proportion of each sector were also presented.

Market Place Participants

Market place participants are the persons who assemble at the periodic market places for exchange of goods, services, ideas or other for socio-cultural purposes. This behaviour shows the importance of a particular group or set of the market centres to the localities and ruralities of remote areas. Thus the market place is a vital interface not only for exchange of goods but also for the personal contact and communication of ideas. The significance of it becomes apparent when it is remembered that the change in ideas is every bit as important as the change in the economy which is all-too-often over emphasised (Wanmali, 1979). It should be borne in mind that people often can not take the most rational and essentially the economically determined decision, which nevertheless is a fundamental premise of the central place theory and all other location theories. A correct objective assessment is always in terms of their perceptions coloured by their preference and prejudices and decided by a host of factors usually not encompassed/encompassable in such studies. These factors and variables relate mostly to the psychological and socio-cultural terms. Shrivastava explicitly poses the question does the individual trader or visitor always maximises his space utility under economic constrains? Does an individual mover always structure the rating of opportunities with distance in mind? These variations are caused by individual conservatism, social bonds, level of knowledge, ability to use such knowledge and economic considerations etc. In short these are socio-cultural and tradition bound constrains on the behavioural options. Particularly the socio-economic and psychological perception of cost and inconvenience of transportation on various routes or to various places is affected by very subtle factors like security, road conditions etc. (Shrivastava, 1978).

Traders as a Market Place Participant

In market gathering which are periodically occur at predecided place and time, two major types of participants were present—the consumers and the traders. Among traders participants Wanmali distinguishes part time and full time traders. Among part time traders-producer sellers and collector seller are identified. This includes farmers, makers of earthen pots, bamboo and wood craft, and vegetable sellers. Full time traders are those selling traders, buying traders and service persons. They are economically entirely based on market business (Wanmali, 1979). Smith described a typology of market place participants (Smith, 1976); accordingly three categories are identified, e.g. full-time farmer trader, part time farmer and non-farmer (Smith, 1976). They are present in the market place either for buy or for sale or for both reason.

Market Cycle

Market cycle means the circle or a set of market days through which itinerant traders moves along in chain or in sequence of the week consisting 7 days. Thus the frequency of market centres promote the cyclic system in the periodic marketing, which reflects the stage of development of the region. It is important to note here that in the region markets are weekly. Thus spatio-temporal synchronisation of the market centres follow the need of the consumers and traders.

A market cycle is deemed to exist when and where several periodic markets are attended in sequence, on which the preference to visit the nearest place has also important bearings (Bromley, 1973; Tamaskar, 1979). This cyclic movement is organised normally with the assumption that there is clash in between the nearby markets. The densly population region may provides number of market cycle. However, this situation is no where in the region.

Traders moving in a market cycle are not necessarily quite aware/concious of this, but they are behaving most rationally in terms of socio-economic cost and benefits. Thus aware or unaware, they are best synchronised of the rural marketing system, so as to eke out sufficient business despite the very meagre demand at any single place. Accordingly, they attend market A on Monday, B on Tuesday, C on Wednesday and so on. This indigenious marketing strategy, however demands that spatial and temporal distances between places are convenient and accessible. While it should be feasible to reach the places conviniently, they shuld also have their market days on consequitive or nearly consequitive days. Thus if one place has its weekly market (*hat*) on monday and a second place has its weekly market, instead on thursday, then there is a distance of two days between them.

As a series of interconnected and interacting places, market cycle may be complete or incomplete. If such a set of markets provides business throughout the week or 5 days in a week, the market cycle is regarded as complete, otherwise a series of only 2-3 market is regarded partial or incomplete. In the region by this criterion that nine complete market cycles are traced with calculating the minimum 5 days in a each market cycle (Fig. 23.2). Among all six are in the central plain one in the south and another is located in north and north-east taking Sagar just beyond the study region. In Bina basin one market cycle was found alongwith the National highway 26 between Lalipur and Sagar. In between Bina and Kurwai system one market cycle is found in ribbon shape. Western part is jointly shared by Basoda and Vidisha tahsil. This area presents the exmaple of actual circumfrencial market cycle. Some itinerant traders moving in this cycle in circumferencial manner by either own transport means like covered ox-cart carrying utencils or horse carrying *kirana* or using private vehicle carrying a bag of plastic shoes. Market cycle in central part follows the road net work. This region is the Betwa-basin. Periodic markets in this region are important trade centre for trading of wheat. Basoda, Vidisha, Kasba Bagrod are the main collection centre of grains located in the central parts.

In the region traders travel the longer distances and carryout business in series, visiting several market in series and reaching back home at the end of itinerary. This example

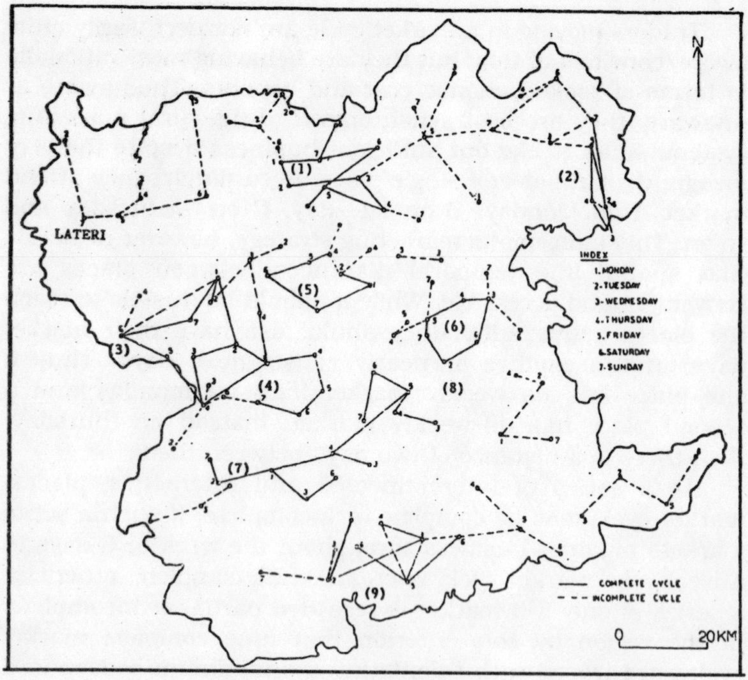

FIG. 23.2: Vidisha Plateau: Market Cycle

is taken from the north western part of region around Shamsabad-Satpara system (Fig. 23.3). Traders of *kirana*, utencils and plastic shoes are identified in this cycle. In the region number of market cycles are incomplete. The thin population and lack of transport means is notable among the factors behind such intruption.

Although there is not any conceptual view in the mind of traders that he is going to join a market cycle but it is a part of his planning as to where he will proceed to attend subsequent market. It is also noticed that there is no application of market cycle in the sale of green vegetables by producer-sellers, they are small farmers bringing a basket — full of vegetable to the market. Although the participation of such traders is always high in each periodic markets, some permanent traders particularly for onion and potatos are moving around the week and throughout the fair weather.

Market cycle or market ring which is particularly the movement adopted by the itinerant traders is also known as

Banji-Bhonri in local dilects. *Banji* means the movement for the purpose of trade and *Bhonri* denotes circuitous travelling. But this terms used after when a shopmen of village visit the surrounding villages where the existance of periodic market is not necessarily available. Horse and ox-cart is the prime means of transport for such itinerancy.

Movement Pattern and Market Cycle

In geographical context of a system of periodic marekt centres, the market cycle denotes a set of periodic markets that stands close enough with one another spatially and temporally; i.e. located at a negotiable distance and having periodic market day/s on sequent days of the weeks. If so these markets attended by itinerant traders sequentially on this respective market days, so that there are important functions available at those markets on the suddenly boomed clientle on its specific day while the traders find ample business throughout the week. Thus this itinerancy of traders among markets of a cycle overcomes at the same constraints of small range of goods/functions usually available at the markets and the large threshold of these goods/functions. Viewed thus the periodic market systems are but rural vassals of Christallerian central place system of region, and market cycle represent an indigenuous compromise, struck by the agency of itinerant trading, between the small range of goods obtaining around rural centres and the large threshold of population (or of business) demanded by the trading functions.

Although, originally itinerancy denotes a cyclic movement from one place to the next, much like the stages of a cycle, it is not necessarily so in practice. In all likelyhood, formerly many a trader itinerancy perhaps presented, by and large, such a circular movement. The present day itinerant traders movement pattern in most cases is radial or nearly so (Fig. 23.3). The causation of this changing pattern is that formerly a trader could trot but a certain limited distance on the horse back or ox-cart or perhaps on foot and market also were regularly spaced nearly that certain distance apart. Therefore, a traders going from A to B on one day and coming back in the evening could not practically attend the market 'C' the next day which may be twice as far away. He perforce had to stay overnight at 'B' in order to avail the market of 'C' next

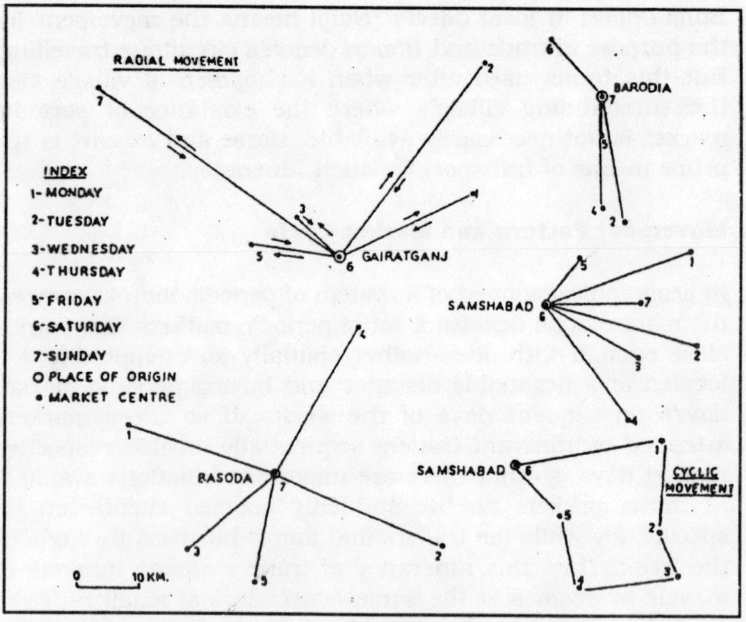

FIG. 23.3: Vidisha Plateau: Patterns of Itinerancy

day. He would come back after 5-6 days to his home village. At variance with this bus and other vehicular means of transport have relagated geographic distances to a position of secondary importance vis-a-vis availability of transport services at appropriate time. Thus a distance of 10-20 km have some weight in regulating the traders itinerancy. The traders can return to the point of origin from long distances as much as 40 to 50 km. Thus coming back from even a long distance to one's home village has become more convenient and feasible than staying overnight out of home. This factor has induced or atleast definately helped the change from cyclic to radial pattern of traders itinerancy.

Traders *vs* Transport

Traders channelised the rural produces to urban centres and manufacture goods the otherway round, and the development infrastructure of market centres depends on the network of transport functionally available in the region. However, one important aspect, which is as to who utilised these transport facilities, as every village does not have road/rail services. If the rail-road communication is available for reaching to periodic market places the real implication is that the market centre is connected to the centres of higher oder markets and the itinerant traders is the person who benefits from such services first. In case of consumers despite the facilities available the expenses is normally higher than the quantity purchased by them. The usefulness of these services is largely by the way of goods and services brought in by the traders. This deserve high appreciation because, due to the lack of transport, only small traders of traditional items reach to the market place by their own conveyance; and from about 5 km range, people mostly come by walking down with the headload of their goods, as vegetable sellers mostly do so.

The mode of transport adopted or available has shown in the Table 23.2

Table 23.2: Visit of Periodic Market by Traders

S. No.	Market Place	Padestrian	Bicycle	Ox-cart	Bus	Rail	Tractor & Trucks	Horse	*Haththela*
1.	Large Town	32	4	28	16	5	—	1	14
2.	Medium Town	43	11	9	32	—	—	2	3
3.	Small Town and very large Villages	24	5	14	52	3	1	1	—
4.	Large Villages	25	7	15	46	—	1	6	—
5.	Medium Villages	41	9	20	21	0.5	1.5	7	—
6.	Small Village (*Hat*)	58	15	4	12	—	—	11	—
	Region	36	8	17	30	1	1	5	2

Source: Field Work - 1983-84.

It is seen that beside paddler traders, bus, rail, tractor, ox-cart, *Hath-thela* (man operated small four wheeler luggage carrier) are the mode of transport using of traders of different goods. In the region highest proportion (36%) of traders is found reaching to the markets on foot carrying the headload of their stalls. This owes largely to the small size of shops and higher proportion of small stall holders. Actually they are those persons who produce small quantity and part time traders. They reach to the market from surrounding villages covering about walkable distance of 6 kms.

Bi-cycle

The use of bicycle is very popular and economic in all over the region. In the periodic market of Vidisha Plateau region 8 per cent of total traders depend upon bicycle for the purpose of reaching market centres with their small stall of cloth and *manihari.* In Kagpur market of Vidisha Distt. the sellers of the readymade garments use bicycle in spite of available bus services, as the distance from Kagpur to Seu or Nateran Village is pretty small. A person who follow this, has the loan based start of Rs. 5000 from Govt./bank and start the business of readymade cloth and periodic markets are only his span of business.

Ox-cart

Ox-cart is a vehicle for all purchasing purposes in rural and remote-rural areas particularly for agriculture, transport for agricultural produces and several domestic purposes. In the region 17 per cent of total traders do come to use ox-cart. The trip taking by ox-cart is multiple and the users of ox-carts are mostly the farmer traders. In Seu maket one metal utensil seller used the covered ox-cart for circumferencial trade and visit even few villages where the market is not held. The farmers use ox-cart for selling their agricultural produces: wheat, gram, *gur* etc. and seasonal horticulture crops: mango, onion, potatos, watermelon, *husk million*, sugarcane etc.

Bus and Rail

In the study region 30 per cent of traders depend on the bus services for attending perioidc markets. However, the small town and larger villages markets have their 52 per cent traders reaching there by bus. This percentage varies from 12 to 16 per cent in small villages.

In sizeable urban places, the periodic market is not very significant for itinerant traders, in that, traders are mostly local person having permanent shops in daily markets and putting up enhanced stalls on periodic market day. They prepare their shops well before a day with sufficient goods as per market day requirements.

In the region the transport services by rail have certain stringent characteristics which tend to restrict its utility for periodic markets. Only in large places, with suitable train timings and stopages are the railway services notably used by the traders. Though on the whole less than one per cent traders resort to railways for visit to periodic markets.

Tractors, trucks, horses and *Hath-thelas* are the other means of transport. Itinerant traders also used horse for carrying their *kirana* shop and visit village to village and offer door to door services. In loacl tongue this form of trading known as *Banji* and itinerary is known as *Bhonri.* The luggage bag is known as *Khurjee* (Panniers). In the periodic markets of Vidisha region only 5 per cent traders use horse for attending the periodic market. Seu, Bichhiya, in Basoda Tahsil, Kagpur in Vidhisha Tahsil and Raisen are the markets where horses were seen in the periodic market.

Spatial Pattern of Market Visit by Traders

Markets particularly a sizeable market, cover a much larger range of area. Some larger centres attract traders from a couple or more km around or sometimes from even far-flung places, whereas some marginally located places are frequently visited by traders from important markets outside the region such as Rahatgarh, Khurai, Bandri, Barodia, from Sagar. These long distance visit by traders is particularly obtained alongwith the important roads e.g. Raisen, Begamganj, Vidisha, Rahatgrah etc. detail analysis of visit is given in the section of transport and market centres.

Conclusion

To investigate the pattern of movement of traders or itinerancy of traders the visual idea is a cyclic movement i.e. circular pattern of movement to the next. Though now a days with the shift of mode of transport infrastructure from walking, horse-back or the ox-cart to vehicular, this is only inadvertantly implicit impression no where has it been explicitly and deponently stated as to what the actual movement pattern of itinerant traders in a given market cycle is. Thus two basic types of itinerant traders movement pattern are discovered—the radial type and the peripherial type as well as various composit of either. In the Vidisha Plateau region of Ganga basin it is hypothesised that formerly the itinerant movement pattern was peripherial except for the initial and the final moves from and to the place of origin or itinerancy. Later this pattern has strongly and steadily tended to be radial from the place of origin and today itinarancy pattern are mostly radial only.

TWENTY-FOUR

Hierarchy of Service Centres: A Case Study of Ujjain District

(MISS) V. PHANSE and (MISS) P. HINGE

The importance of the hierarchic system for planning purposes of Service Centres is undoubted. The idea behind planning is the proper location of social and economic activities over a given space so that a balanced development of the region can be achieved.

Since there exists village dominated agrarian economy in the study area, approximately 95 per cent of the Service Centres are placed very low in the hierarchical system. A modest attempt therefore has been made to identify the hierarchy of Service Centres of Ujjain district on the basis of the centrality index. It may be conceived that with the increase in population of Service Centre, its hierarchical order is also elevated.

The term 'hierarchy' might be used to refer to a ranking of service centres into successive orders which is based either on their sizes and the functions they perform. The idea behind the hierarchical study of service centres is the proper location of social and economic activities over a given space, so that a balance development of a region may be achieved. The services may be rural or urban in character but they play a significant role in implementing development programmes.

Objective

The present study is a modest attempt to identify the hierarchy of service centres of Ujjain district and to study their associated characteristics. "The hierarchy of planning unit may differ in different types of regions, but only that centre will be the appropriate centre which has the potentials of beocming nuclear for future economic, social and political development of the surrounding areas (Shrivastava, 1980).

Area of Study

Ujjain district lies in the mid-western part of Madhya Pradesh, extending from 22°5'N to 23°46' north latitude and from 75°08' to 76°16' east longitude. Thus forming a part of Gangetic plain. There are six tahsils and an equal number of development blocks in Ujjain district inhabited by 11,17002 persons (1981 Census). The present study includes 150 settlements having 1000 and more population along with 8 urban centres. Ujjain city belongs to class I town while the rest belong to class III, IV and V towns. Together there are 158 settlements which have been identified as service centres out of a total of 1127 villages.

The district has a rolling topography with rather fertile black soil. It has agriculture based economy, with more than 77 per cent of the working population engaged in agriculture.

Methodology

For identification of service centres, both primary and secondary data have been used. Secondary data regarding population structure, presence or absence of service centres were collected from 1981 District Census Handbook, District Statistical Office and Block Development Office.

The centrality of a centre largely depends upon the economic activity of the service centre, i.e. the number of persons engaged in non-agricultural activities. This is the first measure of centrality. Similarly the population of a village, small or big, needs certain basic amenities or services. Hence social amenities have been identified as index of centrality. The summation of these two indices bring out the final centrality index of a service centre.

For measuring Functional index the following formula has been used-

$$\text{Functional Index (I.F.)} = \frac{P}{MP} \qquad \text{.........(1)}$$

P = Percentage of working population engaged in

secondary and tertiary activities in a settlement.

MP = The mean percentage of working population engaged in secondary and tertiary activities in selected settlements.

The growth generating functions are those that are available in a few settlements but they are availed of by a large number of settlements. In the present study the qualifying limit for a service centre has been decided on the basis of 6 major groups of functions with 29 sub-functions.

They are—

A: Education:	1) Primary School
	2) Middle School
	3) Higher Secondary School
	4) Adult Education Centre
	5) College
	6) University
B: Administrative:	7) Gram Panchayat
	8) Police Chowky
	9) Police Station
	10) Block headquarters
	11) District headquarters
	12) Commissioner headquarters
C: Health:	13) Primary health centre
	14) Sub-health centre
	15) Family Planning centre
	16) Veterinary Hospital
D: Communication:	17) Post office
	18) Post and Telegraph
	19) Telephone
	20) Head Post office
E: Trade and Commerce	21) Fair price shop
	22) Weekly market
	23) Co-operative Bank
	24) Commercial Bank
	25) Mandi Committee
F: Transport	26) Metalled road
	27) Railway station
	28) Bus stand
	29) Aerostrip

To measure the centrality of selected service centres, weight has been allotted to different sub-functions. The idea is that the greater the scarcity of a service, the more it becomes significant in terms of centrality and the higher the weighage to be awarded. The following formula is used for it.

$$W = \frac{N}{F} \qquad \text{........(2)}$$

W = Weightage to sub-function;
N = Total number of settlements under study;
F = Number of settlements having sub-function.

Accordingly weightage of all sub-functions is thus obtained. If weightages of different sub-functions available in a service centre are aggregated, it will be the aggregated service score value of a settlement. For measuring the social amenities index the following formula has been used-

$$\text{Social Amenities Indix} = \frac{A}{MA} \qquad \text{........(3)}$$

A = Aggregated Service Score value of a settlement;
MA = The mean aggregated Service Score value in the study area.

The final centrality index of a service centre is obtained by the summation of 1st and 3rd formula

Centrality Index (C.I.) = (F.I.) + (S.A.I.)

Accordingly, the centrality index for all 158 settlements has been calculated. In order to measure the change in hierarchical order of the settlements, the centrality index has been measured for 1971 and 1981 of all 158 settlements.

Hierarchy of Settlements

Settlements do vary in size, population structure and number of services they render. In (Figs. 24.1 and 24.2) the centrality index and the log value of population have been taken as two parameters to identify the hierarchy of 158 service centres.

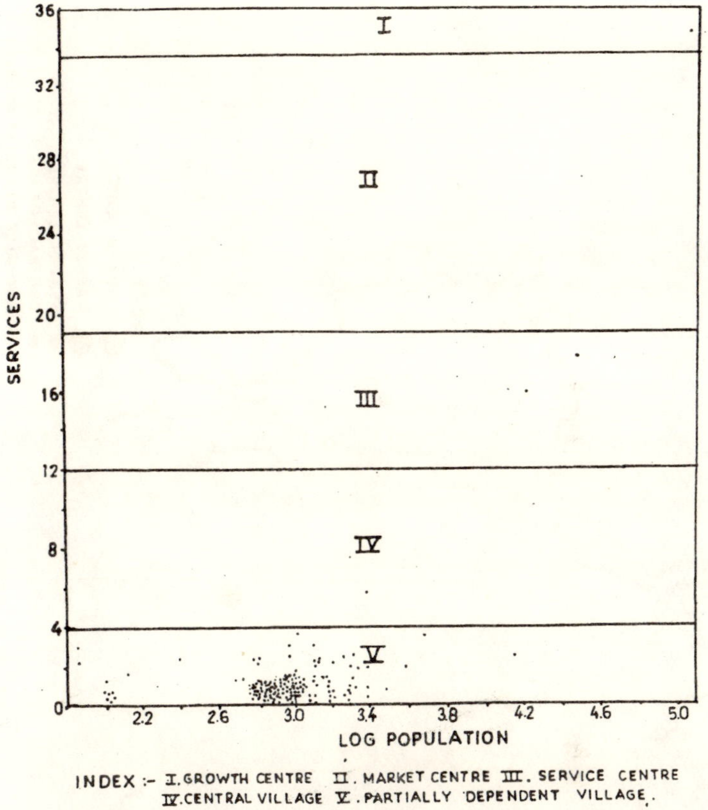

FIG. 24.1: Centrality vs Population Graph

There are four natural break points on the graph which could be used as reference points for classifying service centres into 5 centrality categories - (1) Growth Centre (2) Market Centres, (3) Service Centres, (4) Central villages, (5) Partially dependent villages (Table 24.1).

Characteristics of Service Centres

Growth Centre

In this hierarchical order only Ujjain city, the district and commissioner headquarters is included with 2,78,454 population and 37.33 centrality index. The number of services

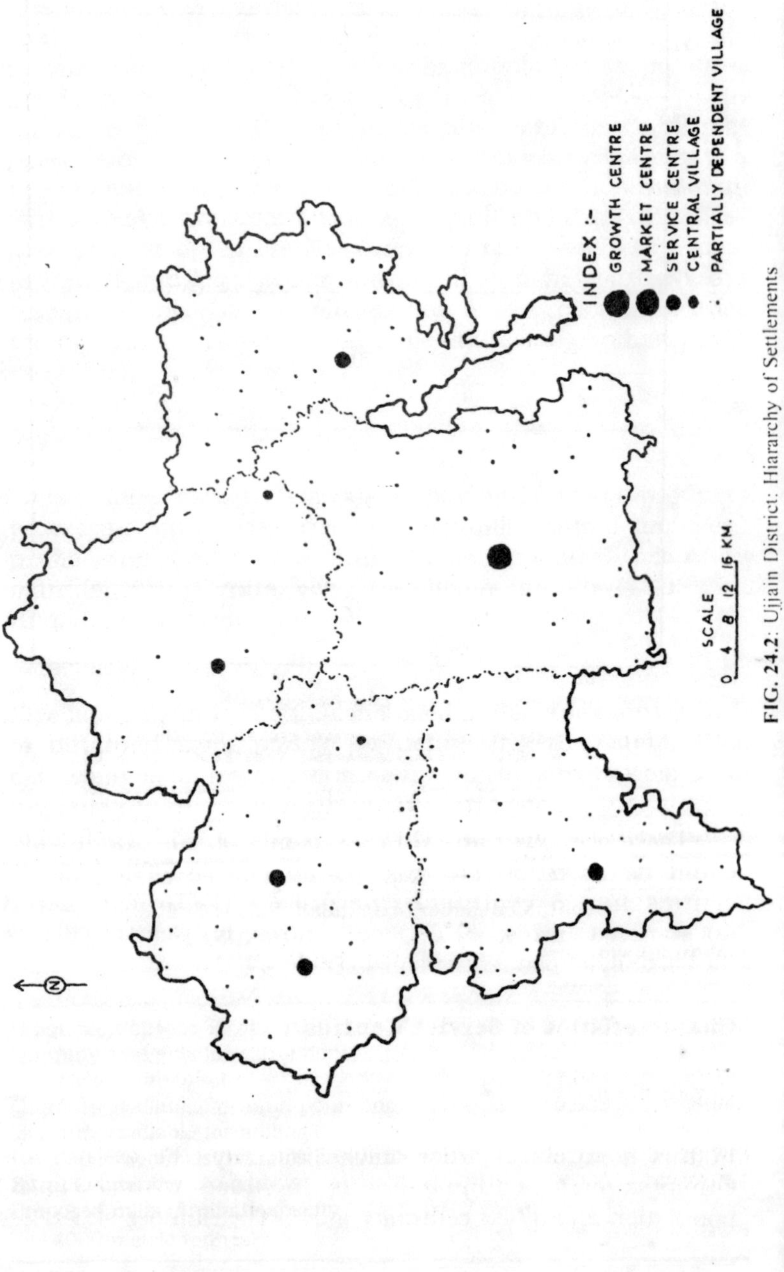

FIG. 24.2: Ujjain District: Hiararchy of Settlements

available in the city are 28.83. 54 per cent of the working population is engaged in secondary and tertiary activities.

Table 24.1: Centrality Score and Associated Settlements

Order	Category	Centrality Index	No.of Settle-ments	Percentage of Settle-ments
I	Growth Centres	> 36	1	0.63
II	Market Centres	14-36	—	—
III	Service Centres	8-14	5	3.18
IV	Central Villages	6-8	2	1.26
V	Partially Dependent villages	6	150	94.93
	Total		158	100.00

Market Centre

It is not much surprising that no settlement of the study area falls in this hierarchical order. In the agrarian economy very few settlements grow into sizeable rank.

Service Centres

There are five urban centres of this order of hierarchy namely Khachrod, Mahidpur, Tarana, Barnagar and Nagda. The population ranges between 15837 (Tarana) to 56602 (Nagda). The centrality index ranges between 10.90 (Tarana) to 12.04 (Mahidpur). They are all tahsil headquarters except Nagda. Nagda is a big industrial town with 99.12 per cent population engaged in secondary and tertiary activities.

Central Villages

Kasba Unhel (Khachrod tahsil) and Ghosla (Mahidpur tahsil) fall in this hierarchical order. The former has a population of 7834 and a centrality index of 6.47; the later has a population of 2103 and centrality index of 7.00.

Partially Dependent Villages

More than 94 per cent (150 villages) of the total service centres of the study area fall in this category. The population of these villages varies between 1020 to 5075 and the centrality index ranges between 0.36 to 4.18. Most of the villages have less than 4 services namely Primary School, Middle School, Gram Panchayat and Fair price shop. The population in secondary and tertiary activities is very insignificant.

Conclusion

(i) A close examination of the graph reveals that there is a close relationship between population-size and centrality index. Ujjain city has highest population (2,78,454) with highest centrality index (37.33). Because as the population grows the pressure for improving the standards and for increasing the number of civic amenities also grows. Being a commissioner and district headquarters, a university centre and a number of textile industries, it has become the Growth Centre of the study area. Thus it not only acts as a powerful magnet but also a nuclie for future economic, social and political development.

(ii) There seems to exist a positive co-relationship between the population, size and the centrality index of the Service Centres. Urban Centres like Nagda, Barnagar, Khachrod, Mahidpur and Tarana have centrality index between 10 to 14 and population between 15 to 57 thousands. Service Centres vary greatly in importance. Ujjain is 266.64 times more central than the last settlement in the hierarchical list.

(iii) Approximately 95 per cent of the settlements fall in Vth hierarchical order. The number of services in these centres is less than 5, while the population ranges between 1 to 4 thousands. It is obvious therefore, that in an agrarian economy where 73.63 per cent of the total populaton is engaged in agriculture, the economic activities are less significant. There seems to be a strong rural impact on the economy of the villages.

(iv) In hierarchical order number II, no settlement of the study area falls, thus creating a wide gap between order number I and III. Ujjain city has 28 services while the urban centres falling in hierarchical order number III have less than 14 services.

(v) Nagda has a population of 56602 and S.A.I. of 6.07 while Barnagar, Khachrod, Mahidpur and Tarana have population not more than 25000, but they have higher S.A.I. than Nagda. The reason being that Nagda is an industrial town with a higher functional index.

(vi) If a comparison is made between 1971-1981, there is little variation in population size as well as in number of services rendered by the Service Centres.

(vii) Places to the north and north-west of Ujjain, to the east and west of Mahidpur and to the north of Barnagar, show a marked absence of service centres. This may be attributed to the absence of transportation lines, specially metalled roads. The people living in these areas have to travel at least 6 to 8 km and in some cases 10 to 12 km to reach a service centre.

TWENTY-FIVE

Socio-economic Implications of Rural Market-Transportation Relations: A Case Study of the Middle Ganga Valley (India)

V.K. SHRIVASTAVA and K.N. TIWARI

Introduction

The chapter examines the results of the mutual relationship between rural market centres and means and modes of transportation and evaluates its impact on the socio-economic development of the region of study. The aim is to propose some hypotheses arrived at through empirical evidences so that they may be further tested and generalization can be made.

The Region of Study

The region of study, i.e. Ghazipur district lies in the middle Ganga Valley in eastern Uttar Pradesh. It extends from 25° 19' N to 25° 54' N latitudes and from 83° 4' east to 83° 58' east longitude (Fig. 25.1). Ghazipur town, the district headquarters, lies close to Varanasi city. It covers an area of 3380 km² and supports a population of 1.94 million (1981). The study region is situated on the rich alluvial deposits of the Ganga which flows through the southern part. Agriculture is the main occupation of the people of the area. The average density of population is 575 persons/km².

The transport network connects this area to Calcutta in the east and to Varanasi in the south west by railway. The road connections are with Varanasi, Gorakhpur (north) and

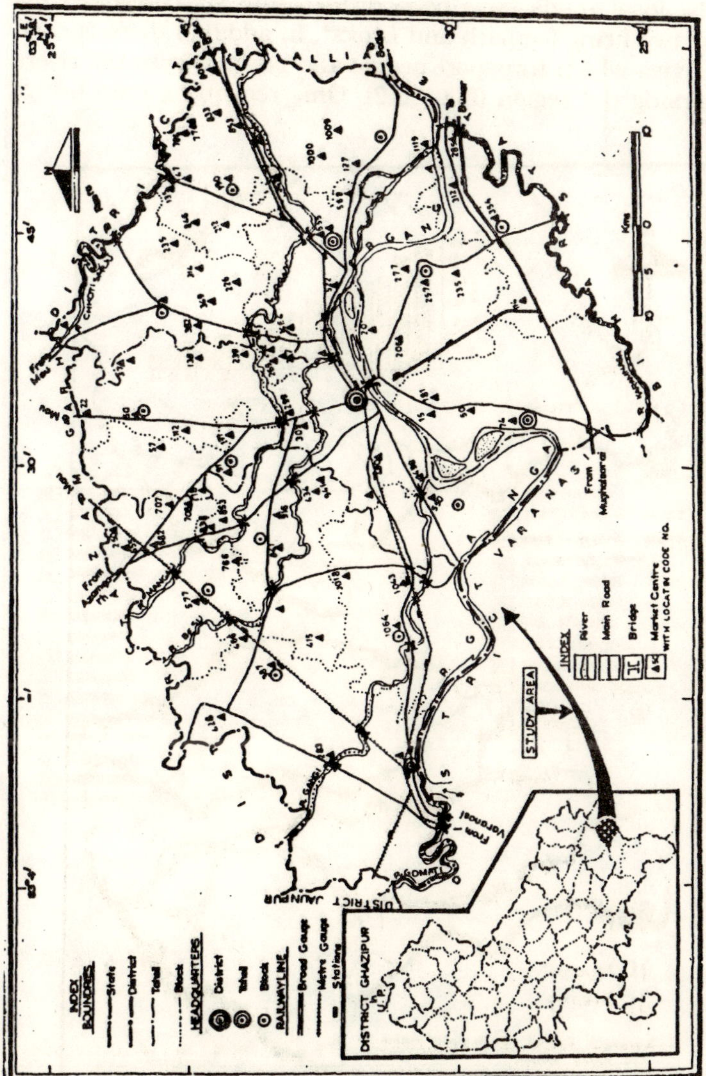

FIG. 25.1: Location Map of District Ghazipur

Calcutta (east). At intra-regional level there are 686 km of metalled and un-metalled roads and 1150 km of canal roads for lower order means of transport. Excepting inter-regional roads, local roads have been divided into six categories the latter two being footpath and *Leaks**. In addition there operate 64 ferries which transport people and goods across the rivers traversing the region (Fig. 25.2). Only recently a road bridge

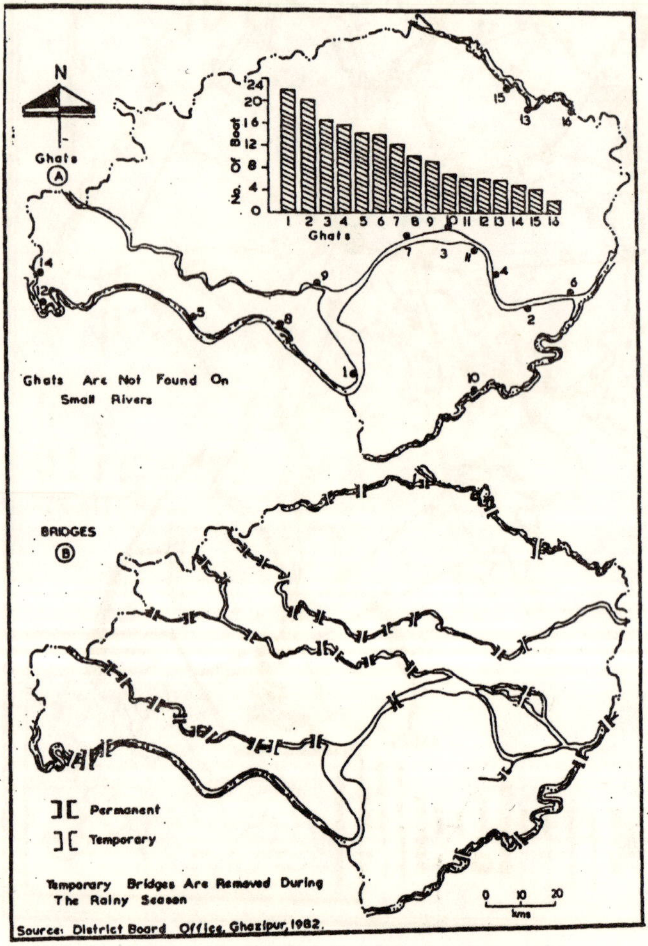

FIG. 25.2: Distribution of Ghats and Bridges, 1962

* 'Leak' is a local term and includes such cart-tracks which are used after harvest for passing through open fields. They are restricted after the fields are sown.

on the Ganga has been constructed near Ghazipur town which has strengthened its north-south connections.

Historical Overview

The history of Ghazipur district dates back to ancient period. It is said to have been occupied by Dravidian people in 5000 to 3000 B.C. (Mukherjee, R.K. 1938). The Aryas migrated towards this area around 2500 B.C. (Mazumdar, 1952). During the Buddha period it formed a part of *kasi Janapada.* During the mediaeval era it was inhabited by tribals in the 11th and the 12th centuries, who were later driven out by *rajputs.* Some of these rulers invited the mughals to quell their rivals which ushered in the mughal rule in this area. Akbar divided this area into *mahals* for revenue collection. In 1764 the district was ceded to the East India Company. The British rule initiated administrative reforms and developed means of transport. Many towns and market places were developed. Ghazipur town was an important river port on the Ganga and the area was famous for opium production.

Development of market centres also dates back to the ancient period as on the Ganga many trading settlements developed due to navigation facilities. During the Buddha period these river ports were inter-connected by road to provide access to the Buddha *mathas* and *stupas* (worship places). The rajput era was marked by feuds and local wars. This inhibited the growth of market centres though a few markets were established by the *rajputs.* Later on the mughals and the British developed the existing market places and rejuvinated the ruined ones. With the development of road and rail transport during the British period market places flourished and later, after the Independence, a full scale development of trade and transport is taking place.

Market Centres

The region of study consists of 85 market centres in all, including rural and urban market centres both. Of these 73 market centres are held periodically, 9 are held daily and only 3 market centres are daily-cum-periodic. The spatial distribution shows a pattern approaching uniformly distributed markets ('R' -1.57073). This follows a uniformly distributed population over the entire area. The superimposition of market location map on the transport network map of the study area reveals that most of the market centres are located along the means of transport, i.e. at bus stops, near railway stations, road-rail crossings etc. (Fig. 25.1). The location has been further influenced by the presence of administrative headquarters, religious places and by the nature of periodicity of markets. In addition to the six categories of market centres identified by Skinner (1964), i.e. Regional city, Local city, Central market town, Intermediate market town, Standard market town, and minor market an additional but lower order category of market centre i.e. *hat* has been identified in the region (Tiwari, 1987).

Market-Transport Relationship

Functional Hierarchy and Means of Transport

The functional hierarchy reveal five orders of market centres. The highest order market centres are few and are located in towns and/or at administrative headquarters. The lower order market centres are more numerous. The functional hierarchy of market centres corresponds with the importance of means of transport with some exceptions. The higher order centres are located at metalled road-rail junctions. The lower order ones are successively located at metalled and un-metalled roads junctions and so on (Appendix-I). It has been observed that an almost exact correspondence between the functional hierarchy and the importance of means of transport is noted among the highest and lowest order market centres, while among the middle order centres this correspondence is either weak or is lacking (Tiwari, 1987).

Flow of Goods and Means/Modes of Transport

Flow of goods is an important element of the study of marketing geography. The amount of goods carried varies according to the importance of the means of transport. On the foot-paths and canal roads the market place visitors mostly travel on foot. They are unable to carry heavy load with them. On the other hand consumers using bicycle, *tonga*, bus etc. on metalled roads can carry heavier loads. In this study the number of consumers arriving by different roads at eight sample market places were counted personally. In addition the amount of goods carried by them either way has been estimated.* Four essential goods i.e. vegetables, foodgrains, *kirana* and clothes were selected for the study. It has been further presumed that the maximum amount carried away from the market by an average consumer may be 5 kg. It is because rural markets are patronised by villagers possessing low purchasing power whose needs are also few.

In this way inflow-outflow charts have been prepared in respect of each of the eight sampled markets (Fig. 25.3).

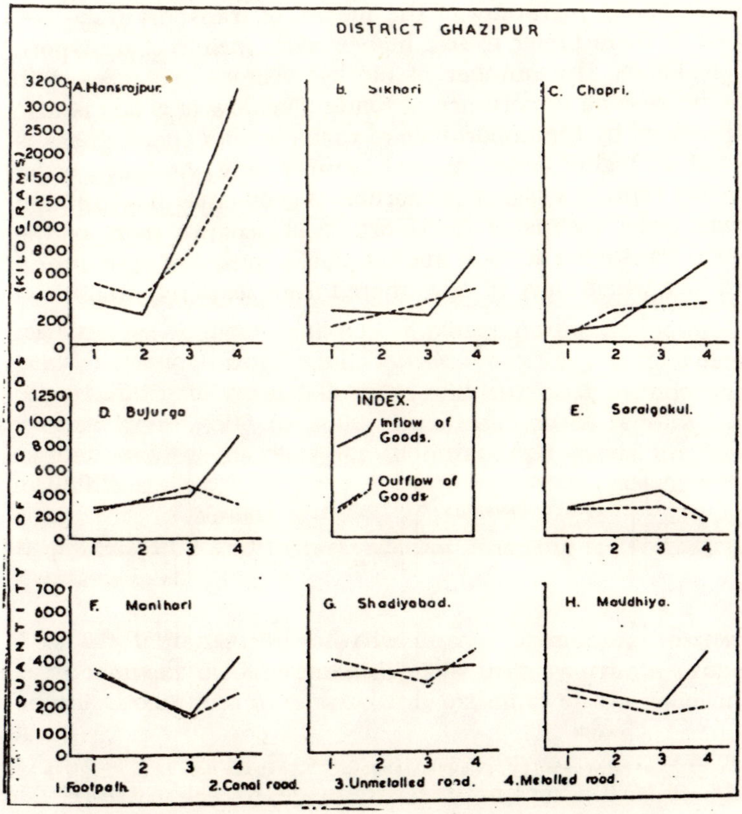

FIG. 25.3: Inflow and Outflow of Goods (Based on Data Collected from Sampled Market Centres of Manihari Block)

---

* It has been presumed that a pedestrian can carry a maximum of 20 kg. load, bi-cycle 40 kg. and bus passenger can carry 50 kg. load.

It has been observed that Hansrajpur, a market centre of third order, is the focal point of ten routes. Nearly 75 per cent of the visitors to this market use bicycle or come on foot. Metalled roads contribute 64 per cent of the total of incoming goods and 52 per cent of the outgoing goods. The amount of goods gets reduced on lower order means of transport. Sikhari, the other market centre is crossed by seven routes (Fig. 25.4). 65 per cent of the total visitors come on foot and 25 per cent use bi-cycle to come to the market. Metalled roads share 60 per cent of the inflow and 46 per cent of the outflow of goods (Table 25.1).

It becomes evident that the market place visitors are aware of the hierarchy of the means of transport they use. Most of them prefer to use higher order means of transport, if available. The number of market visitors decreases with the decreasing importance of roads. The flow of goods is also influenced by the importance of roads but its effectiveness is noted at higher order market centres only. At lower order market centres a higher proportion of goods may flow through lower order means of transport. It is because most of the goods transacted at such market places consist of agricultural produce which have to be gathered from scattered areas.

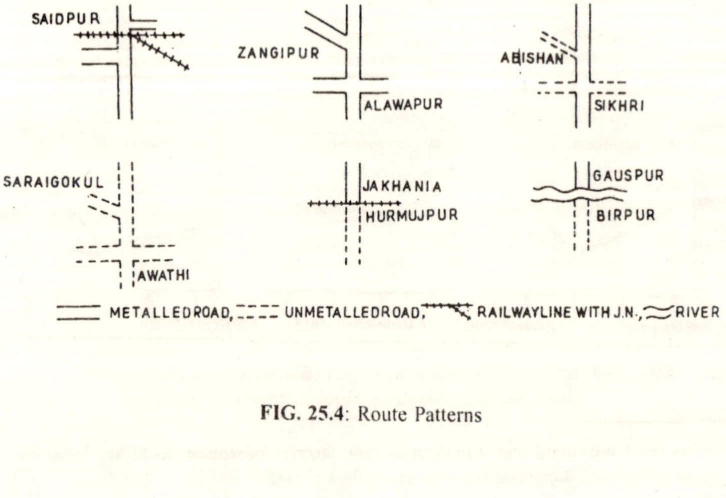

FIG. 25.4: Route Patterns

Table 25.1: The Hierarchy, Means and Modes of Transport at Sampled Markets

Sl. No.	Market Centre	No. of Transport Routes				Mode of transport used by market visitors%			
		Metalled	Unmetalled	Footpath	Canal road	On foot	Bicycle	Bus	Other
1.	Hansrajpur (II)	3	2	3	2	40	35	10	5
2.	Sikhari (III)	2	2	2	—	65	25	5	5
3.	Chhapri (V)	2	—	1	2	60	30	—	5
4.	Buzurga (V)	3	2	4	—	55	25	15	5
5.	Sarai Gokul (IV)	1	3	2	—	79	20	—	10
6.	Manihari (II)	3	1	3	—	40	35	10	15
7.	Shadiabad (III)	1	2	5	—	55	35	5	5
8.	Modhia (V)	1	1	2	—	70	20	5	5

Note.: Hierarchical order in brackerts.

The Emerging Typology

The study of rural market-transportation relationship in the middle Ganga Valley leads to the identification of market centre-transport typologies. The typology is one of the elements that constitute the spatial organization of the study area. The functional characteristics and the related transport net-work, both in static and dynamic aspects, indicate the level of trade and commerce in Ghazipur district and are able to forecast their impact on the socio-economic development of the study area.

The Methodology

The typologies have been identified through on the spot examination of market-transport relations. All metalled roads (from inter-regional to local level) have been grouped together in one category irrespective of the hierarchical status of the market centre they serve. Cart tracks have been included among the un-metalled roads as both of these represent lower order means of transport. Foot paths and canal roads have been kept under one category.

The categorisation of means of transport is followed by the assessment of the modes of transport, the distance covered by them and the amount and the nature of goods transported so that the relative importance of the market centres may be established. For example both metalled and unmetalled roads may connect market centres of lower or higher orders. However, a lower order market centre lying on or very near to metalled road will be more influenced by unmetalled roads because of its functional character. It is because metalled roads may also be used in the import of lower order goods to some extent but the majority of the lower order market place visitors will use unmetalled roads and footpaths due to their very-nature. Thus the mere presence of a metalled road may not add to the functional importance of a market centre.

Similarly, the higher order modes of transport can make use of lower order means of transport but their efficiency will be reduced. For example, a *tanga* may cover 10 to 15 km distance in an hour on a metalled road. It will, on the other hand, cover only 5 to 7 km distance on an unmetalled road. The *tanga walla* is more influenced by the duration of time involved and, therefore, may not like to use the lower order means of transport. In this way the mere availability of higher order mode of transport may not add to the spatial impact of a lower order market centre. Cart tracks, foot paths and canal roads are frequently used by visitors who come to lower order market centres. These paths cannot be used by higher order modes of transport. The market place visitors using these paths travel on foot. Naturally, their area of influence is reduced. Unmetalled roads, on the other hand, are used by bicycles and *tangas* which increase the range of market place visitors using them.

The transport of goods is found to be directly related to market hierarchy and to the importance of the means of transport. Ghazipur district mainly produces consumer goods like food-grains, vegetables and fruits. These items make use of intra-regional modes of transport like tractor trolley, bullock-carts, *tanga* etc. on metalled and unmetalled roads. Higher order goods are imported from cities like Varanasi and Kanpur. These goods follows higher order means of transport and terminate at first or second order market places.

The following typology of market-transportation may thus be identified:

Higher Order Market-Transport Typology

This typology comprises of higher order market centres and metalled road-railway crossing points (Fig. 25.5). The origin/destination places of modes of transport using these paths are of higher order than the order of the market centre which they serve. The rail-road connections provide inter-regional access. The modes of transport may range from bus and trucks to bullock carts and bicycles. The market centres import higher order durable goods from other regions and distribute them at intra-regional level. Agricultural produce are collected at these points. The market centres may also be connected with lower order means of transport.

Medium Order Market-Transport Typology

This typology represents medium category of market centres (Third-fourth order) connected with one metalled road and one or more unmetalled roads or cart-tracks (Fig. 25.6). The

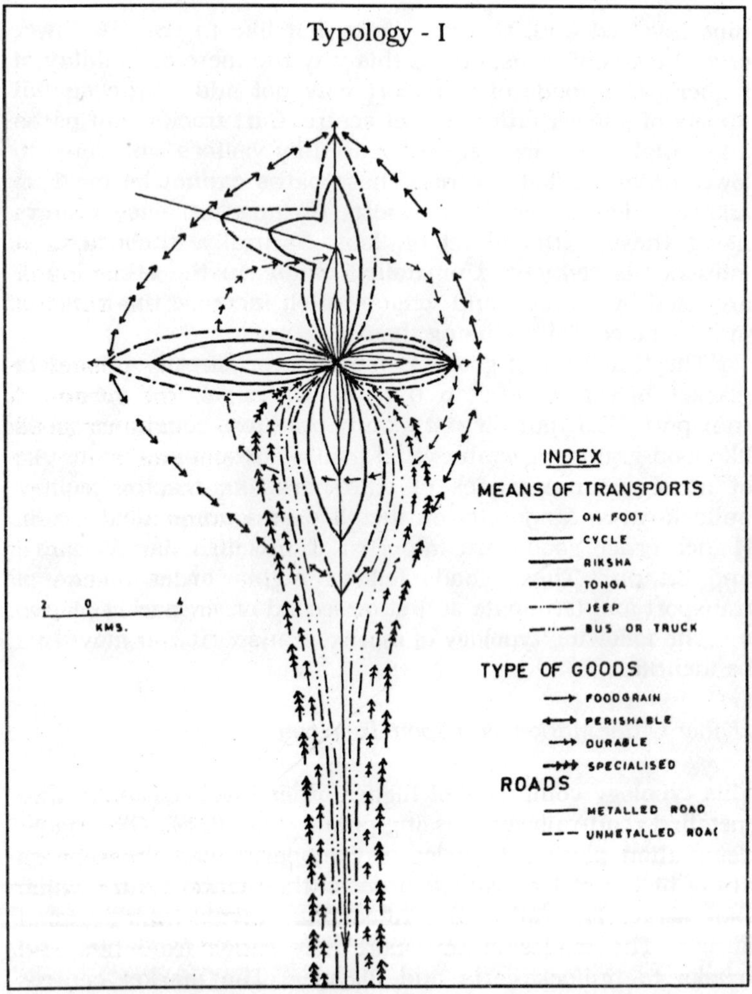

FIG. 25.5: Higher Order Market Centre, Means and Modes of Transport and Goods

metalled road provides connection with market centres of similar or higher order. The modes of transport using these paths are mainly of intra-regional level. These may include taxi car, jeep, tractor trolley, *tanga* and bullock-cart. Consumers scattered all over the market-area make use of these modes of transport. Only a small quantity of goods

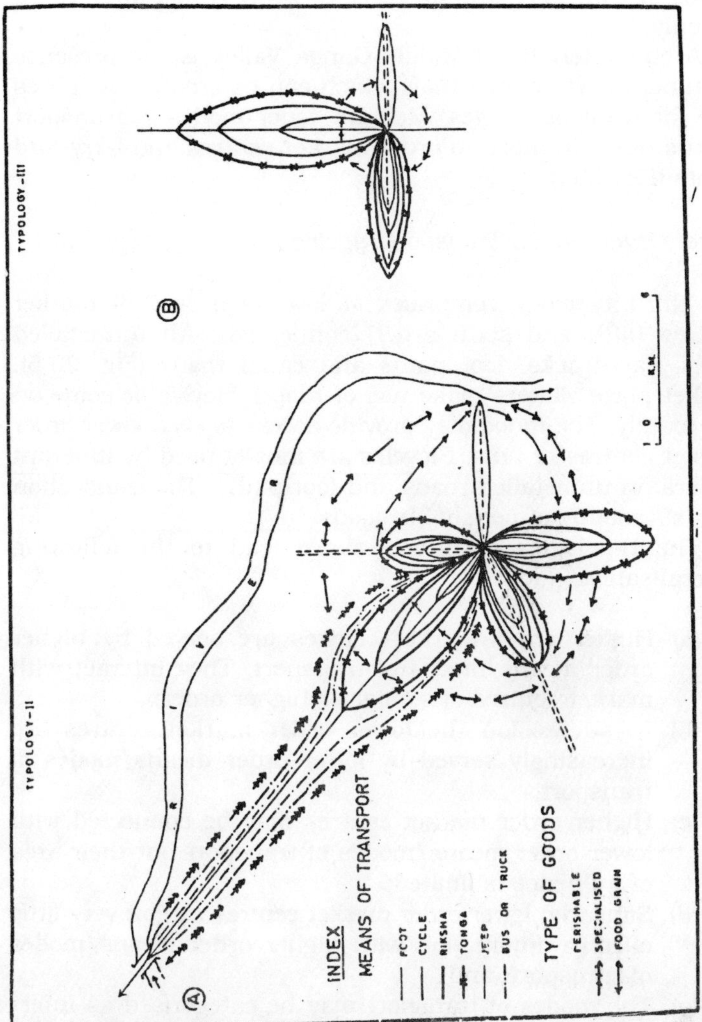

FIG. 25.6: Medium Order and LLower Order Market Centres, Means and Modes of Transport and Goods.

imported from other regions may penetrate these market centres directly. These market centres mainly collected food grains and perishable goods from surrounding areas. The modes of transport usually cover two-way traffic upto 10-15 km only.

A characteristic of Middle Ganga Valley is the presence of numerous rivers or canals which can be crossed by ferries only for want of bridges. Medium order modes of transport shuttle between medium order market centres and ferry-ford points (Fig. 25.3).

Lower Order Market-Transport Typology

The third typology comprises of lower category of market centres (fifth and sixth order) connected with unmetalled roads, cart-tracks, foot paths and canal roads (Fig. 25.5). Market place visitors make use of *tanga*, bicycle or come on foot mainly. The *tanga* may provide access to even lower order market centres or *hats*. Bicycles are mostly used by itinerant traders on unmetalled roads and foot-paths. The transaction consists mainly of perishable goods.

The typologies described above lead to the following generalisation:

(a) Higher order market centres are served by higher order means/modes of transport. They interact with market centres of similar or higher order;
(b) In succession the lower order market centres are increasingly served by lower order means/modes of transport;
(c) Higher order market centres may be connected with lower order means/modes of transport but their area of influence is limited;
(d) Similarly, lower order market centres exhibit very little effective interaction with higher order means/modes of transport; and
(e) The modes of transport may be categorised as inter-regional, intra-regional and local depending on the order of the market centre with which they effectively inter-act. Passenger bus, raill and trucks may be called inter-regional; taxi car, jeep, tractor-trolly, bullock-cart and *tanga* may be called intra-regional

and cycle rikshaw, bicycle may be called local modes of transport.

Conclusion

The Socio-economic Implications

The scope of geography of marketing is very vast. It does not only include the location, structure and functions of market centres but it also studies the impact of market activities on the development of the area which the makets serve. The mere growth of tertiary functions in any area may not be indicative of development because if tertriary activiies deal with consumer goods and engage in horizontal exchange they may not generate income. For development the growth of such tertiary functions is necessary which may be production oriented (Mishra, 1985). It also depends on the nature of goods produced by the area concerned.

The Middle Ganga Valley is a fertile plain where more than 90 per cent of the working population is engaged mainly in agriculture. Traditional method of cultivation and food-grain production are the chief characteristics of the economy of the region. There has been a continuous increase in the agricultural produce of this area since a decade (Tiwari, 1987). It mainly consists of cereals. The production of cash crops has also increased but their relative importance is weak. Empirical study shows that high class farmers are getting lower returns from agriculture. This is because of non-availability of labourers. On the other hand the production of medium class farmers is increasing (Nath, 1982). They have also diversified their production. Thus the study area has witnessed an increasing production of consumer goods.

A rural market centre serves about 40 km^2, area and 2400 population on an average. This ratio taxes the efficiency of periodic markets. It may be mentioned that the traditional market system is vital for the rural development in India (Shrivastava, 1987 a, b). Throughout the country the periodic markets are linked with each other in terms of a hierarchical arrangement. They thus promote a sustained system of service areas. Even though these service areas are of elementary level and their extent is small they do perform some important development functions of a lower level (Mukerji, 1988). Only lower order means of transport connect interior areas. Thus the study area is being exploited by a continuous export of consumer goods (Lal, 1986).

However, the development of transportation and increased production has led to intense market activity. This in turn has brought an awareness of the need of secondary activities related to agriculture, i.e. rice and flour mills, oil mill, *dal* mill, bakeries etc. Market centres have provided potential sites for the development of such secondary activities. Sugar mills, distillaries and paper mills, using sugarcane as raw material, have been initiated at market places which provide good transport connection as well. A cotton mill and some industrial estates are also in the offing. Thus the existence of market centres is promoting trade, commerce and industry. The spatial organization of Ghazipur district is expected to be transformed in the coming decades which may lead to the generation of money and attract investment of capital in the area.

The Hypotheses

The study thus leads to propose the following hypotheses:

(a) There is a direct relationship between the hierarchical order of market centres and means/modes of transport.

(b) The effective impact of higher order means/modes of transport diminishes with the decreasing importance of a market centre.

(c) The origin/destination points of modes of transport show an inverse relationship with the importance of a market centre.

(d) Higher order goods may not make use of lower order means of transport and vice-versa.

(e) The modes of transport may be categorised as inter-regional, intra-regional and local based on the importance of market centre which they serve.

APPENDIX-I

Transport of Goods and Means of Transport

S.N.	Market Centres	Foot Path				Matealled Road				Un-metalled Road				Canal Road				Total	
		No. of traders	Incoming amount kg.	No. of consumers	Outgoing amount kg.	No. of traders	Incoming amount kg.	No. of consumers	Outgoing amount kg.	No. of traders	Incoming amount kg.	No. of consum ers	Outgoing amount kg.	No. of traders	Incoming amount kg.	No. of consumers	Outgoing amount kg.	Incoming Kg.	Out going Kg.
1.	Hansrajpur	18	360	100	500	78	3120	350	1750	46	1150	150	750	11	220	80	400	4850	3400
2.	Sikhari	14	280	29	145	18	720	88	440	9	225	74	370	—	—	—	—	1225	955
3.	Chhapri	5	100	18	90	17	680	68	340	—	—	—	—	7	140	51	255	920	685
4.	Buzurga	13	207	41	205	21	840	59	295	14	350	86	430	—	—	—	—	1450	930
5.	Sarai Gokul	12	240	47	235	3	120	22	110	15	375	44	220	—	—	—	—	633	565
6.	Manihari	17	340	67	335	10	400	50	250	7	175	31	155	—	—	—	—	915	740
7.	Shadiabad	16	320	78	290	9	360	85	325	14	350	58	290	—	—	—	—	1030	905
8.	Modhia	13	260	46	230	10	400	35	175	7	175	28	140	—	—	—	—	835	545

Source: Based of field work, 1986.

TWENTY-SIX

Planning for Integrated Rural Development of Middle Son Basin

R.N. RAI and J.P. RAI

Aim and Objective

The aim and objective of the present research work is to prepare a plan for rural development of the Middle Son Basin. For this purpose a new methodology for the analysis of differences in the levels of development of the study region has been used.

Location

The study region is located between 22°55'-24°55' north latitudes to 82°20'-84°55' east longitudes. It comprises of 11 Tahsils, i.e. Surguja from M.P., Mirzapur from U.P. and Palamau and Ranchi districts from Bihar. It is a tribal and under developed region. The area of this region is 27.8 thousand km^2 and its population is 29.8 lakhs (19981). Before proposing any plan for development, it would be useful first to analyse the theoretical and behavioural aspects of integrated rural development.

Meaning of the Integrated Development

First of all it should be noted that integrated development is not necessarily associated with rural development. It is also a welknown fact that there are two different aspects of the process of rural and urban development. That is the role of infrastructure in rural development and urban relationship in village development. Thus, the term integrated rural development has been used in a wider sense. It may also be emphasised that the study region is already dominated by rural population. Thus, an attempt of development of this region may, is synonomous with rural development.

Rethinking over Integrated Development

In India planning for integrated rural development have mostly been attempted by geographers, for instance, after the seventees Mishra and Sundaram tried to throw some light on theoretical and behavioural aspects of regional development and planning in India. Sen and Wanmali used growth centres in integrated development of Miryalguda Taluka. Moreover, in 1977, V.K.R.V. Rao pointed out the defects in integrated rural development. Shrivastava tried to associate rural development with rural marketing. V.M. Rao made attempts to analyse planning in rural context. Ramchandran used village clusters as a basis for rural development planning and Shrivastava made attempts to associate villages and cities under the banner of rural development.

Conceptual Background

Now in brief, one can say that there is no basic difference in rural and urban development in the frame work of integrated rural development planning and theoretically in central place theory and growth pole theory, both may be useful. However, growth pole theory is so broad that it covers all the related social, economical and geographical theories into one. Central Place theory, in its hierarchical concept, underlines a strategy on the basis of which development planning can be made useful. It is also a wellknown fact that a central place is such a human settlement which supplies goods and services to its surrounding population. Central place basically provides tertiary activities. But, it should, however, be noted that not only cities but rural settlements too, may come in the category of central place which perform tertiary functions. Rural central places are conventionally known as rural marketing centres. They have a conventional functional relationship with village groups. Villages are related with periodic market centres and for higher order functions they have a vertical relationship with daily marketing centres, towns and cities accordingly. Thus, urban development cannot be isolated from the very process of rural development planning, instead it has become an integral part of rural development planning.

It is already known that the determinants of development are distributed according to requirements of the region. For this purpose, some of the central places are denoted as growth points and others as growth centres according to their hierarchical importance.

A model for integrated development of middle Son Basin has been developed in which village groups are associated with periodic market centres. In this way, there is a daily marketing centre over per four periodic marketing centre, which is vertically associated with cities. This model has been constructed on the basis of a hierarchical plan, according to central place theory. There is proposal to associate village higher central places. But, the number of villages can be adjusted according to regional requirements.

Suggestions for Integrated Rural Development

Before we attempt to give any suggestion for integrated rural development of the study region, it would be useful to analyse the existing central place system of the region. Therefore, periodic market centres, daily market centres, cities, growth point and growth centres have been taken as basis. These may be examined as under:

The Existing State of Integration

There are 223 periodic marketing centres in the region. But when the number of villages, their population and dependent area of these centres is examined, integration is found to be weak. There are 21 villages, 1200 population and 124 km^2 area on each market centre (Table 26.1).

There are only 36 daily market centres in the region. Thus, there exist 129 villages, 75000 population and 773 km^2 area on each daily market centre (Table 26.1). However, intra-regional variations are noted. In plateau and tribal regions villages are often large, but their population is less. Thus, the area becomes larger in comparision to the population living on it. On the other hand where population

Table 26.1: Based on Central Place, Village, Population and Area in Middle Son Basin

	Existing					Proposed				
	Growth centre	Growth points	Marketing Town	Daily Markets centres	Periodic Market	Growth centre	Growth point	Marketing town	Daily market centres	Periodic market
Number	2	5	18	36	223	3	8	33	133	534
Village	2328	931	258	129	21	1552	582	141	35	87
Population	1354045	541618	150449	75224	12144	902697	338511	82063	20361	5000
Area (km^2)	13911.5	5568.6	1545.7	772.86	124.76	9274.33	3477.88	843.12	209.12	52.1

is dense the size of villages may be small. However, no fixed ratio can be earmarked among number of villages and central places/market centres.

There are 18 urban market centres in the region. It is noted that in developed parts there are only two urban centres (Chopan and Churk), in an average developed region too, there are two urban centres Surajpur and Vishrampur. However in less developed region there are five centres, i.e. Ghaghra, Balumath, Chandwa, Netarhot and Baikunthpur. Besides this, in the least developed region there exist 9 urban centres (Pipari, Dudhi, Uttari and Dakhini Jharkhund, Pandrihi, Badi Bazar, Chirmi, Kursia and Ramapurganj. Among them, 14 are cities and four are approaching to become cities. Table 26.1 shows that there are 258 villages, 1.5 lakhs population and 1.54 thousand km^2 area per town. It is also clear that there are five growth points (Renukut, Obera, Mahendragarh, Gumla and Latehai) and only two growth centres (Rabartsganj and Ambikapur) in the region. Middle Son Basin is a natural region. At present Ambikapur in the south and Robertsganj in the north can be termed as growth centres. They are situated at the junction of transportation and are administratvie headquarters too. It may be said that not only population but aforesaid functional structure of these urban centres and their capacity to distribute the determinants of development have also been considered in their selection.

However, it is clear that the number of these basic centres for development is so small that the desired rate of development of the region cannot be achieved. Thus, for integrated development of the region upgradation of towns to growth centres is required.

Now, before giving any proposal for the development of central places, it would be useful to assess the impact of existing central place system. It has been related for detailed analysis. Vindhyachal region is most appropriate in this context.

Sampled Region

As it can be seen that there are 23 periodic market centres in Vindhyachal sub-region (Robertsganj). There are thus 57 villages, 39000 population and 275 km^2 area come on each market centre in Vindhyachal region. These main centres are not capable in meeting the desired requirements of development. Besides this, there is no balanced relationship in area and size of the study region. Probably, it is the result of an unequal distribution of standard development centres. Alongwith this, there are spatial gaps in the distribution of market centres in the northern part of the region.

There are 8 daily market centres (Bina, Markundi, Bhindhamganj, Kon, Anpara, Dala, Gurma and Saktinagar) and urban market centres like Pipari, Pudhi, Chura and Chopan in the sampled region. Besides this on the basis of their population and distributive capacity as service centres Obera and Renukot urban centres can also be treated as growth points. Only Robertsganj has been recognised as a growth centre in this region so far. This centre is situated on the junction of means of transportation. It is also a tahsil headquarters which has enough capacity to distribute determinants of development.

A careful observation of the existing condition of the sampled region also reveals the fact that it is necessary to upgrade the number of these centres for the improvement of the process integrated development of Middle Son Basin. Population may be considered as basis, because the size of villages is larger. for this purpose, a periodic market centre may be taken to serve 5000 population to propose a plan for development.

Proposed Plan

Now, according to the proposed plan for integrated rural development it is proposed that the number of periodic market centres be increased from the exisiting 223 to 534 so that the population per periodic market comes to 5000 persons. In this way, there will be 9 villages and 50 km^2 area per market. The proposed framework for development of this region has been mathametically calculated using chi square method (Table 26.2).

We have already taken as our Null hypothesis that there is no relationship between existing plan of central places and their proposed one. The result of χ^2 test is 64.75. According to the table validity of null hypothesis is only 0.1 per cent. It means there is a highly positive correlation (with 99.9 per cent validity) between existing marketing plan and proposed plan.

Then come daily marketing centres next to the periodic marketing centres in the hierarchical system. It is already known that the proposed number of daily marketing cenres is 133, in the region (Table 26.2).

Table 26.2: Existing and Proposed Plan of Marketing Centres in Middle Son Basin

No.	Tahsil	Existing marketing centres	Proposed marketing centres	Existing marketing centres per 100 settlements 'O'	Proposed marketing centres per 100 settlements 'E'
1.	Surajpur	26	54	4.70	9.7
2.	Pal	28	12	5.34	3.56
3.	Mahendragarh	8	14	8.57	6.25
4.	Ambikapur	28	68	4.71	10.22
5.	Samari	7	15	3.59	7.69
6.	Baikuntpur	11	15	4.36	5.95
7.	Robertsganj	12	16	1.17	7.43
8.	Dudhi	11	35	3.87	12.32
9.	Latehar	57	13	7.62	1.73
10.	Gumla	35	9	9.23	2.37

Note : O = Observed, E = Expected.

Formula = $\chi^2 = \frac{(O-E)^2}{E}$ = Result 64.75

Thus there are 35 settlements, about 20,000 population and 207 km² area per daily market. This proposed model has been derived on the fundamental community approach to integrated rural development model. In this model, one daily marketing centre is associated with two periodic market centres. As there comes an average of 8.8 villages per periodical marketing centre, so an average population and area of 35 villages per daily market centre can also be justified.

In the same way a plan of 33 urban market centres has been proposed in Middle Son Basin. There are 140 villages, 82000 population and 843 km² area on each of them. Many of these centres of the study region are small towns and daily market centres.

Growth points have also been proposed according to hierarchical plan of central place system in Middle Son Basin. There is a plan to increase their number from 528, for integrated development of the region. Among these proposed growth points 5 are Tahsil headquarters (Latehar, Surajpur, Mahendragarh, Baikuntpura and Ramanijganj) and remaining 3 (Obra, Renukut and Kursia) are industrial centres, as well as they are main centres for transportation too. There come 582 villages and 3.38 lakhs population on per growth point, which has the capability for fulfilment the requirements of about 3.47 thousand km^2 area.

However, growth points have been taken in vertical order for integrated development. Ambikapur and Robertsganj are famous as growth centres in Middle Son Basin, but Gumla has been also proposed as growth point. All these centres represent their own region. The proposal for these three growth centres is necessary, because, Ambikapur alone can not regulate the distribution system in the whole region, in absence of means of transportation. Its effective administrative area will come under the border of M.P. Other two proposed centre Gumla (Bihar) and Robsertsganj (U.P.) are also adjustant. Any how, it can be assured that Ambikapur can become the only growth centre of the region, if in future, administrative hindrence are removed. It is also a noticeable fact that these centres are changeable and growth point can also function as growth centres, if necessary.

In this way on the basis of growth point theory, there has been proposed a framework, i.e. from periodic marketing centre to growth point, combining the existing status and proposed plan with each other, for integrated development of the region. It will be usefull in context to the aforesaid selected area.

Selected Region

Bindyachal region has been selected in order to make the aforesaid proposed plan, more cognizable. We have already discussed the existing status of the region and its proposed plan is as follows:

There are 23 periodic marketing centres in this region and 111 are proposed according to new plan. In this way, it has been assumed that 124 periodic marketing centres shall fulfill the requirements of about 1.3 thousand villages. In the same way, there has been a proposed 26 daily market centres; Alongwith this, there have been proposed size urban marketing centres (Churk, Chopan, Dudhi, Pipari, Kon and Murkundi). It is already known that at present, except Kon and Murkundi, all of them come into the category of urban centres, but their population is less than 10 thousands of each of them. According to the previous plan, there have been proposed two growth points (Obara and Renukot) in this selected region, of each of their population is more than 2000. They are also capable of regulating distribution system and have transportation capability too. There is a proposal to establish Robertsganj, as a growth centre in the selected region. It is situated on the junction of transportation and is a Tahsil headquarters, as well. Thus, it has a enough capability for the distribution of determinants of developments. Besides this it is in a regular process of development, so there appears a probability of Renukot to become a growth centre in furture.

Now on the basis of above discussion one can say that the proposed Central Place Theory would be useful for integrated rural development. It is also remarkable that central place system provides a basic strategy which helps implementing development plannings.

TWENTY-SEVEN

Planning for Commercial Activities in North Bihar: A Desired Developmental Dimension

NANDESHWAR SHARMA

Commercial Activities

A Link Components of Development

A theoretical comprehension of the phenomenon of development asserts the role of a few necessary components of it. The most obvious primary components of development have been the activities of production and consumption. Production and consumption components contributed to the initiation of the process of development. They have also been contributing towards the present day developmental accomplishments. Developmental dimensions could, however, fail to deliver goods to the necessities of life at desired scales and forms. The production-consumption interface tended to sustain development just at subsistence level. Production was aimed to meet the bare basic needs of consumption essentially at the centre of primary production. The two components interface created a condition in which production pursuit acted just to be the function of consumption and the consumption pursuit failed to prompt production. Development pursuits needed a link component to gear the processes of development through increased production and consumption efficiency. The third component link was found in the emergence of commercial activities—better identified with the exchange system. Things began to reach more easily from containers of producers to baskets of consumers.

Producers began to be benefited to acquire and use commercial inputs at greater ease to be prompted to produce more to meet the growing aspirations of consumers. Production for consumption and consumption for production response caused a desired developmental dimension assisted with commercial activities—the link component. Dimensions of development as a linked stage may be comprehended through the following theoretical model:

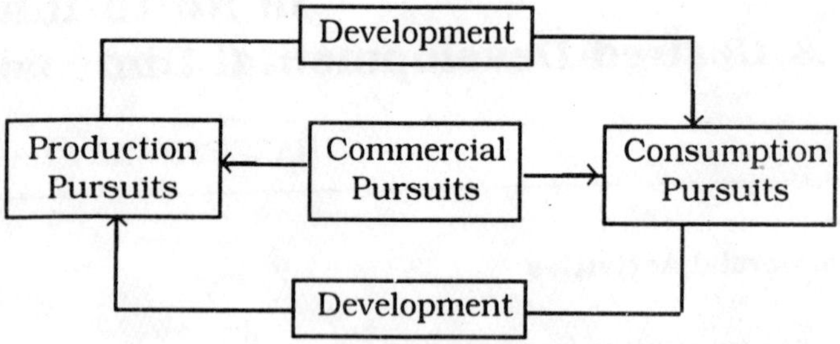

North Bihar

Ecological Setting

Viewed in ecological perspectives North Bihar forms a major segment of the vast Middle Ganga Basin. Hemmed in between Siwaliks in the north and the Ganges in the south and the openness of its eastern boundary into the lower Ganga Basin and that of its western boundary into its Uttar Pradesh counterpart, the region defines its territorial configuration between latitudinal bounds of 25°15'N.-27°30'N. and longitudinal bounds of 83°45'E-88°15' E.

Isotropism tends to determine the ecological dominance of the region. The physiographic isotropism coincides with the vast "isotropic Ganga Basin" in its remarkable absence of "Jarring mound" or "elevated jet" of land to break the surface level monotony and the dominant fluvial ecological setting with mighty rivers the Ganges, the Ghaghra, the Gandak, the Burhi Gandak, the Adhawara group of rivers and the Kosi continually engaged in grounding the land base to create habitability and workability for centuries. The transitional environmental ecology is characterised by summer heat less intense than its drier upper Ganga Basin counterpart and by a condition less moist and enervating than its wetter Lower Ganga Basin counterpart. The Indian Monsoon intends to reign supreme and ideal in this part of the one of the greatest plains of the world—the "Hindusthan Plain".

The ordained ecological setting has tended to make North Bihar transitional at *par excellence.* Ecological transition has acted to form its chief forte to weave the prevailing human and economic panoramas deciding the developmental dimensions of the region. Prongs of development have been responding to attain the degree of closeness to or distance from the desired dimension in not an unfavourable ecological setting.

Prongs of Development

The phenomenon of development appears to be essentially a multi-pronged process. The process of development becomes, in this sense, a sectoral concept. Different sectors of development—primary, secondary and tertiary, for example, tend to create the prongs of regional development. Prongs of development in North Bihar have been an ordained destiny since long. The predominantly fluvial ecology of the area has long tended to provide it with exceedingly dominant rural society and agrarian economy. Economic development has been showing strong bias towards production and consumption largely at subsistence level. The all pervading economic developmental sphere even today prevails, in most part of the area, in continuance of age-old tradition-bound operational mechanism of agricultural production. Agriculture acts to be developmental dominant. Large-scale manufacturing almost absents the developmental scenario with a few exception of Barauni Industrial Complex and agro-based establishments. Developmental panorama of the region may be portrayed to represent the condition as follows.

The panoramic elements compose the syndrome of the ecological constraints which the developmental dimension of North Bihar is put to strain.

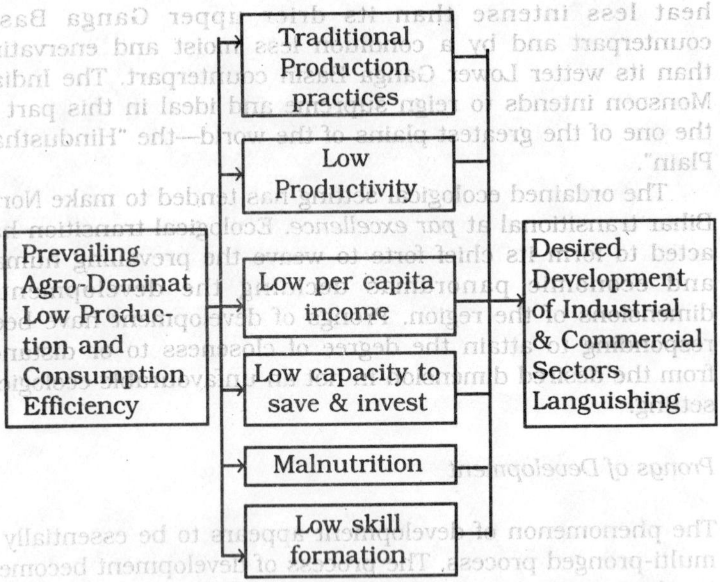

Developmental Dimension

Ecological Constraints

The developmental scenario of North Bihar is exceedingly dominated by rural habitats and agricultural economic base. The entire scenario presents, however, a picture of near despair lacking desired developmental glare. What constraints does the Region confront in its developmental affair?

The flood phenomenon appears to be the ecologically dominant of all the myriad of physico-economic, socio-cultural and politico-organisational constraints. The common experience shows that most of the developmental gains are washed away by recurrent floods every year frequenting some part of the other with differing intensities. The multipronged attack of the flood phenomenon constraining the developmental stages can glaringly been viewed in its ravaged economy, infrastructure and human habitats that the Region is left to inherit. Left after the onslaught of floods, we find submerged fields with crops crumbled, embankments, roads and rails breached and damaged, electric and telephone poles uprooted and laid down, huts and houses deluged and crushed, people broken and despaired to feel the loss of their belongings and doings. And all these to restart in the name of development.

Man-water-nexus asserting to be a necessary ecological condition of the humanization and production in this part of the Ganga Basin has been continually sustained by a combination of Terrigenic, Technogenic and Homogenic nexuses. The terrigenic nexus includes all such natural elements which create the conditions aggravating inundation. The technogenic nexus comprises all such technological or engineering actions which fail to contain the menace of flooding and add to its intensity and the homogenic nexus relates to all such man's reckless developmental actions which impinge upon natural elements resulting in territorial ecological disequilibrium. The elements of technogenic and homogenic forces are, however, inescapably affected by terrigenic forces wich may be comprehended to be the outcome of 3Rs function of Relief, Rain and River. The 3Rs behaviours combine to generate the genetic elements, genetic process and the elemental emits of flooding in the Region. The mechanism of flooding creating the condition of ecological constraints to development may better be comprehended through the flow chart model that follows:

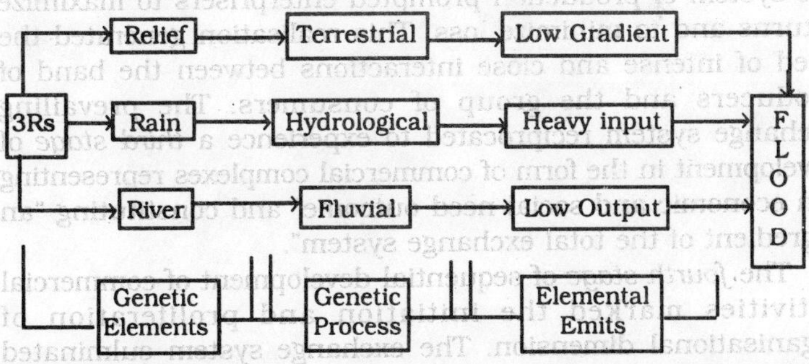

Heavy dependence on agriculture subjects the economy of the Region to be strained under ecological constraints therein. People of the Region are, in majority, subjected to abject poverty in the absence of desired commercial activities.

Commercial Activities

Past Legacy and Contemporary Accomplishment

The system of development has been envisaged to operate effectively as an outcome of the interplay of three fundamental elements of production, exchange and consumption. It was essentially the operation of the subsistence level economy which initiated the *first stage* of the sequential development. The stage happend to be a necessary outcome of primary production-local consumption-interface. It did not, however, mean the total absence of commercial activities. The production-consumption-interface was inherently supported by initial exchange system through barter or local sale and purchase.

Increased awareness to the necessities of life began to put demand for improved exchange system. Commercial activities received the support of the emergence of periodical markets—better known as *hats* or village *mandis*. The Region witnessed a *new state* of development which brought socio-economic changes with the functioning of new commercial centres. These centres acted to serve as the only outlets available to rural masses to be exposed to developmental changes taking place in time and area dimension.

The realisation of the possibility of accruing gains from the system of production prompted enterprisers to maximize returns and to minimize loss. This realisation generated the need of intense and close interactions between the band of producers and the group of consumers. The prevailing exchange system reciprocated to experience a *third stage* of development in the form of commercial complexes representing "an economic and social need outcome" and constituting "an ingredient of the total exchange system".

The *fourth stage* of sequential development of commercial activities marked the initiation and proliferation of organisational dimension. The exchange system culminated in the creation of organised market system which tended to assert its veracity to act as the necessary dominant component of development system at local, sub-regional and regional scales.

From inheriting the initial legacy to tempting present accomplishments commercial activities have tended continually to change their forms and functions both in temporal and spatial perspectives. The mechanism of change may be summarised in the table that follows:

Stage	Form	Function	Periodicity
I	Non-existent	Barter, Local sale + purchase	Irregular
II	*Hats* or village *Mandis* (Periodical Markets)	Exchange outlets for exposure to new developments	Weekly Bi-weekly Tri-weekly
III	Commercial complexes	Intense and close inter-action between producer and consumer.	Increased permanancy and regularity
IV	Organised Market system	Centres of Production and exchange	Organised and Regular

The entire mechanism entailed a sequence which created a condition of (i) transformation of barter and local sale and purchase system of commercial activities into a system of trade and commerce, (ii) emergence of places of convergence of central functions, (iii) establishment of a polarised distribution system, (iv) increased production-consumption-interface, and (v) acceleration in developmental processes through desired maximization of returns and minimization of loss both for producer and consumer.

The formal and functional components of exchange system represent to constitute the commerical infrastructure in regional developmental perspectives. They function to be centres of production. They operate to be places of convergence of central functions. They assert to be the essential link component of the system of development by finding spaital locations as commerical nodes in the formal and infomral channels of distribution of inputs and outputs. The prevailing gaps in the formal, functional and spatial hierarchies tend to delink the elements of exchange system from functioning as a necessary component of desired developmental dimension. The ecological constraints, which North Bihar is subjected to, have inflicted many such gaps. This makes the search for a desired developmental dimension imperative.

Desired Developmental Dimension

The presence of centres of commercial activities has been accepted as a developmental necessity. Their role, as a link component of development, makes the spatial organisational planning of such centres an urgency to achieve a desired developmental dimension. Planning for commercial activities involve the complex issues of spatial and structural relevance. The spatial location, the periodicity, the commodity structure, the socio-economic strucutre, the business structure and people's atitudinal behaviour all combine to relate the task of spatial organisation.

The task of planning commercial activities in North Bihar—a major segment of the Middle Ganga Basin relies on some valid assumptions.

(i) Commercial centres seek location at local, sub-regional and regional scale hierarchies.
(ii) Commercial centres of varying formal hierarchies develop functional hierarchies at a real scale from lower to higher regional units.
(iii) Commercial centres in rural agro-dominant developmental scenario are committed to function as marketing channels for agricultural inputs on the one hand and export channels for produces on the other.
(iv) Commercial centres at relatively higher scales by virtue of their capacity to function as nodes of developmental infrastructure have to diversify sectoral specialisation and selective development.
(v) An integrated exchange system will function to effectuate the desired developmental dimension in the Region.

Periodic markets continue to be of spurious distribution in great numbers in North Bihar. There have now developed a good number of organised commercial complexes also in various forms of urban centres and rural growth centres. To ensure the effective and operative contribution of commercial activities aiming at desired development in the Region the proposals envisage the planning measures:

(i) Identification of existing formal and functional gaps in the distribution and functioning of rural *hats* and *mandis* and their reorganisation in terms of spatial location and periodic permanancy.

(ii) Identification of new commercial activities and places of their location and functioning.

(iii) Increasing the functional viability of commercial centres in terms of creation of opportunities to provide non-agricultural employment, new sources of farm income and accessibility.

(iv) Provision of spatial links at all hierarchies of commercial centres to enhance their locational viability to serve as central places at local, sub-regional and regional scales.

(v) Intensification of marketing landscape through making commercial centres places of location of wider range of goods and services. The increased competition for relatively higher order market centres is envisaged to cause the decline in the number and periodicity of non-viable local *hats* and *mandis* and the stability in their spatial location and functioning as daily markets.

(vi) Making the location and functional operation of market system acceptable all to "Centre-Down Development Paradigm", "Core-Periphery Paradigm" and "Bottom-up Development Strategy" of spatial planning.

(vii) Facilitating exposure of rural consumers to higher order centres to release developmental inputs to rural areas by creating a desired hierarchic network of market centres and transportation.

The operational mechanism of planning for commercial activities is precisely envisaged to create a condition of desirability and satisfaction of those who constitute the components of development. This may be understood in the flow chart model that follows:

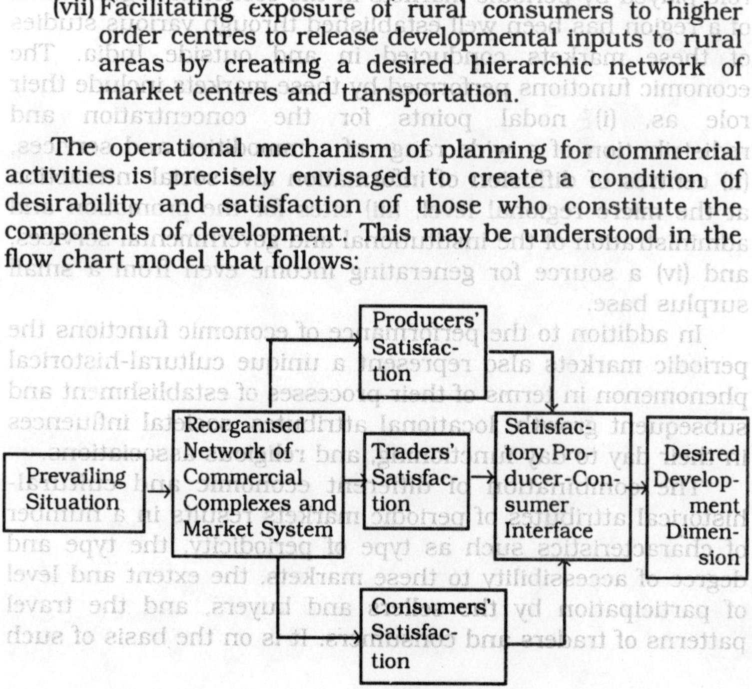

TWENTY-EIGHT

Some Questions on the Persistence of Periodic Markets in Economically Developed Areas

K.D. SHARMA

Periodic markets comprise the lowest level of the marketing system in a region. It is customary to associate the existence and function of periodic markets with developing and less developed economices as conventional features particularly of the rural economic organisation. The importance of the role played by periodic markets in the economic organisation of a region has been well established through various studies of these markets conducted in and outside India. The economic functions performed by these markets include their role as, (i) nodal points for the concentration and redistribution of a wide range of commodities and services, (ii) centres of diffusion of information and social interaction at the micro regional level, (iii) sites for the promotion and administration of the institutional and governmental services, and (iv) a source for generating income even from a small surplus base.

In addition to the performance of economic functions the periodic markets also represent a unique cultural-historical phenomenon in terms of their processes of establishment and subsequent growth, locational attributes, societal influences in their day to day functioning, and religious associations.

The combination of different economic and cultural-historical attributes of periodic markets results in a number of characteristics such as type of periodicity, the type and degree of accessibility to these markets, the extent and level of participation by the sellers and buyers, and the travel patterns of traders and consumers. It is on the basis of such attributes and characteristics that periodic marekts, located in different regions, acquire their distinctive character. Thus as an integral part of the local and regional marekting systems periodic markets reflect the regional socio-economic character and have significant regional developmental implications.

The changes in a market exchange system provide one of the major indicators of economic development. The changes brought about by higher levels of economic development in the permanent markets at the individual as well as the collective market level are well explored and established. However, in view of their customary association with traditional developing economies, the persistence of periodic markets in economically developed regions presents an anomolous situation and a very important aspect in the understanding of the periodic markets-regional economic development relationship.

Objective

The existence of periodic markets in India can be traced back to the pre-Christian era through their mention in the various classical texts. These have continued to exist and function in different areas of the country through various historical periods and in the process of their evolution have acquired distinct regional economic and cultural characteristics. Whereas the existence of periodic markets in such regions as rural Bengal, Orissa, Assam, Bihar, parts of Uttar Pradesh and tribal regions of the country is in accordance with the customary association of such markets with a low level of regional economic development, their persistence in the more developed regions such as Western Uttar Pradesh, Maharashtra and South Bihar, coupled with their occurrence in rural as well as urban areas refutes the direct, simplistic periodic markets-low economic development relationship and raises a number of questions. How far is the purely economic explanation sufficient for explaining the existence of periodic markets? How do periodic markets respond to the changed economic organisation in order to retain themselves? What is the impact of changes in economic thresholds on periodic markets? How does an improved developmental infrastructure, particularly transport network, influence the existing periodic markets? Do periodic markets continue to function in an economically developed region due to the constant availability of specific clientele group patronage? Do periodic markets represent an essentially cultural-historical phenomenon more or less frozen in time and space and thus continue to persist due to the forces of inertia? It is proposed that the answers to these questions based on empirical studies of periodic markets in an economcially developed region in India would help in a better understanding of the periodic markets and thier functioning.

Economic Explanation

There has been an almost singular reliance on explaining the location and functioning of periodic markets within an economic framework. This approach is not restricted to geographers alone. Simply stated, the economic explanation rests on the postulate that periodic marketing will result whenever the threshold requirements exceed the range of a good and with a high density of demand and a low fraction of distance the periodic markets would evolve into dialy markets or permanent shops. This basic argument, either singly or in combination with some others has been applied to the study of periodic markets. However, the explanations provided under this approach are essentially ex-post-facto explanations. Also, the proposition that periodic markets would evolve into daily markets or permanent shops does not stand scrutiny. Rural periodic marekts frequently operate side by side with urban daily markets, and many periodic markets in small towns have a large number of permanent daily traders. Similarly, in many large cities periodic markets exist at daily market sites or as separate weekly markets in addition to urban daily markets.

There is obviously a need for a more detailed, comprehensive economic framework for the understanding of persistence of periodic markets in economically developed areas.

Economic Thresholds

One of the most important reflections of regional economic systems at any given time is provided by the economic thresholds. These can be related to income distribution, population attributes, and accessibility. Economic thresholds are also quite sensitive to the changes brought about in an existing economic system by introduction of inputs generated by the process of economic development. How do periodic markets respond to these changes in the economic thresholds? As a general principle with an increase in the levels of economic development the disparity between the threshold requirements and the range of goods would tend to decrease resulting in a complementary reduction in the periodic element of these markets. Over a period of time the higher level periodic markets would acquire the attributes of permanent markets and their place would be taken over by the lower level markets. A logical extensionof this process is that in this type of vertical mobility the void created at the lowest levels would be filled by new periodic markets.

The existing ground evidence, however, does not fully support this proposition since periodic markets in economically developed regions have shown a great resilience and persistence in maintaining their traditonal characteristics.

Improved Developmental Infrastructure

The process of regional economic development initiates and is subsequently influenced by the developmental infrastructure, particularly transport network. As a major input an improved transport network plays an important role in the movement of goods and people and in providing or improving the existing accessibility to markets. One of the major effects of this component of developmental infrastructure is in causing a strengthening of the existing locational relationships. It also causes new in and out-flows and can result in changes in the orientation of the movement of goods and people. It also helps in the creation and establishment of new nodes and can reduce the locational efficiency of some of the older pre-existing nodes.

The impact of an improved transport network on the market organisation in general has been well investigated. However, the specific response of periodic markets to an improved transport network is yet to be analysed fully. The generalisation that the markets which compete successfully continue to grow further whereas those which lose locational advantages either decline or stop functioning needs a more rigorous analysis so far as periodic markets in economically developed regions are concerned.

Constant Clientele Patronage

The process of economic development is generally associated with an upward vertical mobility of economic classes through a rise in the income levels which in turn effects the purchasing power at the individual client level. Periodic markets are a traditional source of commodities and services at cheaper rates mostly to lower middle and lower income group population. It is generally believed that without the constant availability of patronage from these classes periodic markets, particularly those in urban areas, would not survive, let alone flourish.

In a region undergoing economic development the upward movement of economic groups is a general feature. Whether this type of movement is accompanied by a similar response in the attributes of periodic markets or is it that although the specific membership in an economic class undergoes a change only to be replaced by new entrants to that group or is it that tradition and culture remain the basic determinants of clientele patronage and consumer behaviour and negate the impact of upward economic mobility so far as periodic markets are concerned. An investigation of these aspects would help in understanding the persistence of periodic markets in economically developed regions.

Cultural-Historical Inertia

The existence of periodic markets in diverse types of regions and the generally offered economic explanations for it suggests that these markets possess a very high degree of tenacity to persist. This could be related to an ability to adjust in a changed economic organisation or to the overwhelming influence of cultural-historical inertia which inhibits any kind of response of these markets beyond the local level by ensuring a permanant place for these markets in the cultural ethos of the people. It is suggested that an analysis of this aspect of periodic markets would help in evaluating the extent to which purely economic explanations are valid in understanding the persistence of periodic markets in economically developed regions and would also help in assessing the role of cultural-historical factors in the promotion of tenatious persistence that these markets continue to display.

Summary

Periodic markets have been functioning as conventional centres of collection and redistribution of goods in diverse types of regions through various historical periods. These have been generally associated with developing economies. The economic explanations for the existence of periodic markets suggest that with the achievement of higher levels of economic development these would gradually acquire the attributes of permanent markets because the conditions necessitating their existence would themselves undergo a change. The ground evidence, however, does not support this proposition. The periodic markets have shown considerable tenacity to preserve their inherent attributes and continue to function, temporally as well as spatially side by side their permanent counterparts in the economically developed regions. In the Ganga Plain a classic example of this situation exists in western Uttar Pradesh.

The persistence of periodic markets in economically developed regions points to a need for an asessment of the existing economic explanations. The response of periodic markets to the changed economic organisation needs to be understood with reference to such aspects as changes in economic thresholds, improved transport network, continuous availability of clientele patronage, and the contribution made by cultural-historical factors. It is proposed that such an analysis would help in developing a more comprehensive framwork for an understanding of the phenomenon of periodic markets in economically developed regions.

TWENTY-NINE

Periodic Markets, Central Places and Regional Development: A Case Study of North-eastern Peninsula (India)

MRS. K.R. SHRIVASTAVA

This chapter hypothises that periodic markets and central places play a decisive role in the regional development of backward areas. A physico-cultural unit of the Ganga Basin, also known as Baghelkhand in the north-eastern Madhya Pradesh, has been selected as the study area for the case study (Fig. 29.1). With an area of about 50 thousand sq.km. and a population of about 4.8 million (1991) the region's 45 per cent population consists of tribals. The study area possesses rich tropical forests, minerals, power and human resources.

The chapter examines the spatio-temporal and functional characteristics of central places of the study region. This helps in identifying the factors controlling spatial organisation of the study area. As periodic markets vis-a-vis central places are found to be a part and parcel of the regional economy their role in regional development becomes obvious. The study highlights three main aspects:

(i) Re-organisation of rural space to make it conducive for development,
(ii) The role of market centres as centres of diffusion,
(iii) Streamlining the flow of goods as a means to further the process of development.

The study area is primarily an agricultural region. The

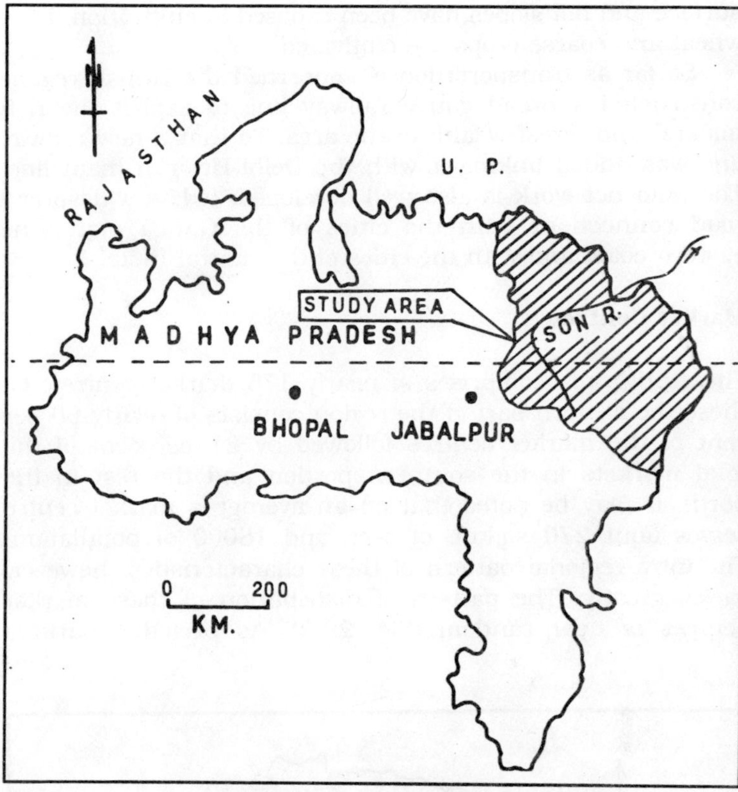

FIG. 29.1: Location of Study Area

forest resources also form part of the economy of local people. The mineral resources comprise of coal which is extracted at commercial scale. In addition rich bauxite deposist, inferior quality iron ore, manganese, limestone etc. are also mined. The Amarkantak Thermal Power Station and Singrauli Super Power Thermal Plant provide power to local industries. The Orient Paper Mill is an important industry of the area. It may also be mentioned that the study area has a rich ancient past. It has experienced phases of socio-economic development intervened with periods of wilderness. The area was ruled by tribal chiefs and remained isolated from the rest of the country due to thick forest cover and highly dissected terrain. River Son and its tributaries have developed flat valley portions where agriculture used to be practised. With the increasing pressure of population now the undulated plateau surface and hill slopes have been exposed to cultivation. Rice, wheat and coarse crops are cultivated.

So far as transportation is concerned the British regime constructed a broad gauge railway line to exploit the rich mineral and forest wealth of the area. To that a new railway line was added linking it with the Delhi-Howrah main line. The road net work is also well developed. It has widespread road connections with the cities of the Ganga plain, the eastern coast and with the cities of the central India.

Market Centres

The study area comprises of nearly 175 market centres. Of these the eastern part of the region consists of nearly 60 per cent of the market centres followed by 21 per cent of the total markets in the southern portion and the rest in the north. It may be noted that on an average a market centre serves aout 270 sq.km. of area and 18000 of population. The intra-regional pattern of these characteristics, however, varies greatly. The pattern of distribution of these market centres is near random (Fig. 29.2). As periodic markets

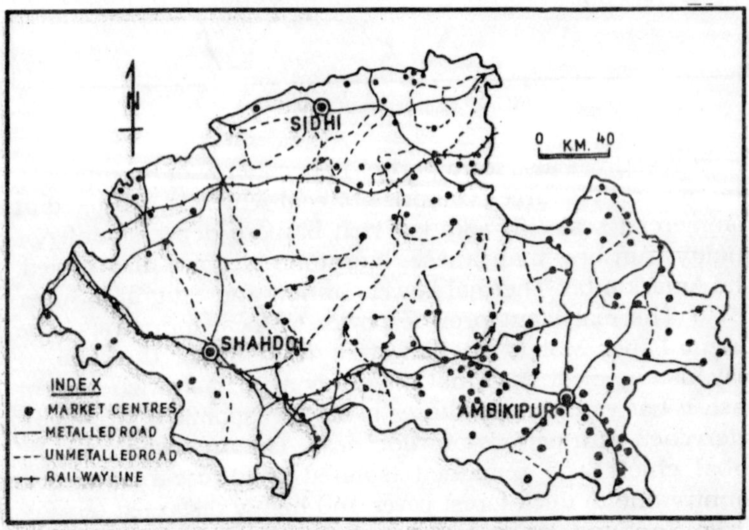

FIG. 29.2: Distribution of Market Centres

predominate market cycles are a common phenomenon. The area signifies itself with incomplete market cycles (Shrivastava, K.R., 1992). An analysis of spatio-temporal organisation using Smith and Bromley's methods reveals a weak organisation of markets and central places of higher order.

A study of the hierarchical nature of market centres has also been attempted before examining the potential of the central places for the development of the study region. The central places of the study region may be arranged in five hierarchical levels. The first order centre is a town and conforms to the level of a local town as per Skinner's classification scheme. The second level centres are small towns served by roads only. The third level centres comprise of town areas and large rurban villages. In the same way fourth order centres are periodic-cum-daily market centres whereas at the lowest level only periodic markets function as central places.

The appraisal of central place system shows that the central places from first to third level of hierarchy interact from national level of centres to inter-regional level central places. This reflects the level of demand of the population of the study region served by central places. From fourth order of hierarchy where periodic-cum-daily market centres operate the functional interaction operates at intra-regional level. The periodic markets, i.e. the centres of lowest level of hierarchy, however, operate at local level. Thus a well organised central place system operates in the study region.

The effectiveness of the central places system as an instrument of delivering means of development may be said to be reflected in the nature of their market area regions. It has been observed that the market area regions of Baghelkhand do not exhibit a nesting pattern as prescribed by the theory of central places. Market areas of the lowest order of central places do nest in the market areas of higher order central places but those of standard market town and of intermediate towns do not conform to a nesting pattern. It has been further observed that market areas either overlap or leave wide unserved space in between.

The Role of Market Centres in Development

It may be observed that the market centres deliver the goods, ideas and tools of development to the region they serve. In this sense market centres function as an institution of development. This aspect is strengthened by the nature of spatio-temporal organisation and by the nature of market area regions. Both these aspects are weak as has been observed above. It has been mentioned that a central place system is in operation in the study region. It is also true that the effectiveness of a central place system as an instrument of development of the area served by them is controlled by the level and nature of vertical exchange mechanism. In the study area it has been observed that in the ara some market centres are able to interact with a central place lying beyond the study area or even beyond the reach of their counterpart. Thus the expected central place functioning for optimal development operates only in parts in the study region. This may adversely affect the process of development of the study region. In the same manner the market area regions either overlap or leave unserved areas in between. Thus the efficiency of market area regions is also not conducive for development in all respects. This calls for a restructuring of the economy of the study area so that the benefits of the existing system of central places could be streamlined to generate and accelerate the process of development.

Periodic Market, Central Places and Development

It has thus been observed that a weak system of central place order is in operation in the study area. Though the identification and re-organisation of functional linkages the system can be made conducive to development.

Five orders of hierarchy of central place system have been identified which are similar to the postulation of Mukerji (Mukerji, 1987). The operation of three hierarchical levels of source regions of goods, as postulated in the model (Fig. 29.3) is observed in the study area itself. The three levels of these regions are local sources, regional sources and supra-regional sources, as discussed earlier. Mukerji has further proposed an idealised model of commodity structure (Fig. 29.4) and has exmined its relationship with development levels. It is observed in Fig. 29.4 that Set I is comprised of low cost, unsphosticated, manufactured goods which are of use to a

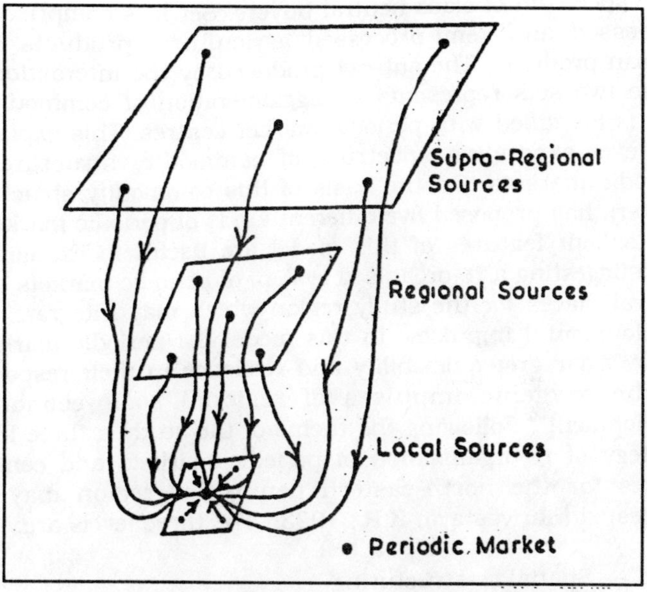

FIG. 29.3: An Idealised Model of Regional Sources and Linkages of Commodity Structure (After Mukerji, A.B.)

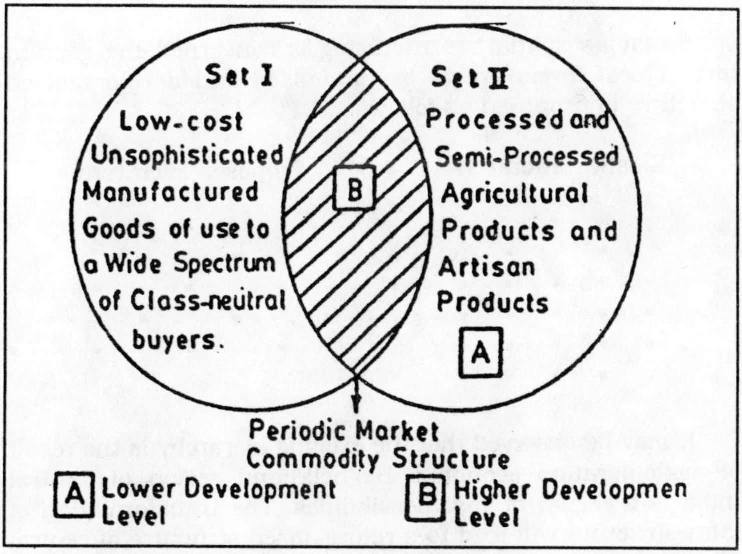

FIG. 29.4: Idealised Model of Commodity Structure of Periodic Market and Relationship with Development Levels

wide spectrum of class-neutral buyers. Set II is comprised of processed and semi-processed agricultural products and artisan products. The sub-set produced by the interaction of these two sets represents an agglomeration of commodities and is identified with periodic market centres. This explains the ever-expanding spectrum of commodity structure of periodic markets. On the basis of this commodity structure Mukerji has proposed five different kinds of periodic markets. The salient features of this model are useful in examining and suggesting a re-organised system of periodic markets and central places for the study region which may integrate the developmental impulses. In this model the periodic markets show "a far greter flexibility and resilence in their response to the oxygenic impulses of regional socio-economic development". Following the theme of the study a three level strategy of re-organisation of periodic markets and central places for the north-eastern peninsular region may be suggested (Shrivastava, K.R., 1993). The three levels are:

A — Spatial re-structuring
B — Socio-economic re-structuring
C — Institutional re-structuring

So far as spatial restructuring is concerned the gaps in hierarchical levels are to be minimised and a re-organised structure is proposed as follows:

Existing Hierarchy Proposed Hierarchy

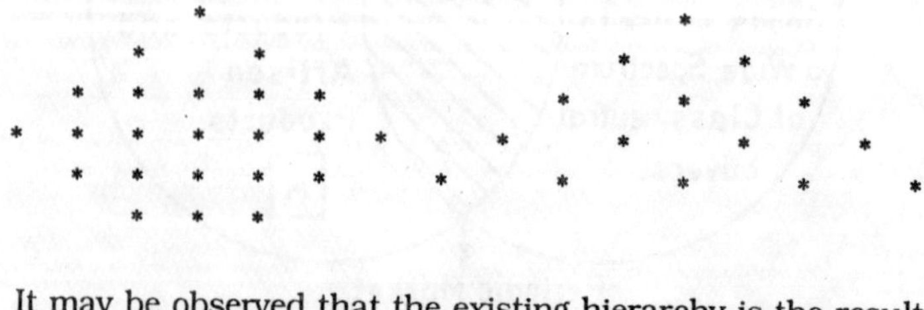

It may be observed that the existing hierarchy is the result of agglomeration economy. Baghelkhand region of Central India is a region of vast possibilities. The transformation of infra-structure will lead to a re-organised strucutre of central places. Periodic markets will transform into daily market centres and the number of market centres will naturally decrease. The process of spatial re-structuring will be perpetuated.

Socio-economic restructuring calls for transformation of the flow of goods, price control mechanism, cost-benefit aspects and the information level of people. Modernisation of the economic system, free flow of goods, de-control on prices and reducing subsidies, and supplementing the informational resources are the measures to be adopted under such situation.

The mechanism of flow of goods in the study region is found to be complex (Shrivastava, K.R., 1982). It is due to the multiplicity of sale point types and due to the intervention of brokers. It leads to multiplication of the cost with less returns to the producers.

In this, context a model regulating the flow of goods may be examined (Fig. 29.5). This model integrates the process of production of agricultural products with the processes of

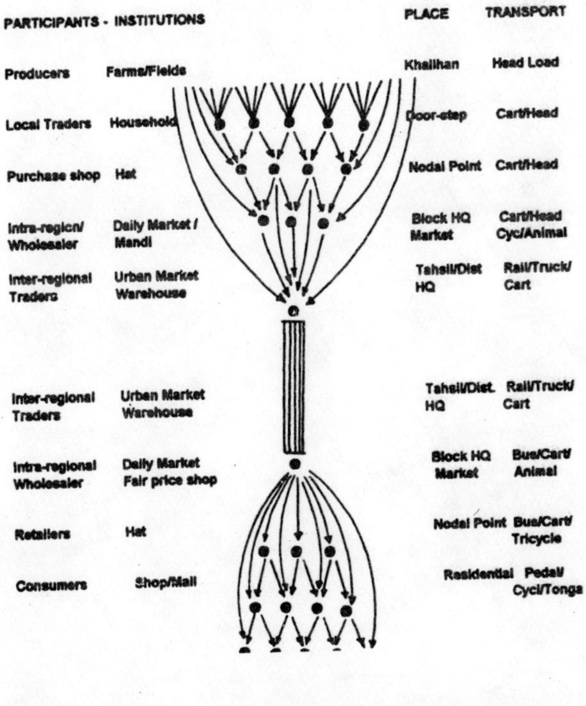

FIG. 29.5: High Labour and Low Capital Input

distribution and consumption of such products. It may be observed that at the production stage labour intensive low capital inputs are required. Through the system of collection and distribution, transport improvement 'shock' as a means to spatial restructuring. Another shock treatment is coming through the advancement of telecommunications. It will definitely improve the level of information available and the awareness of the population. Such reorganisational means will strengthen the role of periodic markets and central places in the process of regional development.

Theme - V

Human Resources, Environment and Economic Development

THIRTY

Levels of Human Resource Development and Economic Growth in a Segment of Middle Ganga Plain

B.R.K. SINHA

The developing regions are currently in the need for developing and utilizing human resources for economic growth. Of the three key resource factors of production — Natural, Human and Cultural, which determine a region's capacity for economic, social, cultural and political growth and development — Human resource factor seems to be crucial one which improves every aspect of life of the people in the society. Human resource is the qualitative value of the people which is utilized in producing a use-value of any description for satisfying needs of the people in the society.

The level of development in any form of an area depends largely upon the levels of working capability of the people of any region. Capability of the people is the productive soical value which they achieve either through formal or non-formal education, on the job training or learning by some other sources with an integration of health and nutrition.

The present work is an outcome of an intensive study of human resource development and utilization in Dhanarua Block, Patna District (Bihar). This Block, spreading over an area of 185.85 km^2, is a segment of the Middle Ganga Plain. This study can be considered as a representative of such studies at national level and will give a new facet in geographic discipline.

Objectives

The objectives of the present study are to:

(i) find out the levels of human resource development in general,
(ii) find out the relationship between the levels of human resource development and the levels of per capita income, and
(iii) extend appropriate suggestions for the development and utilization of human resources for economic growth.

Approach

Approach consists of two parts — Data base and Conceptual base

Data Base

The present work is exclusively based on the primary informations collected from the fourteen villages selected on the basis of stratified random sampling technique. In order to measure perfect differences in the development of human resources, two types of villages — Cultivator Dominated (CD), and Agricultural Labourers Dominated (ALD) were selected. The informations on age and sex, educational achievement, per capita income from all sources, persons involved in economic functions, births and deaths etc. were collected from around 20 per cent households from each village of both categories.

Conceptual Base

This involves the criteria upon which the measurement of the levels of human resource development and economic growth depends.

Measurement of levels of human resource development: Harbison (1973, pp. 12-13) considered educational achievement, school participation ratio, numbers and proportions of persons in the labour force with strategic skills (such as artisan, craftsman, foremen, master farmers, writers, musicians, teachers, artists, engineers, doctors, scientists, administrators, managers, etc.) measure of health and nutrition of the total population and particularly of very young children as indicators of human resource development.

Harbison and Myers (1964, p. 26) considered rate of literacy also as an indicator of human resource development in some studies. Singh, (1982, pp. 12-13) has also taken into account the educational achievement as an indicator of human resource development. Kothari, (1965, pp. 3 and 22) has also stated that the human capital or human resource is the product of education, training and experience and the spread of education is the most potent single weapon of human resource development. Moseman, (1964, p. 121) has also regarded that education of the people is recognized as a direct means of developing human resources.

Above statements show that the levels of human capability (human resource) depend upon the levels of educational achievement. Levels of education (particularly higher level) determine the quality of increasingly sophisticated and ever changing variety of human resources needed in agriculture, industry, administration, services, etc.

Author has also considered educational achievement or levels of education of individuals as indicator for measuring the levels of human resource development in the area. On this basis levels of human resource development have been framed into three categories. First, undeveloped or very low level human resource which is indicated by illiterate people. Second, less developed or low level human resource which is indicated by the educational level of below matriculated. Third, is the high level or developed human resource indicated by the educational levels of matriculate and above including professional/technical. These levels indicate only mental capabilities of the people.

Criteria to Measure Economic Growth: Harbison and Myers, (1964, pp. 34-36) considered Gross National Product (GNP) per capita, percentage of the active population engaged in agricultural occupations (simple but important indicator of the level of economic development in a particular country), public expenditure on all branches of education as indicators of economic growth though they have several limitations.

Author has considered per capita income (from all sources) and fixed a yardstic to measure the levels of economic growth. On this basis author has made three levels of income groups which are — High level, Medium level and Low level.

Analysis and Discussion

Levels of Human Resource Development (HRD)

Since human resource being an active agent brings region to the road of development, the analysis of the levels of Human Resource Development is important and essential.

Table 30.1 and Fig. 30.1 show the differential levels of HRD between Cultivators Dominated (CD) and Agricultural Labourers Dominated (ALD) Villages.

It is clear that the proportion of very low level or undeveloped human resources is sharply higher in the ALD village than that in CD villages. But the reverse is true in the case of other levels of HRD. The proportions of low level or less developed human resources and high level or developed human resources are higher in CD villages than that in ALD

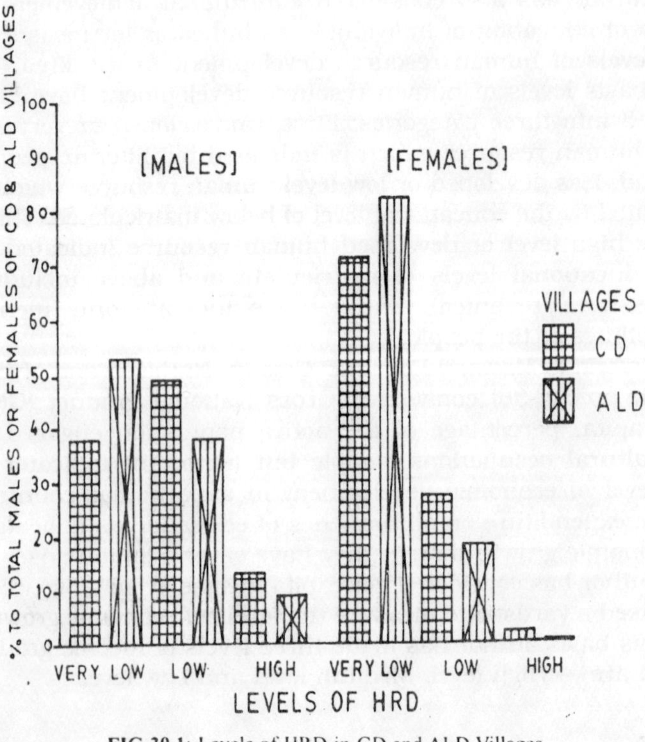

FIG 30.1: Levels of HRD in GD and ALD Villages

Table 30.1: Levels of HRD (1984)

Levels of HRD	Village Dominated by Cultivators		Village Dominated by Agricultural Labours		At Block Level (Total)	
	M	F	M	F	M	F
Very Low	440 (37.70)	674 (70.80)	425 (52.60)	579 (81.90)	865 (43.80)	1253 (75.53)
Low	570 (48.84)	260 (27.31)	307 (37.99)	125 (17.68)	877 (44.40)	385 (23.21)
High	157 (13.45)	18 (1.89)	76 (9.41)	3 (0.32)	233 (11.80)	21 (1.26)
Total	1167	952	808	707	1975	1659

Source : Authors' Survey, 1984.
Note : Bracketed lower figures are percentages to total Males or Females.

villages. This trend of HRD may be considered as the consequence of differential socio-economic conditions and unequal opportunities of social amenities between CD and ALD villages.

The difference among the levels of HRD at Block level is also noticeable, as the proportion of under-developed human resources (particularly in women category) is very high and the proportions of less developed and developed human resources are found lower. All these levels are observed to affect proportionately the socio-economic development of the area.

Levels of HRD and Economic Growth

The levels of HRD and economic growth have been considered as indicators of regional development. The levels of regional development depand largely upon the levels of development and utilization of human resources and its economic returns. Economic returns are calculated in terms of per capita annual income and HRD in terms of working capabilities which are the product of mental and physical development of the people. In this way, the HRD and Economic progress go hand in hand and ultimately lead the region to the road of modernization.

Table 30.2 and Fig. 30.2 apparently show the associationship between the levels of HRD (measured by

Table 30.2: Levels of HRD and Economic Growth (1984)

Levels of per capita income (In Rs.) at village level	Numer of Villages	Levels of HRD: Very low level	Low level	High level	Total Population
Low	1	284	97	12	393
Below 350	(7.14%)	(72.29)*	(24.68)	(3.05)	10.81**
Medium	11	1699	941	164	2804
350-700	(78.57)	(60.59)	(33.56)	(5.85)	77.16
High	2	135	224	78	437
Above 700	(14.29)	(30.89)	(51.26)	(17.85)	12.03
Total	14	2118	1262	254	3634

Source : Author's Survey, 1984.

* Bracketed lower figures are the percentages to total population of respective category of income level.

** Unbracketed lower figures are the percentages to total population (3634) of the Block.

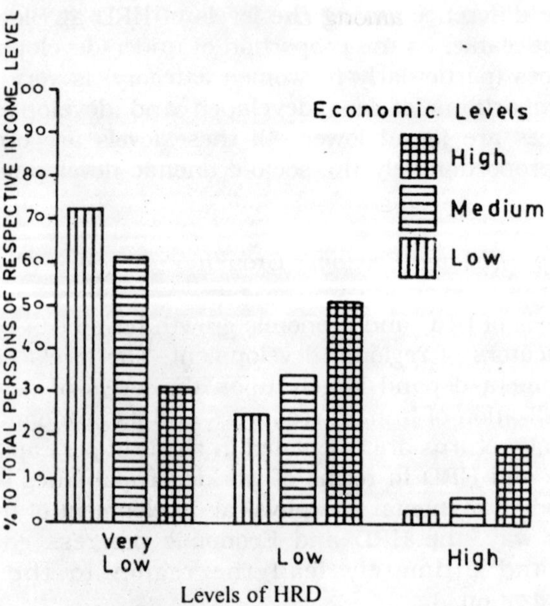

FIG. 30.2: HRD and Economic Levels

educational attainment) and the levels of economic growth (measured by per capita annual income).

Low level income category (below Rs. 360) comprised only 7.14 per cent of the total villages in which the percentage of very low level (undeveloped) human resources was found very high (72.26%) and the percentages of low level (less developed) and high level (developed) human resources were very low i.e. 24.68 and 3.05 per cent respectively. It means that the mental working capacity of the persons falling under the low level economic progress remains very low, and shows low level regional development. Medium level income category (Rs. 350-700) comprised 78.57 per cent of the villages in which the percentage of very low level human resources was again very high and the percentages of low level and high level human resources were low. It shows medium level regional development because of medium level increase in the HRD and per capita income, High level income category (above Rs. 700) comprised only 30.89 per cnet of villages in which the percentage of very low level human resource was less than one-third (30.89%) of the total population resources whereas the percentage of low level was highest (51.26%) and of high level 17.85 per cent. This trend also indicates that the percentage of qualitatively better people remains higher in the higher level income category and lower in the lower level income category. This level shows high level regional development.

It is, therefore, clear that the percentage of undeveloped human resources remains high in the low level economic growth, medium in the medium level economic growth and low in the high level economic growth. This trend indicates that the low level economic development is because of the presence of undeveloped human resources and in absence of developed human resources.

The percentage of less developed human resources remains low in the low level economic growth, medium in the medium level economic growth and high in the high level economic growth. Similarly the percentage of high level human resources remains low in the low level economic growth, medium in the medium level economic growth and high in the high level economic growth. This trend also indicates that the economic development of the area is lower because of lower levels of human resource development and higher because of higher levels of human resource development.

Looking into overall picture it can be stated that the percentage of undeveloped human resources was observed decreasing with increasing levels of economic growth or vice-versa and the percentages of less developed and developed human resources were observed increasing with increasing levels of economic growth or vice-versa.

On the basis of this it can also be stated that the human resource development is low because of less economic growth and less economic growth is because of low development of human resources and human resource development is high because of high economic growth and high economic growth is because of high development of human resources. This is a perfect case of a vicious circle.

On the whole, it can be stated that both the HRD and economic growth are associated with each other and the development of one is dependent upon another.

Some Other Measures of HRD and Economic Growth

Besides above criteria adopted, author considers some other measures also which directly or indirectly indicate the levels of economic and human resource development, though they may bear some limitations. These indicators are as follows:

The study area stands with very high proportion of children (39% boys and 39% girls to total males or females) which may be considered as a potential labour force but at the same time it may be harmful for the area's economic development if the labour force will not be properly utilized. More children are the results of undeveloped and less developed human resources and economic growth.

High birth and death rates indicate region's undeveloped and developing conditions. High birth rate is the result of undeveloped human resources. The National Sample Survey, 16th round (July 1960-June 1961, p. 4) stated that the number of children becomes smaller with higher educational attainment of husband but the decline is sharp particularly with higher educational standard of wife. In the area, birth and death rates have been found higher in ALD villages than that in CD villages which can be considered as the result of differential HRD and economic growth.

Proportion of working force in agricultural sector has been

found exceptionally very high and in non-agricultural sector very low. This is very pronounced particularly in the case of female working force. This indicates very poor HRD and economic growth. Ghosh, (1985, p. 123) has also stated that the developed countries have a high percentage of people in non-agricultural occupations but the under-developed countries have very low percentage of people in such occupations.

It has been found that there has been a slow shift in the participation rate of the working human resources from agricultural to non-agricultural economic activities of the area. This trend indicates a healthy sign of the development of the area. This trend is observed as a result of HRD as non-agricultural sector requires high level of literacy and education than that of agricultural sector. Batra (1978, p. 97), Aperyan, (1979, p. 123) and Ghosh, (1985, pp. 124 and 135) also observed that a shift or movement of working force from agricultural to non-agricultural sectors is a general tendency of region's social, economic, cultural and political progress.

An appreciable proportion of child and superannuated labour utilization has been found particularly in the agricultural economic functions of the area and mot of them are in the category of undeveloped human resources. This is not a good sign for area's economic development.

Proportion of unemployement and underemployment also indicates area's economic, social, cultural and political growth. 52.57 per cent males and 88.67 per cent females were found in the category of non-working force in the year 1984. These figures are more or less equal to the figures of 1971 and 1981. Around 20 per cent males and 27 per cent females from the working force were underutilized and most of them were in the category of undeveloped human resources. Such a higher proportion of unemployment and underemployment stands as obstacle in the way of area's development.

Types of houses in which people of the area live, availability of cereals for year's consumption and capacity to purchase medicines and to have well medical treatment also indicate the economic development of the area. It has been found that there is notable difference in the availability of all these essentials between cultivators and agricultural labourers. The cultivators do not face as much problems regarding such essentials as agricultural labourers face. This is the result of differential economic and human resource development between the CD and ALD villages. This is also a not good sign for area's social, economic, cultural and political development.

Literacy and education are considered as indicators of HRD and socio-economic development of the region. It has been observed that people having better socio-economic status are more literate and educated than those having poor socio-economic status. A high association has been found between the degree of economic progress and the degree of literacy and education. It has been found that there has been an increase in the percentage of literates and educated people from 1971 to 1981 and to 1984 which is a healthy sign for area's development. Similarly, educational and health facilities including educational and health institutions have also been observed as indicators of area's social, economic, cultural and political development.

Human resource formation is another indicator of HRD and economic growth. The rate of human resource formation has been found slow. Only 65 per cent boys and 43 per cent girls in the schooling period of compulsory elementary education (5-14 years) were on the human resource formation and rest boys and girls are off the formation. This is not a good sign of area's socio-economic development.

Since HRD and economic growth are highly associated with each other and the development of one is not possible for want of another one, a well and proper planning should be made for promoting the human resources of the right type, in the right quantity and quality and at the right time which are essentially and urgently needed for area's economic, social, cultural and political devleopment. For achieving such developmental goals all essentials which are under the Purview of minimum needs should be made available to each and everyone in the area. This will ultimately enable the people of the area to live a life under the state of peace and comfort, through utilizing their knowledge, skills, energies, talents and other qualitative values in areas economic functions.

THIRTY-ONE

Socio-economic Development in Upper and Middle Ganga Valley: A Comparative Study

SHEO SHANKAR VERMA and JAI PRAKASH JAISWAL

In this chapter an attempt has been made to measure the levels of spatial pattern of socio-economic development with special reference to Eastern and Western Uttar Pradesh which represent the middle and the Upper Ganga Valley respectively.

Indicators of Socio-economic Development

A group of twenty-seven indicators representing various sectors of the economy has been selected for the measurement of levels of Socio-economic development in thirty-four districts falling in Western and Eastern U.P. Amongst these indicators seven indicators are related to agricultural development, four indicators to the industrial development and remaining sixteen indicators are related to infrastructural facilities. These indicators are as follows:

Agricultural Development

1. *Agricultural Area* — Percentage of net shown area to total area.
2. *Agricultural Intensity* — Area sown more than once as percentage of net sown area.
3. *Commercialization of Agriculture* — Percentage of commercial cropped area to net sown area.
4. *Developoment of Irrigation* — Irrigated area as percentage of net sown area.

5. *Agricultural Productivity* — Per capita agricultural production in rupees.
6. *Consumption of Chemical Fertilizer* — Per hactare fertilizer consumption in kgs.
7. *Tractorization* — Number of tractors per lakh hactare of net sown area.

Industrial Development

1. *Industrial Intensity* — Number of industrial units per lakh of population.
2. *Industrial Workers Intensity* — Percentage of industrial workers to total workers.
3. *Industrial Processing* - Per industrial unit out-put in rupees.
4. *Industrial Productivity* - Per capita industrial production in rupees.

Educational Development

1. *Total Literacy* — Percentage of literate people to total population.
2. *Intensity of Schools* — (i) No. of Primary Schools per lakh of population; (ii) No. of Junior High Schools per lakh of population; (iii) No. of High School and Intermediate Colleges per lakh of population.

Health Development

1. *Intensity of Health Services* — (i) No. of allopathic hospitals and dispensaries per lakh of population; (ii) No. of family planning and child welfare centres per lakh of population. (iii) No. of beds in hospitals per lakh of population.

Transport and Communication Development

1. *Road Density* — Length of roads per 100 km^2 area.
2. *Road Accessibility* — Percentage of village within 3 km distance from any metalled road.
3. *Post Office Intensity* — No. of post offices per lakh of population.

Other Infrastructural Development

1. *Banking Services* — No. of banks per lakh of population.
2. *Alternative Energy Sources* — No. of bio-gas, Gobar Gas Plants per lakh of population.
3. *Electrification* — Percentage of Electrified villages to total inhabited villages.
4. *New Agriculture Technological Innovations* — No. of seeds and Fertilizer stores per lakh of population.

Methodology

In the present case, on the basis of above indicators, an attempt has been made to calculate the composite index of socio-economic development with the help of 'Texonomic Method'

For the calculation of composite index and co-efficient of development, the following formulae have been used:

$$Z_{ij} = \frac{X_{ij} - X_j}{S_j}$$

Where,.

Z_{ij} = the value of *i*th indicator of *j* *r*th region.

X_{ij} = the mean value of *i*th indicator.

S_j = the standard deviation of *i*th indicator.

In each row there will be one point with the shortest or minimum (Z_{oj}) at the corresponding points of the row. The Z_{oj} value shows to be the highest value of *Z* score of a row. Then, the composite index is obtained by using following formula:

$$C_{jo} = \sqrt{\sum_{J=1}^{M} (Z_{ij} - Z_{oj})^2}$$

Where,

C_{jo} = is the composite index for *j*th region

Z_{ij} = is the standized value of various indicators.

Z_{oj} = is the highest or best standardized value of *j*th region.

After calculating the mean and standard deviation of C_{jo} index, a constant value can be find out by subtracting the twice standard deviation from the mean of composite index. This can be written in the following form:

$$C_0 = C_{jo} + 2\, S_{jo}$$

Where,

C_{jo} & S_{jo} are the mean and *S.D.* of composite index (C_{jo}) respectively.

To find out co-efficient of composite index the following formula is used:

$$C\, C_i = 1 - \frac{C_{jo}}{CO}$$

Abbriviation stands the same as above.

In this method the co-efficient of composite index always becomes positive and it ranges from 0 to + 1. The higher value of co-efficient of composite index means the high level of regional development of the region and the less value of (near to Zero) co-efficient indicates the less regional development of the region.

Spatial Patterns of Socio-economic Development in 1985-86

All the districts of the study region are classifed according to their coefficient of development into five categories, viz. highly developed, developed, average, backward and highly backward which is given in the Table 31.1.

It is apparent from the Table 31.1 that out of 34 districts of the study region ten districts are highly developed, Seven districts high developed, four districts average developed, thirteen districts less developed and only one district falls in the category of very backward. The highest co-efficient of development is 0.99 in Ghaziabad district of Western U.P. and the lowest one is 0.19 in Pratapgarh district of Eastern U.P.

Highly Developed

Out of thirty-four districts ten districts of the study area fall in this category of development. Out of these seven districts are in Western U.P. and remaining three districts which are Varanasi, Mirzapur and Gorakhpur are in eastern U.P. In these districts the co-efficient of development is found above than 0.80. The districts under this category comprise of large urban centres where most civic amenities are already available for development. Besides these, the central and state Government are also paying much attention for their rapid progress.

Table 31.1: Classification of Districts according to the Composite Index of Socio-economic Development in 1985-86

Category of Development	Districts	Ranks	Co-efficient of Development
1. Highly Developed (0.8 & above)	Ghaziabad	1	0.99
	Mathura	2	0.98
	Mirzapur	3	0.98
	Meerut	4	0.97
	Varanasi	5	0.96
	Agra	6	0.87
	Muzaffar Nagar	7	0.83
	Gorakhpur	8	0.83
	Saharanpur	9	0.82
	Bulandshahar (10)	10	0.80
2. High Developed (0.6 to 0.8)	Aligarh	11	0.78
	Allahabad	12	0.77
	Bareilly	13	0.69
	Rampur	14	0.65
	Bijnore	15	0.61
	Farrukhabad	16	0.61
	Moradabad (7)	17	0.60
3. Average Developed (0,4 to 0,6)	Faizabad	18	0.59
	Ghazipur	19	0.49
	Jaunpur	20	0,44
	Deoria (4)	21	0,40
4. Less Developed (0.2 to 0.4)	Shahjahanpur	22	0.39
	Ballia	23	0.39
	Sultanpur	24	0.38
	Mainpuri	25	0.37
	Azamgarh	26	0.36
	Etawah	27	0.36
	Etah	28	0.34
	Badaun	29	0.33
	Gonda	30	0.33
	Pilibhit	31	0.32
	Bahraich	32	0.30
	Basti (13)	33	0.27
5. Highly Backward 0.2 & below	Partapgarh (1)	34	0.19

High Developed

Amongst seven districts which fall in this group of development, six are from western U.P. and only one district, i.e. Allahabad is in eastern U.P. The co-efficient of this group is between 0.6 to 0.8 and the districts which come under this category also comprise of large urban centres where transport and communication and other infrastructural facilities are well developed.

Average Developed

Four districts namely Faizabad, Ghazipur, Kanpur and Deoria are moderately developed and these districts are in eastern U.P.

Less Developed

Twelve districts fall under the less developed category. Six districts each of all in western and eastern U.P. respectively. Hence, about 35.3 per cent area of the study region is still backward. The districts of this category are mainly concentrated in eastern, southern parts of West U.P. and in northern, central parts of eastern U.P.

Least Developed

Pratapgarh district of East U.P. is the only district which comes in this category. This district is highly backward in regard to Socio-economic development.

Thus, from the above discussion it is evident that overall Socio-economic progress is concentrated around a few large urban centres. Not only that, there is lop-sided development in the region but the extent of disparity is also very significant because the range of co-efficient of composite index is very wide in the study region. At the same time it is also notable that most of the districts (particularly those of eastern U.P. districts) are concentrated around the lowest value of co-efficient. This situation speaks of the magnitude of the backwardness of the eastern districts in comparison to the western districts of the study region.

Causes for Regional Variations in Socio-economic Development in Eastern and Western U.P.

The districts of eastern U.P. are comparatively less developed than the districts of western U.P. There are many constrains for balanced growth of both the regions under study.

It may be noted that the districts of eastern U.P. do not have enough natural resources except soil, water and small patches of forest, but the relative backwardness of this region cannot be explained in terms of its natural resource endowment as the districts of West U.P. are equally deificient in this regard. Similary, the poverty of eastern U.P. cannot be explained by reffering to the heavy population pressure in this region as density of western U.P. is only marginally lower. Though, there are some differences in demographic characteristics like age-structure, literacy rates, working -non working ratio etc.

The explanation of relative poverty of eastern U.P. may, therefore, be sought in such socio-economic structure, low productivity in agriculture and industry owing to inadequate capital and backward technology, inadequate infra-structure, low degree of urbanisation and unfavourable location position of the region for industries.

Though the economy of both the regions of eastern and western U.P. are primarily based on agriculture yet the dependency on agriculture is much higher in the former region in comparision to the later one. At the same time it is also remarkable that the economic structure of West U.P. is comparatively more diversified. A strong negative association exists between per capita district product and the proportion of workers in agriculture and a positive association between per capita district product and the proportion of workers in manufacturing and services. The differences in per capita product are very strongly associated with difference in labour productivity differences in agricultural productivity seem to be a major factor in inter-regional and inter-district differentials in per capita product.

Eastern U.P. has still subsistance oriented agriculture and area of cash crops like Sugarcane, Oilseed and vegetable etc. is nominal. Very small size and fragmentation of holdings are also impediments in the agricultural development of the eastern region. There is moreover, considerable underemployment in this region and area per cultivator is relatively small. The capacity of investment of capital in agriculture is also comparatively low in eastern U.P. Inadequate development of infrastructural facilities like assured means of irrigation, link roads, banking and credit facilities and other non farm services are also another important constraints for the agricultural development of this region.

Above all, social and cultural factors like rigid social structure, conservative attitudes, weak health of cultivators as well as the prevalence of social attitudes and customs uncongenial to economic development have also been instrumental in keeping the agriculture in a backward form in East U.P. On the other hand, in West U.P. the average size of holding is larger, capital stock and land per worker is more, assured means of irrigation and credit facilities are more developed, besides, the cultivators are more hard worker and willing to adopt new agricultural technology.

West U.P. is comparatively more industrialized than East U.P. But however, the differences in the degree of industrialisation can not be attributed to the availability of local raw materials. As both the regions East and West U.P. are equally deficient in mineral resources and no strong linkage between the industries could be observed. Less Development of social and economic overhead capital is one of the major factors responsible for less industrial development of the Eastern region. Shortage of financial instituion, absence of a vigorous enterpreneurial class, frequent industrial disputes and differences, administrative delays and inefficiency in the department concerned with industries and the failure political leadership to initiate a bold policy of industrial develeopoment of the state are other reason for less industrialization of Eastern Uttar Pradesh.

Besides this, the lack of well developed system of urban centres, which may act as fact of growth, seems to be an other important factor in the Economic backwardness of East U.P. The degree of Urbanisation is very low in this region and big urban centres are few. Thus, in the absence of agglomeration economies provided by big Urban centres, very few Industries are attracted in the Eastern U.P.

Lastly, it is frequently urged that owing to low capacity of investment there are low income levels of its regions. No local vigorous enterpreneurial class has emerged in the State, comparable to Punjab, Gujarat, Tamil Nadu etc. to exploit its industrial potential. In the absence of favourable locational conditions capital has not been attracted from outside. Some of the public sector projects were launched in the state during the first two decades of planning. Investment under the five years plans on per capita basis has been lower in Uttar Pradesh as compared to many other states. Between 1951 and 1974, per capita plan out lay in U.P. amounted to Rs. 283 as compared to Rs. 360 in other states. Flow of funds from the centres has also been meagre in the state. Thus, per capita central assistance during the period of First Three Five Years Plans in U.P. was Rs. 76 as against all state average of Rs. 105. The State Government in its turn has not displayed much vigour in mobilising resources for development has failed to initiate measures on a sufficient scale to correct the problems of regional imbalances in the state.

Although, there has been considerable improvement in respect of various social and economic facilities in the regions of U.P. imbalances, but, however, there is a need of a deliberate and well thought policy for regional development and rectify the regional imbalances which have persisted over the year in the regions of U.P.

THIRTY-TWO

Socio-economic Influences on Electoral Participation in Eastern U.P.: A Case Study of 1984 Parliamentary Election

S.K. DIKSHIT

Election data help to reveal the varying prospects of political parties at national, state and local levels and also general trends in the political system. The results of these elections clearly reveal certain major trends, including the dominance of several parties in the country. The electoral process has brought masses of people into closer contact with the political system, and in turn has brought the political parties into closer contact with the masses. Elections have proved to be powerful instrument of mass education and the political socialization. The Indian experience has proved that they can function in essentially traditional social systems, with an overwhelming illiterate population and still serve the modern political goals of integration, nation building and development.

The spatial variation in electoral participation forms an integral part of electoral studies because it exhibits the level of political consciousness and development which differs from place to place and region to region. It is related to the various features which are responsible for the degree of variation. These factors include the physical and biological characteristics of voters, e.g. sex, the place of residence (urban and rural), education, the status and their living standard and the like. This chapter explores the factors which have been responsible for spatial variation in electoral participation in eastern Uttar Pradesh. The eastern U.P. being comparatively less developed region, having socio-economic diversities, abject poverty, having low per capits income, a low percentage of literacy, urbanization and industrialization. The people mainly residing in the countryside are mostly conservative, traditional and fatalist and divided in many castes and sub-caste groups, inevitably influence the electoral participation. In this chapter four very important variables, i.e. literacy, scheduled caste population, urban and working population have been selected to test the influence of these variables on electoral participation of the region.

Introduction

The introduction of universal adult franchise and its successful practice in our country in face of numerous odds, viz. illiteracy, inexperience, casteism, regionalism and the like has been able to bring social and political development and has granted freedom as well, to the members of religious minorities and other socially and economically depressed classes. The exercise of franchise has always been affected with socio-economic conditions of the region. Taylor and Johnston (1979, 108) have stated that modern elections consist of competition between political parties for the support of the electorate. Although in most voting systems, the actual voting decisions taken by individual voters at the ballot box involves choosing between candidates, in practice, the voter chooses between the parties they represent. Hence, the election of independent or non-party candidate is a very rare event in modern election. The authors have presented an example of Norway and have pointed out that the rural areas consistently have lower turnouts and are slower in catching up with their pre-extension situations. Although the rural areas include much more than the periphery, these findings do imply that mobilization is more difficult in peripheral areas. This can only be fully illustrated, of course, by using a much more detailed ecological breakdown than a simple city/rural one. Weiner *et al* (1977, p. 6) have brought out the comparisons of electoral participation in urban constituencies. They have considered that India's urban constituencies are electorally more politicised than is the countryside. Urban residents tend to vote more than rural dwellers. There are, however, substantial variations which serve to qualify any simple generalizations. Differences in turnout between urban and rural constituencies are generally greatest in the most backward states; that is, those with the lowest level of economic development and least in India's more developed states. Das Gupta and Morris-Jones (1975, p.9) have stated that participation occupies a prominent place in the body of democratic political theory. Participation is the supreme goal and overriding standard; a democracy is good because and insofar as it is a participatory democracy. The participation is relevant not only as a democratic norm but also in many cases as a meausre of the strength of the political system. Declines in electoral participation may be reliable alarm signal, while increases in the same will, if not invariably, often reflect a sense of membership of and involvement in the system. Varma and Narain (173) have discussed the voting behaviour in Rajasthan in the specific context of demographic and socio-economic characteristics, level of political information, various media of communication, exposure to and participation in campaigning, voting preferences and their determinants. They have concluded that non-voters are more among those who are politically less informed and less exposed to various media of communication. In rural constituencies participation is the highest among farmers and the lowest among agricultural labourers, whereas in urban areas participation is higher among population engaged in white-collar occupations than in manual and semi-skilled workers. Mishra *et al* (1982, p.51) have pointed out that electoral participation is associated with political awareness, that is, actual knowledge of political affairs. The number of aware voters is extremely small in tribal areas because education and the use of mass-media are not wide-spread (Table 32.1). Political issues also play an important role in electoral participation.

In the present study 31 constituencies which comprise 15 districts of eastern Uttar Pradesh have been taken to analyse the influence of socio-economic variables on electoral participation. The constituency-wise voter turnout has been shown in the Table 32.1. It clarifies that the average male turnout is much higher than that of female. In comparison to other parts of India the eastern Uttar Pradesh is a region having low percentage of literacy and economic development. This is also a part of low trunout areas of the country. The average turnout of the study area was 48.8 per cent in 1984

Table 32.1: Pattern of Voter Turnout (1984)

Sl. No.	Name of Constituencies	Voter turnout	Male*	Female*
1.	Pratapgarh	43.68	43.48	43.88
2.	Amethi	50.10	58.75	38.90
3.	Sultanpur	42.72	54.16	28.65
4.	Akbarpur	53.49	58.12	48.25
5.	Faizabad	45.59	47.25	43.71
6.	Bahraich	36.84	52.27	17.85
7.	Balrampur	43.87	48.41	38.65
8.	Gonda	35.18	39.76	30.00
9.	Basti	38.24	40.05	35.99
10.	Domariyaganj	53.73	51.73	56.06
11.	Khalilabad	47.42	49.97	44.55
12.	Bansgaon	43.80	47.72	38.98
13.	Gorakhpur	50.69	55.59	44.77
14.	Mahrajganj	54.74	60.16	48.23
15.	Padrauna	49.85	62.09	35.77
16.	Deoria	46.67	56.20	38.85
17.	Salempur	47.52	53.92	40.37
18.	Ballia	52.54	52.54	52.53
19.	Ghosi	53.59	53.64	53.52
20.	Azamgarh	54.61	54.97	54.19
21.	Lalganj	50.54	50.49	50.59
22.	Machhalisahar	50.61	52.70	48.25
23.	Jaunpur	53.25	53.81	52.62
24.	Saidpur	50.73	51.77	49.57
25.	Ghazipur	52.91	52.20	53.69
26.	Chandauli	53.26	56.24	49.90
27.	Varanasi	53.66	56.99	49.94
28.	Robertsganj	49.22	60.09	37.30
29.	Mirzapur	51.94	53.76	49.96
30.	Phulpur	53.52	59.76	45.88
31.	Allahabad	48.06	54.03	40.74
	Total	48.8	53.0	43.92

* Calculated by the author on the basis of election reports.

parliamentary election which is lower than that of country's average (56.92) and state average 49.96 per cent. The frequency distribution of parliamentary constituencies in different categories of voter turnout has been shown in table 13.2.

Table 32.2: Spatial Distribution of Voter Turnout (1984)

Categories	Characteristics	No. of constituencies
< 40 per cent	Ver low	3
40-50	Low	4
45-50	Moderate	7
> 50	High	17
Total	-	31

The above Table 32.2 shows that the high turnout (50%) was found in 17 Constituencies of the region. These were Amethi, Akbarpur, Domariyaganj, Gorakhpur, Ballia, Ghosi, Azamgrah, Lalganj, Machhalisahar, Jaunpur, Saidpur, Chandauli, Varanasi, Mirzapur and Phulpur. The moderate turnour (45 to 50%) was found in 7 constituencies, i.e. Faizabad, Khalilabad, Padrauna, Deoria, Salempur, Robertsganj and Allahabad. The Constituencies of low participation (40 to 45%) were Pratapgarh, Sultanpur, Balrampur and Bansgaon. The very low turnout constituencies are Bahraich , Basti and Gonda. The Table 32.1 indicates that the highest percentage of turnout, i.e. 54.74 was found in Mahrajganj constituency while the lowest, i.e. 35.18 per cent in Gonda constituency.

Socio-economic Influences

To study and analyse the influence of socio-economic variables on electoral participation of the region four variables have been selected on the basis of preceding studies done by various scholars. These variables are literacy, urban population, scheduled caste population and working population. The means of these variables ($\bar{x}$) in eastern Uttar Pradesh are 24.29, 21.43, 7.68 and 31.14 per cent respectively, while the mean of dependent variable ($\bar{y}$) is 48.8 per cent. It has been hypothesised that the areas having higher percentage of literacy, urban population, working population and scheduled caste population are the areas having higher percentage of voter turnout. To test these hypotheses the correlation between socio-economic variables (X) and voter turnout (Y) has been worked out. The product moment coefficient of correlation (r) has been calculated to know the relationship between these variables. The result has been given in Table 32.3.

Table 32.3: Results of Correlation

Variables	Mean of Independent variable ($\bar{x}$)	Coefficient of correlation (*r*)	Variation explained r^2
Literacy	24.29	0.65	42%
S.C. population	21.43	0.339	10%
Urban population	7.68	0.09	Negligible
Working population	31.14	-0.24	5%

Table 32.3 clarifies that the correlation between literacy and voter turnout is found positive. The coefficient of correlation is 0.65, which shows the high correlation between these variables. Thus the hypothesis related to this variable is accepted and proved. In the case of scheduled caste population the correlation coefficient is .339 which shows the poor correlation between S.C. population and voter turnout, but the hypothesis related to this variable is also proved and accepted. The correlation between urban population and voter turnout is negligible, i.e. 0.09 while in the case of working population the low negative correlation is found. The value of the coeffficient is -0.24. It may be said that the areas having higher percentage of literacy, scheduled caste population and urban population are the areas of high turnout. The coefficient of determination has also been calculated which shows that the literacy and scheduled caste population variables are also to explain apparently 42 per cent and 10 per cent variation respectively in the distribution of voter turnout in this region.

Male and Female Turnout

A comparative study of male and female turnout has been made to analyse the influence of this variable on the voter participation. It is apparently seen in the Table 32.1 that in the most of the cases the male turnout is higher than female turn out. In few of the constituencies i.e. 4 out of 31, female turnout is found higher in comparison to the male. These constituencies are Pratapgarh, Domariyaganj, Lalganj and Ghazipur. It shows the growing consciousness of the female population about their voting rights in this region.

Conclusion

On the basis of the preceding study and analysis of the voter turnout and influences of socio-economic variables on voter turn out it is concluded that there exists a close relationship between literacy and voter turnout while in the case of scheduled caste population and in case of urban population it is found to be poor. It may be said that the areas having higher percentage of literacy, urban population, male population and scheduled caste population are high voter turnout areas in eastern Uttar Pradesh while the areas having higher percentage of working population are low voter turnout areas of the region.

THIRTY-THREE

The Changing Scene of Rural Environment (Social Aspect)

J.S. VERMA and VISHWA NATH

The concept of rural transformation means a process through which rural poverty is alleviated by sustained increases in the productivity and income of low-income rural workers and households. Rural transformation is intended for the economic development for the growing rural population, it is aimed at increasing production and raising productivity and hence the required services and institutions. To achieve this, greater interaction between the modern and traditional sector of technology is insisted

The nature and extent of any rural transformation programmes or project will always reflect the political, social and economic circumstances of the particulars country or region. As already referred earlier that geography deals with man-environment interactional relationship. The science of habitat transformation consider whole world as one family to promote peace and bone among the human community at global level (Singh, and Rana, 1980).

It is notable that the concept of IRD and RHT (Rural Habitat Transformation) should be generally considered similar to each other, while is also considered with ecological and environmental issues in addition to the integration of sectors and policies in span of time and dimension.

The social transformation of a rural society in a developing country like India involves many complex of socio-political issues. The first and often the most obvious problem is the pattern of land holding. If a small group of land-lords own and control a considerable proportion of total land and a majority of the rural population consists of small farmers, tenants or landless workers, the majority will have little hope of any improvement in their life until they obtain a fare share of the land through land reforms.

But the second and in a sense a more important aspect of rural transformation or change is the nature of social relationship. Land reforms can impose ceiling on larger holdings and redistribute land to poor tenants or landless workers, but they may not be themselves change the social relationship between the medium land lords who are below the prescribed ceiling and their tenants and the resumed land may be a very small proportion of the tenants and land less workers. The social transformation of a rural society can begin only when the land reforms are drastic enough not only in achieving a more equitable distribution of all the available land but in changing the nature of social relationship in a manner that will eliminate or minimise exploitation and create greater equality based on egalitarian ethics.

The third crucial aspect of social change is more positive one. Even after land has been redistributed and the negative feature of the old system reflect in inequitable relationship have been changed, there will be need for a new relationship in which the new land holders can work together to improve not only their land with increasing water resources but also to improve the common social relationship and organise a dynamic rural community.

Objective and Methodology

The main objective of this chapter is to analyse changing feature of social system in rural community of the study area and then to discuss the changing pattern of rural ecology.

The study of above theme will be reflected on the following grounds:

(a) The basic information has been studied from the Census of India and reports of differnet decades with the aim to measure the effect and rate of socio-economic changes during the post-Independence period.

(b) The major part of the study area Distt. Basti (U.P.) lies in the *Tarai* region of Uttar Pradesh which is one of the most backward district of the state and was under effective control and inhabited by different Rajput clan. For an analysis of the processes and pattern of organizational system and problems of ecodevelopment, an operational method is adopted.

(c) Strategies and prospects for rural social development will be projected on the result of an intensive field work.

Regional Personality

The study area distt. Basti (U.P.) is located between 26°23' to 27°30'N latitude and 82°17' to 83°30' E longitude in the middle part of the middle Ganga plain. It is a backward and highly populated (35.78 lac) with 6929 habited villages.

Transformation of Joint Family System

Though joint family system in the villages of this area was more effective since Vadic period and was functioning in an organizational system. But due to some of its weakness today it is disorganizing. This disorganizational trend may be good or bad we like or dislike it, but today in this modernizing age the disorganization of joint family system can not be checked. There are different reasons of joint family disorganisation in this area, for example —

(1) Industrial revolution
(2) Development of means of transportation
(3) Growth of Population
(4) Western culture and education
(5) Attitude of individualism
(6) Ideology of freedom and equality
(7) Family conflict and poverty.

These are common factors of family disorganization in the rural area. After Independence of the country traditional socio-economic system has been transformed in different ways. The Family disorganizational pattern is different among the social groups (Table 33.1).

The cases of family disorganization, family conflict and sepration of family is higher (80.40%) in Scheduled and Backward Caste (75.94%) than forward caste (60.13%). But the economic development is highest (98.03%) in forward and Backward Caste (88.77%) than lower caste (41.13%). (Table 33.2).

Table 33.1: Family Structure

(Percentage)

Social Group	PresentFamily structure		What should be the present family structure Collection of views	
	Joint	Isolated	Joint	Isolated
1. Forward Caste	84.97	15.03	67.32	32.68
2. Backward Caste	81.28	18.72	71.12	28.28
3. Scheduled Caste	54.61	45.39	43.26	56.74
Total in study Area	74.63	25.37	61.74	38.26

Table 33.2: Family Sepration and Economic Development

(Percentage)

Social Group	Sepration since last 30 years		Economic Development after Independence	
	Seprated	Not Seprated	Developed their Economy	Not Developed their Economy
1. Forward cast	60.13	39.87	98.03	1.93
2. Backward cast	75.94	24.06	88.77	12.23
3. Scheduled cast	84.40	15.60	41.13	58.87
Total in study Area	73.39	26.61	77.75	22.25

Source : Based on field study.

Transformation of Jajmani System

Jajmani system is an importment labour division system in rural India. There are some expectation of special social services from few particular caste for other groups of the society. The people belonging barber, washerman, brahmin (*Purohit*) etc. castes are bound to provide their services to families from which they are related since a long time on the basis of exchanging services for some gifts, like grain, and other goods. But due to improvment in literacy and socio-economic conditions of the rural family the traditional *Jajmani* system is also reducing. (Table 33.3 and 33.4).

Table 33.3: Present Situation of Traditional Jajmani System

(Percentage)

Social Groups under which the servicer are working		Caste		Jajmani System		Jajmani System is either increasing or decreasing	
		Working	Not working	Working	Not woking	Increas-ing	Decreas ing
1.	F.C.	90.20	9.8	92.16	7.84	37.9	62.10
2.	B.C.	81.82	18.18	77.00	23.00	31.02	68.98
3.	S.C.	41.13	58.87	39.71	60.29	17.73	82.27
	Total	72.55	27.45	70.90	29.10	29.31	70.69

Source : Based on field study.

Table 33.4: Reason of Leaving Jajmani System of Some Castes

(Percentage)

Reason	Barber	Washerman
Feeling of complexes	4.55	3.57
Education	37.88	45.00
Jajmani himselves left the services of these groups due to unskilled work	28.03	14.29
Working on cash wages	28.78	31.42

Now the cast relating jajmani system are establishing their work at nearest town or any road crossing or they are migrating to the cities. The old rate of goods barter is not applicable now, so that barber and washerman are providing their services on cash on their shops of saloon or pressing cloths.

The Table 33.5 shows that traditional mutual co-operation and other characteristics are decreasing (55.1%) while internal conflict, castism, co-operative works in villages of the study area are decreasing rapidly.

Attitude of 98.7 per cent of the population of the study area is in the favour of family planning and they are adopting different means of birth control and now the rural population also visit to hospital for their treatment.

TABLE 33.5: Transformated Rural Social Environment

(Percentages)

Mutual Co-operation		Internal conflict		Cases		Castism		Co-operative Attitude	
Incr.	Decr.	Incr.	Decr.	Incr.	Decr.	Incr.	Decr.	Incr.	Decr.
44.9	55.1	75.89	24.11	51.14	48.86	74	26	41.79	58.21

Rural Living Standard as an Index of Social Transformation

The improvement in living standard is higher in forward (100%) and backward (96.24%) caste in comparison to lower castes. It is notable that each and every group member of the society of the study area, whose living standard has been improved has built either *pucka* house or purchased cycle, watches, radio, scooter, agricultural land etc. Listening of radio and television has also influenced in the transforming of socio-economic life of the rural people.

Though, the socio-economic status is transforming in the villages of this area on one side, but below mentioned factors are disorganizing the social environment of the village life -

(a) Consolidation scheme,
(b) Partism due to castism,
(c) Election of village Pradhan,
(d) Illiteracy,
(e) Literacy,
(f) Social injustification,
(g) Family disorganization,
(h) Rural conflict or communal misunderstanding, and
(i) unequal distribution of land and income.

Thus these changes in social system and living standard of people show glimpses of social transformation.

THIRTY-FOUR

Geography of Violent Crimes of the Lower Chambal Basin

S.S. KATARE

Violent Crimes have been a feature of North-India. An analysis of decennary average of dacoity cases reported during 1969-78 reveals that high incidence (1200to 5300) is found in Uttar Pradesh, Bihar and West Bengal. Moderate incidence (250 to 500) is found in Maharashtra, Madhya Pradesh and Assam. Modest incidence (100 to 250) is found in Andhra Ptadesh, Gujarat. Karnataka, Orissa and Rajasthan. Low incidence (Below 100) is found in the remaining parts of the country (Katare,1981,p. 155).

A comparision reveals that violent crimes are much higher in North-Central States, than in the selected southern States, rates for kidnapping, dacoity and robbery are specially high.

Table 34.1: Violent Crimes per 10,000 People in 1971

Sates	Total crime	Murder	Homicide not amt. to murder	Rape	Kidnap-ping and Abduction	Dacoi--ty	Rob-bery
North-Central							
Uttar-Pradesh	26.63	.40	.11	.07	.35	.68	1.13
Madhya-Pradesh	21.13	.41	.00	.10	.22	.10	.25
Southern-States							
Kerala	13.88	.20	.00	.o2	.03	.02	.06
Tamilnadu	144.43	.20	.00	.01	.05	.00	.03

Source: Dutta, Noble and Singh, 1979, p.105.

Violent crimes have risen in the northern districts of Madhya Pradesh during 1957-1971 (Table 34.1).

Table 34.2: Average Figures for Five Years

Offences	1957 to 1961	1961 to 1966	1967 to '71
Murders	134	73	64
Dacoities	208	130	91
Kidnappings	71	171	201

Source: P.H.Q. Police Records

An Analysis of the above data reveals that the cases of dacoities have shown a downward trend while kidnappings have shown an upward trend. The cases of murders have fallen because they create hatred among the people and call for a strong action of the government. Thus,with the passage of time mode of operation of dacoits have changed.

Spatial Patterns of Violent Crimes in the Chambal Basin

Terrain governs the incidence of violent crimes in the lower Chambal basin. Spatial patterns of crimes confirm the regional occurrences. Murder, dacoity and kidnapping are more rural than other crimes. Violent crimes are mainly concentrated in the transitional lowlands. The Chambal basin is full of ravines with labrinthine gullies and deep gorges, which provide most safe hideouts and opportunities for carrying out a guerrilla warfare. The luxuriant forests, jungle terrain and the Khohs of the Vindhyan hills are ideally suited to the secret movements of the gangs and provide temporary suitable shelter. The plateau region does not attract the gangs for the obvious reason that the nature of topography is such as to afford no hiding places of convenient movement.

A characteristic spatial pattern observed has been mentioned as under:

The Ravine Belts Serve as a Habitat to the Criminals

The ravine belts of the lower Chambal, the Yamuna and the Pahuj rivers have been a refuge and a notorious habitat of the dacoits and all types of criminals. This region is a contact zone of the older landmass of the peninsular India and the vast alluvial Gangetic plains of Northern India. It is an open gateway to the Gangetic plains from the highlands of the Vindhyas many rivers have their origin in the Vindhyas and flow through this region and have eroded soils.

The rivers of this region, flow parallel to each other and are connected with each other by streams, pastures and woodlands forming a vast area for criminal avtivities. These rivers are fordable during summer and winter. The gangs can cross over from one part to another. A great strech of these rivers and their tributaries provides safer routes and the ravines provide short-cuts to reach their destinations. Means of transport and communication are negligible or sparase, isolating it from other parts of the country. The dacoits have created an institution of harbourers, supporters and helpers all along these ravine belts.

The concentration of violent crimes is higher at the confluence of rivers, along the ravine belts and forests and on the common district and state boundaries. The inhabitant of the badlands are ill fed, ill clothed, ill housed and illiterate as they are isolated and away from the civilizing influence of the modern society. Thus, these ravine belts serve as the life lines to the dacoits. During monsoons, deep ravines turns into rivulets and interior parts of the lowlands become inaccessible.

The Great Ravine Belt of the Sindh, the Pahuj, the Vaisali, the Kunwari and the Chambal Rivers

At the conflunce of these rivers, there lies a vast and most confusing ravine zone, where higher concentratoin of violent crimes is found. To the south of it, lies the Bharkua highland. The Pahuj, the Kunwari and the Sindh rivers provide the districts of Jalaun. Bhind, Gwalior, Jhansi, Datia, Etawah and Morena with common natural boundaries. It is habitat of warlike clans of thakurs like Parihars, Bhadorias and Tomars.

The Ravine Belts of the Kunwari and the Asan

This belt stretches more than one hundred miles continuously having a width of the one mile all along the river banks before meeting the Great Ravine Belt. It is a life line for dacoits and a breeding ground of dacoits. The violent crimes occur along these rivers and their subsidiary streams. It suffers from great caste prejudices.

The Ravine Belt of the Chambal River

The Chambal has created a confusing belt of ravines over five miles in width, running its whole length along its bank in Morena and Bhind district. The highlands of Sheopur and Sabalgarh meet this belt from the south and the highlands of Dholpur and Karauli from the north and form a bottleneck in the Western part of Morena district. While in the eastern part of Morena, Bhind, Etawah and Jalaun districts, the ravine belts of the Yamuna and the Kunwari run almost parallel whose subsidiary streams come closer. At the confluence of these rivers, there is a vast belt of ravines.

Violent crimes are concentrated on the head of ravines and along the forests, but deeper gorges of ravines are free from crimes in the Chambal belt between Dholpur-Karauli highland and Sheopur-Sabhalgrah highlands. The Chambal ravine belt between the Yamuna and the Kunwari rivers is badly affected by crimes as the ravine belts come closer, making the area completely isolated and insecure.

The Ravine Belt of the Pahuji River

The concentration of violent crimes is found along the Pahuj river in Bhind district.

The Transitional Lowlands Serve Sustenance to Criminals

The transitional lowlands lying between various river belts serve as a means of sustenance to the dacoits. Violent crimes are highly concentrated in such lowlands. The vast and prosperous transitional lowlands are less affected by violent crimes, while the smaller and isolated transitional lowlands are highly affected by violent crimes and they provide safe ground for the sustenance of the criminals.

(1) The transitional lowlands of the Kunwari and the Asan rivers is a highly dacoity infested zone. The low land of Vijaipur is highly infested as it is inhabited by Thakur,

Kachhis and Ahir communities. But in Jora-Sihonia part, the violent crimes are concentrated along the river belts and the forests.

(2) The transitional lowlands of the lower Chambal and the lower Kunwari rivers provide an ideal and safe ground for the criminal activities of dacoits. The Chambal and the Yamuna rivers have isolated them from the rest of the country.

(3) *The lowlands of Gwalior-Gird*: Violent crimes are concentrated along the Sankh, the Morar, the Karu and the Vaisali rivers and along the forests. It is inhabited by Gujars.

(4) *The lowlands of Tomarghar*: The violent crimes are found along the belts of the Kunwari and the Chambal rivers. The dacoity menace decreases with the increasing distance of the ravine belts. It is inhabited by Tomars who are most powerful and no gang can survive against their will.

(5) *The lowlands of Bhind*: The occurrence of violent crimes are less because of the high accessibility, good economy, urban influence and bigger settlements.

(6) *The lowlands of the Pahuj and the Sindh rivers:* The occurrence of violent crimes is limited to the ravine belts. The distance from the ravine belts determine the occurrence.

(7) *The lowland of Sikarwari*: Being isolated, it has been a breeding place of dacoits. It is inhabited by Sikarwars, Gujars and Chamars. It is poor and inaccessible.

(8) *The lowlands of the East Parbati and the Sindh rivers*: It is prosperous zone. Dacoits commit offences here only when they are forced to stay in the nearby highlands. Crimes are limited along the rivers and forests.

(9) *The lowland of the Parbati River*: The frequency of violent crimes is quite less in this zone. Only dacoities take place at great intervals.

The Vindhyan Highlands as a Sheltering Region

The Vindhyan highlands are thick and bushy and there are various Khohs and waterpoints in them. The settlements are sparse, isolated and inhabited by the aboriginals. The gangs take shelter in this region.

(1) *The highlands of Kandhar and Singhpur*: It is a narrow belt of fifteen miles. Active gang activity is found only when gangas pass through this narrow belt.

(2) *The highlands of Gwalior-Gird:* It is full of dense and

bushy forests and numerous Khohs abound here. It is a narrow belt of forest with 15 to 20 miles in width. Active gang movement is found here while they pass through it from Pahargarh forest to the Asan river.

(3) *The highlands of Sheopur and Pahargarh*: It is full of dense forests, deep Khohs and rugged terrain. It is completely isolated. It is connected with the lowlands by deep valleys. The gangs movement is found here when they move through the adjoining river valleys.

The Datia Plateau

It lies between the lowlands of the Sindh and the Pahuj, and hence serves as a gateway to the gangs. It is rarely visited by gangs as no natural shelter occurs here.

The crimes reality is immensely varied and complex. In order to understand its true nature, it is imperative to understand i.e., nature of physical environment and nature of man. The nature of man depends upon his roots in the specific ordering of his society. His nature is what his culture conditions to be. An understanding to the cultural presuppositions of a people is what is involved understanding their social context and the individuals placed in it. An investigation into the natural environment and the social traditions of the lower Chambal basin has been attempted.

The rivers have been the cradle of civilization but paradoxically enough the Chambal has been a breeding ground of criminals. Violent crimes have been the permanent features of the valley with a long standing history of violence. It has been the march zone of Indian history, across which armies of conquest have swept and within which diverse cultures have clashed (Dutt, Noble and Singh, 1979, p. 11). It has presented a scenario of great political upheavals, worst social disorders and violent criminal activities. The extremist formations like the maralldars, the rebels, Pindaries, Thugs, dacoits and revolutionaries have cropped up time and again since 1019 A.D. Thus, there have always been gradations amongst these evildoers, each class in turn despising the next beneath it in the criminal scale (Cox, 1925, p. 31). These social and political conflicts have influenced the life of the inhabitants and each limited the other in turn. The outcome thereof has been the criminalization of the Chambal basin.

The lower Chambal basin, lying between the Gangetic Plain and the Peninsular tableland, extends from 25° 28' N to 28° 52'N of latitude and 78° 28' E to 79° 7'E of longitude. It covers Bhind, Morena, Gwalior, Shivpuri and Datia of Madhya Pradesh; Agra, Etawah, Mainpuri, Jalaun and Jhansi of Uttar Pradesh and sub-division of Dholpur in Bharatpur, district, Karauli in Madhopur district and Shahabad in Kota district of Rajasthan. The region is sharply bounded by the Vindhyan scarps. Mainly, there are two scarped features, facing towards the East over Bundelkhand and towards the North-West flanking the left bank of the Chambal. A scraped block occupies the Tahsils of Dholpur and Karauli (Rajasthan). The lower Chambal, occupying a strike valley, cuts across the scarps, and is superimposed on them. Gullying along the lower Chambal and its tributaries suggest a slight recent rejuvenation.

The superficial alluvial deposits, covering the funnel of the lower Chambal basin, form an outlying and marginal portion of the Gangetic plains. Presumably, the Chambal and its tributaries have smoothered the old rugged surface of the Peninsular Foreland and have deposited recent alluvium. The prevailing formation is some form of sandy clay. The dominant features of relief are flood plain bluffs and belt of ravines and badlands formed by gully erosion. The terrain is criss-crossed by a mass of deep ravines of the Chambal, the Yamuna and the Pahuj. They have formed a funnel shaped region isolating it from the rest of the country.

Most of the soils of this region are formed by river deposits, which belong mainly to the Indo-Gangetic alluvium. The surface texture grades into sandy loam to loam and clay-loam to clay. These soils are pale brown to yellowish brown and dark grey brown to dark brown. Reddish brown soils are generally found along the scarplands. There are gravelly clays and are slightly alkaline. Soil erosion is very grave. The severely gullied and ravined land along the river courses show how the uncontrolled water condition coming from the upstrean has thrown large areas out of cultivation. It is estimated that 1.38 lakh hectares of land in Rajasthan, 1.13 lakh hectares in U.P. and 1.5 lakhs hectares in M.P. are under the ravines in this region.

The summer is hot, dry and scorching. The winter is mild. The monsoons are unreliable. The rainfall is maximum during the rainy season. However, slight rainfall occurs during the winter season. The annual average rainfall is 30 inches. The rainfall is highly variable and droughts and dearths are frequent. The region is worse off than the arid North-West India. The semi-arid conditions prevail here.

The hilly tracts are covered with forests of semi-Zerophytic variety. Open scrub is confined to riverine tracts. Vegetation is scanty on the alluvial deposits and rare in the arable lands. Grasses are confined to hills, waterbunds and barren lands.

It is a historical region where anarchy prevailed and rule of law defied successfully throughout its history. The behaviour of individuals and personality of the society got shaped under these circumstances. Usual loot and robbery have been the way of life. The warrior clans forming the great bulk of the population adopted plunder as a means of their livelihood due to the measure for a quick and easy acquisition of money and material by force. Hamilton (1920, p. 372) mentions that the Jats, Gujars, Rajputs, Aheers, Lodhas, Pathans, Mewaties, Meenas, Buddicks, Thugs, Cozauks, Chumas, Khaukrobes, had been from time immemorial addicted to open and secret plunder, it is not to be wondered that criminal offences are not wholly eradicated. Thus, age old traditions hardly die as they became a part of their specific culture.

The population of dacoity infested areas in Madhya Pradesh is roughly 54.52 lakhs. Eighty-five per cent of this population lives in villages. The density of population in this areas is 196 persons per square miles. The percentage of literacy is 10.27 and that of employment 46.39. The bulk of population is engaged in cultivation either as owner of land or as agricultural labour. The total population of the five district of Uttar Pradesh exposed to dacoity menace is 60 lakhs. The density of population in this area is 542 persons per sq.mile. The percentage of literacy and employment are 22.09 and 35.75 respectively. In Rajasthan, the population of dacoity infested areas is roughly 29.42 lakhs. Eighty-five per cent of the population lives in villages. The density of population is 245 persons per sq.mile. The percentages of literacy and employment are 15.55 and 46.37, respectively. There is no noticeable backwardness in this region as compared to other regions of India.

The male-female ratio of northern district of M.P. shows

that women fall short of man. Female figures per thousand males are 866 Gwalior, 854 Bhind, 842 Morena, 889 Shivpuri and 895 Datia. It has led to moral degeneration in the society. People do not observe any code in having sexual intercourse with women of any caste and creed. Sexual offences against women of higher castes are not tolerated and avenged by murdering the culprit.

The social organization is based on Hindu Varna system, in which the Brahmins and Thakurs are placed superior. Other castes like *Baniya*, Rajput, Kachhi, Ahir, Kurmi, Kunbi, Lodhas, Kayastha, Dhobi, Teli, Kumhar, Chamar, Basore are placed below them. Other depressed castes are Bagri, Balai, Beria, Bhangi, Kanjar, Khatik, Koli, Barar and Bargonda and the prominent aboriginal tribes are the Gujars, Kirars, Mainas, Kols and Bhils. A minor community of Mohammadans like Sheikhs and Pathans also reside in the basin. There are various clans of Rajputs like the Madas of Sawai Madhopur, Pawars of Sheopur, Sikarwars of Sikarwari, Tomars of Tomarghar, Gujars of Gujarghar, Bhadorias of Bhadawar, Bhind, Bah and Etawah, Chouhans of Kacchwai, Sagar and Mainpuri, the Kacchwahas of the Asan lowlands and the Parihars of Sahson and Sandaus Parganas of Etawah. These clans trace their descent from the ancestors who were once the ruling families of Delhi, Rajasthan and Central India. They are too proud of their heritage. It has been a refuge for the political fugitives. The Moghuls could never subdue them. These local Chiefs were entrusted with revenue collecting rights. It was a symbol of prestige for them. The Britishers left the maintenance of law and order to these local rulers. After Independence, these powerful chiefs and rulers were divested of their ruling rights. These partial clans were recruited in the army and police but it has been discontinued later, which has deplated their economy further. It led to the weakening of the authority of the social heads and the respect they formerly commanded.

The caste system is deeply ingrained. The unity of caste, clans and groups produced rivalries and ill feelings. Hostality and hatred inflame passions and violence. The lower caste groups are economically, socially and politically in the ascendent and on the offensive, they are bursting with brashness of the newly prosperous and newly assertive gains in perpetuity to advance further. Each caste remains isolated from the rest and has little affected by change. Thus, the social fabric of society has been fragmented and breaking apart. Usually, cases of disputes arise over the possession of land. Recourse to legal procedure is lengthy. Uneducated people hardly wait for such a justice. They settle their disputes by force. Those committing such acts take to ravines and become outlaws (Dubey, p.3).

Social fragmentation into castes, creeds, clans and groups is found within limits. A broad unity is observed in customs, practices, beliefs and faiths. Majority of people follow Hindu religion. They order their individual life by following *Dharmic* tradition. Although at the same time, they follow social tradition at a different level. Thus divergent views prevail in the masses regarding contradiction appearing in these two approaches.

The social customs and beliefs are medievel and feudal. The family is an important social and economic unit. It serves not only to satisfy the biological instincts of the sex and perpetuation of race but also functions as an important unit in the quest for livelihood. It conserves and transmits social customs and traditions, ideals and values to the succeeding generations. In the economic pursuits all the members of the family contribute all they can and the Head of the Family looks after the material needs of its members. Joint family provides security. The head of the family rules with strictness and unquestioned obedience. Elders are respected in hierarchial order. The social functions are important obligations. Family cohesiveness and consciousness is strong. Male children are desired more than the female ones because they bring honour to the family. The social organisation is idential throughout the valley.

The village is an important social unit and consists of a number of families. The homesteads are clustered together in a locality. The number of families inhabiting the villages varies considerably from one place to another. The residents of these villages constitute a recognisable local group. The land area of every village is well defined and there are several sizes of villages. Habitation is clustered in the transitional lowlands. The majority of villages are situated close to the ravines or at spots where the rivers overlook them. Water requirements compel the people to reside on the river banks. Each village had council of elders, which was presided over by the village headman. Now-a-days, Gram Panchayats have been formed according to the Panchayat Act. Each village has its own member to represent it. These Gram Panchayats have become not bed of politics, caste rivalries and troubles, defeating the purpose of their existence. Local politicians seek help of the dacoits in securing votes during elections and in return they give protection and material help. Local elections are fought on caste basis and the gangs of their own cast supoort their respective caste candidates as caste groups provide shelter and protection to the dacoits. Political leaders patronise dacoits to maintain their hold in the society.

Summary

Crime pattern shows that violent crimes have been a nature of nothern India. The lower Chambal basin has been antisocial region where primitive formations have taken roots. The natural environment and social setting have created favourable conditions for the origin, growth and development of criminal gangs and, hence, it has a long-standing history of violence.

Bibliography

Agarwal, P.C. & Z.T. Khan (1983). "Spatial Analysis of the Levels of Regional Development in M.P.", pp 315-24 in P. Pandey (ed.), *Modern Geographical Trends*, New Delhi: Today and Tomorrow. (5)

Ahmed, Nafis (1975). *A New Economic Geography of Bangladesh*, Vikas Publishing House Pvt. Ltd., New Delhi (8).

Alam, S.M. (1963). "Commerical Structure of the Cities of Hyderabad and Secunderabad", *Journal of the Osmania University, Arts, Commerce, Law & Education*, I, pp.1-10, Hyderabad (17).

Aperyan, V. (1979). *Manpower, Resources and Population under Socilaism*, Progress Publisher, Moscow, (28).

Audholia, B.S. and R.C. Choubey (1967). "Madhya Pradesh" in Kapoor, T.N. (ed.), *Industiral Development in the States of India*, p. 247 (10).

Babu, C.M. (1979). *Sugarcane*, Indian Press Pvt. Ltd., New Delhi (8).

Bagchi, R. and K.N. Mukherjee, (1983). *Diagnostic Survey of West Bengal (North)*, 0.60, Calcutta, Department of Geography, University of Calcutta (4).

Batra, V.P. (1978). *The Economy of Human Resources*, B.R. Publishing Corporation, Delhi (29).

Baquee, A.H.M.A. (1980). "A Spatio-temporal Analysis of Rural Markets in Dacca district", *Oriental Geographer*, January and July, 1975 and 1976, 52-61, Dhaka, Bangladesh (13).

Berry, B.J.L. (1967). *Geography of Market Centres and Retail Distribution*, p. 62, Englewood Cliffs, N.J. Prentice Hall (17).

Bhatnagar, P.P. (1965). "Special Report on Kanpur City", *Census of India - 1961, Vol. XV, Uttar Pradesh, Part X*, p.4, Govt. Printing Press, Allahabad (17).

Bromley, R.J. (1973). "The Spatial Behaviour and Temporal Synchronisation of Periodic Markets", *Swansea Geographer,* Vol. 2 pp. 15-25 (23).

Chang, H.T. (1977). "Integrated Rural Devleopment in 'Rural Development Technology. An Integrated Approach". *Proceedings of International Conference A.I.T. Bangkok* (ed.) G. Singh, J.H. de Geod, pp. 10-11 (12).

Chaturvedi, B. (1989). "Understanding India — Key to Reform of Society", *Times of India,* Dec. 24, New Delhi (33).

Choubey, R.N. (1988). *Population and Food Supply in Uttar Pradesh.* Unpublished Ph.D. Thesis, Dr. H.S. Gour University, Sagar, India (2).

Christaller, W.C. (1933). "Dieztralen Otre in Suddentschland". Translated by Buskin, C.W. (1966), *Central Places in Southern Germany,* Prentice Hall, Englewood Cliffs New Jersey, USA (13, 20).

Clarke, P.J. and A.C. Evans, (1954). "Distance of Nearest Neighbour as a Measure of Spatial Relationship", *Ecology,* 85, pp. 445-46 (14).

Clark, W.A.V. (1968). "Consumer Travel Patterns and the Concept of Range", *Annals of the Association of American Geographers,* Vol. 58, p. 396 (17).

Cox, E.C.B. (1925). *Police and Crime in India,* Stanley Paul & Co., London (33).

Dacey, M.F. (1960). "The Spacing of River Towns", *Annals of Association of American Geographers,* 50, pp. 59-61, and a note on the derivation of nearest neighbour distance, *Journal of Regional Science,* 2, 1960, pp. 81-87 (22).

Das, A.K. and T. Benerjee, (1984). "Betal vis-a-vis Paddy", in Roy S.K. *et al., Proceedings of the National Workshop on Betelvine,* Calcutta, Agricultural Society of India (19).

Dasgupta, B. & Morris Jones, W.H. (1975) *Patterns and Trends in Indian Politics.* Allied Pub. New Delhi.

Datta, T.N. (1980). "Regional Variations in the Level of Development of Madhya Pradesh", *Geographical Review of India,* Vo. 42, No. 3, p. 254 (5).

De, N.K. (1984). *Measurring Land Potentials in Developing Countries,* The University of Burdwan, Burdwan (7).

Dharam Narain (1965). *Impact of Price Movement on Areas Under Selected Crops in India, 1900-1939,* Cambridge University Press, New Delhi (3).

Dharam Narain, (1988). *Studies on Indian Agriculture,* ed. by

K.N. Ray, Amartya Sen, C.H. Hanumantha Rao, Oxford Press, New Delhi (3).

Dixit, R.S. (1979). *Market Centres and their Spatial Development in the Umland of Kanpur*, Unpublished D.Phil. Thesis, Allahabad University, Department of Geography (19).

Dixit, R.S. (1983). "Spatial Distribution of Market Centres in the Umland of Kanpur Metropolis", *Geographical Review of India.*, Vol. 45, No. 1, March, 39-54, Calcutta, India (13).

Dixit, R.S. (1984). "Market Cycles: The Case of the Bundlekhand Region", *Indian Journal of Marketing Geography*, Vol. 2, 102-105, Gorakhpur, India (13).

Dixit, R.S. (1984a). *Spatial Organisation of Market Centrs in Hamirpur Disrict, U.P. (India)*, Research Project Report, New Delhi, Indian Council of Social Science Research (19).

Dixit, R.S. (1984b). *Market Centres and their Spatial Development in the Umland of Kanpur*, Allahabad, Kitab Mahal (19).

Dixit, R.S. (1988). *Spatial Organization of Market Centres*, Pointer Publishers, Jaipur (19).

Dixit, R.S. (1989a). *Periodic Marketing in an Urban Environment, Mahoba (U.P.), India— A Study in 'Geography of Commercial Activities'*, Research Project Report, University Grants Commission, New Delhi (19).

Dixit, R.S. (1989b). "Consumer Change - Attitude and Behaviour: The Case of a Developing Economy, Mahoba, U.P. (India)", in Howarh, E.B. (ed.), Papers on Retail Development and Consumer Behaviour, *Proceedings of the Oxford Symposium*, Oxford, Trade and Society Collection (19).

Dixit, R.S. (1990). "Betel Leaf Chewing in Mahoba (U.P.)", *The Deccan Geographer*, XXVIII, June, (19).

Dube, R.S. (1989). *Population Pressure and Agrarian Change*, Jaipur: Rawat Publishers, (2).

Dube, R.S. and R.P. Mishra (1984). "Evaluation of Foodgrain Availability in India", *Asian Geographer*, Vol. 3(1) (2).

Dube, R.S. (1987). *Agricultural Geography: Issues and Applications*, New Delhi, Gyan Publishing House.

Dubey, K.C. (Unpublished). "A Study of the Dacoits of the Chambal Valley of Agra Region", Paper presented in the *5th World Congress of Psychiatry*, Mexico (34).

Dutt, A.K., A.G. Noble, and S. Singh, (1979). "Is There A North-Central Sub-Culture of Violence in India", *The National Geographical Journal of India*, Vol.XXV, Part 2, June, B.H.U., Varanasi (34).

Dutt, A.K. and G. Venugopal, (1983). "Spatial Patterns of Crime Among Indian Cities", *Geoforum*, Vol. 14, No.2, Pergamen Press Ltd (34).

Fagerlund, V.G. and R.H.T. Smith, (1970). "A Preliminary Map of Market Periodicity in Ghana", *Journal of Developing Areas*, Vol.4 April, 333-348 (13).

Gedam, D.A. (1980). "Hierarchy of Periodic Market Centres in the Wardha Valley of Maharashtra", *Indian journal of Landscape System*, Vol.3, No.1 and 2 September, 27-38, Calcutta, India (13).

Ghosh, B.N. (1985). *Fundamentals of Population Geography*, Sterling Publishers Pvt. Ltd., New Delhi (29).

Giles, B.D. (1951). *Agriculture and Price Mechanism*, ed. by T. Wilson and P.W.S. Andrews, Oxford Press, New Delhi (3).

Gormsen, E. (1985). "Role of Market Places in Developing Countries" in '*Agricultural Markets in Semiarid Tropics*', Proceedings of Internation workshop held at I.C.R.I.S.A.T. Centre, Patencheru, Hyderabad, India, 1983, pp. 22-28, (15).

Hamilton, Walter (1920). (Reprint-1971) *Description of Hindostan and the Adjacent Countries*, Vol.I, Oriental Publishers, New Delhi, (34).

Harbison, F.H. and Charles A. Myers, (1964). *Education, Manpower and Economic Growth: Strategies of Human Resources Development*, McGraw Hill Book Company, New York, (29).

Harriss, B. (1974). The Role of Punjab Wheat Markets on Growth Centres, *Geographical Journal*, 140, pp. 52-71, (15).

Hay, A.M. (1971). "Notes on the Economic Basis for Periodic Marketing in Developing Countries", *Geograpical Analysis*, pp. 393-410, (28).

Hill, P. and R.H.T. Smith, (1972). "The Spatial and Temporal Synchronization of Periodic Markets: Evidences from Four Emirates in Northern Nigeria", *Economic Geography*, Vol-48, July, 345-355, (13).

Jain, A.K. (1987). *Marketing in an Agricultural Region : A*

Geographical Study of Periodic Markets in Vidisha Plateau, M.P., Unpublished. Ph.D. Thesis, Dr. H.S. Gour University, Sagar, (23).

Jain, C.K. (1988). *Patterns of Agricultural Development in Madhya Pradesh*, New Delhi, Northern Book Centre, (2).

Jaysawal, H. (1968). "Achieving Higher Oil Seeds and Pulses Production", *Yojana*, Vol.31, No.24 (4).

John, P.V. (1968). *Some Aspects of the Structure of Indian Agricultural Economy*, 1947-48 to 1961-62, Asia Publishing House, New Delhi (3).

Johnson, E.A.J. (1970). *The Organization of Space in Developing Countries*, Harvard University, Press, p. 3, (15).

Johnson, E.A.J. (1965). *Market Towns and Spatial Development in India*, National Council of Applied Economic Research, New Delhi, p. 60, (15).

Katare, S.S. (1981). "A Gloomy Decade of Dacoity in India", *Indian Journal of Criminology*, Vol.9, No.2, July, Madras, (34).

Katare, S.S. (1968). *Patterns of Dacoity in Madhya Pradesh*, Ph.D. Thesis, Accepted by University of Sagar, Sagar, (34).

Kothari, V.N. (1965). "Rapporteur, Investment in Human Resources", *Papers read at the Indian Economic Conference, Banaras*, Popular Prakashan, Bombay, (29).

Kulkarni, G.S. & A.P. Kulkarni, (1973). "Some Aspects of the Urban Infrastructure in Municipal Towns of Maharashtra", *Urban Geography in Developing Countries*, ed., R.L. Singh, (24).

Lal, V.N. (1986). "Role of Commercial Activities in a Rural Market: A Case Study of Raipur Market in Ghazipur District", in Shrivastava, V.K. (Ed.), *Commercial Activities and Rural Development in South Asia*, Concept Publishing Company, New Delhi, (25).

Lohani, B.N. (1980). "Environmental Impacts of Rural Transformation Activities and that Assessment in R.H.T. in World Forontiers", *National Geographical Society of India*, Varanasi, Singh, R.L. (ed.) p. 68, (32).

Majumdar, D.N. (1962). *Social Contours of an Indian City*, p.42, Bombay, India Publishing House, (17).

Mazumdar, R.C. (1960). *The History and Culture of Indian People*, Vol.I, Calcutta, (25).

Mishra, S.N. *et al.*, (1982). *The Tribal Voting Behaviour: A Case Study of Bihar Tribes*. Concept Publishing, New Delhi.

Misra, R.P. and R.S. Dube, (1984). *Nutritional Availability Patterns in Madhya Pradesh,* (2).

Misra, R.P. (1989). *Population and Food Supply in Madhya Pradesh,* Northern Book Centre, New Delhi, (2).

Misra, R.P. *et al.* (1974). *Regional Development Planning in India,* Vikas Publishing House, Delhi, pp. 140-41, (26).

Misra, V.C. & S.K. Shukla, (1980). "Regional Disparities of Industrialisation in Madhya Pradesh", p. 139, *Uttar Bharat Bhoogol Patrika,* Vol.16, No.2, (11).

Mishra, T.K. (1987). "On Streamlining Agricultural Marketing", *Yojana,* Vol.31, No.20 (November 1-14), pp.10-14, (20).

Moseman, A.H. (1964). *Agricultural Sciences for the Developing Nations,* Radha Krishna Prakashan, Delhi, (29).

Moseley, M.J. (1974). *Growth Centres in Spaial Planning,* Pergaman Press, Oxford, (26).

Mukerji, A.B. (1988). "Periodic Markets of India: Characteristics and Developmental Implications", in V.K. Shrivastava, ed., *Commercial Activities and Rural Development in South Asia,* Concept Publishing Company, New Delhi, (28).

Mukerji, R.K. (1938). *The Changing Face of Bengal,* Calcutta, (25, 35).

Murdie, R. (1965). "Cultural Differences in Consumer Travel", *Economic Geography,* Vol.41, pp.211-33, (17).

Nath, V. (1982). *Marketing and Social Structure in Awadh Plain (North),* Ph.D. Thesis, Gorakhpur University, (unpublished), (22,25).

Naik, D.N. and S.C. Patnaik, (1987). "Study of Marketing of Potato in Puri District of Orissa", *Agricultural Marketing,* (April-June). pp.19-24, (20).

Pantulu, V.R. (1967). "A Plan for Development of Fishing Industry in Sundarbans", *C.I.F.R.I.,* Barrackpore, West Bengal, (10).

Polly Hill (1966). "Notes on Traditional Market Authority and Market Periodicity in West Africa", *Journal of African History,* pp.295-311, (28).

Potter, D. (1955). 'The Bazar Merchant' in *Social Forces in the Middle East,* Ithaca, N.Y., (17).

Raza, Moonis. *Levels of Regional Development in India,* p.8, (11).

Ramachandran, H. (1982). *Behaviour in Space,* Concept Publishing House, New Delhi, pp.1, 2, 15, (18).

Ramachandran, H. (1980). *Village Clusters and Rural Development*. Concept Publishing Company, New Delhi, (26)

Ram Surat (1986). *Geography of Wholesaling: A Case Study of Agricultural Mandis of Eastern U.P.*, Unpublished Ph.D. Thesis, Department of Geography, University of Gorakhpur, Gorakhpur, (14).

Rao, V.N. (1980). *Rural Development and Village Perspective for Planning for Development*, Sterling, New Delhi, (26).

Rao, V.K.R.V. (1977). "Some Neglected Factors in Integrated Rural Development", XVI, Convocation Address, Indian Agricultual Research Institute, New Delhi, January, (26).

Ray, D.M. (1986). "Cultural Differences in Consumer Travel Pattern Behaviour in Eastern Ontario", *Annals of the Associaton of American Geographers*, Vol.58, p.396, (17).

Rejuan, H.B. (1981). *Regional Variation of Sugarcane Yield and Sucrose Recovery in Bangladesh*, M.Sc. Thesis, D.U. Dhaka, (8).

Riddell, J.B. (1974). Periodic Markets in Sierra Leone, *Annals of the Association of American Geographers*, Vol.64, pp.541-548, (15).

Roychowdhury, K.C. (1964). "Prospect of Better Utilization of Goran and Mangrove Barks from Sundarbans for Tanning Industry", *Directorate of Forest, Planning and Statistical Cell*, Calcutta, (10).

Roy, S.K. *et al.* (1984). *Peroceedings of the National Workshop on Betelvine*, Calcutta, The Agricultural Society of India, (19).

Sarkar, Asit Kumar (1989). "Applications of Remote Sensing Techniques for Acquisition of Geographical Information", *Applied Geography*, National Atlas & Thematic Mapping Organisation, Calcutta, (7).

Sartaj Aziz (1978). *Rural Development and Land Reforms in China*, Macmillon Press Ltd. London and Basigastoka, Hongkong, p.25-36, (32).

Scott, P. (1970). *Geography and Retailing*, London, Hutchinson, University Library, p.134, (17).

Sen, L.K., S. Wanmali, *et al.* (1971). *Planning Rural Growth Centres for Integrated Area Development: A Case Study of Miryalguda Taluka*, N.I.C.D., Hyderabad, (12,26).

Sen, L.K., R.N. Tripathi, G.K. Mishra and A.L. Thaha (1975). *Growth Centres in Raichur*, N.I.C.D. Hyderabad, (26).

Sharma, S.K. (1981). "Problems of Rural Economic Development in the Baghelkhand Plateau, M.P.", *The Geographer*, 28, 2, pp. 57-68, (5).

Sharma, S.K. (1988). "Regional Resource Base and Pattern of Economic Development in M.P., India", pp. 123-144 in V. Vidyanath & R. Ram Mohan Rao eds., *Development of India's Resource Base*, New Delhi, Gyan Publishing House, (5).

Shrivastava, K.R. (1982). *Periodic Markets and Central Places in Baghelkhand Region*, Ph.d. Thesis, Rani Durgawati Vishwavidyalaya, Jabalpur, (29).

Shrivastava, K.R. (1992). "Spatio-Temporal Organisation of Market Centres in Baghelkhand Region", *Maharastra Bhoogol Shastra Sanshodhan Patrika*, Vol.VI, No.2, 1992, (29).

Shrivastava, K.R. (1993). "Reorganisation of Economy in Tribal Areas: A Model", in Phanse, V. (ed.), *Scenario of the Evaluation and Exploitation of Tribal Resources*, M.P.S.T., Indore, (29).

Shrivastava, V.K. (1978). "Theoretical Norms and Interpretation of Market Place Participants Spatial Behaviour", *National Geographer*, Vol.13 (2), pp.117-34, (23).

Shrivastava, V.K. (1977). "Periodic Markets and Rural Development Bahraich District : A Case Study", *National Geographers*, Vol. 12(1), pp.47-55, (26).

Shrivastava, V.K. (1980). "Central Place Theory in an Indian Context", *Indian Journal of Regional Science*, Vol.XII, pp.195 206, (26).

Shrivastava, V.K. and I.Richard (1978). "Regional Distribution of a Rural Settlements : An Analytical Study", *Uttar Bharat Bhoogol Patrika*, Vol.II, No.2, Dec., pp.54-64, (25).

Shrivastava, V.K. (1982). "Approaches to Planning and Regionalization of Settlement", in Mandal & Peters (eds.), *Urbanization and Regional Development*, Concept Publishing Company, pp.311-20, (26).

Shrivastava, V.K. (1987). *Geography of Marketing and Rural Development*, Inter-India, New Delhi, (25).

Shrivastava, V.K. (1987). "Traditional Marketing Systems and Rural Development in India", *Retail Trade with Regard to the Present-Day Changes: The Facts and Their Analysis*, Liege, Ed. Schoumaker, B.M. (25).

Singh, A.K. (1981). *Patterns of Regional Development, A Comparative Study*, Sterling Publishers Pvt. Ltd., New Delhi, pp.246-47, (30).

Singh, S. (1984). "Measuring the Levels of Development, A Taxonomic Approach", *Indian Journal of Regional Science*, Vol.XVI, p.88, (30).

Singh, J.P. (1982). *Human Resources of North-Eastern India*, Inter-India Publications, Delhi, (29).

Singh, Kashi N. (1973). "Central Places and Development Strategy in Varanasi Region: A Spatial Functional Approach", *Urban Geography in Developing Countries*, (ed.) R.L. Singh, (24).

Singh, Surendra (1977). Function Facility Ratio in the Rural Growth Centres of Rohilkhand (U.P.)", *The Geographical View Point*, Vol.VIII, No.1 & 2, pp.38, 42, (24).

Singh, R.L. and P.B. Rana (1980). "Transformation Model for Rural Development, A Geographical Appraisal at Special Inequality Productivity" in *National Geographical Society of India, Research Publication* No.30, p.23, (33).

Singh, U.P. 91982). "Evolution and Growth of Industrial Landscape in Damodar Valley, Bihar", pp.153-162, *Institute of Indian Geographers*, Vol.4, No.2, July, (11).

Skinner, G.W. (1964). "Marketing and Social Structure in Rural China", *Journal of Asian Studies*, Vol.24, pp.195-228, (22,25).

Smith, R.H.T. (1976). "Periodic Market Place and Travelling Traders in Developing Countries", in *Readings in Planning and Developments*, (Ed.), V.L.S. Prakesh Rao, Indian Geographical Society, Madras, pp.214-24, (23).

Srivastava, R.C. (1990). "Periodic Markets and Intra-Urban Mobility: A Case Study of Kanpur Metropolis" in R.N.P. Sinha (ed.), *Environment and Human Response: Selected Essays in Geography*, Concept Publishing Company, New Delhi, (17).

Srivastava, R.C. and J. Ali (1980). "Identification of Basic Planning Units for Integrated Area Development— Patha Area of Bundelkhand: A Case Study", *Transactions, Indian Council of Geographers*, Vol. 8, Dec., p.3.

Srivastava, R.C. and J.P. Gupta, (1979). "Consumer Travel Patterns in the Periodic Markets of Kanpur Metropolis", *National Geographer*, Vol. XIV, No.2, pp.147-58, (17).

Srivastava, R.C. (1982). "Consumer Buyer Behaviour in the

Periodic Markets of Kanpur Metropolis", in (ed.) R.B. Mandal and G.L. Peters, *Urbanization and Regional Development*, Concept Publishing Company, New Delhi, pp.217-41, (17).

Stine, J.H. (1962). "Temporal Aspects of Tertiary Production Elements in Korea", in F.R. Pitts, (ed.), *Urban Systems and Economic Development*, Eugene, pp.68-88, (28).

Stone, B. (1975). *Successful Direct Marketing Method*, Chicago, Rapp, Collins, Stone and Alder Inc., (20).

Sultana, R. (1982). "Bangladesh Gramin Hat Bazarer Sthanik Bistoran", *Bhugol Patrika* No.1, 13-20, Jahangirnagar University, Savar, Dhaka, Bangaldesh, (13).

Sultana, R. (1985-86). "Some Geographical Aspects of Rural Markets — Savar Upazila", *Journal of the Bangladesh National Geographical Association*, Vol-13 & 14 Nos. 22,60-78, Dhaka, Bangladesh, (13).

Sundaram, K.V. (1983). *Geography of Underdevelopment*, New Delhi, Concept Publishing Company, p.161, (5).

Suresh, R. (1971). "Parade—A Periodical Market of Kanpur", *The Geographical Knowledge*, Vol. VI, No.1 & 2, p.56-65, (17).

Sur, Suchit (1982). "Pineapple Cultivation in North Bengal: 1941-75", *North Bengal University Review* (Humanities & Social Sciences) Vol.3, No.1, June, pp.35-52, N. Bengal University, Raja Rammohunpur, (4).

Symanski, R. (1971). *Periodic Markets of Andean, Colombia*, Unpublished Ph.D. Thesis, Syracuse University, New York, U.S.A., (13).

Syamnaski, R. and M.J. Webber, (1973). "Periodic Markets: An Economic Location Analysis", *Economic Geography*, Vol.42, No.3, p.211, (17).

Tamaskar, B.G. (1979). "Geographic Perspective on Periodic Marketing System and Network in the Chhatishgarh Plain", *Geographical Review*, Vol. 40 (1) pp.15-24, (23).

Taylor, P.J. & Johnston R.J. (1979). *Geography of Elections*. Penguin Books, England.

Tiwari, K.N. (1987). *Market Centres and Transpotation: A Case Study of Ghazipur District*, Ph.D. Thesis accepted by University of Gorakhpur, Gorakhpur, (25,35).

Tiwari, P.D. & C.K. Jain (1989). *Modernization of Agriculture and Food Availability in India*, New Delhi, Northern Book Centre, (5, 23).

Tripathi, D.N. (1988). *Samanvit Gramin Vikas— Tahsil Amethi: Ek Prkartik Adhyayan*, Unpublished Ph.D. Thesis, Avadh University, Faizabad, (12).

Usami, Y. (1989). "Economic Analysis of Betelvine Cultivation" in H.Ishihara (ed.), *Markets and Marketing in West Bengal and East Nepal*, Nagoya, Nagoya University, Department of Geography, (19).

Varma, S.P. & Narain, I. (1977), *Voting Behaviour in Changing Societies*, National Publishers. New Delhi.

Vishwa Nath (1982). *Marketing and Social Structure in Awadh Plain (North)*, Ph.D. Thesis accepted by University of Gorakhpur, Gorakhpur, (unpublished), (25).

Wanmali, S. (1979). "Periodic Markets, Periodic Marketing and Rural Development in India", *Mangement and Labour Studies*, Vol.5 (1), pp.1-15, (23).

Wanmali, S. (1981). *Periodic Markets and Rural Development*, B.R. Publishers, New Delhi, (23).

Webber, M.J. and Richard Symanski (1973). "Periodic Markets: An Economic Locational Analysis", *Economic Geography*, pp. 213-27, (28).

Weiner, M., *et al.*, (1977). *Electoral Politics in Indian States: The Impact of Modernization*. Manohar Books, New Delhi.

Wheeler, P.T. (1960). "Travelling Vans and Mobile Shops in Sutherland", *Scottish Geographical Magazine*, 76, pp. 147-55, (17).

INDEX